SOCIAL NEUROSCIENCE

Key Readings in Social Psychology

General Editor: ARIE W. KRUGLANSKI, University of Maryland at College Park

The aim of this series is to make available to senior undergraduate and graduate students key articles in each area of social psychology in an attractive, user-friendly format. Many professors want to encourage their students to engage directly with research in their fields, yet this can often be daunting for students coming to detailed study of a topic for the first time. Moreover, declining library budgets mean that articles are not always readily available, and course packs can be expensive and time-consuming to produce. **Key Readings in Social Psychology** aims to address this need by providing comprehensive volumes, each one of which will be edited by a senior and active researcher in the field. Articles will be carefully chosen to illustrate the way the field has developed historically as well as current issues and research directions. Each volume will have a similar structure to include:

• an overview chapter, as well as introduction to sections and articles
• questions for class discussion
• annotated bibliographies
• full author and subject indexes

Published Titles

The Self in Social Psychology	Roy F. Baumeister
Stereotypes and Prejudice	Charles Stangor
Motivational Science	E. Tory Higgins and Arie W. Kruglanski
Social Psychology and Human Sexuality	Roy F. Baumeister
Emotions in Social Psychology	W. Gerrod Parrott
Intergroup Relations	Michael A. Hogg and Dominic Abrams
The Social Psychology of Organizational Behavior	Leigh L. Thompson
Social Psychology: A General Reader	Arie W. Kruglanski and E. Tory Higgins
Social Psychology of Health	Peter Salovey and Alexander J. Rothman
The Interface of Social and Clinical Psychology	Robin M. Kowalski and Mark R. Leary
Political Psychology	John T. Jost and James Sidanius
Close Relationships	Harry T. Reis and Caryl E. Rusbult

Titles in Preparation

Attitudes	Richard E. Petty and Russell Fazio
Group Processes	John Levine and Richard Moreland
Language and Communication	Gün R. Semin
Persuasion	Richard E. Petty and Russell Fazio
Social Cognition	David L. Hamilton
Social Comparison	Diederik Stapel and Hart Blanton
Social Neuroscience	John T. Cacioppo and Gary Berntson

For continually updated information about published and forthcoming titles in the Key Readings in Social Psychology series, please visit: **www.keyreadings.com**

SOCIAL NEUROSCIENCE
Key Readings

Edited by

John T. Cacioppo
University of Chicago

Gary G. Berntson
Ohio State University

Psychology Press
New York and Hove

Published in 2005 by
Psychology Press
270 Madison Avenue
New York, NY 10016
www.psypress.com

Published in Great Britain by
Psychology Press
27 Church Road
Hove, East Sussex
BN3 2FA
www.psypress.co.uk

Psychology Press, is an imprint of the Taylor & Francis Group.
Printed in the United States of America on acid-free paper.

Cover image by Mike Agliolo/Photo Researchers, Inc.

10 9 8 7 6 5 4 3 2

Library of Congress Cataloging-in-Publication Data

Social neuroscience: key readings/edited by John T. Cacioppo and Gary G. Berntson.
   p. cm. — (Key readings in social psychology)
Includes bibliographical references and index.
ISBN 1-84169-098-8 (hardback: alk. paper) — ISBN 1-84169-099-6 (pbk.: alk. paper)
1. Neuropsychology. 2. Social psychology. I. Cacioppo, John T. II. Berntson, Gary G. III. Series.
QP360.S595 2004
153—dc22

2004009959

Contents

About the Editors

John T. Cacioppo is the Tiffany and Margaret Blake Distinguished Service Professor of psychology at the University of Chicago. He is the author of over 270 articles, and among his books are *Attitudes and Persuasion, Emotional Contagion, Principles of Psychophysiology, Foundations in Social Neuroscience,* and *Handbook of Psychophysiology.* He is a recipient of the National Academy of Sciences Troland Research Award, the Society for Personality and Social Psychology's Campbell Award, the Society for Psychophysiological Research's Award for Distinguished Scientific Contributions to Psychophysiology, and the American Psychological Association's Distinguished Scientific Contribution Award.

Gary G. Berntson is a professor of psychology, psychiatry, and pediatrics, as well as a member of the Neuroscience Graduate Faculty at the Ohio State University. His research is highly interdisciplinary and ranges from clinical studies in humans to neurophysiological investigations in animals.

Acknowledgments

The authors and publishers are grateful to the following for permission to reproduce the articles in this book:

Reading 1: H. Damasio, T. Grabowski, R. Frank, A. M. Galaburda, and A. R. Damasio, The Return of Phineas Gage: Clues about the Brain from the Skull of a Famous Patient. *Science*, New Series, 264, 1102–1105. Copyright © 1994 by the American Association for the Advancement of Science. Reprinted with permission.

Reading 2: S. W. Anderson, A. Bechara, H. Damasio, D. Tranel, and A. R. Damasio, Impairment of Social and Moral Behavior Related to Early Damage in Human Prefrontal Cortex. *Nature Neuroscience*, 2 (11), 1032–1037. Copyright © 1999 by Nature Publishing Group. Reprinted with permission.

Reading 3: H. Yamasaki, K. S. LaBar, and G. McCarthy, Dissociable Prefrontal Brain Systems for Attention and Emotion. *Proceedings of the National Academy of Sciences*, 99 (17), 11447–11451. Copyright © 2002 by the National Academy of Sciences. Reprinted with permission.

Reading 4: J. P. Mitchell, T. F. Heatherton, and C. N. Macrae, Distinct Neural Systems Subserve Person and Object Knowledge. *Proceedings of the National Academy of Sciences*, 99 (23), 15238–15243. Copyright © 2002 by the National Academy of Sciences. Reprinted with permission.

Reading 5: J. Moll, R. de Oliveira-Souza, I. E., Bramati, and J. Grafman, Functional Networks in Emotional Moral and Nonmoral Social Judgments. *NeuroImage*, 16 (3-1), 696–703. Copyright © 2002 by Elsevier. Reprinted with permission.

Reading 6: J. Liu, A. Harris, and N. Kanwisher, Stages of Processing in Face Perception: An MEG Study. *Nature Neuroscience*, 5 (9), 910–916. Copyright © 2002 by Nature Publishing Group. Reprinted with permission.

Reading 7: J. V. Haxby, M. I. Gobbini, M. L. Furey, A. Ishai, J. L. Schouten, and P. Pietrini, Distributed and Overlapping Representations of Faces and Objects in Ventral Temporal Cortex. *Science*, 293, 2425–2430. Copyright © 2001 by the American Association for the Advancement of Science. Reprinted with permission.

Reading 8: E. D. Grossman and R. Blake, Brain Areas Active during Visual Perception of Biological Motion. *Neuron*, 35, 1167–1175. Copyright © 2002 by Elsevier. Reprinted with permission.

Reading 9: A. Puce and D. Perrett, Electrophysiology and Brain Imaging of Biological Motion. *Philosophical Transactions of the Royal Society of London Series B-Biological Sciences*, 358, 435–445. Copyright © 2003 by the Royal Society of London. Reprinted with permission.

Reading 10: G. Buccino, F. Binkofski, G. R. Fink, L. Fadiga, L. Fogassi, V. Gallese, R. J. Seitz, K. Zilles, G. Rizzolatti, and H. J. Freund, Action Observation Activates Premotor and Parietal Areas in a Somatotopic Manner: An fMRI Study. *European Journal of Neuroscience*, 13 (2),

400–404. Copyright © 2001 by Blackwell Publishing. Reprinted with permission.

Reading 11: L. Carr, M. Iacoboni, M. Dubeau, J. C. Mazziotta, and G. L. Lenzi, Neural Mechanisms of Empathy in Humans: A Relay from Neural Systems for Imitation to Limbic Areas. *Proceedings of the National Academy of Sciences*, 100 (9), 5497–5502. Copyright © 2003 by the National Academy of Sciences. Reprinted with permission.

Reading 12: F. Castelli, F. Happé, U. Frith, and C. Frith, Movement and Mind: A Functional Imaging Study of Perception and Interpretation of Complex Intentional Movement Patterns. *NeuroImage*, 12 (3), 314–325. Copyright © 2000 by Elsevier. Reprinted with permission.

Reading 13: R. Saxe and N. Kanwisher, People Thinking about Thinking People: The Role of the Temporo-Parietal Junction in "Theory of Mind." *NeuroImage*, 19 (4), 1835–1842. Copyright © 2003 by Elsevier. Reprinted with permission.

Reading 14: A. K. Anderson, K. Christoff, D. Panitz, E. De Rosa, and J. D. E. Gabrieli, Neural Correlates of the Automatic Processing of Threat Facial Signals. *The Journal of Neuroscience*, 23, 5627–5633. Copyright © 2003 by the Society for Neuroscience. Reprinted with permission.

Reading 15: J. S. Winston, B. A. Strange, J. O. O'Doherty, and R. J. Dolan, Automatic and Intentional Brain Responses during Evaluation of Trustworthiness of Faces. *Nature Neuroscience*, 5 (3), 277–283. Copyright © 2002 by Nature Publishing Group. Reprinted with permission.

Reading 16: A. G. Sanfey, J. K. Rilling, J. A. Aronson, L. E. Nystrom, and J. D. Cohen, The Neural Basis of Economic Decision-Making in the Ultimatum Game. *Science*, 300, 1755–1758. Copyright © 2003 by the American Association for the Advancement of Science. Reprinted with permission.

Reading 17: R. Bar-On, D. Tranel, N. L. Denburg, and A. Bechara, Exploring the Neurological Substrate of Emotional and Social Intelligence. *Brain*, 126, 1790–1800. Copyright © 2003 by Oxford University Press. Reprinted with permission.

Reading 18: D. Morgan, K. A. Grant, H. D. Gage, R. H. Mach, J. R. Kaplan, O. Prioleau, S. H. Nader, N. Buchheimer, R. L. Ehrenkaufer, and M. A. Nader, Social Dominance in Monkeys: Dopamine D2 Receptors and Cocaine Self-Administration. *Nature Neuroscience*, 5 (2), 169–174. Copyright © 2002 by Nature Publishing Group. Reprinted with permission.

Reading 19: K. N. Ochsner, S. A. Bunge, J. J. Gross, and J. D. E. Gabrieli, Rethinking Feelings: An fMRI Study of the Cognitive Regulation of Emotion. *Journal of Cognitive Neuroscience*, 14 (8), 1215–1229. Copyright © 2002 by the Massachusetts Institute of Technology. Reprinted with permission.

Preface

Neuroscientists and cognitive scientists have collaborated for more than a decade with the common goal of understanding how the mind works. These collaborations have helped unravel puzzles of the mind including aspects of perception, imagery, attention, and memory. Many aspects of the mind, however, require a more comprehensive approach to reveal the mystery of mind-brain connections. The topics of attraction, altruism, aggression, affiliation, attachment, and attitudes represent a small sampler from the top of the alphabet alone. Social neuroscience, therefore, has emerged to address fundamental questions about the mind and its dynamic interactions with the biological systems of the brain and body and the social world in which it resides. It is concerned with the relationship between neural and social processes, including the intervening information processing components and operations at both the neural and the computational levels of analysis. As such, work in social neuroscience builds on work in the neurosciences, cognitive sciences, and social sciences. The premise underlying this book is that more complex aspects of the mind and behavior will benefit from yet a broader collaboration of neuroscientists, cognitive scientists, and social scientists.

The field of social neuroscience encompasses studies ranging from social cognition, motivation, and emotion to interpersonal and group processes, and to social influences on health and mortality. One is as likely to find relevant animal and computational models as human studies, and the methodologies—which support measurements ranging from the gene to cultures—are even more diverse. Attempting to canvas the full scope of social neuroscience would deprive the reader of the rich depth and coherence that can come from multilevel analyses of some of the most fascinating questions humanity has asked about itself and the human mind. We, therefore, limited our scope to human studies of a single question in one area—"Is there anything special about social" cognition?"—although we also included several studies of brain lesions where appropriate.

The readings are organized to reveal a series of facets of what might be special about *social* information processing. Following an overview, readings in the next three sections show that the brain determines social behavior, that there are dissociable systems in the brain for social and nonsocial information processing, and that there may be dissociable systems in the brain for face and object processing. In the next two sections, readings demonstrate that there are dissociable systems in the brain for the perception of biological and nonbiological movement, and that the perception of biological movement can automatically elicit imitation (mimicry) and empathy. Readings in the next three sections address possible means by which the brain constructs inferences about the mental states of others, utilizes information about others from multiple parallel streams of information processing, and ultimately formulates preferences and decisions to negotiate the social world. We end with two readings to illustrate that research showing social cognition is instantiated in biological (e.g., brain) processes does not mean that it is fixed and immutable by an individual's genotype.

Work on this volume was made possible by funding from the National Science Foundation BCS-0086314, an institution that has tirelessly supported efforts to bridge the abyss across the social, cognitive, and neurosciences for many years; the support of Paul Dukes at Psychology Press; and the assistance of Judy Runge in the preparation of the manuscript. We hope the reader will enjoy getting to know the field of social neuroscience and its potential in the century ahead.

John T. Cacioppo
University of Chicago

Gary G. Berntson
The Ohio State University

PART 1

Volume Overview: Analyses of the Social Brain through the Lens of Human Brain Imaging

John T. Cacioppo • University of Chicago

Gary G. Berntson • The Ohio State University

Among the major evolutionary advances in humans is the striking development of the human cerebral cortex, especially the frontal and temporal regions. The cerebral cortex is a mantle of between 2.6 to 16 billion neurons with each neuron receiving 10,000 to 100,000 synapses in their dendritic trees (e.g., Pakkenberg, 1966). The frontal and temporal lobes constitute 32% and 23% of the cerebral cortex, respectively, rendering the sensorimotor cortices that dominate most mammalian brains to minority status in the human brain. The expansion of the frontal regions in the human brain is largely responsible for the human capacity for reasoning, planning, and performing mental simulations, and an intact frontal region contributes to the human ability to reason, remember, and work together. The temporal regions, in turn, play essential roles in social perception and communication. The neocortex, in particular, is a recent development in evolutionary time, and the means for guiding behavior through the environment, albeit in a more rigid and stereotyped fashion, emerged prior to neocortical expansion. These evolutionarily older systems likely also play a role in human information processing and behavior (Berntson, Boysen, & Cacioppo, 1993; Smith et al., 2003).

Human information processing capacities remain woefully insufficient even with the expansion of the cortices, however. The sensory load from the physical environment is minor in comparison to the quantity and complexity of the information that comes from other individuals, groups, alliances, and cultures—as well as the potential for benevolence or treachery from each. It is perhaps understandable why social cognition is not an objective information process but instead is rife with the operation of self-interest, self-enhancement, and self-protective processes (Cacioppo & Berntson, 2004). For instance, because there is more information than can possibly be processed, people tend to search for and attend to evidence that confirms what they already believe to be true (Snyder & Swann, 1978). Information processing is biased in ways that protects the self from symbolic as well as actual threats and promotes reproductive success (e.g., Jones & Berglas, 1978). People believe they know how long things they choose will make them feel good or bad, but in fact they grossly overestimate the duration of these feelings (Wilson et al., 2000). Subtle reminders of their mortality can push people to promote defensive information processing, such as blaming the victim and enacting risky behaviors, as if to prove to themselves that the world is just and threats do not apply to them (Pyszczynski, Greenberg, & Solomon, 1999). In fact, people are not particularly good at knowing the causes of their feelings or behavior (Nisbett & Wilson, 1977). They believe they know that opposites attract, just as assuredly as they know that its logical opposite is also true (i.e., birds of a feather flock together). People overestimate

their strengths and underestimate their faults (Ross & Sicoly, 1979); they overestimate how important is their input, how pervasive are their beliefs, and how likely is a desired event to occur (McGuire, 1981), all while underestimating the contributions of others and the likelihood that risks in the world apply to them (Ross, Greene, & House, 1977). Events that unfold unexpectedly are not reasoned as much as they are rationalized (Aronson, 1968), and the act of remembering is far more of a biased reconstruction than an accurate record of actual events (Roediger, Buckner, & McDermott, 1999; McDonald & Hirt, 1997). Mental simulation of alternative outcomes— made possible through the expansion of the frontal cortices—can dramatically influence our evaluations and decisions, so much so that the counterfactual reasoning of silver medalists in the Olympic Games leave them, on average, less happy with their achievements than bronze medalists (Medvec, Madey, & Gilovich, 1995). These biases in social cognition are automatic in the sense that they are spontaneous, their implementation does not require cognitive effort, and they are ubiquitous in that they represent normative processing. They represent emergent properties from the operation of the human brain, sculpted by adaptive and reproductive successes and failures (Cacioppo & Berntson, 2004).

During most of the past century, the nuances of social cognition and social processes, including unconscious processes, were plumbed through the clever experimental designs and measures of verbal reports, judgments, and reaction time. These methodologies were limited in what they could reveal about social processes, however.

Social cognition and behavior are often affect-laden or habitual, and nuances deriving from these features proved difficult to capture fully using subjective measures and response latencies to semantic (e.g., lexical decision) tasks (Zajonc, 1980). In a recent *Annual Review of Neurosciences*, LeDoux observed:

> It is widely recognized that most cognitive processes occur unconsciously, with only the end products reaching awareness, and then only sometimes. Emotion researchers, though, did not make this conceptual leap. They remained focused on subjective emotional experience . . . The main lesson to be learned . . . is that emotion researchers need to figure out how to escape from the shackles of subjectivity if emotion research is to thrive. (LeDoux, 2000, p.156)

The same is true in social psychology (Berntson & Cacioppo, 2000; Cacioppo & Berntson, 1992, 2004). The study of automatic and implicit processes became popular in social psychology in the 1990s, but as important as these developments were, the richness of the information provided remained quite limited. The purpose of this book is to introduce students to a new and developing approach to address these questions—an approach termed *social neuroscience* (Cacioppo & Berntson, 1992).

In social neuroscience, theory and methods in the neurosciences constrain and inspire hypotheses in the behavioral and social sciences, foster experimental tests of otherwise indistinguishable theoretical explanations, and increase the comprehensiveness and relevance of social and behavioral theories. Whereas a measure of reaction time may provide information about differences in the time it takes to perform specific mental operations, metabolic and

electrophysiological images of brain activity may provide moment by moment information about when and where social cognition is unfolding in the brain, and from this one can infer what is the nature of the information processing operation being performed moment by moment in the brain. Parallel series of information processing operations, in theory, are as tractable as a single series of information processing operations—making it possible to examine the brain as it does two (or more) things at the same time.

The field of social neuroscience stretches far beyond social cognition, human studies, or brain imaging methodologies (see Cacioppo et al., 2002). Rather than canvassing the full scope of social neuroscience, however, we selected the current readings to illustrate work within a limited area that is shaping scientific thought about a classic question in social psychology: Is there anything special about "social" cognition? We next review illustrative evidence bearing on this question to provide a context for the readings that follow.

Social Processes and Behavior: Multipurpose or Specialized Neural Mechanisms

One of the fundamental questions in the field is whether specific social constructs, processes, and representations have a definable neural locus. Is social information processed by specialized neural circuitry? Two complementing strategies are typically used to address this question: (1) one can examine the function or functions associated with a particular neural locus or region to determine if it exclusively serves social information processing, or (2) one can place the focus on a specific social process or function to examine the different ways in which this function might be achieved.

In a seminal thesis based primarily on neurophysiological recordings in nonhuman primates, Brothers (1990) proposed that the superior temporal sulcus (STS) is involved in integrative processing of conspecifics' behavior, and the amygdala and orbitofrontal cortex are subsequently involved in specifying the socioemotional relevance of social information. Kanwisher (e.g., Kanwisher, 2000; Kanwisher, McDermott, & Chun, 1997), using functional magnetic resonance imaging (fMRI) data, emphasized the role of the fusiform gyrus in face processing, and Damasio and colleagues (e.g., Damasio, 1994), focusing primarily on data from humans with brain lesions, have emphasized the role of the frontal (ventromedial prefrontal, orbitofrontal) cortex, amygdala, and somatosensory cortex (insula, SI, SII) in social perception, cognition, and decision-making. Adolphs (2003, see Figure 1) has drawn from these literatures and brain lesion data to suggest that social cognition draws upon neural mechanisms for perceiving, recognizing, and evaluating stimuli, which are then used to construct complex central representations of the social environment. These central processes involve the fusiform gyrus and the STS in the temporal region, as well as the amygdala, orbitofrontal cortex, anterior and posterior cingulate cortices, and right somatosensory-related cortices. Like nonsocial information processing, the central processes of social cognition modulate effector systems including the motor and premotor cortices,

basal ganglia, hypothalamus, and periaqueductal gray.

Disputes have emerged, however, regarding whether certain nuclei (e.g., fusiform gyrus) function to process social information (e.g., faces; Kanwisher, 2000) or more generic forms of information (e.g., objects about which there is expertise; Gauthier et al., 2000; cf. Farah et al., 1998) and about the specific contribution to social cognition made by various nuclei. These disputes depend in part on the conceptualization of brain localization and what it is that is localized.

The adaptive value of social recognition and communication contributed to the evolution of the human brain's preparedness for facial recognition and language acquisition, but these same information-processing operations may be useful in all kinds of information processing tasks confronting people in contemporary societies. However, the evolutionary function or functions that led to the rise of a particular neural system in the human brain do not place strict constraints on the stimuli, tasks, or functions that may be served today by the system. That is, a structure that already exists can take on a new function, or an established process may be co-opted for other purposes. This extended adaptation of an existing structure or system is termed *exaption* and may contribute to the appearance that there is nothing special in the brain regarding social cognition.

Ideas about the anatomical basis of functional localization in the cortex have been debated for hundreds of years, until research on primary sensory cortices (e.g., Munk, 1881; Tunturi, 1952) and on somatosensory regions (e.g., Schaltenbrand

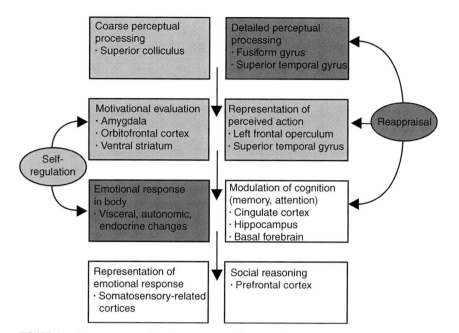

FIGURE 1 ■ Processes and brain structures that are involved in social cognition. It is possible to assign sets of neural structures to various stages of information processing. However, the flow of social information defies any simple scheme for at least two reasons: It is multidimensional and it is recursive. A single process is implemented by a flexible set of structures, and a single structure participates in several processes, often during distinct windows of time. Processing routes differ in terms of their automaticity, cognitive penetrability, detail of the representations they involve, and processing speed. The structures outlined in this figure share some core features of a social information processing system: selectivity (they make distinctions between different kinds of information), categorization and generalization, and the incorporation of past experience. Several of the components of social cognition (inside the gray shaded area) contribute to social knowledge. Reappraisal and self-regulation are particular models of feedback modulation whereby evaluation and emotional response to social stimuli can be volitionally influenced. (From Adolphs, R. [2003]. *Neuroscience Reviews, 4,* 165–178. With permission.)

& Woolsey, 1964) refuted the hypothesis that the brain was a homogeneous tissue that depended on total mass to carry out functions. The more recent discovery of mirror neurons in monkeys also cautions against a premature assignment of function to structures, and at the same time illustrates the potential brain localization of social information processing. Mirror neurons are a class of neurons in the ventral premotor cortex of monkeys (area F5, among others) that become active when the monkey makes a particular action or when it observes another individual making a similar action (Rizzolatti, Fogassi, & Gallese, 2001). The same neurons also respond on perceiving an object that affords specific kinds of motor behaviors (Grezes & Decety, 2002; Rizzolatti & Fadiga, 1998), but they do not otherwise tend to respond to the presentation of an object of an action, or to the mimicking of an action in the absence of the object. Kohler et al. (2002) recorded from individual neurons in the F5 area of monkeys homologous to Broca's area in humans. They found that individual neurons responded when the monkey performed specific motor behaviors, when the monkey observed other individuals performing the same behavior, and when the monkey heard but could not see the same behavior being performed by another. These results indicate that visual and audiovisual mirror neurons code not the visual analysis of the action per se but the goal and meaning of the actions of both oneself and others, as well as the perspective one takes on those actions (Ruby & Decety, 2001). Studies employing fMRI suggest that similar functions may also be represented in the premotor cortex of humans (Grezes et al., 2003).

Recall that the somatosensory cortices dominate most mammalian brains but in the human brain the frontal and temporal lobules constitute over half the cerebral cortex. The well-defined localization of sensory and motor functions poses as a hypothesis but does not prove that more complex integrative processing by the brain is similarly compartmentalized. Brothers (1990), for instance, suggested that the amygdala was an essential component of a set of nuclei involved in social cognition. The evidence that led to this suggestion is illustrated by Dicks, Myers, and Kling (1969), who subjected a sample of free-roaming rhesus monkeys to bilateral amygdalectomy before returning them to their social groups. Dicks et al. (1969) found that these monkeys invariably were ostracized and most perished without the support of their troop. This led to the view that the amygdala was essential for the normal perception and production of expressive displays and behaviors, and that damage to the amygdala undermined an animal's capacity for effective social interactions.

Using macaque monkeys, Amaral and colleagues (Amaral et al., 2003; Prather et al., 2001) examined the role of the amygdala in social cognition using a more circumscribed lesion of the amygdala and quantitative measures of dyadic social interactions. Amaral et al. (2003) observed the social behavior of monkeys with ibotenic acid lesions of the amygdala and controls matched for age, sex, and dominance. Results revealed that the lesion of the amygdala appeared to have produced a socially uninhibited monkey. For instance, the lesioned monkeys did not go through the normal period of evaluation of the other monkeys before engaging in social interactions. As a result, the lesioned monkeys initiated greater amounts of affiliative social behavior than the control monkeys. Amaral et al. (2003) also found differences in how the control animals interacted with the lesioned animals. Rather than shunning the lesioned monkeys because of their early and non-normative forwardness toward the control monkeys, the control monkeys generated more affiliative social behaviors toward the lesioned than the control monkeys. "The inevitable conclusion from this study is that in dyadic social interactions, monkeys with extensive bilateral lesions of the amygdala can interpret and generate social gestures and initiate and receive more affiliative social interactions than controls" (Amaral et al., 2003, p. 238). Amaral and colleagues have posited that the amygdala functions to suppress the engagement of objects and conspecifics while an evaluation of the potential threat is conducted. In the absence of a functioning amygdala, conspecifics are not regarded as potentially dangerous or the social context is regarded as safe, and, hence, social interactions are engaged.

Amaral et al. (2003) further reviewed evidence that the amygdala plays this role in threat appraisals generally, not only in the evaluation of potential dyadic partners. The latency to retrieve a food reward from in front of a stimulus object is slowed in normal animals when the stimulus has fear-provoking qualities (e.g., rubber snake), but the latency of lesioned monkeys was not altered by potential dangers in the environment. Prather et al. (2001) evaluated whether the amygdala was essential not for the emission of social behaviors but for the learning of social behaviors. Young monkeys underwent the same bilateral lesion of the amygdala at 2 weeks of age. Steps were taken to insure opportunities for normal social development and to avoid the behavioral differences associated with nursery rearing. Results reveal interactions with the mother that are similar for lesioned and control animals. The lesioned animals also showed little fear of normally fear-provoking objects (e.g., rubber snake), although they did show more less social interaction and more fear grimaces, screams in novel dyadic social interactions. Most social behaviors, however, were indistinguishable between lesioned and control animals.

In sum, the question is not whether, but where and how activity in the brain serves a social process that has the potential to inform theory in the social and brain sciences. The research on the essential role of the amygdala in social cognition is illustrative of the general thesis that, even though

the dramatic expansion of the human brain may have been fueled by the complexities of social interactions and communication, the central processes in the brain may not be specialized, or at least not specialized exclusively, for social information processing. Cortical and subcortical areas may be active in a wide range of behavioral functions but across those functions the networks in which they participate may be quite different. With these nuances in mind, knowing which brain structures or systems are involved, especially when used in combination with a sophisticated understanding of the roles or functions of these structures and systems, fosters the construction of crucial tests among competing hypotheses and leads to new hypotheses about the structure and function of specific social processes, representations, and constructs. The readings in this book are designed to stimulate and to provoke just such thinking, and thereby, promote a deeper and more comprehensive understanding of social cognition, emotion, and behavior.

To simplify methodological variations, we have given preference to human research that employs fMRI. When one first reads an article in which functional brain imaging measurements are reported, one may be both impressed by the apparent ability of this new technology to image the inner workings of the normal human brain, and bewildered by the esoteric language of nuclear physics. To prepare readers for the articles that follow, we thought it would be useful to review, in nontechnical language, what fMRI is measuring, how and why the blood oxygen level dependent (BOLD) response is assumed to be related to neuronal activity. In addition, we will offer understandable definitions for the abstruse Ts—Tesla, T1, T2, TR, and TE—and why we should care what they are.

Like other approaches, however, fMRI studies are informative regarding questions within certain contexts. Readers interested in some of the limitations as well as potential of fMRI studies might wish to see Cacioppo et al. (in press), Jezzard, Matthews, & Smith (2001), Sarter, Berntson, & Cacioppo (1996), and Zald & Curtis (in press).

What Is fMRI Measuring?

Although the relationship is complex (Heeger & Ress, 2002), there is a coupling between neuronal activity and the local control of blood flow and oxygenation in the brain. The current model of the hemodynamic response posits that a transient increase in neuronal activity within a region of the brain begins consuming additional oxygen in the blood proximal to these cells but also causes local vasodilation. As a result, blood near a region of local neuronal activity soon has a higher ratio of oxygenated to deoxygenated hemoglobin than blood in locally inactive areas. The BOLD fMRI provides a measure of these hemodynamic adjustments and—by inference—the transient changes in neuronal activity in the proximal brain tissue (cf. Buckner, 1998; Heeger & Ress, 2002; Liao et al., 2002; Raichle, 2000).

If this is difficult to visualize, think of a time when you have picked up something heavy such as dumbbells, a particularly heavy stack of books, or

the Sunday edition of *The New York Times*. This neuromuscular action is accompanied by an increased rate of oxygen utilization in the muscles in your arms. The initial muscular exertion results in reduction in the ratio of oxygenated to deoxygenated hemoglobin in your arm muscles, followed quickly by an increase in blood flow to the working muscles and an increase in the ratio of oxygenated to deoxygenated hemoglobin. Accompanying the increase in blood flow to the working muscles of your arms is a slight increase in blood volume in these regions. This is why, after putting down whatever heavy object you lifted, you might have noticed that your arms felt bigger and the veins in your arms were more visible. Note that this change in blood flow increases the ratio of oxygenated to deoxygenated hemoglobin in this region and does so when there is muscular exertion, whether or not work is actually performed (that is, whether the muscle exertion produced any movement). The ratio of oxygenated to deoxygenated hemoglobin in the region increases depending on exertion, metabolism, and vasodilation, not work per se.

For introductory purposes, the enhanced local blood flow and oxygenation that serves as the basis for brain imaging using fMRI can be viewed as occurring in this fashion—an initial brief period of deoxygenation upon activation of a brain region, followed by a slower increase in oxygenation to that region that peaks approximately 4–12 seconds following the onset of the task-induced brain activation. More specifically, the basis for the BOLD response is both the greater oxygen extraction and the greater blood flow to active brain tissue.[1] At rest, oxygen extraction from blood in the brain is about 40%. During activation, blood flow to the region increases about 30% and oxygen extraction increases about 5%. Imagine a capillary in the brain at rest that contains 100 molecules of deoxyhemoglobin (dHB) and 100 molecules of oxyhemoglobin (HB). At rest, 40% of oxygen is extracted from the capillary, which leaves 140 molecules of dHB and 60 molecules of HB. The ratio of dHB/HB is 2.3.

When the brain tissue served by this capillary is activated, two additional molecules of HB are extracted (5% of the 40 HB molecules that were extracted at rest), and blood flow to the region increases by 30%. This yields 172 molecules of dHB (130 molecules of dHB that flowed into the region plus the 42 molecules that were extracted from the HB molecules) and 88 molecules of HB (130 HB molecules that flowed to the region less 42 that were extracted). The ratio of dHB/HB becomes 1.9—which means more oxygen has reached the brain region than is needed, and the proportion of oxygenated hemoglobin is larger during activation than at rest—a task-evoked blood oxygen level dependent response.

Origins of the MRI signal. The basis for the fMRI signal is the fact that certain nuclei (e.g., hydrogen) have an intrinsic magnetic dipole moment.[2] A hydrogen nucleus consists of a single proton that spins. Think of this hydrogen nucleus (proton) as a spinning top that essentially either spins right side up or upside down and, like a top, tends to wobble around that upward or downward alignment. Because much of the human brain is water, hydrogen nuclei are incredibly plentiful. How plentiful? There are more than $4 * 10^{19}$ water protons/mm^3 in the human brain (Jezzard et al., 2001). If a hydrogen nucleus were equivalent to 1 ft, the number of hydrogen nuclei within 1 cubic mm of brain tissue would be equivalent to 304.24 billion trips around the earth's equator. If a hydrogen nucleus were to be a single second, the number of hydrogen nuclei within a cubic mm of brain tissue (a cube of tissue four-hundredths of an inch high by four-hundredths of an inch wide by four-hundredths of an inch deep) would be the equivalent of 1278 billion years. Suffice it to say that from the perspective of quantum physics, 1 cubic mm of brain tissue is packed with hydrogen nuclei.

An MRI instrument creates a strong magnetic field (termed an applied magnetic field) that is homogeneous, which means all nuclei within the MRI instrument are exposed to the same applied magnetic field—usually 1.5 to 3 Tesla in contemporary brain imaging studies. A Tesla is a measure of magnetic flux density, or in simpler terms, the strength of the magnetic field created by the MRI scanner. The earth has a magnetic field but we hardly notice it in everyday life unless one is using a compass to navigate. A 3 Tesla magnetic field is about 60,000 times the strength of the earth's magnetic field (Bandettini et al., 2000).

Placing an individual's head into an MRI scanner for an fMRI study, to the physicist, is equivalent to placing a very large number of hydrogen nuclei into

---

[1]We thank Ana Solodkin from the University of Chicago for these statistics and this example.

[2]The term magnetic moment, or magnetic dipole moment, refers to the maximum torque that any given system of poles/charges can experience in a uniform magnetic/electric field of unit strength.

a strong, homogeneous magnetic field produced by the magnet. When this is done, a small percentage of these spinning hydrogen nuclei reorient their spin axis to align (parallel or antiparallel) to this magnetic field.[3] These nuclei precess (think of it as wobble) around this alignment much as a spinning top might wobble around its center of gravity. The parallel alignment is a state of relatively low energy, so slightly more spins reside at this than any other orientation in a strong magnetic field. That is, a hydrogen nucleus whose spin is oriented parallel to the applied magnetic field (think of it as a top spinning upright) is said to be relaxed or in a low energy state, and a hydrogen nucleus whose spin is oriented against the magnetic field (think of it as a top spinning upside down) is said to be in an excited or high energy state. Importantly, the transition from a low to high energy state is accompanied by the *absorption* of energy in the radiofrequency (RF) range, whereas a transition from a high to low energy state is accompanied by *emission* of energy in the RF range. This is actually quite intuitive; moving from a relaxed to excited state requires the input of energy, whereas the transition from an excited to relaxed state requires the release of energy. In fMRI imaging, the scanner injects a pulse of RF energy to excite these nuclei and raise them out of their low energy states. When the RF pulse is terminated, the hydrogen nuclei return to their lower energy states, and in so doing *emit* RF energy that is measured by the scanner.

The RF energy absorbed by the hydrogen nuclei perturbs their spin and alters the wobble. The frequency of the wobbling (precession) of these hydrogen nuclei is a function of the strength of the magnetic field (higher magnetic field strengths produce higher frequency wobbles). Any given magnetic field will produce a signature precess (wobble) frequency, which is called its Larmor frequency. The Larmor frequency is also the resonant frequency for these nuclei. What this means will become clear shortly. Of course, a human brain contains more than hydrogen nuclei, and the applied magnetic field affects these other nuclei, as well. But their frequency of precession differs from hydrogen nuclei, which means the MRI can be tuned to detect and quantify specifically the RF signals from hydrogen nuclei (Bandettini et al., 2000).[5] Moreover, the relative abundance of hydrogen nuclei in the brain and their high sensitivity for magnetic resonance signal make hydrogen nuclei ideal candidates for brain imaging studies.

If a radio signal is now injected at the resonant (i.e., the Larmor) frequency for hydrogen nuclei, the energy will be absorbed by some of these nuclei (i.e., the nuclei will become excited), causing some

---

[3]Not all nuclei align to the magnetic field because their spins become randomized by thermal motion. The number of nuclei that align is about 3 per million per Tesla. Given there are approximately $4 * 10^{19}$ nuclei in a cubic mm of brain tissue, there is still a very large number of nuclei that change their alignment as a result of being placed in a magnetic field.

[4]Electromagnetic energy can be described in terms of a stream of photons, each traveling in a wave-like pattern, moving at the speed of light and carrying some amount of energy. The difference between radio waves, visible light, and gamma rays is the energy of the photons. RF waves have photons with low energies and the longest wavelength. Microwaves have a little more energy than radio waves, infrared has still more, then visible, ultraviolet, X-rays, and gamma rays.

---

[5]The Larmor frequency in a 1.5 Tesla applied magnetic field is 64 MHz, whereas in a 3 Tesla field it is 128 MHz.

to align in the opposing orientation. Think of it as a spinning top that is pulsed with an external source of energy and flips so that it is now spinning at a different orientation.

The hydrogen nuclei that absorbed the RF energy from the brief pulse in an MRI scanner will dissipate this energy and return to their more stable (lower energy) state (e.g., parallel to the applied magnetic field) when the RF pulse terminates. As these nuclei transition from a high to low energy state, these hydrogen nuclei emit an RF signal at their signature frequency (i.e., 64 MHz in a 1.5 Tesla magnetic field, 128 MHz in a 3 Tesla field). The emission of this RF signal is the MRI signal that is recorded in fMRI studies.[6] Excited spins regain 66% of their equilibrium magnetization over a period called T1 and 95% of their equilibrium magnetization over three T1 periods. (T1 refers to the time constant for the exponential decay of excitation of the nuclei.) Importantly, the T1 for a water molecule will depend on the local chemical environment (e.g., different parts of the brain). For instance, T1 is longer for water in the cerebrospinal fluid than for water in tissue.

No detector could tell where such a signal is coming from if that is all that was involved. However, if a range of frequencies were included in the radio pulse, the only frequency that would be absorbed (i.e., within limits, excite or move some of the protons to higher energy states) and then returned (i.e., emitted on dissipation or relaxation of the protons to lower energy states), is the RF signal that is at the Larmor frequency for a particular hydrogen nucleus. (Recall from above that this signature frequency is a function of the applied magnetic field.) Coils, or devices that can generate additional small, local magnetic field gradients or differences, are used to slightly shift the Larmor frequency across brain areas, and permit the scanner to recognize the location of the signal by its frequency.[7] It is simpler to envision this process in one-dimensional than two-dimensional or three-dimensional space, but the notion of how one localizes the RF signal from relaxing hydrogen nuclei works generally the same in these higher dimensional spaces. Rather than thinking about where the hydrogen nuclei might be within the three dimensional brain, therefore, we will consider the simpler example of how to locate their position along a single line.

A 3 Tesla MRI scanner produces a homogeneous, constant 3 Tesla magnetic field. Therefore, all of the hydrogen nuclei along any single line will have a resonant frequency of 128 MHz. If an RF pulse excited some of these nuclei and their emissions were recorded as they relaxed, detecting a 128 MHz emission would not tell you where along the line the emissions originated. If, however, a coil is positioned at an angle to this line of hydrogen nuclei and the coil applies a second but much smaller magnetic field, the local magnetic field for the hydrogen nuclei along this line will differ slightly

---

[6]In most brain imaging studies, the strong signal from protons in fat is ignored or edited from the image. This means that in MRI and fMRI, it is the distribution of protons in tissue water that is imaged (Jezzard et al., 2001).

[7]Coils are used because when electricity flows through a coiled conductor, a magnetic field is generated. Hence, one can design coils whose magnetic flux density can be specified and can be turned on and off quickly.

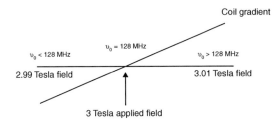

FIGURE 2 ■ MRI and the localization of RF emissions from hydrogen nuclei in water in the human brain, illustrated along one dimension. An MRI scanner applies a large (e.g., 3 Tesla), homogeneous applied magnetic field. An RF pulse is used to excite some of the hydrogen nuclei, which absorb RF energy at a frequency that is a specific function of the magnetic field applied to the hydrogen nuclei. For instance, the resonance frequency for hydrogen nuclei in a 3 Tesla magnetic field is 128 MHz. A coil is also used to produce small variations in the applied magnetic field along the line of imaging. This produces slightly different applied magnetic fields along the line of hydrogen nuclei, and causes their resonance frequency to vary slightly. When the RF signals emitted by these hydrogen nuclei are measured, a decomposition of this measured signal provides information on the strength and location of each of the component signals—that is, where along the line the signal originated and how much signal originated at each point along the line.

(see Figure 2). For instance, the applied magnetic field of the hydrogen nuclei that fall below the coil may exist in a magnetic field slightly higher than 3 Tesla, and those that fall above the coil may exist in a field slightly lower than 3 Tesla. Because the frequency of the wobble of the hydrogen nuclei depends on the strength of the magnetic field, the frequency at which these nuclei wobble will differ, with higher resonant frequencies at the end where the local magnetic field is higher, and lower resonant frequencies at the end where the local magnetic field is slightly lower. When an RF pulse of varying frequencies is applied briefly in the MRI scanner, the hydrogen nuclei along this line will absorb the RF energy that matches its resonant (Larmor)

frequency. When the RF pulse ends, the excited hydrogen nuclei transition from high to low energy states (i.e., relax), as described earlier. In doing so, these nuclei emit RF frequencies at their resonant frequencies, which differ depending where they are along our hypothetical line of hydrogen nuclei. These emitted RF frequencies are then quantified by the scanner.

The quantified RF signals will be the sum of many different RF signals, so this complex signal needs then to be decomposed into frequency components using mathematical procedures such as the fast Fourier Transform. Which frequencies are present in this decomposed signal provides information about *where* along the line hydrogen nuclei had been excited and relaxed, and the power recorded at that RF would provide information about the strength of the signal. So that allows structural localization, but does it permit measurement of brain *activity*?

Functional MRI. Shortening the interpulse delay (TR) in a pulse sequence means the same thing as increasing the rate at which radio-frequency pulses are applied to the sample. As the TR shortens, the emitted RF signals from regions of the brain with a shorter T1 (e.g., tissue) will increase relative to parts of the brain with a longer T1. Within any specific region of the brain, an excited, spinning, wobbling resonating hydrogen nucleus, if isolated, would dissipate energy with a time constant of T1. In a real sample, however, one is measuring the simultaneous emissions from a huge number of nuclei. When dealing with more than a trillion protons spinning per cubic mm across different regions of the brain,[8] the nuclei are each continuously experiencing very small changes in local magnetic fields (i.e., "inhomogeneities"). These varying magnetic fields result in an exchange of energy between the hydrogen nuclei, which results in a dephasing of these nuclei and a reduction in the intensity of the summoned resonance signal (emitted RF signals) from these nuclei. That is, some of these nuclei will emit RF signals in phase, while the emissions of others will fall out of phase (i.e., "dephase") as a function of predictable factors. When the nuclei are all oscillating together, they are said to have high coherence. Local inhomogeneities

at the atomic scale result in a loss of coherence in the phases of the resonance emissions of the hydrogen nuclei, which produces an exponential loss of intensity for the summed resonance signal from all of the nuclei together. Consequently, the measured radio-frequency signal decays more quickly when there are local inhomogeneities in the magnetic field because each hydrogen nucleus is exposed to a slightly different magnetic field strength during excitation and their radio-frequency emissions interfere with each other resulting in the net RF signal diminishing more quickly than those in more homogeneous magnetic fields. The time constant for the exponential function describing the period of dephasing is referred to as T2 (Jezzard et al., 2001).

It follows from the above that T2 is an intrinsic property of nuclei in a particular chemical environment. Increasing the delay before signal detection in a pulse sequence is referred to as lengthening the TE. This has the effect of increasing the strength of the radio-frequency signals from nuclei with a relatively long T2 (e.g., brain grey matter) relative to those with a short T2 (e.g., brain white matter). This is because the exponential decay of the signal from the latter nuclei results in a more precipitous drop in signal strength than does the exponential decay over the same TE when the time constant (T2) is relatively long (Bandettini et al., 2000; Jezzard et al., 2001).

The rate at which the signal decays (i.e., T2) depends upon physical and physiological factors. Most important for investigators using fMRI for brain imaging, the signal decays more quickly in the presence of deoxyhemoglobin than oxygenated

---

[8]If a hydrogen nucleus was the size of a top (about 3 cubic in.), fitting the same number of tops as hydrogen nuclei one finds in a single cubic mm of brain tissue would take approximately 2 quadrillion cubic mi.

hemoglobin (blood). This is because oxygenated hemoglobin is less paramagnetic than dexoygenated hemoglobin (recall that hemoglobin contains iron), and produces a more homogeneous magnetic field, greater spin coherence (i.e., less cancellation of the emitted radio-frequency signals), and a stronger MRI signal. BOLD fMRI techniques are designed to measure primarily changes in the inhomogeneities of the magnetic field within each small volume of tissue resulting from these variations in blood oxygenation and—by inference—neuronal activity (cf. Heeger & Ress, 2002). As one might expect, the signal changes are quite small – 0.5-5.0% at 3 Tesla, for instance,[9] but techniques have been developed to produce signal-to-noise ratios adequate to be detectable (e.g., Cohen & Bookheimer, 1994). The essential point here is that an increase in the concentration of deoxygenated hemoglobin causes a decrease in image intensity, whereas a decrease in deoxygenated hemoglobin causes an increase in image intensity.

The information one gets from an fMRI scan depends upon how and when magnetic gradients and RF pulses (i.e., pulse sequences) are applied. A common fMRI technique for studying the time course of signal intensity changes in the brain is fast echo planar imaging (EPI), which makes it possible to acquire a complete two-dimensional image in as little as 40 ms following a single excitation of the spin system and multislice volumes of MR images

within a single repetition time (i.e., TR; see Zald & Curtis, in press). It is, however, sensitive to a number of artifacts (e.g., movement). For this reason, the temporal resolution of the fMRI was initially limited by the need to block experimental conditions. This limitation has been lessened by the demonstrated feasibility of selective averaging techniques (Buckner et al., 1996). Ultimately, the temporal resolution of the fMRI is limited by the fact that the blood flow response typically lags the actual electrical signal by 1–2 sec, peaks in 4–12 sec, and does not track activity on a msec-by-msec basis. That is, the blood flow response is influenced by activity levels over some time interval (a few hundred msec or more) and, thus, is less temporally specific than the neuronal activity with which it is associated. For many investigations, this temporal imprecision is of little or no importance. In studies in which higher temporal resolution is required, fMRI studies can be complemented by event-related brain potential (ERP) studies.

Interpretation of fMRI data. A series of functional scans are usually collected during a baseline and during the performance of one or more tasks. Typically, the functional images for each participant are realigned to correct for the participant's movement, and then coregistered with a structural (T1 weighted) image (e.g., a high resolution MRI image of the individual's brain). If required, the images are spatially normalized to align brains across participants, and statistical analyses are performed to identify areas that have been activated by the experimental manipulation. The results are then displayed on individual or average structural images. Averaging images across brains can also

---

[9]Higher strength magnetic fields (e.g., 3 Tesla MRIs) produce greater excitation of the nuclei and stronger MRI signals but they can also be more sensitive to artifacts and, in some instances, result in net loss in signal contrast, especially in regions near air (e.g., orbitofrontal cortex).

produce artifacts, so the presentation of images from individual brains, at least in supplementary materials, is often advisable (see Brett, Johnsrude, & Owen, 2002). How one should perform statistical tests on such a large multivariate dataset, characterized by correlated dependent variables and violations of sphericity assumptions, is important but beyond the scope of this introduction.

An important point to remember when reading fMRI studies is that brain regions depicted as "active" refer to areas of the brain that showed task-related increases in deoxygenation and oxygenation, an indicator of the activation of nearby brain tissue. This is a relative, not an absolute, measure. One can tell that the brain activation is task-related either because the strength of the BOLD response during a task is greater than resting baseline or because the strength of the BOLD response during a task differs from the BOLD response during another task that differs from the first by, for instance, only one information processing operation. Task minus baseline contrasts point to the active regions of brain associated with the performance of the task vs. resting, whereas contrasts between two tasks point to the active brain regions associated with the performance of the information processing operation that differs between the two tasks.

It will be helpful to have a brain atlas when reading fMRI studies to help visualize the brain regions and their structural relationships to one another. One such atlas that might be useful is the whole brain atlas, available on the Internet at www.med.harvard.edu/AANLIB/home.html. A medical dictionary may also be helpful, and these,

too, can be found on the internet (e.g., medical-dictionary.com/). A few directional terms are essential to understand when studying the brain, however, so we cover them here. First is a pair of terms tied to a spatial reference. *Anterior* refers to the front or in front of, whereas *posterior* refers to the back or the back part of. There are also three dimensions (axes) that are used to specify topographical relations defined in terms of a body-reference frame in bilaterally symmetrical animals (including humans): (a) *rostrocaudal axis*, which refers to the beak/tail dimension in nonhuman animals and the human body, and to the dimension ranging from the forebrain (*rostral*) to the spinal cord (*caudal*) in the human central nervous system; (b) *dorsoventral axis*, which refers to the back (*dorsal*) and belly (*ventral*) dimension of the body, and to the back (dorsal) and front (ventral) dimension in the human brain and spinal cord; and (c) the *mediolateral axis*, which refers to the middle or toward the middle (*medial*) and toward the sides (*lateral*) in both the body and brain. This terminology can be confusing, because of the alternative frames of reference, as the mapping between the spatial and body reference frames is different for quadrapeds and bipeds. For humans, however, anterior is generally considered to be synonymous with ventral and posterior with dorsal. There also are three orientations in which one might slice or depict the brain: (a) an *axial* orientation means the brain is sliced top to bottom; (b) a *coronal* orientation means the slices are made ear to ear or any plane parallel thereto; and (c) a *sagittal* orientation means the slices are made in the median plane (front to back in the direction an arrow would travel through the brain) or any plane parallel thereto.

Finally, remember the fact that there is brain activation associated with a psychological state or process is not particularly informative—we take as a given that the brain underlies psychological activity. Where and when brain activation occurs is informative, however, because we are beginning to understand what kinds of information processing are performed in various parts of the brain. By studying the neural substrates of a social or psychological process, we should be able to learn more about the component information processing operations and sources of errors and biases in these operations (Cacioppo et al., in press).

REFERENCES

Adolphs, R. (2003). Cognitive neuroscience of human social behaviour. *Neuroscience Reviews, 4,* 165–178.

Amaral, D. G., Capitanio, J. P., Jourdain, M., Mason, W. A., Mendoza, S. P., & Prather, M. (2003). The amygdala: Is it an essential component of the neural network for social cognition? *Neuropsychologica, 41,* 235–240.

Aronson, E. (1968). Dissonance theory: Progress and problems. In R. P. Abelson, E. Aronson, W. J. McGuire, T. M. Newcomb, M. J. Rosenberg, & P. H. Tannenbaum (Eds.), *Theories of cognitive consistency: A sourcebook* (pp. 5–27). Chicago: Rand McNally.

Bandettini, P. A., Birn, R. M., & Donahue, K. M. (2000). Functional MRI: Background, methodology, limits, and implementation. In J. T. Cacioppo, L. G. Tassinary, & G. G. Berntson (Eds.), *The handbook of psychophysiology* (pp. 978–1014). New York: Cambridge University Press.

Berntson, G. G., Boysen, S. T., & Cacioppo, J. T. (1993). Neurobehavioral organization and the cardinal principle of evaluative bivalence. *Annals of the New York Academy of Sciences, 702,* 75–102.

Berntson, G. G., & Cacioppo, J. T. (2000). Psychobiology and social psychology: Past, present, and future. *Personality and Social Psychology Review, 4,* 3–15.

Brothers, L. (1990). The social brain: A project for integrating primate behavior and neurophysiology in a new domain. *Concepts in Neuroscience, 1,* 27–51.

Buckner R. L., Bandettini P. A., O'Craven K. M., Savoy R. L., Petersen S. E., Raichle M. E., & Rosen B. R. (1996).

Detection of cortical activation during averaged single trials of a cognitive task using functional magnetic resonance imaging. *Proceedings of the National Academy of Science, 93*(25):14878–14883.

Buckner, R. L. (1998). Event-related fMRI and the hemodynamic response. *Human Brain Mapping, 6,* 373–377.

Cacioppo, J. T., & Berntson, G. G. (1992). Social psychological contributions to the decade of the brain: Doctrine of multilevel analysis. *American Psychologist, 47,* 1019–1028.

Cacioppo, J. T., & Berntson, G. G. (2004). Social neuroscience. In M. Gazzaniga (Ed.), *The new cognitive neuroscience* (3rd edition). Cambridge, MA: MIT Press.

Cacioppo, J. T., Berntson, G. G., Adolphs, R., Carter, C. S., Davidson, R. J., McClintock, M. K., McEwen, B. S., Meaney, M. J., Schacter, D. L., Sternberg, E. M., Suomi, S. S., & Taylor, S. E. (2002). *Foundations in social neuroscience.* Cambridge, MA: MIT Press.

Cacioppo, J. T., Berntson, G. G., Lorig, T. S., Norris, C. J., Rickett, E., & Nusbaum, H. (2003). Just because you're imaging the brain doesn't mean you can stop using your head: A primer and set of first principles. *Journal of Personality and Social Psychology, 85,* 650–661.

Cohen, M. S., & Bookheimer, S. Y. (1994). Localization of brain function using magnetic resonance imaging. *Trends in Neurosciences, 17,* 268–277.

Damasio, A. R. (1994). *Descartes' error: Emotion, reason, and the human brain.* New York: Grosset/Putnam.

Dicks, D., Myers, R. E., & Kling, A. (1969). Uncus and amygdalalesions: Effects on social behavior in the free ranging rhesus monkey. *Science, 165,* 69–71.

Farah, M.J. (1994). Neuropsychological inferences with an interactive brain: A critique of the "locality" assumption. *Behavioral and Brain Sciences, 22,* 287–288.

Gauthier, I., Skudlarski, P., Gore, J. C., & Anderson, A. W. (2000). Expertise for cars and birds recruits brain areas involved in face recognition. *Nature Neuroscience, 3,* 191–197.

Grezes, J., Armony, J. L., Rowe, J., & Passingham, R. E. (2003). Activations related to "mirror" and "canonical" neurones in the human brain: An fMRI study. *Neuroimage, 18,* 928–937.

Grezes, J., & Decety, J. (2002). Does visual perception of the object afford action? Evidence from a neuroimaging study. *Neuropsychologia, 40,* 212–222.

Heeger, D. J., & Ress, D. (2002). What does fMRI tell us about neuronal activity? *Nature Reviews: Neuroscience, 3,* 142–151.

Jezzard, P., Matthews, P. M., & Smith, S. M. (2001). *Functional MRI.* Oxford: Oxford University Press.

Jones, E. E., & Berglas, S. (1978). Control of attributions about the self through self-handicapping strategies: The appeal of alcohol and the role of under achievement. *Personality and Social Psychology Bulletin, 4,* 200–206.

Kanwisher, N. (2000). Domain specificity in face perception. *Nature Neuroscience, 3,* 759–763.

Kanwisher, N., McDermott, K. B., & Chun, M. (1997). The fusiform face area: A module in human extrastriate cortex specialized for face perception. *Journal of Neuroscience.*

Kohler, E., Keysers, C., Umilta, M. A., Fogassi, L., Gallese, V., & Rizzolatti, G. (2002). Hearing sounds, understanding actions: Action representation in mirror neurons. *Science, 297,* 846–848.

LeDoux, J. (2000). Emotion circuits in the brain. *Annual Review of Neuroscience, 23,* 155–184.

Liao, H., Worsley, K. J., Poline, J. B., Aston, J. D., Duncan, G. H., & Evans, A. C. (2002). Estimating the delay of the fMRI response. *NeuroImage, 16,* 593–606.

McDonald, H. E., & Hirt, E. R. (1997). When expectancy meets desire: Motivational effects in reconstructive memory. *Journal of Personality and Social Psychology, 72,* 5–23.

McGuire, W. J. (1981). The probabilogical model of cognitive structure and attitude change. In R. E. Petty, T. M. Ostrom, & T. C. Brock (Eds.), *Cognitive responses in persuasion* (pp. 291–308). Hillsdale, NJ: Erlbaum.

Medvec, V. H., Madey, S. F., & Gilovich, T. (1995). When less is more: Counterfactual thinking and satisfaction among Olympic medalists. *Journal of Personality & Social Psychology, 69,* 603–610.

Munk, H. (1881). *Uber die funktionen der grosshirnrinde* [*About the functions of the cortex*]. Berlin: Hirschwald.

Nisbett, R. E., & Wilson, T. D. (1977). Telling more than we can know: Verbal reports on mental processes. *Psychological Review, 84,* 231–259.

Pakkenberg, H. (1966). The number of nerve cells in the cerebral cortex of man. *Journal of Comparative Neurology, 128,* 17–20.

Prather, M. D., Lavanex, P., Mauldin-Jourdain, M. L., Mason, W. A., Capitanio, J. P., Mendoza, S. P., et al. (2001). Increased social fear and decreased fear of objects in monkeys with neonatal amygdala lesions. *Neuroscience, 106,* 653–658.

Pyszczynski, T., Greenberg, J., & Solomon, S. (1999). A dual-process model of defense against conscious and unconscious death-related thoughts: An extension of terror management theory. *Psychological Review, 106,* 835–845.

Raichle, M. E. (2000). A brief history of human functional brain mapping. In A. W. Toga & J. C. Mazziotta (Eds.), *Brain mapping: The systems* (pp. 33–77). San Diego: Academic Press.

Rizzolatti, G., & Fadiga, L. (1998). Grasping objects and grasping action meanings: The dual role of monkey rostroventral premotor cortex (area F5). *Novartis Foundation Symposium, 218,* 81–95.

Rizzolatti, G., Fogassi, L., & Gallese, V. (2001). Neurophysiological mechanisms underlying the understanding and imitation of action. *Nature Reviews: Neuroscience, 2,* 661–670.

Roediger, H. L., Buckner, R. L., & McDermott, K. B. (1999). Components of processing. In J. K. Foster & M. Jelicic (Eds.), *Memory: Systems, process, or function?* (pp. 31–65). New York: Oxford University Press.

Ross, L., Greene, D., & House, P. (1977). The "false consensus effect": An egocentric bias in social perception and attribution processes. *Journal of Experimental Social Psychology, 13,* 279–301.

Ross, M., & Sicoly, F. (1979). Egocentric biases in availability and attribution. *Journal of Personality and Social Psychology, 37,* 322–336.

Ruby, P., & Decety, J. (2001). Effect of subjective perspective taking during simulation of action: A PET investigation of agency. *Nature Neuroscience, 4,* 546–550.

Sarter, M., Berntson, G. G., & Cacioppo, J. T. (1996). Brain imaging and cognitive neuroscience: Toward strong inference in attributing function to structure. *American Psychologist, 51,* 13–21.

Schaltenbrand, G., & Woolsey, C. N. (1964). *Cerebral localization and organization; proceedings of a symposium sponsored by the World Federation of Neurology, held at Lisbon, Portugal, October, 1960.* Madison: University of Wisconsin Press.

Smith, N. K., Cacioppo, J. T., Larsen, J. T., & Chartrand, T. L. (2003). May I have your attention please: Electrocortical responses to positive and negative stimuli. *Neuropsychologia, 41,* 171–183.

Snyder, M., & Swann, W. B., Jr. (1978). Hypothesis-testing processes in social interaction. *Journal of Personality and Social Psychology, 35,* 656–666.

Tunturi, A. R. (1952). A difference in the representation of auditory signals for the left and right ears in the isofrequency contours of right ectosylvian auditory cortex of the dog. *Journal of Comparative and Physiological Psychology, 168,* 712–727.

Wilson, T. D., Wheatley, T., Meyers, J. M., Gilbert, D. T., & Axsom, D. (2000). Focalism: A source of durability bias in affective forecasting. *Journal of Personality and Social Psychology, 78,* 821–836.

Zajonc, R. B. (1980). Feeling and thinking: Preferences need no inferences. *American Psychologist, 35,* 157–193.

Zald, D. H., & Curtis, C. (in press). Functional neuroimaging. In M. Eid & E. Diener (Eds.), *Handbook of psychological measurement: A multimethod perspective.* Washington, DC: American Psychological Association.

PART 2

The Brain Determines Social Behavior: The Story of Phineas Gage

There is an intuitive appeal to viewing a social psychological construct or research enterprise as more legitimate, respectable, or "scientific" if the social psychological measure, process, or representation is shown to covary with some event in the brain. Nevertheless, investigations that simply show there are changes in brain activation which correspond to some aspect of social cognition, emotion, or behavior contribute little because no scientific theory would predict otherwise. There is ample evidence that the self and social behavior are maintained despite the loss of various appendages, visceral organs, and personal relationships but are terminated by the cessation of activity in the human brain and that this is so even when the heart continues to beat.

This was not always evident, of course. The earliest localization of mental faculties and bodily processes was based on blood, or essences supposedly carried in the blood, rather than the brain. This misconception is understandable, as the loss of consciousness and life could clearly be demonstrated to follow dramatic losses of blood. By the 2nd century A.D., however, Galen had firmly planted the faculties of reason within the brain. A few well-publicized clinical cases in the 19th century called attention to the role of the brain, particularly the frontal and temporal regions, in social cognition, affect, and behavior. Among these was the case of Phineas Gage, a young American railroad construction supervisor, who in 1848 accidentally detonated a dynamite blast, rocketing his tamping rod through his cheek, eye, and skull and decimating the orbitofrontal and sections of the ventromedial cortex of his brain. The case of Phineas Gage is recounted in the first reading by Damasio et al. (1994).

The second reading by Anderson et al. (1999) also concerns the cognitive, social, and behavioral effects of prefrontal cortex lesions. Whereas Phineas Gage was 25 years of age when he sustained his brain injury, Anderson et al. (1999) examined the long-term consequences of damage to the prefrontal cortex that occurred during infancy. The fascinating similarities and differences in the deficits that emerge from these readings illuminate the importance and specific functions of the prefrontal cortex in social learning as well as social cognition, emotion, and behavior.

Both readings provide unequivocal evidence for a principle articulated in the volume introduction—the brain determines social processes and behavior, and the study of where and how the brain does this informs and expands our understanding of social psychology. The cases covered in these readings also illustrate two of three additional principles in social and cognitive neuroscience: (1) the lesion of circumscribed areas of the brain could cause the loss of specific mental or nervous functions in humans; (2) activity in circumscribed areas of the brain could reflect specific mental or nervous functions in humans; and (3) the human brain is not a dispassionate information processing organ but a socioemotional processing organ, as well. Brain lesion studies of the type illustrated in this section speak to the first and third principles, whereas brain imaging studies such as those in the subsequent sections of this reader speak to the second and third principles.

The Return of Phineas Gage: Clues about the Brain from the Skull of a Famous Patient

Hanna Damasio, Thomas Grabowski, Randall Frank,
Albert M. Galaburda, and Antonio R. Damasio*

When the landmark patient Phineas Gage died in 1861, no autopsy was performed, but his skull was later recovered. The brain lesion that caused the profound personality changes for which his case became famous has been presumed to have involved the left frontal region, but questions have been raised about the involvement of other regions and about the exact placement of the lesion within the vast frontal territory. Measurements from Gage's skull and modern neuroimaging techniques were used to reconstitute the accident and determine the probable location of the lesion. The damage involved both left and right prefrontal cortices in a pattern that, as confirmed by Gage's modern counterparts, causes a defect in rational decision making and the processing of emotion.

On 13 September 1848, Phineas P. Gage, a 25-year-old construction foreman for the Rutland and Burlington Railroad in New England, became a victim of a bizarre accident. In order to lay new rail tracks across Vermont, it was necessary to level the uneven terrain by controlled blasting. Among other tasks, Gage was in charge of the detonations, which involved drilling holes in the stone, partially filling the holes with explosive powder, covering the powder with sand, and using a fuse and a tamping iron to trigger an explosion into the rock. On the fateful day, a momentary distraction let Gage begin tamping directly over the powder before his assistant had had a chance to cover it with sand. The result was a powerful explosion away from the rock and toward Gage. The

*H. Damasio and A. R. Damasio are in the Department of Neurology, University of Iowa Hospitals & Clinics, Iowa City, IA 52242, and the Salk Institute for Biological Research, San Diego, CA 92186–5800, USA. T. Grabowski and R. Frank are in the Department of Neurology, University of Iowa Hospitals & Clinics, Iowa City, IA 52242, USA. A. M. Galaburda is in the Department of Neurology, Harvard Medical School, Beth Israel Hospital, Boston, MA 02215, USA.

fine-pointed, 3-cm-thick, 109-cm-long tamping iron was hurled, rocket-like, through his face, skull, brain, and then into the sky. Gage was momentarily stunned but regained full consciousness immediately thereafter. He was able to talk and even walk with the help of his men. The iron landed many yards away (*1*).

Phineas Gage not only survived the momentous injury, in itself enough to earn him a place in the annals of medicine, but he survived as a different man, and therein lies the greater significance of this case. Gage had been a responsible, intelligent, and socially well-adapted individual, a favorite with peers and elders. He had made progress and showed promise. The signs of a profound change in personality were already evident during the convalescence under the care of his physician, John Harlow. But as the months passed it became apparent that the transformation was not only radical but difficult to comprehend. In some respects, Gage was fully recovered. He remained as able-bodied and appeared to be as intelligent as before the accident; he had no impairment of movement or speech; new learning was intact, and neither memory nor intelligence in the conventional sense had been affected. On the other hand, he had become irreverent and capricious. His respect for the social conventions by which he once abided had vanished. His abundant profanity offended those around him. Perhaps most troubling, he had taken leave of his sense of responsibility. He could not be trusted to honor his commitments. His employers had deemed him "the most efficient and capable" man in their "employ" but now had to dismiss him. In the words of his physician, "the equilibrium or balance, so to speak, between his intellectual faculty and animal propensities" had been destroyed. In the words of his friends and acquaintances, "Gage was no longer Gage" (*1*). Gage began a new life of wandering that ended a dozen years later, in San Francisco, under the custody of his family. Gage never returned to a fully independent existence, never again held a job comparable to the one he once had. His accident had made headlines but his death went unnoticed. No autopsy was obtained.

Twenty years after the accident, John Harlow, unaided by the tools of experimental neuropsychology available today, perceptively correlated Gage's cognitive and behavioral changes with a presumed area of focal damage in the frontal region (*1*). Other cases of neurological damage were then revealing the brain's foundation for language, motor function, and perception, and now Gage's case indicated something even more surprising: Perhaps there were structures in the human brain dedicated to the planning and execution of personally and socially suitable behavior, to the aspect of reasoning known as rationality.

Given the power of this insight, Harlow's observation should have made the scientific impact that the comparable suggestions based on the patients of Broca and Wernicke made (*2*). The suggestions, although surrounded by controversy, became the foundation for the understanding of the neural basis of language and were pursued actively, while Harlow's report on Gage did not inspire a search for the neural basis of reasoning, decision-making, or social behavior. One factor likely to have contributed to the indifferent reception accorded Harlow's work was that the intellectual atmosphere of the time made it somewhat more acceptable that there was a neural basis for processes such as movement or even language rather than for moral reasoning and social behavior (*3*). But the principal explanation must rest with the substance of Harlow's report. Broca and Wernicke had autopsy results, Harlow did not. Unsupported by anatomical evidence, Harlow's observation was the more easily dismissed. Because the exact position of the lesion was not known, some critics could claim that the damage actually involved Broca's so-called language "center," and perhaps would also have involved the nearby "motor centers." And because the patient showed neither paralysis nor aphasia, some critics reached the conclusion that there were no specialized regions at all (*4*). The British physiologist David Ferrier was a rare dissenting voice. He thoughtfully ventured, in 1878, that the lesion spared both motor and language centers, that it had damaged the left prefrontal cortex, and that such damage probably explained Gage's behavioral defects, which he aptly described as a "mental degradation" (5).

Harlow only learned of Gage's death about 5 years after its occurrence. He proceeded to ask Gage's family to have the body exhumed so that the skull could be recovered and kept as a medical record. The strange request was granted, and Phineas Gage was once again the protagonist of a grim event. As a result, the skull and the tamping iron, alongside which Gage had been buried, have been part of the Warren Anatomical Medical Museum at Harvard University.

As new cases of frontal damage were described in this century, some of which did resemble that of Gage, and as the enigmas of frontal lobe function continued to resist elucidation, Gage gradually acquired land-mark status. Our own interest in the case grew out of the idea that Gage exemplified a particular type of cognitive and behavioral defect caused by damage to ventral and medial sectors of prefrontal cortex, rather than to the left dorsolateral sector as implicit in the traditional view. It then occurred to us that some of the image processing techniques now used to investigate Gage's counterparts could be used to test this idea by going back in time, reconstituting the accident, and determining the probable placement of his lesion. The following is the result of our neuroanthropological effort.

We began by having one of us (A.M.G.) photograph Gage's skull inside and out and obtain a skull x-ray (Figure 1.1) as well as a set of precise measurements (6) relative to bone landmarks. Using these measurements, we proceeded to deform linearly the three-dimensional reconstruction of a standard human skull (7) so that its dimensions matched those of Phineas Gage's skull. We also constructed Talairach's stereotactic space for both this skull and Phineas Gage's real skull (8). On the basis of the skull photographs, the dimensions of the entry and exit holes were scaled and mapped into the deformed standard skull. Based on measurements of the iron rod and on the recorded descriptions of the accident, we determined the range of likely trajectories of the rod. Finally, we simulated those trajectories in three-dimensional space using Brainvox (9). We modeled

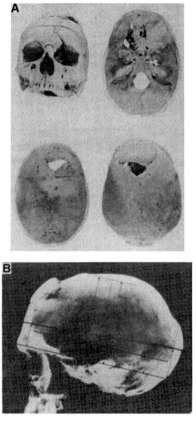

FIGURE 1.1 ■ Photographs of (A) several views of the skull of Phineas Gage and (B) the skull x-ray.

the rod's trajectory as a straight line connecting the center of the entry hole at orbital level to the center of the exit hole. This line was then carried downward to the level of the mandibular ramus. The skull anatomy allowed us to consider entry points within a 1.5-cm radius of this point (20 points in all) (Figure 1.2).

Possible exit points were determined as follows: We decided to constrain the exit point to be at least 1.5 cm (half the diameter of the rod) from the lateral and posterior margins of the area of bone loss (Figure 1.3) because there were no disruptions of the outer table of the calvarium in these directions (Figure 1.1 lower right panel). However, we accepted that the rod might have passed up to 1.5 cm anterior to the area of bone

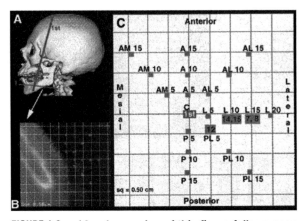

FIGURE 1.2 ■ (*A color version of this figure follows page 146.*) View of the entry-level area with the *a priori* most likely first trajectory. (A) Skull with this first vector and the level (red) at which entry points were marked. (B) View of a segment of section 1. On the left is the mandibular ramus, and on the right is the array of entry points. (C) Enlargement of the array of entry points. One additional point was added (L20) to ensure that every viable entry point was surrounded by nonviable points. Nonviable vectors are shown in red and viable vectors with labels identifying their exit points are shown in green. Abbreviations: A, anterior; L, lateral; P, posterior; AM, anteromesial; AL, anterolateral; PL, posterolateral; C, central.

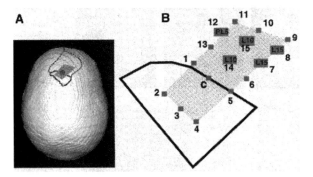

FIGURE 1.3 ■ (*A color version of this figure follows page 146.*) (A) View from above the deformed skull with the exit hole and the anterior bone flap traced in black. The blue circle represents the first vector tested, and the gray surface represents the area where exit points were tested. (B) Schematic enlargement of the exit hole and of the area tested for exit points. The letter C marks the first tested vector (blue). The numbers 1 through 15 mark the other exit points tested. Red indicates nonviable vectors, green indicates viable vectors, and the label identifies the entry point. Note that the *a priori* best fit C was not viable.

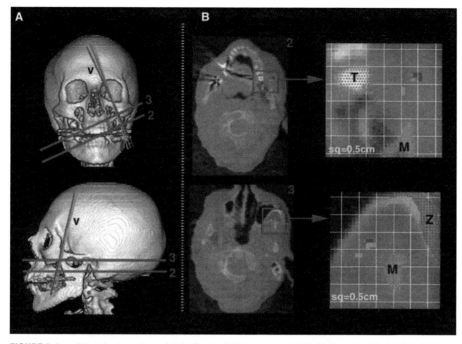

FIGURE 1.4 ■ (*A color version of this figure follows page 146.*) (A) Front and lateral skull views with the projection of the five final vectors (V). The two red lines show the position of the two sections seen in (B). (B) Skull sections 2 and 3: examples of two bottleneck levels at which the viability of vectors was checked. Next to each section is an enlargement of the critical area. Abbreviations: T, missing tooth; M, intact mandible; Z, intact zygoma with a chipped area (light blue).

loss because inspection of the bone in this region revealed that it must have been separated completely from the rest of the calvarium (Figure 1.1). Furthermore, the wound was described as an inverted funnel (*1*). We tested 16 points within the rectangular-shaped exit area that we constructed (Figure 1.3).

The trajectory connecting each of the entry and exit points was tested at multiple anatomical levels. The three-dimensional skull was resampled in planes perpendicular to the best *a priori* trajectory (C in Figs. 1.2 and 1.3). We were helped by several important anatomical constraints. We knew that the left mandible was intact; that the zygomatic arch was mostly intact but had a chipped area, at its medial and superior edge, that suggested the rod had grazed it; and that the last superior molar socket was intact although the tooth was missing. Acceptable trajectories were those

which, at each level, did not violate the following rules: The vectors representing the trajectories could not be closer than 1.5 cm from the mid-thickness of the zygomatic arch, 1 cm from the last superior molar, and 0.5 cm from the coronoid process of the mandible (*10*). Only seven trajectories satisfied these conditions (Figure 1.4). Two of those seven invariably hit the anterior horn of the lateral ventricle and were therefore rejected as anatomically improbable because they would not have been compatible with survival (the resulting massive infection would not have been controllable in the preantibiotic era). When checked in our collection of normal brains, one of the remaining five trajectories behaved better than any other relative to the lower constraints and was thus chosen as the most likely trajectory. The final step was to model the five acceptable trajectories of the iron rod in a three-dimensional reconstruction

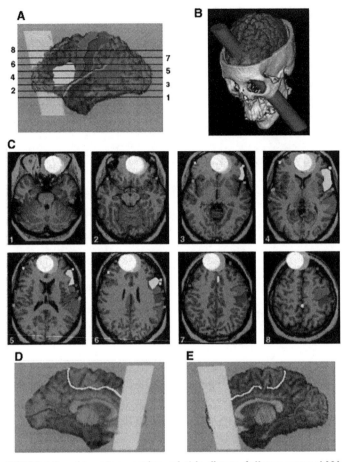

FIGURE 1.5 ■ (A color version of this figure follows page 146.)
Normal brain fitted with the five possible rods. The best rod is highlighted
in solid white [except for (B), where it is shown in red]. The areas
spared by the iron are highlighted in color: Broca, yellow; motor, red;
somatosensory, green; Wernicke, blue. (A) Lateral view of the brain.
Numbered black lines correspond to levels of the brain section shown in
(C). (D and E) Medical view of left and right hemispheres, respectively,
with the rod shown in white.

of a human brain that closely fit Phineas Gage's
assumed brain dimensions (*11*). Talairach's stereotactic warpings were used for this final step.

The modeling yielded the results shown in
Figure 1.5. In the left hemisphere, the lesion involved the anterior half of the orbital frontal cortex
(Brodmann's cytoarchitectonic fields 11 and 12),
the polar and anterior mesial frontal cortices
(fields 8 to 10 and 32), and the anterior-most
sector of the anterior cingulate gyrus (field 24).

However, the lesion did not involve the mesial aspect of field 6 [the supplementary motor area
(SMA)]. The frontal operculum, which contains
Broca's area and includes fields 44, 45, and 47,
was also spared, both cortically and in the underlying white matter. In the right hemisphere, the lesion involved part of the anterior and mesial orbital region (field 12), the mesial and polar frontal
cortices (fields 8 to 10 and 32), and the anterior
segment of the anterior cingulate gyrus (field 24).

The SMA was spared. The white matter core of the frontal lobes was more extensively damaged in the left hemisphere than in the right. There was no damage outside of the frontal lobes.

Even allowing for error and taking into consideration that additional white matter damage likely occurred in the surround of the iron's trajectory, we can conclude that the lesion did not involve Broca's area or the motor cortices and that it favored the ventromedial region of both frontal lobes while sparing the dorsolateral. Thus, Ferrier was correct, and Gage fits a neuroanatomical pattern that we have identified to date in 12 patients within a group of 28 individuals with frontal damage (*12*). Their ability to make rational decisions in personal and social matters is invariably compromised and so is their processing of emotion. On the contrary, their ability to tackle the logic of an abstract problem, to perform calculations, and to call up appropriate knowledge and attend to it remains intact. The establishment of such a pattern has led to the hypothesis that emotion and its underlying neural machinery participate in decision making within the social domain and has raised the possibility that the participation depends on the ventromedial frontal region (*13*). This region is reciprocally connected with subcortical nuclei that control basic biological regulation, emotional processing, and social cognition and behavior, for instance, in amygdala and hypothalamus (*14*). Moreover, this region shows a high concentration of serotonin S_2 receptors in monkeys whose behavior is socially adapted as well as a low concentration in aggressive, socially uncooperative animals (*15*). In contrast, structures in the dorsolateral region are involved in other domains of cognition concerning extrapersonal space, objects, language, and arithmetic (*16*). These structures are largely intact in Gage-like patients, thus accounting for the patients' normal performance in traditional neuropsychologic tests that are aimed at such domains.

The assignment of frontal regions to different cognitive domains is compatible with the idea that frontal neurons in any of those regions may be involved with attention, working memory, and the categorization of contingent relationships regardless of the domain (*17*). This assignment also agrees with the idea that in non-brain-damaged individuals the separate frontal regions are interconnected and act cooperatively to support reasoning and decision making. The mysteries of frontal lobe function are slowly being solved, and it is only fair to establish, on a more substantial footing, the roles that Gage and Harlow played in the solution.

REFERENCES AND NOTES

1. J. M. Harlow, *Pub. Mass. Med. Soc.*. 2, 327 (1868).
2. P. Broca, *Bull. Soc. Anthropol.* 6, 337 (1865); C. Wemicke, *Der aphasische Symptomencomplex* (Cohn und Weigert, Breslau, Poland, 1874). A remarkable number of basic insights on the functional specialization of the human brain, from motor function to sensory perception and to spoken and written language, came from the description of such cases mostly during the second half of the 19th century. The cases usually acted as a springboard for further research, but on occasion their significance was overlooked, as in the case of Gage. Another such example is the description of color perception impairment (achromatopsia) caused by a ventral occipital lesion, by D. Verrey [*Arch. Ophthalmol. (Paris)* 8, 289 (1888)]. His astonishing finding was first denied and then ignored until the 1970s.
3. Reasoning and social behavior were deemed inextricable from ethics and religion and not amenable to biological explanation.
4. The reaction against claims for brain specialization was in fact a reaction against phrenological doctrines, the curious and often unacknowledged inspiration for many of the early case reports. The views of E. Dupuy exemplify the attitude [*Examen de Quelques Points de la Physiologie du Cerveau* (Delahaye, Paris, 1873); M. MacMillan, *Brain Cognit.* 5, 67 (1986)].
5. D. Ferrier, *Br. Med. J.* 1, 399 (1878).
6. The first measurements were those necessary to construct Gage's Talairach stereotactic space and deform a three-dimensional, computerized tomography skull: the maximum length of the skull, the maximum height of the skull above the inion-glabella line, the distance from this line to the floor of the middle fossa, the maximum width of the skull, and the position of the section contour of Gage's skull relative to the inion-glabella line. The second measurements were those necessary to construct the entry and exit areas: on the top external view, the measure of edges of the triangular exit hole; on the internal view the distances from its three corners to the mid-sagittal line and to the nasion; the distance from the borders of the hole to the fracture lines seen anteriorly and posteriorly to this hole; and the dimensions of the entry hole at the level of the orbit.

7. Thin-cut standard computerized tomography image of a cadaver head obtained at North Carolina Memorial Hospital.

8. We introduced the following changes to the method described by P. Fox, J. Perlmutter, and M. Raichle [*J. Comput. Assist. Tomogr.* 9, 141 (1985)]. We calculated the mean distance from the anterior commissure (AC) to the posterior commissure (PC) in a group of 27 normal brains and used that distance for Gage (26.0 mm). We also did not consider the AC-frontal pole and the PC-occipital pole distances as equal because our group of normals had a mean difference of 5 mm between the two measures, and Talairach himself did not give these two measurements as equal [J. Talairach and G. Szikla, *Atlas d'Anatomie Stereotaxique du Telencephale* (Masson, Paris, 1967); J. Talairach and P. Tournoux, *Co-Planar Stereotaxic Atlas of the Human Brain* (Thieme, New York, 1988)]. We introduced an anterior shift of 3% to the center of the AC-PC line and used that point as the center of the AC-PC segment. This shift meant that the anterior sector of Talairach's space was 47% of the total length and that the posterior was 53%. We had no means of calculating the difference between the right and left width of Gage's brain; therefore, we assumed them to be equal.

9. H. Damasio and R. Frank, *Arch. Neurol.* 49, 137 (1992).

10. There were two reasons to allow the vector this close to the mandible: (i) The zygomatic arch and the coronoid process were never more than 2 cm apart; (ii) we assumed that, in reality, this distance might have been larger if the mouth were open or if the mandible, a movable structure, had been pushed by the impact of the iron rod.

11. The final dimensions of Phineas Gage's Talairach space were as follows: total length, 171.6 mm; total height, 111.1 mm; and total width, 126.5 mm. Comparing these dimensions to a group of 27 normal subjects, we found that in seven cases at least two of the dimensions were close to those of Phineas Gage [mean length, 169.9 mm (SD, 4.1); mean height, 113.6 (SD, 2.3), mean width, 125 (SD, 3.9). The seven brains were fitted with the possible trajectories to determine which brain areas were involved. There were no significant differences in the areas of damage. The modeling we present here was performed on subject 1600LL (length, 169 mm; height, 115.2 mm; width, 125.6 mm).

12. Data from the Lesion Registry of the University of Iowa's Division of Cognitive Neuroscience as of 1993.

13. P. Eslinger and A. R. Damasio, *Neurology* 35, 1731 (1985); J. L. Saver and A. R. Damasio, *Neuropsychologia* 29, 1241 (1991); A. R. Damasio, D. Tranel, H. Damasio, in *Frontal Lobe Function and Dysfunction*, H. S. Levin, H. M. Eisenberg, A. L. Benton, Eds. (Oxford Univ. Press, New York, 1991), pp. 217–229; S. Dehaene and J. P. Changeux, *Cereb. Cortex* 1, 62 (1991).

14. P. S. Goldman-Rakic, in *Handbook of Physiology; The Nervous System*, F. Plum, Ed. (American Physiological Society, Bethesda, MD, 1987), vol. 5, pp. 373–401; D. N. Pandya and E. H. Yeterian, in *The Prefrontal Cortex: Its Structure, Function and Pathology*, H. B. M. Uylings, Ed. (Elsevier, Amsterdam, 1990); H. Barbas and D. N. Pandya, *J. Comp. Neurol.* 286, 253 (1989).

15. M. J. Raleigh and G. L. Brammer, *Soc. Neurosci. Abstr.* 19, 592 (1993).

16. M. Petrides and B. Milner, *Neuropsychologia* 20, 249 (1982); J. M. Fuster, *The Prefrontal Cortex* (Raven, New York, ed. 2, 1989); M. I. Posner and S. E. Petersen, *Annu. Rev. Neurosci.* 13, 25 (1990).

17. P. S. Goldman-Rakic, *Sci. Am.* 267, 110 (September 1992); A. Bechara, A. R. Damasio, H. Damasio, S. Anderson, *Cognition* 50, 7 (1994); A. R. Damasio, *Descartes' Error: Emotion, Reason and the Human Brain* (Putnam, New York, in press).

18. We thank A. Paul of the Warren Anatomical Museum for giving us access to Gage's skull. Supported by National Institute of Neurological Diseases and Stroke grant PO1 NS 19632 and by the Mathers Foundation.

Impairment of Social and Moral Behavior Related to Early Damage in Human Prefrontal Cortex

Steven W. Anderson, Antoine Bechara, Hanna Damasio, Daniel Tranel and Antonio R. Damasio*

The long-term consequences of early prefrontal cortex lesions occurring before 16 months were investigated in two adults. As is the case when such damage occurs in adulthood, the two early-onset patients had severely impaired social behavior despite normal basic cognitive abilities, and showed insensitivity to future consequences of decisions, defective autonomic responses to punishment contingencies and failure to respond to behavioral interventions. Unlike adult-onset patients, however, the two patients had defective social and moral reasoning, suggesting that the acquisition of complex social conventions and moral rules had been impaired. Thus early-onset prefrontal damage resulted in a syndrome resembling psychopathy.

It is well established that in adults who have had normal development of social behavior, damage to certain sectors of prefrontal cortex produces a severe impairment of decision-making and disrupts social behavior, although the patients so affected preserve intellectual abilities and maintain factual knowledge of social conventions and moral rules.[1-6] Little is known for certain, however, about the consequences of comparable damage occurring before the maturation of the relevant neural and cognitive systems, namely in infancy, because such cases are exceedingly rare. Information about the early onset condition is vital to the elucidation of how social and moral competencies develop from a neurobiological standpoint. A number of questions have arisen in this regard. First, would early-onset lesions lead to the appearance of persistent defects comparable to those seen in adult-onset lesions, or would further development and brain plasticity reduce or cancel

* All of the Department of Neurology, Division of Behavioral Neurology and Cognitive Neuroscience, The University of Iowa College of Medicine, Iowa City, Iowa 52242, USA.

the effects of the lesions and prevent the appearance of the defects? Second, assuming early-onset lesions cause a comparable defect, would there be a dissociation between disrupted social behavior and preserved factual social knowledge, as seen in the adult-onset condition, or would the acquisition of social knowledge at factual level be compromised as well? We addressed these questions by investigating two young adults who received focal nonprogressive prefrontal damage before 16 months of age.

Results

The evidence presented here is based on detailed histories obtained from medical and school records, as well as legal documents, extensive interviews with the patients' parents, clinical and experimental cognitive tasks and neuroimaging studies.

Clinical Evidence

The first patient (subject A) was 20 years old at the time of these studies and was ambidextrous. She had been run over by a vehicle at age 15 months. At the time of the accident, she appeared to recover fully within days. No behavioral abnormalities were observed until the age of three years, when she was first noted to be largely unresponsive to verbal or physical punishment. Her behavior became progressively disruptive, so much so that, by age 14, she required placement in the first of several treatment facilities. Her teachers considered her to be intelligent and academically capable, but she routinely failed to complete assigned tasks. Her adolescence was marked by disruptive behavior in school and at home (for example, failure to comply with rules, frequent loud confrontations with peers and adults). She stole from her family and from other children and shoplifted frequently, leading to multiple arrests. She was verbally and physically abusive to others. She lied chronically. Her lack of friends was conspicuous. She ran away from home and from treatment facilities. She exhibited early and risky sexual behavior leading to a pregnancy at age 18. Contingency management in residential treatment facilities and the use of psychotropic medication were of no help. After repeatedly putting herself at physical and financial risk, she became entirely dependent on her parents and on social agencies for financial support and oversight of her personal affairs. She did not formulate any plans for her future and she sought no employment. Whenever employment was arranged, she was unable to hold the job due to lack of dependability and gross infractions of rules. Affect was labile and often poorly matched to the situation, but superficial social behavior was unremarkable. She never expressed guilt or remorse for her misbehavior. There was little or no evidence that she experienced empathy, and her maternal behavior was marked by dangerous insensitivity to the infant's needs. She blamed her misdeeds and social difficulties on other people, and she denied any difficulties with cognition or behavior.

When first seen by us, the second patient (subject B) was 23 years old. He had undergone resection of a right frontal tumor at age three months. He had an excellent recovery and there were no signs of recurrence. Developmental milestones were normal and he was left handed. In early grade school, mild difficulties were noted with behavior control and peer interactions, but he was not especially disruptive in school or at home. By age nine, however, he showed a general lack of motivation, had limited social interactions, usually exhibited a neutral affect and suffered from occasional brief and explosive outbursts of anger. His work habits were poor, and tutoring was recommended. He was able to graduate from high school, but perhaps because of the loss of structure for daily activities, his behavioral problems escalated after graduation. Left to himself, he limited his activities to viewing television and listening to music. His personal hygiene was poor and his living quarters were filthy. He consumed large quantities of foods with high fat and sugar content, and became progressively more obese. He also displayed abnormal food choices, for instance, eating uncooked frozen foods. Given his frequent absences, tardiness and general lack of dependability, he could not hold a job. He showed reckless financial behavior which resulted in large debts, and engaged in poorly planned petty thievery. He frequently threatened others and occasionally engaged in physical assault. He lied frequently, often without apparent motive. He had no lasting friendships and displayed little empathy. His sexual behavior was irresponsible. He fathered a child in a casual relationship, and did not fulfill his paternal obligations. He was dependent on his parents for financial support and legal guardianship. He showed no guilt or remorse for his behavior and could not formulate any realistic plans for his future.

Both patients were raised in stable, middle-class homes by college-educated parents who devoted considerable time and resources to their children. In neither case was there a family history of neurologic or psychiatric disease, and both patients had socially well-adapted siblings whose behavior was normal. The neurological evaluation was normal in both patients, except for their behavioral defects.

Neuropsychological Evidence

Comprehensive neuropsychological evaluations (Table 2.1) revealed normal performances on measures of intellectual ability (for example, fund of general information, ability to repeat and reverse random sequence of digits, mental arithmetic, verbal reasoning, nonverbal problem solving, verbal and visual anterograde memory, speech and language, visuospatial perception, visuomotor abilities and academic achievement). As in the case of patients with adult-onset lesions, the behavioral inadequacy of the two patients with early-onset lesions cannot be explained by a failure in basic mental abilities.

The patients were asked to perform several cognitive tasks designed to assess their ability to plan and execute multi-step procedures, use contingencies to guide behavior, reason through social dilemmas and generate appropriate responses to social situations. Both patients had significant impairments on these tasks. They failed to show normal learning of rules and strategies from repeated experience and feedback (Wisconsin Card

TABLE 2.1. Standardized Neuropsychological Test Data

		Subject A	Subject B
WAIS-R			
	Information	37	63
	Digit span	25	37
	Arithmetic	37	63
	Similarities	37	25
	Block design	75	75
	Digit symbol	25	25
RAVLT			
	Trial 5	78	11
	30 min. recall	99	68
JLO		40	57
Complex figure test			
	Copy	21	39
	30 min. recall	32	66
WRAT-R			
	Reading	86	63
	Spelling	81	63
	Arithmetic	32	58
COWA		43	15
WCST			
	Categories	>16	>16
	Persev. errors	1*	88
TOH			
	Trial 1	7*	7*
	Trial 2	1*	51
	Trial 3	1*	1*
	Trial 4	1*	1*
	Trial 5	1*	1*

WAIS-R, Wechsler Adult Intelligence Scale-Revised; RAVLT, Rey Auditory Verbal Learning Test; JLO, Judgment of Line Orientation; WRAT-R, Wide Range Achievement Test-Revised; COWA, Controlled Oral Word Association; WCST, Wisconsin Card Sorting Test; TOH, Tower of Hanoi. All tests were administered according to standardized procedures.[27,28,29] Test performances are represented as percentile scores and impairment is indicated by an asterisk.

Sorting Test, Subject A; Tower of Hanoi, both subjects). They also had significant impairments of social-moral reasoning and verbal generation of responses to social situations (Figure 2.1). Moral reasoning was conducted at a very early ('preconventional') stage, in which moral dilemmas were approached largely from the egocentric perspective of avoiding punishment.[7] This stage of moral reasoning is characteristic of 10-year-olds, and is surpassed by most young adolescents. The patients demonstrated limited consideration of the social and emotional implications of decisions, failed to identify the primary issues involved in

a)

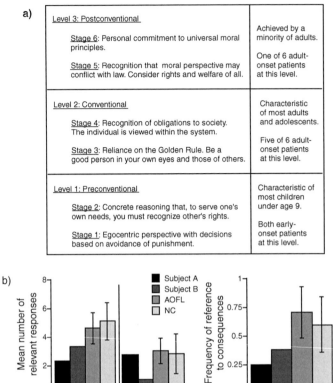

Level 3: Postconventional	
Stage 6: Personal commitment to universal moral principles. Stage 5: Recognition that moral perspective may conflict with law. Consider rights and welfare of all.	Achieved by a minority of adults. One of 6 adult-onset patients at this level.
Level 2: Conventional	
Stage 4: Recognition of obligations to society. The individual is viewed within the system. Stage 3: Reliance on the Golden Rule. Be a good person in your own eyes and those of others.	Characteristic of most adults and adolescents. Five of 6 adult-onset patients at this level.
Level 1: Preconventional	
Stage 2: Concrete reasoning that, to serve one's own needs, you must recognize other's rights. Stage 1: Egocentric perspective with decisions based on avoidance of punishment.	Characteristic of most children under age 9. Both early-onset patients at this level.

b)

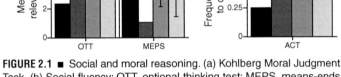

FIGURE 2.1 ■ Social and moral reasoning. (a) Kohlberg Moral Judgment Task. (b) Social fluency; OTT, optional thinking test; MEPS, means-ends problem solving; ACT, awareness of consequences.

social dilemmas and generated few response options for interpersonal conflicts. Their performance was in stark contrast to that of patients with adult-onset prefrontal damage, who can access the 'facts' of social knowledge in the format used in the laboratory (verbally packaged, outside of real life and real time[8]).

To explore the decision-making process further, the patients participated in a computerized version of the Gambling Task.[9,10] This task simulates real-life decision-making in the way it factors uncertainty of rewards and punishments associated with various response options. Unlike normal controls, but precisely as patients with adult-onset prefrontal lesions, both patients failed to develop a preference for the advantageous

response options. They failed to choose options with low immediate reward but positive long-term gains; rather, they persisted in choosing response options which provided high immediate reward but higher long-term loss (Figure 2.2).

The electrodermal skin conductance response (SCR) was used as a dependent measure of somatic-state activation, according to methods described elsewhere.[11] After repeated trials, normal controls begin to generate anticipatory SCRs when pondering the selection of a risky response (a response which may lead to long-term punishment). However, both patients failed to acquire these anticipatory SCRs, although they did show normal SCRs to a variety of unconditioned stimuli. Again, these findings were similar to

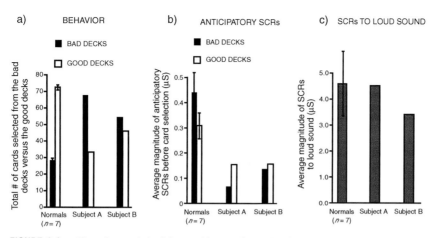

FIGURE 2.2 ■ Experimental decision-making and psychophysiology. (a) Responses on the gambling task. (b) Anticipatory skin conductance responses (SCRs). (c) SCRs to an unconditioned stimulus (sudden onset of 110-dB noise).

those from patients with adult-onset prefrontal damage.[11]

Neuroimaging Evidence

The patients were studied with research-protocol magnetic resonance imaging, which permitted reconstruction of their brains in three dimensions using the Brainvox technique and subsequent analysis of their anatomical defects. Both patients had focal damage to prefrontal regions, and had no evidence of damage in other brain areas (Figure 2.3). The lesion in subject A was bilateral and involved the polar and ventromedial prefrontal sectors. The lesion in subject B was unilateral, located in the right prefrontal region, and involved the polar sector, both medially and dorsally. The lesions of both patients were located in sites whose damage in adults is known to produce the emotional and decision-making defects discussed above.[2,3,12] Most frequently, these defects are caused by ventromedial and bilateral lesions, but the condition also has been noted with exclusively right, medial or lateral prefrontal lesions. The critical issue seems to be dysfunction in the medial prefrontal cortices (which can be caused either by direct cortical damage or white matter undercutting)

and the sparing of at least one dorsolateral prefrontal sector.

Discussion

We begin by acknowledging that our sample was small, but our findings accord with the only two other recorded instances of patients with early onset frontal lobe damage,[13,14] both with life-long behavior dysfunction, although in neither case is there precise neuroanatomical information. (One case, from 1947, predates modern neuropsychological and neuroimaging techniques, and lesions of the other are not described satisfactorily and may not be confined to the prefrontal region.) The sample is valuable, nonetheless, because of its rarity, and the evidence is offered in the hope that it calls attention to other existing cases and facilitates their study and the extension of the preliminary investigation noted here.

In answer to the first question we posed, the evidence presented above suggests that patients with early-onset prefrontal lesions in bilateral ventromedial or right sectors resembled patients with comparable adult-onset lesions in a number of ways. In early-onset patients, emotional responses to social situations and behavior in situations that

a)

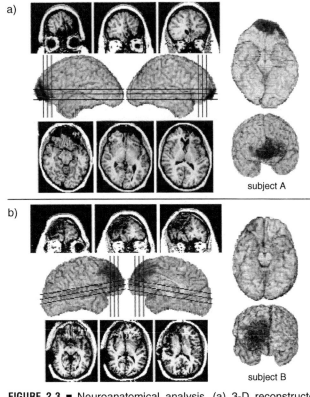

subject A

b)

subject B

FIGURE 2.3 ■ Neuroanatomical analysis. (a) 3-D reconstructed brain of patient I (subject A). There was a cystic formation occupying the polar region of both frontal lobes. This cyst displaced and compressed prefrontal regions, especially in the anterior orbital sector, more so on the left than on the right. Brodmann areas 11, 10 and 9 bilaterally, and 46 and 47 on the left, were involved. Additionally, there was structural damage in the right mesial orbital sector and the left polar cortices (Brodmann areas 11, 47 and 10). (b) 3-D reconstructed brain of patient 2 (subject B). There was extensive damage to the right frontal lobe, encompassing prefrontal cortices in mesial, polar and lateral sectors (Brodmann areas 10, 9, 46 and 8.) Both the lateral half of the orbital gyri and the anterior sector of the cingulate gyrus were damaged. (Brodmann areas 12, 24 and 32.) The cortex of the inferior frontal gyrus was intact (Brodmann areas 44, 45 and 47), but the underlying white matter was damaged, especially in the anterior sector.

require knowledge of complex social conventions and moral rules were inadequate. But whereas the early-onset patients were comparable, at first glance, to patients with adult-onset prefrontal lesions, a comprehensive analysis reveals several distinctive features. First, the inadequate social behaviors were present throughout development and into adulthood; second, those behavioral defects were more severe in early-onset patients; third, the patients could not retrieve complex, socially relevant knowledge at the factual level.

The greater severity of impairment in these two subjects was especially notable. The adult-onset prefrontal-lesion patients we studied ($n > 25$)

generally do not show the sort of antisocial behavior noted in the early-onset patients, for example, stealing, violence against persons or property. Beyond the acute period, the disruptive behavior of adult-onset patients tends to be more constrained, although impulsiveness and susceptibility to immediately present environmental cues leave them at risk of violating the rights of others. More often than not, the victims are the adult-onset patients themselves, not others, and their social and moral ineptitude can hardly be described as antisocial.

Patients with impairments of social behavior caused by adult-onset lesions of the pre-frontal cortex acquire varied aspects of socially relevant knowledge during normal development, and usually have had decades of appropriate application of such knowledge to social situations before incurring brain damage. As shown here and previously, following lesion onset in adulthood, they can continue to access socially relevant knowledge at the level of declarative facts,[5] and they can even solve social problems when presented in a laboratory setting, that is, in a verbal format, outside of real time. This distinction might explain why the two patients described here seemed to show less of a sense of guilt and remorse relative to their conduct than do adult-onset patients. Admittedly, however, this is a clinical impression, and we have no controlled measurement yet to substantiate it.

The mechanisms whereby adult-onset patients fail in social behaviors are still under investigation, but we have suggested that an important mechanism of the defect is the disruption of the systems that hold covert, emotionally related knowledge of social situations.[2,9] Emotionally related knowledge is presumed to bias the reasoning process covertly, namely, by enhancing attention and working memory related to options for action and future consequences of choices, as well as to bias the process overtly, by qualifying options for action or outcomes of actions in emotional terms. When emotionally related knowledge, covert or overt, is no longer available or cannot be retrieved, as shown in experiments involving failure of anticipatory psychophysiological responses,[10,11] the declarative recall of socially relevant facts

either does not occur or is insufficient to ensure adequate social behavior in real-life and real-time circumstances. Given that early-onset patients failed in both emotionally related and factual modes of retrieval, it is possible that they never acquired socially relevant knowledge, either in emotional or factual modes, and that their profound behavioral inadequacy is explained by an absence of the diverse knowledge base necessary for social and moral behavior.

The cognitive and behavioral defects present in these patients arose in the context of stable social environments that led to normal and well-adapted social behavior in their siblings. In spite of extensive exposure to appropriate social behavior in their home and school environments, and in spite of the relevant instruction, the patients failed to acquire complex social knowledge during the regular development period. Moreover, they failed to respond to programs aimed at correcting their inappropriate behavior during adolescence and young adulthood. This is an intriguing finding. Although comparison of different complex functions should be cautious, it is noteworthy that patients with early damage to language cortices, including those who undergo ablations of the entire left cerebral cortex at ages comparable to those at which our patients acquired their lesions, emerge into adolescence and adulthood with language defects whose magnitude seems smaller than the defects we encounter in the prefrontal patients described here. That the magnitude of compensation seemed smaller in our patients suggests that neural systems impaired by their lesions were critical for the acquisition of social knowledge, at least in the manner in which that acquisition traditionally occurs. It is possible, for instance, that by destroying a critical cortical control for the punishment and reward system, the acquisition of knowledge that depends on the coordinated contributions of punishment and reward situations becomes severely compromised. Should this be the case, it is possible that other neural systems might be recruited for the learning and processing of social knowledge, provided appropriate behavioral or pharmacological interventions could be developed. For example, cognitive-behavioral strategies that rely on a different balance of punishment and reward contributions might prove successful, and administration of neuromodulators such as serotonin and dopamine might conceivably help those interventions.

The cognitive and behavioral profiles resulting from early prefrontal damage resembled, in several respects, the profiles resulting from adult-onset damage. Unlike adult-onset patients, however, early-onset patients could not retrieve complex social knowledge at the factual level, and may never have acquired such knowledge. Overall, the profiles of early-onset patients bore considerable similarity to those of patients with psychopathy or sociopathy ('Conduct Disorder' or 'Antisocial Personality Disorder', according to DSM-IV nosology[15]), another early onset disorder characterized by a pervasive disregard for social and moral standards, consistent irresponsibility and a lack of remorse. Psychopathy may be associated with dysfunction in prefrontal regions,[16–18] especially in persons without predisposing psychosocial risk factors.[18] Also of note, children with antisocial tendencies have deficiencies of moral reasoning relative to age-matched controls,[19,20] and abnormal psychophysiological arousal and reactivity are found in adults with antisocial behavior.[21] The behavior of our patients differed from the typical profile of psychopathy in that our patients' patterns of aggression seemed impulsive rather than goal-directed, and also in the highly transparent, almost child-like nature of their transgressions and their attempts to cover them.

In conclusion, early dysfunction in certain sectors of prefrontal cortex seems to cause abnormal development of social and moral behavior, independently of social and psychological factors, which do not seem to have played a role in the condition of our subjects. This suggests that antisocial behavior may depend, at least in part, on the abnormal operation of a multi-component neural system which includes, but is not limited to, sectors of the prefrontal cortex. The causes of that abnormal operation would range from primarily biological (for instance, genetic, acting at the molecular and cellular levels) to environmental. Further clarification of these questions requires not only additional studies in humans, relying on both lesions and functional neuroimaging, but also experimental studies in developing animals, such as those demonstrating defects in social interactions of neonate monkeys with lesions of the amygdala and inferotemporal cortex.[22]

Methods

The behavioral histories were based on evidence obtained from medical and school records and legal documents, as well as extensive interviews with the patients' parents. Participants in this research provided informed consent in accord with the policies of the Institutional Review Board of the University of Iowa College of Medicine. Neuroimaging analysis was conducted by an investigator blind to neuropsychological information, on the basis of thin-cut T1 weighted magnetic resonance (MR) images using Brainvox.[23,24]

Comprehensive clinical neuropsychological evaluations were conducted according to standardized procedures (Table 2.1). Assessment of social knowledge and moral reasoning was based on four measures, Standard Issue Moral Judgement (SIMJ),[7] the Optional Thinking Test (OTT),[25] the Awareness of Consequences Test (ACT),[25] and the Means-Ends Problem Solving Procedure (MEPS).[26] All of these procedures involve standardized verbal presentation to the subject of moral dilemmas or social situations, and require verbal responses.

In the SIMJ task, a subject is presented with a conflict between two moral imperatives (a man must steal a drug in order to save his wife's life). The subject is asked to describe the protagonist's proper actions and their rationale through a series of standard questions (for example, "Should he steal the drug?", "Is it right or wrong for him to steal it?" or "Why do you think that?"). Responses were scored according to explicit criteria to allow staging of specific levels of moral development. The OTT is designed to measure the ability to generate alternative solutions to hypothetical social dilemmas (for instance, two people disagree on what TV channel to watch). A series of probes are used to elicit as many potential solutions as the subject could produce. The number of discrete relevant alternative solutions is scored. The ACT is intended to sample a subject's spontaneous consideration of the consequences of actions. Hypothetical predicaments involving temptation to transgress ordinary rules of social conduct are presented (for instance, receiving too much money in a business transaction through a mistake), and the subject must describe how the scenario evolves, including the protagonist's thoughts prior to the action and the subsequent events. Scoring reflects the frequency with which the likely consequences of response options are considered. The MEPS is intended to measure a subject's ability to conceptualize effective means of achieving social goals. Scoring is based on the number of effective instrumental acts described as methods of achieving goals in hypothetical scenarios (for example, how to meet people in a new neighborhood).

In the Gambling Task, subjects are presented with four decks of cards (named A, B, C and D) and instructed to select cards from the decks in a manner to win as much play money as possible. After each card selection, they are awarded some money, but certain selections are also followed by a loss of money. The magnitude of the yield of each deck and the magnitude and frequency of punishment associated with each deck are controlled such that choosing from the decks with low initial reward turns out to be the most advantageous strategy over a long series of selections.[9] Subjects are required to make a series of 100 card selections, but they are not told in advance how many card selections they will be allowed to make. Cards can be selected one at a time from any deck, and subjects are free to switch from any deck to another at any time and as often as they wish. The decision to select from one deck or another is largely influenced by schedules of rewards and punishment. These schedules are pre-programmed and known to the examiner, but not to the subject. They are arranged in such a way that every time a card is selected from deck A or B, the subject gets $100, and every time a card deck is selected from C or D, the subject gets $50. However, in each of the four decks, subjects encounter unpredictable money loss (punishment). The punishment is set to be higher in the high-paying decks, A and B, and lower in the low-paying decks, C and D. In decks A and B, the subject encounters a total loss of $1,250 in every 10 cards. In decks C and D, the subject encounters a total loss of $250 in every

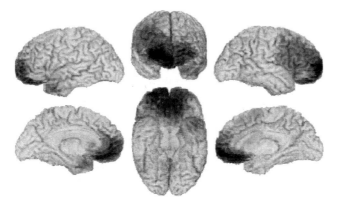

FIGURE 2.4 ■ Control subjects with adult-onset prefrontal damage. The overlap of lesions in the 6 patients with adult-onset lesions is depicted on a normal reference brain. Lesions of individual subjects were transferred onto the reference brain using MAP-3.[24] Darker shade indicates a higher number of overlapping subjects. The areas involved include all sectors damaged in the target subjects.

10 cards. In the longer term, decks A and B are disadvantageous because they cost more (a loss of $250 in every 10 cards). Decks C and D are advantageous because they result in an overall gain in the end (a gain of $250 in every 10 cards[6]).

The methods for the psychophysiological recordings (Figure 2.2) are described.[11] Response selection in the gambling task was temporally linked by computer to ongoing SCR recordings, and SCRs generated in the four seconds before behavioral response selection were considered to be anticipatory responses. The normal control subjects (three male, four female) were matched to the target subjects for age and education. The control subjects with adult onset prefrontal damage (three male, three female) were selected from our database on the basis of lesion location, in order to provide representation of adult-onset damage to prefrontal areas including, and more extensive than, the areas of damage in the early-onset cases (Figure 2.4). Lesions were due to a vascular event ($n = 3$) or resection of a meningioma ($n = 3$). Age of lesion onset ranged from 26 to 51 years, and subjects were studied at least one year following onset.

Acknowledgments

Supported by the National Institute of Neurological Diseases and Stroke Grant PO1 NS19632 and the Mathers Foundation.

REFERENCES

1. Damasio, A. R., Tranel, D. & Damasio, H. in *Frontal Lobe Function and Dysfunction* (eds. Levin, H. S., Eisenberg, H. M. & Benton, A. L.) 217–229 (Oxford Univ. Press, New York, 1991).
2. Damasio, A. R. *Descartes' Error.* (Grosset/Putnam, New York, 1994).
3. Damasio, A. R. The somatic marker hypothesis and the possible functions of the prefrontal cortex. *Philos. Trans. R. Soc. Lond. B Biol. Sci. 351*, 1413–1420 (1996).
4. Grafman, J. in *Structure and Functions of the Human Prefrontal Cortex* (eds. Grafman, J., Holyoak, K.J. & Boller, F.) 337–368 (1995).
5. Shallice T. & Burgess, P. W. Deficits in strategy application following frontal lobe damage in man. *Brain 114*, 727–741 (1991).
6. Stuss, D. T. & Benson, D. F. *The Frontal Lobes* (Raven, New York, 1986).
7. Colby, A. & Kohlberg, L. *The Measurement of Moral Judgment* (Cambridge Univ. Press, New York, 1987).
8. Saver, J. & Damasio, A. R. Preserved access and processing of social knowledge in a patient with acquired sociopathy due to ventromedial frontal damage. *Neuropsychologia 29*, 1241–1249 (1991).
9. Bechara, A., Damasio, A. R., Damasio, H. & Anderson, S. W. Insensitivity to future consequences following damage to human prefrontal cortex. *Cognition 50*, 7–15 (1994).
10. Bechara, A., Damasio, H., Tranel, D. & Damasio, A. R. Deciding advantageously before knowing the advantageous strategy. *Science 275*, 1293–1295 (1997).
11. Bechara, A., Tranel, D., Damasio, H. & Damasio, A. R. Failure to respond autonomically to anticipated future outcomes following damage to prefrontal cortex. *Cereb. Cortex 6*, 215–225 (1996).
12. Damasio, A. R. & Anderson, S. W. in *Clinical Neuropsychology*, 3rd edn. (eds. Heilman, K. M. & Valenstein, E.) 409–460 (Oxford Univ. Press, New York, 1993).
13. Ackerly, S. S. & Benton, A. L. Report of a case of bilateral frontal lobe defect. *Assoc. Res. Nerv. Ment. Dis. 27*, 479–504 (1947).
14. Price, B. H., Daffner, K. R., Stowe, R. M. & Mesulam, M. M. The comportmental learning disabilities of early frontal lobe damage. *Brain, 113*, 1383–1393 (1990).
15. American Psychiatric Association. *Diagnostic and Statistical Manual of Mental Disorders* 4th edn. (APA, Washington, District of Columbia, 1994).
16. Deckel, A. W., Hesselbrock, V. & Bauer, L. Antisocial personality disorder, childhood delinquency, and frontal brain functioning: EEG and neuropsychological findings. *J. Clin. Psychol. 52*, 639–650 (1996).
17. Kuruoglu, A. C. *et al.* Single photon emission computerised tomography in chronic alcoholism. *Br. J. Psychiatry 169*, 348–354 (1996).
18. Raine, A., Stoddard, J., Bihrle, S. & Buchsbaum, M. Prefrontal glucose deficits in murderes lacking psychosocial deprivation. *Neuropsychiatry Neuropsychol. Behav. Neurol. 11*, 1–7 (1998).
19. Campagna, A. F. & Harter, S. Moral judgment in sociopathic and normal children. *J. Pers. Soc. Psychol. 31*, 199–205 (1975).
20. Blair, R. J. R. Moral reasoning and the child with psychopathic tendencies. *Pers. Individ. Diff. 22*, 731–739 (1997).
21. Scarpa, A. & Raine, A. Psychophysiology of anger and violent behavior. *Psychiatr. Clin. North Am. 20*, 375–394 (1997).
22. Newman, J. D. & Bachevalier, J. Neonatal ablations of the amygdala and inferior temporal cortex alter the vocal response to social separation in rhesus macaques. *Brain Res. 758*, 180–186 (1997).

23. Damasio, H. & Frank, R. J. Three-dimensional *in vivo* mapping of brain lesions in humans. *Arch. Neurol. 49*, 137–143 (1992).

24. Frank, R. J., Damasio, H. & Grabowski, T. J. Brainvox: An interactive, multimodal visualization and analysis system for neuroanatomical imaging. *Neuroimage 5*, 13–30 (1997).

25. Platt, J. J. & Spivack, G. *Measures of Interpersonal Problem-Solving for Adults and Adolescents* (Department of Mental Health Sciences, Hahnemann Medical College, Philadelphia, 1977).

26. Platt, J. J. & Spivack, G. *Manual for the Means-Ends Problem Solving Procedure* (Widener University Institute for Graduate Psychology, Chester, Pennsylvania, 1975).

27. Lezak, M. *Neuropsychological Assessment* 3rd edn. (Oxford Univ. Press, New York, 1995).

28. Davis, H. P., Bajsjar, G. M. & Squire, L. R. *Tower of Hanoi Test—Colorado Neuropsychology Tests Version 2.0.* (Western Psychological Services, Los Angeles, 1995).

29. Heaton, R. K. et al. *Wisconsin Card Sorting Test Manual* (Psychological Assessment Resources, Odessa, Florida, 1993).

PART 3

Dissociable Systems for Attention, Emotion, and Social Knowledge

The readings in the previous section suggested that the human brain is not simply a dispassionate information processing organ but an organ responsible for socioemotional information processing, as well. A premise underlying work in cognitive and social neuroscience is that there is a close, causal, relation between information processing operations (both cognitive and affective) and the operation of specific nervous system circuits. Consequently, lesions of circumscribed areas of the brain may cause loss or alterations of specific mental or nervous functions in humans, and activity in circumscribed areas of the brain may reflect specific mental or nervous functions in humans. Although there are often theoretical disputes regarding what precisely constitutes a mental function, or the system responsible for a mental function, there is general agreement regarding several broad domains of knowledge that can be distinguished from one another (e.g., person knowledge, object knowledge). Recent brain imaging studies have been applied to these domains of knowledge to examine whether processing items from different domains of knowledge are served by separable networks in the human brain.

We begin with a reading by Yamasaki, LaBar, and McCarthy (2002) on the separability of prefrontal systems for attention and emotion. Their essay illustrates how it is just as important to correctly specify the psychological functions as it is to correctly measure the associated regions of brain activation. They report evidence not only suggesting that attention and emotion are governed by different systems, but that attentional processing involves areas in the dorsal prefrontal cortex, emotional processing involves areas in the ventral prefrontal cortex, and that these streams of information processing are integrated in the anterior cingulate gyrus.

In the second reading, Mitchell, Heatherton, and Macrae (2002) examine whether semantic knowledge about objects are represented or processed differently in the brain than semantic knowledge about individuals. Mitchell and colleagues found that person knowledge and object knowledge are subserved by distinct regions of the brain and, further, that social knowledge involves regions including the medial prefrontal cortex and

superior temporal sulcus—areas discussed in Part 1, the Volume Overview.

Humans are not only endowed with the capacities for attention, emotion, and social perception but also with a sense of fairness and justice that saturates interpersonal interactions and civilized societies. Moll et al. (2002) explore whether emotional moral reasoning and equally emotional but nonmoral reasoning involve dissociable neural networks. Their results accorded a special role in moral reasoning to structures involved in other forms of social cognition, namely, the medial orbitofrontal cortex, temporal pole, and superior temporal sulcus (see Part 1, Volume Overview). Together, the readings in this section raise the possibility that there may be something special about *social* cognition.

Dissociable Prefrontal Brain Systems for Attention and Emotion

Hiroshi Yamasaki*[†], Kevin S. LaBar[‡], and Gregory McCarthy*[§]

The prefrontal cortex has been implicated in a variety of attentional, executive, and mnemonic mental operations, yet its functional organization is still highly debated. The present study used functional MRI to determine whether attentional and emotional functions are segregated into dissociable prefrontal networks in the human brain. Subjects discriminated infrequent and irregularly presented attentional targets (circles) from frequent standards (squares) while novel distracting scenes, parametrically varied for emotional arousal, were intermittently presented. Targets differentially activated middle frontal gyrus, posterior parietal cortex, and posterior cingulate gyrus. Novel distracters activated inferior frontal gyrus, amygdala, and fusiform gyrus, with significantly stronger activation evoked by the emotional scenes. The anterior cingulate gyrus was the only brain region with equivalent responses to attentional and emotional stimuli. These results show that attentional and emotional functions are segregated into parallel dorsal and ventral streams that extend into prefrontal cortex and are integrated in the anterior cingulate. These findings may have implications for understanding the neural dynamics underlying emotional distractibility on attentional tasks in affective disorders.

Keywords: novelty, prefrontal cortex, amygdala, cingulate gyrus.

*Brain Imaging and Analysis Center, Duke University Medical Center, Durham, NC 27710; †Department of Integrative Physiology, National Institute for Physiological Sciences, Okazaki 444–0806, Japan; ‡Center for Cognitive Neuroscience, Duke University, Durham, NC 27708; and §Department of Veterans Affairs Medical Center, Durham, NC 27705.

The prefrontal cortex (PFC) is a heterogeneous brain region whose expansion in primates contributes to increased flexibility and control of cognition and comportment. Whether the PFC is divided into domain-specific regions has come under close scrutiny. A traditional approach to this question has involved contrasting spatial versus object processing to determine whether the PFC is organized along a dorsal-ventral axis analogous to posterior visual neocortex (1). However, electrophysiological studies in monkeys (2, 3) and neuroimaging studies in humans (4–7) have produced conflicting evidence for such a functional parcellation.

An alternative organization of PFC has been proposed in recent neuroanatomical models. Mayberg (8) postulated that ventral regions of PFC are specialized for "vegetative-somatic" functions, whereas dorsal regions are specialized for "attentional-cognitive" functions. This model further posits that the rostral anterior cingulate gyrus acts as an interface between the two processing streams. Mood disorders are hypothesized to reflect failure of coordinated interaction among these PFC compartments. Other anatomical models support the distinction between a dorsal attentional control system and a ventral emotional arousal system that relay information from posterior parietal cortex and amygdala into dorsal and ventral sectors of the PFC, respectively (9, 10).

In the present study, functional MRI (fMRI) was used to test whether attentional and emotional functions are compartmentalized into distinct prefrontal systems in the human brain. An attention-demanding target detection task ("visual oddball" paradigm) was modified from our previous studies in which subjects discriminated rare targets embedded in a stream of frequent standard stimuli (11, 12). Responses to the attentional targets were segregated from responses to two categories of trial unique task-irrelevant distracters presented intermittently and distinguished by their emotional salience. The distracter categories were equated for presentation frequency and other aspects of stimulus novelty that could potentially drive activation of PFC.

Methods

Thirteen right-handed neurologically healthy subjects participated in the study. All subjects provided written informed consent for a protocol approved by the Duke University Institutional Review Board. Before analysis, data from three subjects were discarded because of excessive head movement. The remaining 10 subjects (four males) ranged in age from 20 to 22 yr.

Experimental Design

An imaging session consisted of 10 runs, each containing 132 stimuli presented singly at the center of a back-projection screen with an onset-to-onset interval of 3,000 ms and a duration of 2,000 ms. A fixation cross was presented in the interval between stimuli. Standards consisted of squares of varying sizes and colors and were presented on 84% of trials. Targets consisted of circles of varying sizes and colors. Emotional distracters consisted of pictures selected primarily from the International Affective Picture System (IAPS; University of Florida, Gainesville, FL) and included unpleasant themes of human violence, mutilation, and disease. Neutral distracters consisted of pictures of ordinary activities and were equated to the emotional distracters with respect to mean luminance, chromatic features, and overall complexity of the scene. All distracters contained human figures and were chosen on the basis of 9-point arousal (1 = low/9 = high) and valence (1 = negative/9 = positive) scales provided in the IAPS norms and in a pilot group of undergraduate students. The range of arousal ratings for the distracters was as follows: emotional, 5–8; neutral, 1–3. The range of valence ratings was as follows: emotional, 1–3; neutral, 4–6. Thus, the ratings for the chosen pictures did not overlap across the stimulus categories. No individual distracter or target was repeated in an imaging session. Targets, emotional distracters, and neutral distracters comprised ≈8, 4, and 4%, respectively, of the stimuli in a given list. Successive targets and distracters were pseudorandomly distributed and separated by a 12- to 51-s interval (mean 18s). A total of 106 targets and 50 each of the emotional and neutral stimuli were presented in a session.

Subjects were required to press a button with the right index finger on detecting a circle (attentional target) and to press another button with the right middle finger for all other stimuli. Subjects were also required to silently count the number of targets presented during each list and to report that count at the list's conclusion. Stimuli were projected on a 10-in-wide screen located within the open magnet bore directly behind the subject's head. Subjects viewed the stimuli through mirrored glasses. Behavioral responses were acquired by using a fiber optic button box. Reaction times and accuracy were measured by customized experimental control software.

MRI Acquisition

Images were acquired by using a 1.5-T General Electric Signa NVi scanner equipped with 41-mT/m gradients. The subject's head was immobilized by using a vacuum cushion and tape. The anterior (AC) and posterior commissures (PC) were identified in the midsagittal slice of a localizer series, and 34 contiguous slices were prescribed parallel to the AC-PC plane for high-resolution T1-weighted structural images [repetition time (TR) = 450 ms; echo time (TE) = 20 ms; field of view (FOV) = 24 cm; matrix = 256^2; slice thickness = 3.75 mm] and gradient echo echoplanar images (TR = 3s; TE = 40 ms; FOV = 24 cm; matrix = 64^2; flip angle = 90°; slice thickness = 3.75 mm; resulting in 3.75-mm^3 isotropic voxels) sensitive to blood oxygenation-level-dependent contrast. An additional series of oblique T1-weighted structural images perpendicular to the AC-PC were also acquired by using the parameters specified above.

fMRI Data Analysis

Head motion was detected by center of mass measurements, and the data of three subjects were discarded because of head motion greater than 3 mm. Compensation for the interleaved slice acquisition was performed by using cubic spline interpolation of each voxel's time course with

realignment to the TR onset. Epochs synchronized to the onset of targets, emotional distracters, and neutral distracters were extracted from the continuous time series of image volumes following the method of Kirino et al. (12). Epochs containing two images preceding and five images following each stimulus type were segregated and averaged. The average MR signal values were converted to percent signal change relative to the 6-s prestimulus baseline.

The primary analysis was based on anatomical regions of interest (ROIs) drawn on each subject's high-resolution coronal structural images. These ROIs included the superior frontal gyrus, middle frontal gyrus, inferior frontal gyrus, cingulate gyrus, superior temporal gyrus, amygdala, hippocampus, intraparietal sulcus, supramarginal gyrus, and fusiform gyrus in each hemisphere. The group-averaged data showed no significant activation in the superior frontal gyrus, superior temporal gyrus, or hippocampus, so these ROIs were not considered further. Following the method of Jha and McCarthy (13) (see their figures 2 and 3), each ROI was drawn on a slice-by-slice basis, and each slice was indexed relative to the AC so that the distribution of activation within a ROI could be evaluated and summarized across subjects. For example, ROIs for the major gyri of the PFC were drawn on eight slices ranging from 7.50 to 33.75 mm anterior to the AC. Mean signal change for all voxels within each ROI was then computed for each time point and plotted to visualize the hemodynamic response profile for each ROI during each stimulus condition. The percent signal change at time points 3, 6, 9, 12, and 15 s poststimulus for each ROI was analyzed by repeated-measures ANOVA followed by post hoc analyses using the Student-Newman-Keuls test to further evaluate main effects due to stimulus category (target, emotional distracter, neutral distracter). An α level of 0.05 was used to determine significant activity in all contrasts.

In addition to the primary ROI analysis, a secondary voxel-based analysis was performed. After corrections for motion and temporal alignment, each subject's time series of whole-brain volumes was coregistered to a standard echoplanar template by using SPM99 (Wellcome Department of Neurology, London, U.K.). Epochs time-locked to stimulus onsets were excised and averaged in the manner specified above, such that each subject contributed a mean epoch of volumes for each of the target, emotional, and neutral categories. As the volumes for each subject were in a common spatial coordinate system, t tests were then applied to compare the signal change for each voxel over a collapsed 6- to 9-s poststimulus period. Contrasts were defined for targets versus emotional distracters and neutral versus emotional distracters. This secondary analysis was performed both as a check on the ROI analysis and to determine whether other brain regions not measured in our primary analysis were differentially influenced by the stimuli.

Results

Behavioral Performance

A repeated-measures ANOVA revealed a main effect of stimulus type [$F(3,27) = 43.12$, $P < 0.0001$] on reaction time. Post hoc Student-Newman-Keuls analysis showed that reaction times to targets (691 ± 146 ms), neutral distracters (680 ± 153 ms), and emotional distracters (728 ± 156 ms) were significantly longer than to standards (536 ± 157 ms). Reaction times to emotional distracters were significantly longer than for all other stimulus types. None of the fMRI activation in our ROIs correlated with reaction times across subjects.

fMRI Results: Prefrontal Cortex

ROI analysis of the activation profile in the middle frontal gyrus (MFG) showed a main effect of stimulus type at 3 s [$F(2,18) = 9.86$, $P < 0.0002$] and 6 s [$F(2,18) = 18.71$, $P < 0.0001$] (Figure 3.1B). Post hoc comparisons revealed that attentional targets elicited a larger signal than either emotional or neutral distracters, which did not differ significantly from each other. In 9 of 10 subjects, targets evoked greater activation in the right hemisphere. Figure 3.1A shows the anterior-posterior distribution of MFG activation by targets. Targets produced the strongest response in the

most anterior slices (22.50- to 33.75-mm anterior to the AC) with relatively little activation obtained more posteriorly. There was a trend for targets to evoke larger responses in the right hemisphere ($P = 0.09$).

In marked contrast to the results for the MFG, the ROI analysis of the inferior frontal gyrus (IFG) revealed strong activation by emotional distracters and lesser activation by neutral distracters at 6 s [$F(2,18) = 18.55$, P < 0.0001] and 9 s [$F(2,18) = 14.71$, P < 0.0002] (Figure 3.1C). Post hoc tests showed that at the anterior IFG emotional distracters evoked more robust activity than neutral distracters that, in turn, evoked stronger activity than targets. Responses to emotional distracters were largest in the segment of the IFG located 18.75–22.50 mm anterior to the AC, i.e., more posteriorly than the maximum activity in MFG evoked by targets. At this more posterior IFG locus, targets and neutral distracters evoked little activity (Figure 3.1D). The double dissociation between the role of MFG and IFG relative to attentional targets and emotional distracters was confirmed as an interaction in a two-way within-subjects ANOVA [$F(2,18) = 87.60$, $P < 0.00001$].

Qualitative inspection of the data from these PFC regions revealed a surprising feature. Namely, the MFG region activated by targets was deactivated by emotional distracters, and the anterior IFG region activated by distracters was relatively deactivated by targets (Figures 3.1B and C). Deactivations in these ROIs were confirmed by post hoc t tests computed to test negative deviations from zero signal change. Bilateral signal suppression in MFG by emotional distracters was significant at 6 s [$t(9) = -3.35$, $P = 0.009$]. Bilateral signal suppression in IFG by targets was marginally significant at 9 s [$t(9) = -2.20$, $P = 0.056$], which was predominantly driven by the left hemisphere [$t(9) = -2.76$, $P = 0.02$]. A similar trend was observed in left IFG at 6 s [$t(9) = -1.88$, $P = 0.093$].

fMRI Results: Other Brain Regions

Strong and selective activation to targets was also observed at 6 s poststimulus in posterior parietal

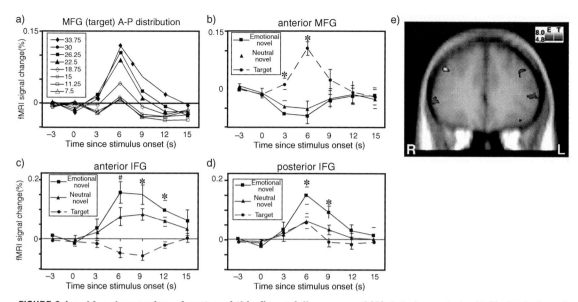

FIGURE 3.1 ■ (A color version of part e of this figure follows page 146.) Anterior-posterior (A-P) distribution of prefrontal cortex activation. (a) MFG activation by attentional targets. Numbers in the box indicate relative distance from the anterior commissure in mm. (b–d) Mean fMRI signal change (±SEM) for the anterior MFG, anterior IFG, and posterior IFG, respectively. In a–d, data from the right and left hemispheres are collapsed. Note change in vertical scale across regions. Asterisks indicate time points where (b) targets evoked more activation than distracters, (c) distracters evoked more activation than targets, and (d) emotional distracters evoked more activation than neutral distracters or targets. The pound sign in c indicates the time point where emotional distracters evoked more activation than neutral distracters, which in turn evoked more activation than targets. (e) Group-averaged t test results ($P < 0.001$ uncorrected) for the contrast between emotional distracters (plotted in blue spectrum) and attentional targets (plotted in red spectrum). Attentional target activity was observed in left MFG (BA 9/46; Talairach coordinates $-36, 35, 30$) and right MFG (BA 9/46; 44, 35, 31). Emotional distracter activity was observed in left IFG (BA 45/47; $-51, 33, 4$) and right IFG (BA 45/47; 55, 33, 0). The coronal section in e shows the single prefrontal slice where differential activation between attentional targets and emotional distracters was most remarkable. However, peak activation to emotional distracters was located ≈ 1 cm more posteriorly within IFG. R, right hemisphere; L, left hemisphere.

cortex, including the intraparietal sulcus [$F(2,18)$ = 38.47, $P < 0.0001$] (Figure 3.2A) and supramarginal gyrus [$F(2,18) = 19.16, P < 0.0001$] (Figure 3.2B). The posterior cingulate gyrus was also strongly activated by targets (see *Results*) (Figure 3.2C). None of these areas showed significant differences between emotional and neutral distracters.

In contrast to these dorsal areas, ventral brain regions did not respond to target stimuli but showed differential engagement to the distracters as a function of their emotional content. Emotional distracters evoked significant activity in the amygdala relative to neutral distracters and targets at 6 s [$F(2,18) = 11.73, P < 0.0006$] (Figure 3.2D).

Emotional distracters also evoked more activation in the fusiform gyrus than did targets at 3 s [$F(2,18) = 14.27, P < 0.0002$], 6 s [$F(2,18) = 56.74, P < 0.0001$] and 9 s [$F(2,18) = 19.43, P < 0.0001$] (Figure 3.2E). Post hoc tests revealed significantly more fusiform activity to emotional than neutral distracters at 6 s. The ROI analysis did not show any hemispheric asymmetry effects in these structures.

To test Mayberg's (8) hypothesis regarding the integrative role of the anterior cingulate gyrus, cingulate ROIs were drawn by subdividing the gyrus into four sectors according to horizontal distance from the AC. Each cingulate region included four slices. In each region at 6 s,

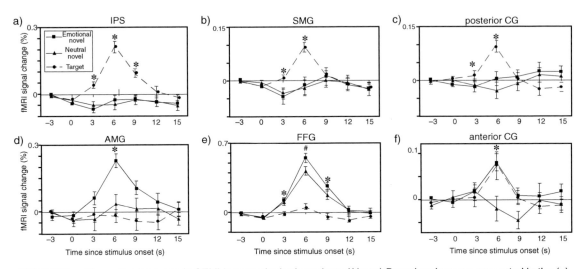

FIGURE 3.2 ■ Mean signal change (±SEM) in posterior brain regions. (*Upper*) Dorsal regions are presented in the (a) intraparietal sulcus (IPS), (b) supramarginal gyrus (SMG), and (c) posterior cingulate (CG). (*Lower*) Ventral regions are presented in the (d) amygdala (AMG), (e) fusiform gyrus (FFG), and (f) anterior CG (from 18.75 to 7.5 mm rostral to the AC). Data from the right and left hemispheres are collapsed. Note change in vertical scale across regions. Asterisks indicate time points where (a–c) targets evoked more activation than distracters, (d) emotional distracters evoked more activation than neutral distracters or targets, (e) distracters evoked more activation than targets, and (f) targets and emotional distracters evoked more activation than neutral distracters. The pound sign in e indicates where emotional distracters elicited stronger responses than neutral distracters, which in turn elicited stronger responses than targets.

repeated-measures ANOVAs with two independent variables (stimulus condition and hemisphere) were computed. In range from 18.75 to 7.5 mm anterior to the AC, a main effect of stimulus type was found [$F(2,18) = 6.66, P < 0.007$] (Figure 3.2F). Post hoc comparisons indicated that both emotional distracters and targets evoked larger activation than neutral distracters. In range from 3.75 mm anterior to 7.5 mm posterior to the AC, similar effects were observed [$F(2,18) = 14.45, P < 0.0002$]. Of all brain regions we examined, these portions of the cingulate gyrus [corresponding to Brodmann's area (BA) 24] were the only areas with equivalent responses to attentional and emotional stimuli. In range from 11.25 to 22.5 mm posterior to the AC, there were no significant results. In range from 26.25 to 37.5 mm posterior to the AC, a main effect of stimulus type was observed [$F(2,18) = 14.17, P < 0.0003$]. In contrast to anterior regions of the cingulate gyrus, here targets generated larger responses than either

emotional or neutral distracters, similar to the pattern seen in MFG and posterior parietal cortex.

Discussion

Behavioral studies have long shown that emotional stimuli can modulate the allocation of attentional resources (14, 15). The neural systems mediating the interaction between emotional and attentional functions, though, have not been well characterized. Previous studies have compared brain activation during attentional tasks to task-relevant stimuli with different levels of emotional meaning, as in the emotional Stroop interference paradigm (16, 17). These studies have supported a role for the rostral anterior cingulate when a pre-potent emotional reaction diverts processing resources away from a simultaneous competing task-appropriate response. The present study took an alternate approach to this topic. Here, subjects performed an attentional target detection task while novel stimuli, parametrically varied for emotional arousal levels, were intermittently presented. Making the emotional stimuli task irrelevant enabled a dissociation of attentional and emotional operations into their constituent networks, while simultaneously revealing where those networks intersected in the brain. Our results indicate that these faculties are segregated into dissociable dorsal and ventral processing streams that extend into the PFC and integrate in the anterior cingulate gyrus.

A Ventrolateral PFC Interface for Emotional Arousal

Neuropsychological reports have revealed dissociations across patient populations regarding the role of dorsal and ventral regions of PFC for cognitive and emotional functions, respectively (18, 19). Our findings provide evidence for this double dissociation in the healthy human brain. However, in the present study, activation to emotional distracters was strong in ventrolateral rather than ventromedial PFC, an area that has been emphasized in recent neuropsychological work. Neuroanatomical studies of the limbic forebrain have identified two parallel pathways by which emotionally arousing stimuli processed in the amygdala potentially interface with PFC (9). The first pathway is the canonical medial circuit linking the basal amygdala with ventromedial orbitofrontal cortex (BA 11), rostral insula, and subgenual portions of the anterior cingulated gyrus (BA 25). A second lateral pathway interconnects inferotemporal cortex and basal amygdala with ventrolateral PFC (BA 10/47) and rostral anterior cingulate (BA 24/32). The distracters in our task engaged the components of this latter circuit, with increasing levels of activation as a function of stimulus arousal (Figures 3.1 and 3.2).

Two accounts have been generated to explain the differential engagement of medial versus lateral sectors of ventral PFC during emotional tasks. The first hypothesis is that negatively valent stimuli engage medial sectors, whereas positively valent stimuli engage lateral sectors (20). An alternative hypothesis is that internally generated emotional states and motivated behaviors preferentially elicit ventromedial PFC, whereas externally triggered ones depend on lateral regions (21, 22). The results of the present experiment and our prior study using auditory cues (23) are consistent with the latter interpretation. One must keep in mind, though, that fMRI susceptibility artifacts have precluded observation of a reliable signal in the medial circuit, and a direct test of these two accounts remains to be undertaken.

Defining the Role of PFC in Stimulus Novelty and Memory Encoding

A number of electrophysiological studies conducted in normal subjects (24, 25), patients with prefrontal lesions (26–28), and epilepsy patients with implanted electrodes (29) have implicated the involvement of PFC in novelty detection. Little attention, however, has been paid to the properties of novel stimuli that are critical for engaging PFC. Our findings suggest that IFG activation to novel distracters depends on their emotional salience particularly in more posterior regions of the IFG (Figure 3.1D). Trial unique task-irrelevant novels that were neutral in emotional content also activated the anterior IFG, but the signal change was approximately 50% of that evoked by emotionally arousing novels (Figure 3.1C). The neutral and emotional distracters were equated for at least four aspects of novelty: presentation history (habituation or repetition effects), presentation frequency (rarity of occurrence relative to other task events), stimulus complexity (including presence of human figures), and lower-order perceptual features (distinguishing colors, luminance, size, etc.). Therefore, these stimulus properties could not account for the differential engagement of IFG across novel categories. The anterior-posterior distribution of IFG activation to novel scenes— ≈2 cm anterior to the AC—was the same as that seen in our previous study using alerting novel sounds (23). In combination, these results argue for a multimodal representation of sensory cues with high emotional salience in IFG.

The foregoing discussion has implications for understanding which features of novel sensory events make them particularly memorable. Several neuroimaging experiments using "subsequent memory" paradigms have shown that stimuli engaging IFG during their initial encoding are selectively retained over time (30, 31). The qualities of the stimuli coded in IFG that facilitate memory retention are unknown. The region of IFG whose activity predicts subsequent recollection overlaps with that observed to novel stimuli in the present report. Thus, the engagement of IFG may reflect an encoding mechanism that promotes stimuli into long-term storage as a function of their arousal value to the individual. However, we note that the same posterior IFG region (Figure 3.1D) was also strongly activated by arousing environmental sounds (23), such as gun shots and breaking glass, suggesting that emotional arousal may be the critical factor in evoking activity in this region.

Role of Dorsolateral PFC in Attention and Cognition

Attentional targets evoked significant activation in MFG, in consort with the parietal cortex and posterior cingulate gyrus, but novel stimuli did not, consistent with our prior work (11, 12). The MFG activation was maximal in a region more than 3 cm anterior to the AC, similar to that observed in our auditory study (23). Thus, both the IFG region activated by novels and the MFG region activated by targets appear to be multimodal in nature. The specific task-relevant computations performed within MFG remain unclear. We have shown activity in this area regardless of whether subjects mentally count the targets or respond to them with a button-press response (12). Thus, a specific task requirement to remember particular stimuli is not a necessary prerequisite for engaging this area.

A Clinical Model of Emotional Distraction on Attention-Demanding Tasks

An unexpected outcome of this study was that the fMRI signal from the MFG region sensitive to attentional targets was suppressed or deactivated in response to emotional distracters. Similarly, the fMRI signal from the IFG region sensitive to emotional distracters was suppressed in response to attentional targets (Figure 3.1C). Analogous deactivations in posterior ROIs were not observed. This pattern supports Drevets and Raichle's (32) observation that neural activity is reduced in some areas required for emotional processing during higher cognitive processes and *vice versa*.

A reciprocal relationship between dorsal and ventral PFC may provide a neural substrate for cognitive—emotional interactions and their dysregulation in mental illness. A hallmark of many affective disorders is the inability to maintain attentional focus on task-relevant operations in the face of prepotent distracting stimuli. Some subjects in our sample showed delayed reaction times to standards immediately after the emotional distracters, indicating a more protracted period of distraction than that seen to the emotional stimuli themselves. This pattern was less prominent to standards after neutral distracters. Thus, both the behavioral and neural effects of task-irrelevant stimulation were modulated by the arousing quality of the distracting material rather than to distraction or novelty per se. Our results provide support for Mayberg's (8) dual-stream theory of mood regulation, at least in healthy subjects. Failure to coordinate the PFC compartments mediating attention, emotion, and their interaction may provide a neural substrate underlying emotional distractibility in clinical populations.

Acknowledgments

This work was supported by Department of Veterans Affairs, National Institute of Mental Health Grants MH-05286 and MH-60451; the National Alliance for Research on Schizophrenia and Depression (K.S.L.); and the Japan Foundation for Aging and Health (H.Y.)

Abbreviations

PFC, prefrontal cortex; fMRI, functional MRI; AC, anterior commissure; PC, posterior commissure; ROI, region of interest; MFG, middle frontal gyrus; IFG, inferior frontal gyrus; BA, Brodmann's area.

REFERENCES

1. Ungerleider, L. G. & Mishkin, M. (1982) in *Analysis of Visual Behavior*, eds. Ingle, D. J., Goodale, M. A. & Mansfield, R. J. W. (MIT Press, Cambridge, MA), pp. 549–586.
2. Wilson, F. A. & Rolls, E. T. (1993) *Exp. Brain Res.* 93, 367–382.
3. Rao, S. C., Rainer, G. & Miller, E. K. (1997) *Science* 276, 821–824.
4. Smith, E. E., Jonides, J., Koeppe, R. A., Awh, E., Schumacher, E. H. & Minoshima, S. (1995) *J. Cognit. Neurosci.* 7, 337–356.
5. McCarthy, G., Puce, A., Constable, R. T., Krystal, J. H., Gore, J. C. & Goldman-Rakic, P. (1996) *Cereb. Cortex* 6, 600–611.
6. Owen, A. M., Stern, C. E., Look, R. B., Tracey, I., Rosen, B. R. & Petrides, M. (1998) *Proc. Natl. Acad. Sci. USA* 95, 7721–7726.
7. D'Esposito, M., Postle, B. R., Ballard, D. & Lease, J. (1999) *Brain Cognit.* 41, 66–86.
8. Mayberg, H. S. (1997) *J. Neuropsychiatr.* 9, 471–481.
9. Mega, M. S., Cummings, J. L., Salloway, S. & Malloy, P. (1997) *J. Neuropsychiatr. Clin. Neurosci.* 9, 315–330.
10. Mesulam, M.-M., ed. (2000) *Principles of Behavioral and Cognitive Neurology* (Oxford Univ. Press, New York), pp. 1–120.
11. McCarthy, G., Luby, M., Gore, J. & Goldman-Rakic, P. (1997) *J. Neurophysiol.* 77, 1630–1634.
12. Kirino, E., Belger, A., Goldman-Rakic, P. & McCarthy, G. (2000) *J. Neurosci.* 20, 6612–6618.
13. Jha, A. P. & McCarthy, G. (2000) *J. Cognit. Neurosci.* 12, 1–16.
14. Easterbrook, J. A. (1959) *Psychol. Rev.* 66, 183–201.
15. LaBar, K. S., Mesulam, M.-M., Gitelman, D. R. & Weintraub, S. (2000) *Neuropsychologia* 38, 1734–1740.
16. George, M. S., Ketter, T. A., Parekh, P. I., Rosinsky, N., Ring, H., Casey, B. J., Trimble, M. R., Horwitz, B., Herscovitch, P. & Post, R. M. (1994) *Hum. Brain Mapp.* 1, 194–209.
17. Whalen, P. J., Rauch, S. L., Etcoff, N. L., McInerney, S. C., Lee, M. B. & Jenike, M. A. (1998) *J. Neurosci.* 18, 411–418.
18. Bechara, A., Damasio, H., Tranel, D. & Anderson, S. W. (1998) *J. Neurosci.* 18, 428–437.
19. Stuss, D. T., Levine, B., Alexander, M. P., Hong, J., Palumbo, C., Hamer, L., Murphy, K. J. & Izukawa, D. (2000) *Neuropsychologia* 38, 388–402.
20. Northoff, G., Richter, A., Gessner, M., Schlagenhauf, F., Fell, J., Baumgart, F., Kaulisch, T., Kötter, R., Stephan, K. E., Leschinger, A., *et al.* (2000) *Cereb. Cortex* 10, 93–107.
21. Chen, Y.-C., Thaler, D., Nixon, P. D., Stern, C. E. & Passingham, R. E. (1995) *Exp. Brain Res.* 102, 461–473.
22. Lane, R. D., Reiman, E. M., Axelrod, B., Yun, L.-S., Holmes, A. & Schwartz, G. E. (1998) *J. Cognit. Neurosci.* 10, 525–535.
23. Hinton, S. C., MacFall, J. R. & McCarthy, G. (1999) *Neuroimage* 9, S793.
24. Daffner, K. R., Mesulam, M. M., Scinto, L. F. M., Cohen, L. G., Kennedy, B. P., West, W. C. & Holcomb, P. J. (1998) *NeuroReport* 9, 787–791.
25. Opitz, B., Mecklinger, A., Friederici, A. D. & von Cramon, D. Y. (1999) *Cereb. Cortex* 9, 379–391.
26. Knight, R. T. (1984) *Electroencephalogr. Clin. Neurophysiol.* 59, 9–20.
27. Yamaguchi, S. & Knight, R. T. (1991) *Electroencephalogr. Clin. Neurophysiol.* 78, 50–55.
28. Daffner, K. R., Mesulam, M. M., Holcomb, P. J., Calvo, V., Acar, D., Chabrerie, A., Kikinis, R., Jolesz, F. A., Rentz, D. M. & Scinto, L. F. M. (2000) *J. Neurol. Neurosurg. Psychiatr.* 68, 18–24.
29. Baudena, P., Halgren, E., Heit, G. & Clarke, J. M. (1995) *Electroencephalogr. Clin. Neurophysiol.* 94, 251–264.
30. Brewer, J. B., Zhao, Z., Desmond, J. E., Glover, G. H. & Gabrieli, J. D. E. (1998) *Science* 281, 1185–1187.
31. Wagner, A. D., Schacter, D. L., Rotte, M., Koutstaal, W., Maril, A., Dale, A. M., Rosen, B. R. & Buckner, R. L. (1998) *Science* 281, 1188–1191.
32. Drevets, W. C. & Raichle, M. E. (1998) *Cognit. Emot.* 12, 353–385.

Distinct Neural Systems Subserve Person and Object Knowledge

Jason P. Mitchell*, Todd F. Heatherton[‡], and C. Neil Macrae[‡]

Studies using functional neuroimaging and patient populations have demonstrated that distinct brain regions subserve semantic knowledge for different classes of inanimate objects (e.g., tools, musical instruments, and houses). What this work has yet to consider, however, is how conceptual knowledge about people may be organized in the brain. In particular, is there a distinct functional neuroanatomy associated with person knowledge? By using event-related functional magnetic resonance imaging (fMRI), we measured neural activity while participants made semantic judgments about people or objects. A unique pattern of brain activity was associated with person judgments and included brain regions previously implicated in other aspects of social-cognitive functioning: medial prefrontal cortex, superior temporal cortex, intraparietal sulcus, and fusiform gyrus. These regions were generally marked by relatively little change from baseline brain activity for person judgments along with significant deactivations for object judgments. Together, these findings support the notion that person knowledge may be functionally dissociable from other classes of semantic knowledge within the brain.

Among the most intriguing findings in cognitive neuroscience is that different categories or classes of objects are often associated with distinct neuroanatomical regions. Both neuropsychological and functional neuroimaging research have converged on the observation that perception of, and semantic knowledge about, particular classes of inanimate stimuli (e.g., tools, musical instruments, and houses) are subserved by distinct areas of the human brain (1–8).

*Department of Psychology, Harvard University, William James Hall, Cambridge, MA 02138; and ‡Department of Psychological and Brain Sciences, Center for Cognitive Neuroscience, Dartmouth College, Moore Hall, Hanover, NH 03755.

Although the exact basis of this neuroanatomical localization remains open to debate, most researchers concur that the brain contains some kind of category-specific neural architecture. Indeed, this observation has prompted some theorists to suggest that the mind may have evolved dedicated neural circuits to deal with knowledge pertaining to certain categories of objects; specifically, objects that have biological relevance or significance to people (e.g., conspecifics, tools, and plants) (4). The benefits of such a modular system reside in the rapid and relatively error-free manner in which semantic knowledge can be selected and deployed. Were distinct classes of information to share a similar neuroanatomical location, interitem competition might compromise (e.g., slow down) the selection process.

In the current experiment, we examined the neural substrates of a class of semantic knowledge that earlier work on category specificity has largely ignored, namely, other people. Although neural regions that subserve the *perception* of persons (e.g., body parts and faces) have been characterized (9–16), research has yet to investigate how the brain represents general knowledge about the internal, unobservable attributes of social agents. Person knowledge differs from knowledge about inanimate objects in a number of potentially important respects. Most obviously, the attributes used to describe persons differ substantially from those used to describe inanimate objects. Whereas a person may be described as *anxious* or *devious*, inanimate objects rarely engender such a description. One basic feature of person knowledge is that it frequently refers to the mental states of others, states that cannot be directly observed but may instead require generalization from one's own internal psychological properties (i.e., theory of mind). Finally, the application of person knowledge demands a flexibility that is typically unnecessary for most classes of object knowledge (e.g., people must frequently track interactions among independent agents acting in complex social settings).

To the extent that: (i) conspecifics are arguably the most important stimulus class to humans; and (ii) person knowledge differs in several important

ways from semantic knowledge about inanimate objects, we expect the representation of person knowledge in the human brain to conform to the category-specific neural organization observed in object semantics. To this end, we used event-related functional MRI (fMRI) to test the prediction that the brain represents person knowledge in a distinct manner from knowledge about inanimate objects. Adopting a paradigm from related research on the organization of semantic memory, the current experiment compared the brain activity associated with semantic judgments about people with that associated with comparable judgments about inanimate objects.

Materials and Methods

Fourteen paid volunteers from the Dartmouth College community (7 male and 7 female; age range, 18–27) participated in this experiment. All participants were right-handed, native English speakers with no history of neurological problems. All gave informed consent according to the procedures approved by the Committee for the Protection of Human Subjects at Dartmouth College. Data from one female participant were discarded because of problems with the acquisition of images during the functional scans.

Imaging Procedure

Imaging was conducted by using a 1.5-tesla GE Signa scanner. An Apple Powerbook G3 computer running PSYSCOPE V.1.2.5 (17) controlled stimulus presentation and recorded participants' behavioral responses by means of a keypress interfaced with a PSYSCOPE button box (Carnegie Mellon University, Pittsburgh). Stimuli were projected onto a screen at the end of the magnet bore that participants viewed by way of a mirror mounted on the head coil. A pillow and foam cushions were placed within the head coil to minimize head movements.

We first collected a high-resolution T1-weighted structural scan (SPGR) followed by four functional runs of 250 axial scans (20 slices; 5 mm thick; 1 mm skip). Functional images were collected by using a gradient spin-echo echo-planar pulse sequence (repetition time = 2,000 ms; echo time = 35 ms; flip angle = 90°, 3.75 × 3.75 in-plane resolution). The duration of each functional run was 8 min and 20 s.

Behavioral Procedure

Participants responded to visually presented noun-adjective pairs (4,000 ms duration) by pressing one of two response buttons if the adjective could ever be true of the noun (left forefinger) or another button if it could not (right forefinger). Nouns were the name of a person (e.g., *David, Emily*) or an object from the categories clothing (e.g., *glove, shirt*) and fruit (e.g., *grape, mango*). Half of the adjectives could appropriately describe a person (e.g., *assertive, energetic, fickle, nervous*) but not any of the objects, whereas the remaining half of the adjectives could describe one class of objects, but not persons or the other class of objects (e.g., clothing: *patched, threadbare*; fruit: *sundried, seedless*). To ensure that participants made use of general semantic knowledge about different classes of targets, they were further instructed to decide the appropriateness of the adjective for hypothetical exemplars of the noun (e.g., for a hypothetical person named David, not an individual they might know with that name). Each trial began with a fixation cross presented for 250 ms. A target noun was then presented alone for 1,000 ms (36-point New York font), after which an adjective was also presented (36-point Helvetica font). The noun-adjective pair remained onscreen for an additional 2,750 ms, during which the participant's behavioral response was recorded. Each fMRI run consisted of 50 trials in which the adjective was appropriate to the noun and 50 trials in which it was not. A pseudorandom order of trial types and a variable interstimulus interval (250–6,000 ms) was used to optimize estimation of the event-related fMRI response (18). During interstimulus intervals, participants passively viewed a fixation crosshair, which defined the baseline.

MRI Data Analysis

Preprocessing and statistical analysis of the fMRI data were performed by using SPM99 software (Wellcome Department of Cognitive Neurology). To allow the magnetic field to reach equilibrium, the first four time points (8 s) of each functional run were discarded. Preprocessing included slice timing and motion correction, normalization to the MN1305 stereotactic space (interpolating to 3-mm cubic voxels), and spatial smoothing with an 8-mm Gaussian kernel. An automated segmentation algorithm (Stanford University) identified gray matter voxels from each participant's T1-weighted anatomical scan, and subsequent statistical modeling was restricted to these voxels. Statistical analyses were performed by using the general linear model in which the event-related design was modeled by using a canonical hemodynamic response function and its temporal derivative. Comparisons of interest were implemented as linear contrasts. This analysis was performed individually for each participant, and contrast images for each participant were used in a second-level analysis treating participants as a random effect. Peak coordinates were identified by using a statistical criterion of at least 19 contiguous voxels exceeding a voxel-wise threshold of $P < 0.001$. A Monte Carlo simulation (www.wjh.harvard.edu/~slotnick/scripts.htm) of our brain volume demonstrated that this cluster extent cutoff provided an experimentwise threshold of $P < 0.05$, corrected for multiple comparisons.

Regions of interest (ROIs) were defined from clusters that survived these thresholding criteria, and peristimulus hemodynamic time courses were extracted for each of these ROIs on a participant-by-participant basis (representing percent signal change in each condition relative to the fixation baseline). One sample, two-tailed t tests (random effects, threshold of $P < 0.01$) were used to test whether signal change at the time point corresponding to the peak response differed significantly from baseline in each region.

Results

Analysis of the reaction time data showed that participants made semantic judgments about Persons significantly faster than comparable judgments about Objects [means, Ms: 900 ms vs. 1,019 ms, $t(12) = 3.92$, $P < 0.002$, $r = 0.49$]. In addition, faster responses were returned on "yes" than "no" trials [Ms: 870 ms vs. 980 ms, $t(12) = 6.29$, $P < 0.0001$, $r = 0.67$]; however, because this response type factor did not impact on the fMRI data, imaging analyses were collapsed across "yes" and "no" trials.

To examine whether judgments about persons and objects were associated with different patterns of neural activity, we compared the event-related BOLD (blood oxygen level-dependent) signal associated with Person trials to that associated with Object trials. This comparison yielded distinct patterns of brain activity for each type of target. *Object > Person* comparisons (Table 4.1 and Figure 4.1) demonstrated greater activity in left inferior frontal gyrus (LIFG), left inferotemporal (IT) cortex, left posterior parietal cortex, left superior frontal gyrus, and bilateral insula cortex. LIFG modulation was observed in multiple regions extending the entire extent of the inferior frontal gyrus. No significant activation differences were observed between fruits and items of clothing.

TABLE 4.1. Significant Peak Locations in *Object > Person*

				t value	
Anatomic label	x	y	z	Object	Person
R. insula	36	23	−6	5.70†	3.20*
L. insula	−33	24	−6	6.42†	4.40†
L. inf. frontal gyrus	−53	30	12	3.67*	1.34
	−50	19	27	4.80†	3.22*
	−50	41	−2	3.65*	1.40
	−50	7	22	5.26†	3.15*
	−50	24	4	4.34†	1.64
	−48	8	36	4.11*	2.56
	−59	8	38	4.29*	3.41*
	−45	−1	33	4.48†	3.04
L. inf. temporal	−53	−59	−5	2.98	0.31
	−50	−53	−10	4.53†	2.18
L. post. parietal	−30	−67	50	5.00†	3.21*
L. sup. frontal gyrus	−9	17	43	3.96*	2.88

Coordinates are from the Talairach and Tournoux atlas (49). Object and Person columns display the t value associated with the area's peak hemodynamic response relative to passive baseline for Object and Person trials, respectively; *, $P < 0.01$; †, $P < 0.001$; R, right; L, left; inf, inferior; post, posterior; sup, superior.

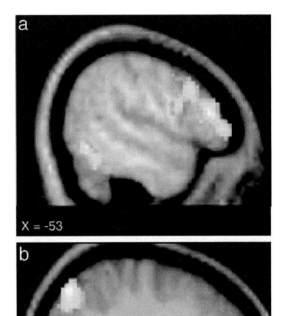

FIGURE 4.1 ■ (*A color version of this figure follows page 146.*) Activation maps show brain areas to be more active during Object trials than during Person trials. Regions of modulation included the left inferior prefrontal cortex and the left IT cortex (a), as well as the left posterior parietal and the left insula cortex (b). See Table 4.1 for the Talairach and Tournoux (49) atlas coordinates.

In sharp contrast, *Person > Object* comparisons (Table 4.2 and Figure 4.2) were associated with modulation in a very different set of brain areas that included dorsal and ventral aspects of the medial prefrontal cortex (MPFC), right intraparietal sulcus (IPS), right fusiform gyrus (FuG), left superior temporal (ST) and medial temporal (MT) cortex, left motor cortex, and regions of the occipital cortex bilaterally.

To further investigate the neural response in regions modulated by Object and Person judgments,

TABLE 4.2. Significant Peak Locations in
Person > Object

Anatomic label	x	y	z	*t* value Object	*t* value Person
Dorsal MPFC	0	54	21	−5.40†	−1.36
Ventral MPFC	3	39	0	−5.55†	−3.41*
	12	36	0	−4.39†	−2.81
R. fusiform	30	−51	−3	−2.08	−0.92
R. intraparietal sulcus	63	−33	33	−3.19*	−0.89
	60	−33	21	−3.67*	−0.46
R. occipital	48	−63	12	−3.70*	−1.64
L. sup. temporal	−60	−6	−3	−0.65	1.61
	−60	−12	−12	−0.45	1.37
L. med. temporal	−66	−24	−12	−1.55	0.25
	−66	−18	−15	−0.78	0.39
L. motor	−45	−27	63	−1.57	−2.22
	−30	−39	60	−0.41	−1.49
	−33	−36	69	−1.12	−1.71
	−30	−27	69	−1.46	−2.29
L. occipital	−51	−75	21	−3.07*	−0.80
	−15	−99	21	−2.10	−0.96

Coordinates are from the Talairach and Tournoux atlas (49). Object and Person columns display the *t* value associated with the area's peak hemodynamic response relative to a passive baseline for Object and Person trials, respectively. Negative *t* values represent deactivations relative to baseline; *, $P < 0.01$; †, $P < 0.001$; L, left; R, right; MPFC, medial prefrontal cortex; sup, superior; Ed, medial.

we examined the hemodynamic time course in each of the regions described above (Figure 4.3). Beyond the observed neuroanatomical differences between Object and Person judgments, these two sets of brain regions were associated with qualitatively different hemodynamic responses. Whereas regions identified from *Object > Person* comparisons uniformly produced signal changes above baseline (Table 4.1 and Figures 4.3a and b), regions identified from *Person > Object* comparisons were generally marked by nonsignificant or modest changes from baseline in response to Person targets, along with significant deactivations in response to Objects (Table 4.2 and Figures 4.3c and d). Indeed, the brain regions associated with activations above baseline for Person trials were almost entirely a subset of those demonstrating activations for Object trials, except for some activations unique to Person trials in bilateral basal ganglia, bilateral occipital lobe, and left cerebellum. In all cases, these unique Person trial activations were in voxels adjacent to Object trial activations and appeared generally to be serving the motoric and perceptual demands of the experimental task.

Finally, because Person trials were associated with significantly faster reaction times than Object trials, we conducted a secondary analysis to rule out the possibility that time course differences were spuriously produced by differences in the relative difficulty of the Person and Object judgments. Specifically, for each functional scan we selected 20 Object trials and then selected a subset of 20 Person trials matched to the Object trials for reaction time. The resulting average reaction time for Object trials (1,051 ms) was nearly identical to that for Person trials (1,047 ms). We then reanalyzed the fMRI data by using these trials and subsequently compared the peak signal change for time courses associated with Person and Object trials in each of the regions obtained in the primary analysis. Of the 17 peak activations observed in *Person > Object* comparisons, only a single region did not continue to demonstrate a significant difference ($P < 0.05$) after matching for time on task. This was the left MT region centered at −66, −18, −15, which was only marginally significant, $P < 0.11$. Of the 14 peak activations observed in *Object > Person* comparisons, all regions continued to demonstrate a significant difference after matching for time on task. Differences were particularly stable in MPFC (for *Person > Object*) and LIFG (for *Object > Person*), where we obtained a significance level of $P < 0.01$ for all comparisons after matching for time on task.

Discussion

The results of this experiment demonstrate a qualitative dissociation between the brain areas subserving semantic judgments about people and inanimate objects. This dissociation was evidenced both by the neuroanatomical localization of different brain areas modulated by Object and Person judgments (Figures 4.1 and 4.2) as well as by qualitative differences in the nature of the hemodynamic time courses underlying these modulations (Figure 4.3).

Neuroanatomically, *Object > Person* comparisons yielded regions (LIFG, IT, and posterior

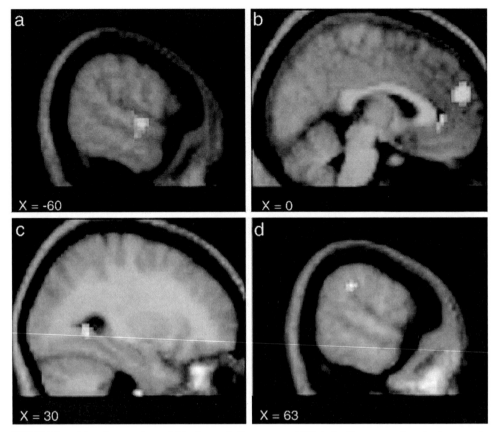

FIGURE 4.2 ■ (*A color version of this figure follows page 146.*) Activation maps show brain areas to be more active during Person trials than during Object trials. Regions of modulation included the left temporal sulcus (a), the dorsal and ventral MPFC (b), the right FuG (c), and the right parietal temporal-occipital junction (d). See Table 4.2 for the Talairach and Tournoux (49) atlas coordinates.

parietal cortex) that were highly consistent with earlier neuroimaging research on semantic memory and object recognition. LIFG activation has consistently been observed across a range of tasks that require use of semantic knowledge, including object naming and categorization, exemplar generation, abstract/concrete word decisions, and tests of factual knowledge (19–22). In addition, activation in the IT region was almost identical to that observed in a previous study in which participants were required to make semantic judgments about tools versus animals (8), and similar activations throughout IT have been associated with a range of object perception/naming tasks (5–7). Finally, earlier work has also implicated posterior

parietal cortex during the maintenance of object information before a behavioral response (23) and during tactile object recognition tasks (24).

In the same way, *Person > Object* comparisons identified regions (dorsal and ventral MPFC, the IPS, the ST region, and FuG) that converge with earlier work suggesting that these areas participate in a range of social-cognitive tasks (25). For example, a number of studies have observed modulation in dorsal MPFC in tasks that require self-monitoring or the attribution of mental states to others (26–28), as well as during retrieval of personally relevant memories (29, 30). In addition, patient studies have linked ventral MPFC to activities that involve the rapid, flexible use of social knowledge,

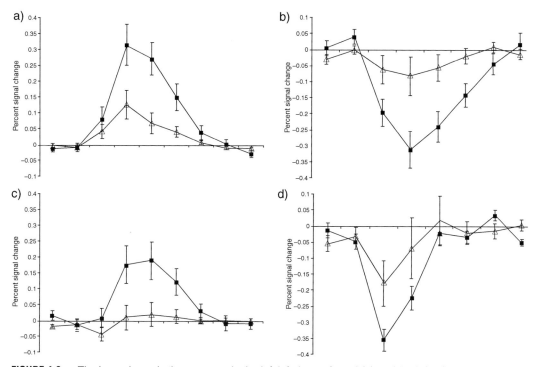

FIGURE 4.3 ■ The hemodynamic time courses in the left inferior prefrontal (a) and the left inferior temporal cortex (c) were characterized by activations above baseline for Object trials (filled squares) and either modest or nonsignificant activations for Person trials (open triangles). In contrast, the dorsal medial prefrontal (b) and right lateral parietal cortices (d) were characterized by significant deactivations for Object trials, along with no significant modulations for Person trials, a pattern typical for areas identified in *Person > Object* comparisons. Time courses were calculated by collapsing across multiple clusters within a neuroanatomical region (except for the dorsal medial prefrontal cortex, for which only one cluster was identified). The scale is seconds (one second per hash mark). Error bars display the standard error of the mean.

such as gender stereotyping (31) and the integration of emotion with thoughts and behavior (32–35). Similarly, the IPS, ST, and FuG have consistently been linked to the perception of socially relevant stimuli, such as eye gaze, biological motion, body parts, and faces. For instance, several recent studies have observed IPS modulation when people assume the physical perspective of another individual (36) or perceive targets displaying direct eye gaze (15, 37), tasks that have been linked to theory of mind and its associated cognitive functions. Likewise, the ST region (the superior temporal sulcus and adjacent areas of the superior and inferior temporal gyri) has been shown to play an important role in the perception of social stimuli, including head and mouth movements, changes in

eye gaze, body parts, and emotional expression (9–12). Finally, the modulation we observed in FuG corresponds closely to a region, dubbed the fusiform face area (FFA), that previous research suggests is selectively responsive to perception of, imagery for, and identification of faces (13–16, 38). We note that, although participants never reported engaging in visual imagery for the person trials, these IPS, ST, and FuG modulations may nevertheless have been associated with participants' spontaneous generation of mental images of body parts and faces.

Importantly, Object and Person trials were also associated with qualitatively different hemodynamic time courses. Whereas *Object > Person* modulations took the form of activations above the baseline, modulations associated with *Person > Object* comparisons were typically deactivations. More specifically, these *Person > Object* modulations were produced by consistent deactivations for Object trials along with nonsignificant or modest modulations for Person trials. As such, these data raise a question about how to interpret the observation that Person judgments consistently produced little change from a passive baseline condition.

One framework in which to consider these results originates in the observation that, when at rest, some brain regions are characterized by relatively high rates of metabolic activity (29, 39, 40). That is, the resting brain consistently assumes a preferred configuration of metabolic activity, with some regions routinely displaying higher levels of activity than others. Interestingly, of the four neuroanatomical regions with notably high resting metabolic rates, three were observed in the current study for *Person > Object* comparisons: dorsal MPFC, ventral MPFC, and lateral parietal areas that include the IPS (medial parietal/precuneus regions constitute the fourth high-metabolism region, which we did not observe across comparisons in this experiment).

Recently, Raichle and colleagues (28, 40, 41) have argued that such tonically high metabolic rates may reflect high levels of spontaneous mental processing that take place during rest. To the extent that metabolic activity in a brain region corresponds to the engagement of mental operations subserved by that region, high metabolic rates suggest that some brain regions engage in continuous, active processing during resting states. Intriguingly, three of the four highest resting metabolic rates are found in brain regions, dorsal and ventral MPFC and lateral parietal cortex (including the IPS), that have consistently been linked to social-cognitive processes such as the simulation of other minds, the flexible use of social and moral knowledge, self-referent memory, emotion regulation, and the perception of socially relevant stimuli (15, 25–27, 30–37, 40, 43–48). Whereas these studies have typically reported MPFC and/or lateral parietal *increases*, it is important to note that these increases have

consistently been observed relative to some other active task, thereby obscuring whether any changes occur relative to a resting baseline (see References 30, 40, and 47 for exceptions in MPFC). That social thought and perception appear to be subserved by areas with high resting metabolic rates suggests that social-cognitive processes constitute an important component of the brain's resting state of activity.

Because regions with high metabolic rates are actively engaged during resting states (such as the passive fixation conditions that often define the fMRI baseline), they consistently deactivate across a range of active cognitive tasks (39). When obliged to perform an active task, the brain typically suspends baseline processes, producing deactivations in the regions subserving those processes. However, because researchers have focused almost exclusively on the functional significance of activations above baseline, relatively little is known about the exact nature of the default baseline processes taking place during rest. The limits imposed by restricting interpretation to activations above baseline suggests that a different analytic approach is required when investigating a region associated with high resting metabolic rate and consistent deactivations across tasks. Because such regions are tonically engaged in the processes they subserve, they are unlikely to produce activations above a resting baseline; one may imagine a neural ceiling effect, of sorts. Instead, if a region is known to deactivate during many active tasks, then identifying conditions that produce no change from baseline can help to characterize the kind of processing operations that may occur spontaneously during rest. More specifically, if one experimental condition produces the kind of deactivation typical for a particular region whereas a second condition produces little or no deviation from baseline, one may tentatively conclude that the processes uniquely engaged by the second task overlap (at least in part) with the ongoing, default processes of that region.

The results of the current study demonstrate exactly such a pattern in dorsal MPFC, ventral MPFC, and lateral parietal regions. That is, Object trials produced significant deactivations across all three of these regions, replicating the deactivations that are consistently observed in these regions. In contrast, Person trials did not significantly modulate activity in either dorsal MPFC or lateral parietal cortex/IPS and only modestly modulated activity in ventral MPFC. Taken together, these two characteristics of the observed MPFC and lateral parietal modulations suggest that the processes subserving semantic judgments about social targets overlap considerably with default processes engaged during resting baseline. By yielding a significant deactivation below baseline, ventral MPFC only partly conformed to the idealized pattern of results. However, the observation that Person judgments did not overlap considerably with baseline ventral MPFC activity may not be terribly surprising. Whereas ventral MPFC has been linked to the *use* of social knowledge in real time, its role in representing abstract social knowledge seems to be minimal. Indeed, patients with ventral MPFC lesions can usually articulate social traits and the norms that govern social life, although they appear impaired at making appropriate use of such explicit information in their everyday life (31).

In summary, the results of the present investigation suggest that distinct networks of brain regions subserve the representation of semantic knowledge about people and objects. Although the areas participating in the representation of object knowledge have been characterized extensively in both neuropsychological and neuroimaging work, the current study is, to the best of our knowledge, the first to identify a network of regions that specifically subserve person knowledge. One interesting future direction will be to disentangle whether person-sensitive regions respond simply to the presence of socially relevant stimuli or whether they subserve some specialized cognitive operations brought to bear when thinking about people (e.g., representing the internal states of other intentional agents). We speculate that the semantic system for person knowledge may prove to rely on a neural architecture structurally similar to that underlying object knowledge: temporal areas such as the ST region and FuG may subserve

perception and identification of socially relevant stimuli in the environment (as IT areas do for object perception), whereas MPFC areas may represent more elaborate semantic information about the descriptive characteristics or internal mental states of social agents (akin to the role of LIFG in nonsocial semantics). Person knowledge may also have a unique contribution from the lateral parietal/IPS region, which may partly support theory of mind representations (15, 37). While this initial study points out the functional neuroanatomical dissociation between the systems supporting object and person knowledge, continuing research guided by these hypotheses will certainly be needed to characterize the nature of these systems more fully.

Acknowledgments

We thank Lila Davachi, Souheil Inati, Orville Jackson, Bill Kelley, Tammy Laroche, Anat Maril, Rebecca Saxe, Scott Slotnick, Anthony Wagner, and Carrie Wyland for their advice and assistance. This work was supported by National Science Foundation Grant BCS 0072861 and predoctoral National Research Service Award F31 NH65053.

Abbreviations

fMRI, functional MRI; LIFG, left inferior frontal gyrus; MPFC, medial prefrontal cortex; ST, superior temporal; MT cortex, medial temporal cortex; IT cortex, inferotemporal cortex; FuG, fusiform gyrus; IPS, intraparietal sulcus.

REFERENCES

1. Caramazza, A. & Shelton, J. R. (1998) *J. Cognit. Neurosci.* 10, 1–34.
2. Martin, A., Wiggs, C. L., Ungerleider, L. G. & Haxby, J. V. (1996) *Nature* 379, 649–652.
3. Martin, A. (2001) in *Handbook of Functional Neuroimaging of Cognition*, eds. Cabeza, R. & Kingstone, A. (MIT Press, Cambridge, MA), pp. 153–186.
4. Shelton, J. R. & Caramazza, A. (2001) in *The Handbook of Cognitive Neuropsychology: What Deficits Reveal About the Human Mind*, ed. Rapp, B. (Psychology Press/Taylor & Francis, Philadelphia), pp. 423–443.

5. Haxby, J. V., Ishai, A., Chao, L., Ungerleider, L. G. & Martin, A. (2000) *Trends Cognit. Sci.* 4, 3–4.

6. Haxby, J. V., Gobbini, M. I., Furey, M. L., Ishai, A., Schouten, J. L. & Pietrini, P. (2001) *Science* 293, 2425–2430.

7. Ishai, A., Ungerleider, L. G., Martin, A., Schouten, J. L. & Haxby, J. V. (1999) *Proc. Natl. Acad. Sci. USA* 96, 9379–9384.

8. Chao, L. L., Haxby, J. V. & Martin, A. (1999) *Nat. Neurosci.* 2, 913–919.

9. Allison, T., Puce, A. & McCarthy, G. (2000) *Trends Cognit. Sci.* 4, 267–278.

10. Perrett, D. I., Harries, M. H., Mistlin, A. J., Hietanen, J. K., Benson, P. J., Bevan, R., Thomas, S., Oram, M. W., Ortega, J. & Brierley, K. (1990) *Int. J. Comp. Psychol.* 4, 25–55.

11. Puce, A., Allison, T., Bentin, S., Gore, J. C. & McCarthy, G. (1998) *J. Neurosci.* 18, 2188–2199.

12. Narumoto, J., Okada, T., Sadato, N., Fukui, K. & Yonekura, Y. (2001) *Brain Res. Cognit. Brain Res.* 12, 225–231.

13. Kanwisher, N., McDermott, J. & Chun, M. M. (1997) *J. Neurosci.* 17, 4302–4311.

14. McCarthy, G., Puce, A., Gore, J. C. & Allison, T. (1997) *J. Cognit. Neurosci.* 9, 605–610.

15. Hoffman, E. A. & Haxby, J. V. (2000) *Nat. Neurosci.* 3, 80–84.

16. Halgren, E., Dale, A. M., Sereno, M. I., Tootell, R. B., Marinkovic, K. & Rosen, B. R. (1999) *Hum. Brain Mapp.* 7, 29–37.

17. Cohen, J., MacWhinney, B., Flatt, M. & Provost, J. (1993) *Behavioral Research Methods, Instruments, and Computers* 25, 257–271.

18. Dale, A. M. (1999) *Hum. Brain Mapp.* 8, 109–114.

19. Cabeza, R. & Nyberg, L. (2000) *J. Cognit. Neurosci.* 12, 1–47.

20. Maril, A., Wagner, A. D. & Schacter, D. L. (2001) *Neuron* 31, 653–660.

21. Wagner, A. D., Schacter, D. L., Rotte, M., Koustaal, W., Maril, A., Dale, A. M., Rosen, B. R. & Buckner, R. L. (1998) *Science* 281, 1188–1191.

22. Gabrieli, J. D. E., Poldrack, R. A. & Desmond, J. E. (1998) *Proc. Natl. Acad. Sci. USA* 95, 906–913.

23. Mecklinger, A., Bosch, V., Gruenewald, C., Bentin, S. & von Cramon, D. Y. (2000) *Hum. Brain Mapp.* 11, 146–161.

24. Deibert, E., Kraut, M., Kremen, S. & Hart, J. (1999) *Neurology* 52, 1413–1417.

25. Adolphs, R. (2001) *Curr. Opin. Neurobiol.* 11, 231–239.

26. Castelli, F., Happé, F., Frith, U. & Frith, C. (2000) *NeuroImage* 12, 314–325.

27. Frith, C. D. & Frith, U. (1999) *Science* 286, 1692–1695.

28. Gusnard, D. A. & Raichle, M. E. (2001) *Nat. Rev. Neurosci.* 2, 685–694.

29. Maguire, E. A. & Mummery, C. J. (1999) *Hippocampus* 9, 54–61.

30. Kelley, W. M., Macrae, C. N., Wyland, C. L., Caglar, S., Inati, S. & Heatherton, T. F. (2002) *J. Cognit. Neurosci.* 14, 785–794.

31. Milne, E. & Grafman, J. (2001) *J. Neurosci.* 21, 1–6.

32. Damasio, A. R., Tranel, D. & Damasio, H. C. (1991) in *Frontal Lobe Function and Dysfunction*, eds. Levin, H. S., Eisenberg, H. M. & Benton, A. L. (Oxford Univ. Press, New York), pp. 217–229.

33. Damasio, A. R. (1994) *Descartes' Error* (Grosset/Putnam, New York).

34. Anderson, S. W., Bechara, A., Damasio, H., Tranel, D. & Damasio, A. R. (1999) *Nat. Neurosci.* 2, 1032–1037.

35. Bechara, A., Dolan, S., Denburg, N., Hindes, A., Anderson, S. W. & Nathan, P. E. (2001) *Neuropsychologia* 39, 376–380.

36. Zacks, J., Rypma, B., Gabrieli, J. D. E., Tversky, B. & Glover, G. H. (1999) *Neuropsychologia* 37, 1029–1040.

37. Calder, A. J., Lawrence, A. D., Keane, J., Scott, S. K., Owen, A. M., Christoffels, I. & Young, A. W. (2002) *Neuropsychologia* 40, 1129–1138.

38. O'Craven, K. & Kanwisher, N. (2000) *J. Cognit. Neurosci.* 12, 1013–1023.

39. Shulman, G. L., Fiez, J. A., Corbetta, M., Buckner, R. L., Miezen, F. M., Raichle, M. E. & Petersen, S. E. (1997) *J. Cognit. Neurosci.* 9, 648–663.

40. Gusnard, D. A., Akbudak, E., Shulman, G. L. & Raichle, M. E. (2001) *Proc. Natl. Acad. Sci. USA* 98, 4259–4264.

41. Raichle, M. E., MacLeod, A. M., Snyder, A. Z., Powers, W. J., Gusnard, D. A. & Shulman, G. L. (2001) *Proc. Natl. Acad. Sci. USA* 98, 676–682.

42. Fletcher, P. C., Happé, F., Frith, U., Baker, S. C., Dolan, R. J., Frackowiak, R. S. J. & Fritch, C. D. (1995) *Cognition* 57, 109–128.

43. Gallagher, H. L., Happé, F., Brunswick, N., Fletcher, P. C., Frith, U. & Frith, C. D. (2000) *Neuropsychologia* 38, 11–21.

44. George, M. S., Ketter, T. A., Parekh, P. I., Herscovitch, P. & Post, R. M. (1996) *Biol. Psychiatry* 40, 859–871.

45. Goel, V., Grafman, J., Sadato, N. & Hallet, M. (1995) *NeuroReport* 6, 1741–1746.

46. Moll, J., de Oliveira-Souza, R., Eslinger, P. J., Bramati, i.e., Mourao-Miranda, J., Andreiuolo, P. A. & Pessoa, L. (2002) *J. Neurosci.* 22, 2730–2736.

47. Pardo, J. V., Pardo, P. J. & Raichle, M. E. (1993) *Am. J. Psychiatry* 150, 713–719.

48. Reiman, E. M., Lane, R. D., Ahern, G. L., Schwartz, G. E., Davidson, R. J., Friston, K. J., Yun, L.-S. & Chen, K. (1997) *Am. J. Psychiatry* 154, 918–925.

49. Talairach, J. & Tournoux, P. (1988) *Coplanar Stereotaxic Atlas of the Human Brain* (Thieme, New York).

Functional Networks in Emotional Moral and Nonmoral Social Judgments

Jorge Moll,* Ricardo de Oliveira-Souza,* Ivanei E. Bramati,* and Jordan Grafman[†]

Reading daily newspaper articles often evokes opinions and social judgments about the characters and stories. Social and moral judgments rely on the proper functioning of neural circuits concerned with complex cognitive and emotional processes. To examine whether dissociable neural systems mediate emotionally charged moral and nonmoral social judgments, we used a visual sentence verification task in conjunction with functional magnetic resonance imaging (fMRI). We found that a network comprising the medial orbitofrontal cortex, the temporal pole and the superior temporal sulcus of the left hemisphere was specifically activated by moral judgments. In contrast, judgment of emotionally evocative, but non-moral statements activated the left amygdala, lingual gyri, and the lateral orbital gyrus. These findings provide new evidence that the orbitofrontal cortex has dedicated subregions specialized in processing specific forms of social behavior.

Keywords: moral judgment; fMRI; orbitofrontal; acquired sociopathy; frontal lobes.

Introduction

Humans routinely judge the social behavior of others (Brothers, 1997). These judgments can be made on the basis of moral beliefs or can be just an interpretation of an actor's intention and the several possible outcomes of that intention (Colby et al., 1990; Haidt, in press). Such complex social judgments rely on the proper functioning of brain networks dedicated to processing stimuli endowed with social and emotional significance (Eisenberg et al., 1995; Damasio et al., 2000). The integration

*Neuroimaging and Behavioral Neurology Group (GNNC), Hospitals D'Or and LABS, Rio de Janeiro, RJ, Brazil; and

†Cognitive Neuroscience Section, National Institute of Neurological Disorders and Stroke, Bethesda, Maryland.

of cognitive evaluation with emotional bias allows humans to more confidently judge the social consequences of other people's actions (Fletcher et al., 1995; Frith and Frith, 1999). Damage to these systems may lead to distinct social behavior abnormalities (Eslinger and Damasio, 1985; Adolphs, 1999). The neural systems underlying these social abilities include the orbitofrontal cortex (OFC), the temporal neocortex and the amygdala (Brothers, 1997; Adolphs et al., 1998; Adolphs, 1999). While numerous functional imaging studies in humans have demonstrated cortical and limbic activation when subjects visually process social (see Adolphs, 1999, for a review) or emotional stimuli (Reiman et al., 1997; Lane et al., 1999), only a few have examined complex social cognition (Hoffman and Haxby, 2000; Golby et al., 2001). Investigations of patients with autism (Frith and Frith, 1999) and psychopaths (Blair, 1995) suggest that different aspects of social cognition can be selectively impaired. For example, although autistic individuals have generally impaired social behavior (Frith and Frith, 1999), psychopaths are impaired on a subset of social behaviors that require moral appraisals (Blair, 1995).

The neurological and neuropsychiatric literature is also informative in regard to the organization of the human social brain. There is increasing evidence that primary psychopaths comprise a particularly severe subgroup of antisocial individuals whose deviant behaviors are related to structural and functional brain abnormalities (Raine et al., 2000; Kiehl et al., 2001). Acquired brain damage in previously normal individuals can also lead to a set of related clinical syndromes reminiscent of primary psychopathy (Tranel, 1994). The antisocial behavior of these patients may result from sheer impulsiveness and goal neglect to recurrent flagrant criminal and evil actions that represent a bizarre change from their premorbid personality styles (Brower and Price, 2002). Like primary psychopaths, such "acquired sociopaths" often retain the ability to tell right from wrong and to articulate sound statements on morality and social appropriateness, that stands in sharp contrast to their behavior in real life. The damage in such cases falls within an extended area that encompasses the polar and mediobasal divisions of the frontal lobes (Kandel and Freed, 1989), the temporal poles (Miller et al., 1999) and several basal forebrain structures that are interconnected by the medial forebrain bundle and extend from the ventromedial hypothalamus caudally to the amygdala and septal area rostrally (Adolphs et al., 1998; Flynn et al., 1988; Gorman and Cummings, 1992).

In previous reports (Oliveira-Souza and Moll, 2000; Moll et al., 2001), we addressed the brain networks involved in the processing of sentences with or without moral content using fMRI in normal subjects. A selective network of brain regions was more active when subjects judged moral as opposed to factual statements. These regions included the ventral-anterior and medial sectors of the prefrontal cortex (frontopolar and medial frontal gyri), right anterior temporal cortex, left angular gyrus, and globus pallidus. Moreover, while the emotional valence of stimuli seemed to be directly related to the activations in right anterior temporal lobe and subcortical nuclei, it played only an ancillary role in the prefrontal cortex activation. Despite such compelling evidence, since our previous study design did not include emotional stimuli as an independent, nonmoral, experimental condition, it is difficult to conclude which brain regions were distinctively recruited by emotion processing as opposed to moral judgment. Another recent fMRI study (Greene et al., 2001) reported similar activation of the anterior prefrontal cortex in response to complex moral judgments. This study did not include a nonmoral emotional condition either and, thus, the reported activations could have been induced by emotional processing. Besides, the increased attentional and decision-making demands of the moral-emotional condition might be associated with slower reaction times, which could by themselves have led to increased prefrontal activation (de Zubicaray et al., 2001). In our previous reports (Oliveira-Souza and Moll, 2000; Moll et al., 2001), we employed a measure of judgment difficulty and found equivalent judgment difficulty for moral and nonmoral stimuli, favoring the view that cognitive effort was not decisively involved in the brain activation patterns. Notwithstanding these observations, the issue of which brain regions are specifically engaged when normal subjects judge moral and nonmoral, emotionally charged situations remains unsettled.

Here we employed functional MRI to address the role of emotional valence and moral content in social judgments. For this purpose, normal subjects were requested to judge statements pertaining to three main conditions: emotionally unpleasant statements without moral connotations, emotionally unpleasant statements with moral connotations, and emotionally neutral statements. Scrambled statements were included as a baseline condition. By including an experimental condition evocative of emotions devoid of moral connotations, we intended to explore the differential effect of emotional valence and moral judgment on brain activation. An additional feature of the present study was that statements pertaining to all experimental conditions described human actions unfolding in social scenarios. Based on the evidence that different kinds of social abilities and emotional processing may be dissociated in cases of brain damage (Eslinger and Damasio, 1985; Blair, 1995), we hypothesized that the judgment of unpleasant-moral and unpleasant-nonmoral social situations would lead to distinct patterns of corticolimbic activation. More specifically, we expected that the anterior sectors of the prefrontal cortex, as shown by our previous study (Moll et al., 2001), would be preferentially activated by moral judgments when compared with judgments of emotional situations without moral connotations. We also predicted that the judgment of unpleasant scenarios devoid of moral content would activate brain regions that mediate basic unpleasant emotions, such as the amygdala.

Materials and Methods

Subjects

Seven healthy right-handed adults (three males, mean age of 30.3 ± 4.7 years, 14.9 ± 2.0 years of education), with no history of neuropsychiatric disorders, participated in the fMRI study. An independent group of seven subjects whose age, level of education and gender distribution did not differ from the fMRI subjects (age: $t = 1.76$, $P = 0.11$; education: $t = 1.13$, $P = 0.28$; gender: $x^2 = 1.40$, $P = 0.56$), was recruited for a supplemental behavioral study. All subjects gave written informed consent and did not receive financial compensation. The study was conducted in the Hospital Barra D'Or and approved by the hospital's Institutional Review Board and Ethics Committee.

Stimuli and Task

Subjects were asked to read short statements that were visually presented through LCD goggles (Resonance Technologies, Inc., CA) and to covertly judge them as being either right or wrong. We chose the words "certo" and "errado," the Portuguese equivalents of "right" and "wrong" because, as in English, they allow moral, factual, and structural connotations. Subjects understood that they were intended to use right or wrong attributions in a broadly defined manner. By limiting the output of their cognitive operations to only two categories ("right" or "wrong"), we expected to force each participant to make standard decisions regardless of the specific content of each sentence.

Rationale behind Moral and Nonmoral Judgments

The distinction between moral and nonmoral judgments relies on psychological constructs that can be objectively assessed and have been extensively validated across different cultures (Snarey, 1985; Colby et al., 1990). A further distinction between nonmoral social norm violations and moral-social violations has also been supported by empirical evidence. This distinction forms the basis of the concept of conventional and moral transgressions, whose psychological bases have been worked out in normal individuals, psychopaths and in patients with autism, in both adults and children (Blair, 1995, 1996; Fisher and Blair, 1998).

Experimental Conditions

Three main conditions included structurally similar neutral (NTR), moral (M), and nonmoral (NM)

TABLE 5.1. Sample Statements

Nonmoral neutral (NTR)
  He never uses the seat belt.
  The elderly sleep more at night.
  Fat children should make a diet.
  The painter used his hand as a paintbrush.
  Judges use white uniforms.
Nonmoral unpleasant (NM)
  He licked the dirty toilet.
  The elderly are used to eating living toads.
  Pregnant women often throw up.
  People don't have tatoos inside their eyeballs.
  Judges often eat rotten food.
Moral (M)
  He shot the victim to death.
  The elderly are useless.
  Criminals should go to jail.
  The father never treated his son as a slave.
  The judge condemned the innocent man.
Scrambled (SCR)
  Sons push use eat work.
  Kick like poor rain old have.
  Life turn of shoes drink was brother.
  Your drive building must meat.
  Day daughter less ground parents loose.

statements (see Table 5.1 for a sample of the statements). NTR statements described relatively unemotional situations, NM statements described emotionally aversive scenarios without moral content, while M statements described emotional situations designed to evoke moral attitudes and feelings. All statements described scenarios and people acting in different settings, and, thus, each of the NTR, NM, and M statements deployed explicit social contexts. An additional condition made up of scrambled statements (SCR) was added to serve as a low level baseline. Subjects covertly judged all the sentences in a categorical fashion as right or wrong. After fMRI scanning, the sentences were presented again, this time in a randomized, unblocked fashion, and subjects were asked to overtly judge them as right or wrong by referring to their impressions while in the scanner. Subjects also rated the degree of moral content and of the positive or negative emotional impact of each statement on 4-point Likert scales. They were instructed that moral content meant issues of values, rights, justice, responsibilities and principles regarding peace and care for others (Colby et al., 1990; Gilligan, 1993). Subjects were encouraged to make a short verbal commentary about each statement. These com-

ments were scored by two judges who used a predefined lexicon of words that expressed basic or moral emotions. The identification of basic in contrast to moral emotions in these descriptions was based on concepts firmly grounded in a large body of empirical research (Haidt, in press). This procedure helped us ascertain that the statements employed in the moral condition suited our purposes as moral-eliciting stimuli.

Each condition was composed of a set of 24 statements that were presented in blocks of three at a time. Stimuli were displayed for 5 s and were separated by 5 s of a blank screen. A pilot study showed that this presentation rate allowed subjects to comfortably read and judge each sentence. The eight blocks of each condition followed a fixed pseudorandomized order. A fixation crosshair was displayed for 15 s between each block to allow a complete return of the BOLD signal to baseline. Scrambled sentences were generated by randomly reordering words sampled from the other conditions, being semantically meaningless and grammatically incorrect ("nonsense"). Subjects were not informed beforehand about the content of the sentences, yet they were asked to "try and get their meaning and to judge all of them, regardless of how weird they might sound." This was meant to encourage subjects to stick to the scrambled sentences and prevent their attention from wandering. To minimize the effects of planning and to prevent the subjects from reasoning about the future, the situations depicted in all statements referred to the present or past only.

Behavioral Measures

To obtain a measure of task difficulty, seven subjects not participating in the fMRI experiment judged the blocked 24 NTR, M, NM, and SCR statements. These blocks were administered in a randomized order across subjects. The time to judge each block was recorded as a response time (RT) and taken as a proxy for task difficulty. Although collecting responses during fMRI data acquisition would be more desirable, MR compatible response devices were not available in our institution at the time this study was completed. Although we could have obtained RTs from the same subjects by repeating the task after fMRI scanning, we pondered that subjects' attitudes to repeated stimuli would not necessarily reflect their naïve responses. For this reason, a different group of subjects matched for age, gender, education and cultural background was employed. This approach has been successfully adopted in previous functional imaging studies (Bottini et al., 1994).

Ratings for moral content, emotional impact, and mean response times were assessed with analysis of variance. Pairwise comparisons of means were evaluated post hoc with the least significant difference test. The association between emotional impact and moral content in the M condition was assessed with the Phi coefficient. Computations were performed using *Statistica*, v. 5.5 (StatSoft, 1999).

fMRI Procedures and Data Analysis

Anatomic (3D-GRE T1-weighted images, 1.25 mm) and functional data (BOLD-EPI imaging, TR/TE = 4980/66 ms, 128 × 128, FOV = 256 mm, thickness/gap = 5/0.25 mm, 16 slices) were obtained with a 1.5 MRI scanner (Siemens Vision, Germany). Data acquisition was synchronized with stimulus presentation. Functional datasets were 3D motion-corrected. Slice time correction, temporal smoothing, linear trend

removal and spatial normalization (3-D Gaussian kernel = 4 mm) were performed. Datasets were co-registered and Talairach transformed (Talairach and Tournoux, 1998). Activation maps were analyzed with statistical parametric methods (Friston et al., 1995) contained in Brain Voyager v. 3.9 (Brain Innovation, Maastricht, The Netherlands). Regressors representing the experimental conditions were modeled with a hemodynamic response filter entered in a multiple regression analysis, using a fixed-effects model. Significance was assessed using a threshold corresponding to $P < 0.001$ (uncorrected) at the voxel level and a three-dimensional cluster extent threshold of 100 mm³ to protect against Type I errors associated with multiple statistical comparisons (Forman et al., 1995). Smaller activated clusters (50–100 mm³) were reported when they fell in a region where an *a priori* hypothesis predicted activation (OFC and medial prefrontal cortex, amygdala and anterior temporal cortex). Levels of statistical significance for each activated cluster are reported in Table 5.2. Results were overlaid on averaged anatomical data from all subjects and on partially inflated three-dimensional templates of a sample subject.

TABLE 5.2. Anatomical Locations and Coordinates of Activations

Brain region, Brodmann area[a]	Center Talairach coordinates			Cluster P value	Cluster volume[b]
	X	Y	Z		
M vs NTR[c]					
L Medial OFC, 10/11[d]	−10	46	−12	0.0002	171
L Temporal pole, 38	−33	19	−23	0.001	50[e]
L STS, 21/22[d]	−47	−40	−2	0.0004	148
NM vs NTR[c]					
R Fusiform G, 19[f]	31	−66	−20	0.0004	139
R Inf Occ G, 19	28	−88	−22	0.001	100
R Lingual G, 17/18[f]	5	−72	0	0.000001	1750
Bilat Calcarine S, 17	−11	−88	2	0.000004	247
L Amygdala[f]	−20	−12	−6	0.000001	253
L Lingual G, 17/18[f]	−23	−64	−15	0.000001	1068
L Lateral OFC, 11/47[f]	−26	32	−1	0.001	108
L Fusiform G, 19[f]	−34	−62	−11	0.00003	206

[a]OFC, orbitofrontal cortex; STS, superior temporal sulcus; G, gyrus; S, sulcus; Inf, inferior; Occ, occipital; L, Left; R, right; Bilat, bilateral.
[b]Cluster volumes of at least 100 mm³.
[c]M, NTR, and NM correspond to moral, neutral, and nonmoral social conditions, respectively.
[d]Also activated in the M vs NM comparison.
[e]Cluster volume below 100 mm³.
[f]Also activated in the NM vs M comparison.

Results

Behavioral

Moral content was rated significantly higher in the M (2.12 ± 1.41) in comparison to the NTR (0.07 ± 0.37) and NM (0.27 ± 0.82) conditions [$F(2,499) = 228.9, P < 0.00002$]. The M and NM statements were designed so that they had negative emotional valence. This was validated by subject ratings of those same statements at debriefing. The emotional valence of the NTR condition approached zero (−0.05 ± 0.98), whereas the net emotional valence for both the M (−2.02 ± 1.26) and NM (−0.88 ± 1.20) conditions was negative. The NM and M conditions differed significantly from the NTR condition in degree of emotional impact [$F(2,497) = 138.23, P < 0.0001$]. M sentences were rated as having a higher emotional impact than NM sentences ($P < 0.0001$). There was a significant relationship between moral content and emotionality of statements ($r = 0.44, p < 0.0001$), suggesting that moral judgment interacts with the perceived emotionality of the stimulus. Judgments in the M condition were described more frequently with moral terms (e.g., "pity" and "indignation") than with basic emotion words (123 × 53) in contrast to judgments in the NM condition, in which primary emotion words (e.g., "disgust") were used more often (136 × 1) (Phi = 0.70, $P < 0.0001$). This result indicated that the M sentences were effective in eliciting moral concerns. There was an overall difference in judgment times across trials ([$F(3,18) = 3.42, P < 0.04$]. Post hoc analyses showed that this difference was due to slower RT in the SCR condition (92.3 ± 33.5 s, $P < 0.03$). Mean RT did not statistically differ for the NTR (75.3 ± 20.7 s), M (73.7 ± 24.3 s), and NM (76.7 ± 25.3 s) conditions, suggesting that judging them recruited equivalent degrees of effort.

Brain Activation

Compared with the NTR condition, the M and NM conditions evoked distinct brain activation patterns (Figures 5.1a and 5.1b and Table 5.2). The NM condition induced activation of the left

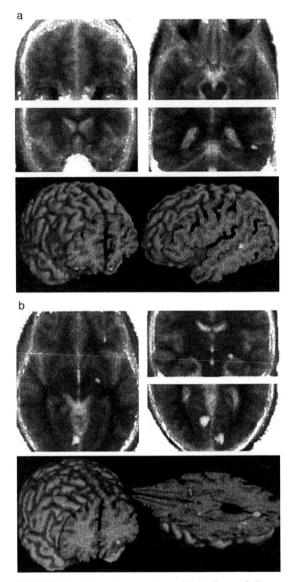

FIGURE 5.1 ■ (A color version of this figure follows page 146.) Brain regions activated by emotionally evocative moral (M) and nonmoral (NM) judgments compared to neutral (NTR) ones. Activations were overlaid on sections through an averaged brain from all subjects with inverted grayscale and on 3-D renderings of a reference brain. (a) M vs NTR condition. Activated regions were in the left orbitofrontal cortex (OFC) and in the superior temporal sulcus and the left temporal pole. (b) NM vs NTR condition. Activated regions were in the left amygdala and lateral OFC, and bilaterally in the visual cortex.

amygdala and left lateral OFC as well as of several regions of the ventral visual cortex (lingual, inferior occipital and fusiform gyri). The M condition induced activation of the left medial OFC (gyrus rectus and medial orbital gyrus), left temporal pole, and the cortex of the superior temporal sulcus (STS), close to the angular gyrus.

When the M condition was compared to the NM condition, the same activations in the medial OFC (101 mm³, $P < 0.001$) and STS (1063 mm³, $P < 10^{-6}$) were seen. The left temporal pole activation was no longer observed. In the opposite NM vs M comparison, the left amygdala (242 mm³, $P < 4 \times 10^{-6}$) and the lateral orbital gyrus (207 mm³, $P < 3 \times 10^{-5}$) remained active, along with the visual cortex (lingual and fusiform gyri). Notably, with the exception of a limited

sector of the STS that has been previously implicated in processing visual social cues (e.g., Hoffman and Haxby, 2000), other sectors of the temporal lobe were not activated when M and NM conditions were contrasted to each other. This is in agreement with the role of temporal lobe structures in semantic comprehension (Zahn et al., 2000), and indicates that semantic processing was well matched in these conditions. Mean signal changes and standard errors from the medial and lateral OFC, amygdala, primary visual cortex and STS cortex in each experimental condition, averaged across subjects, are displayed in Figure 5.2.

In order to investigate the effects of right vs wrong categorical judgments on brain activation, we computed Kendall's correlation coefficient between the percentage of BOLD signal increase in

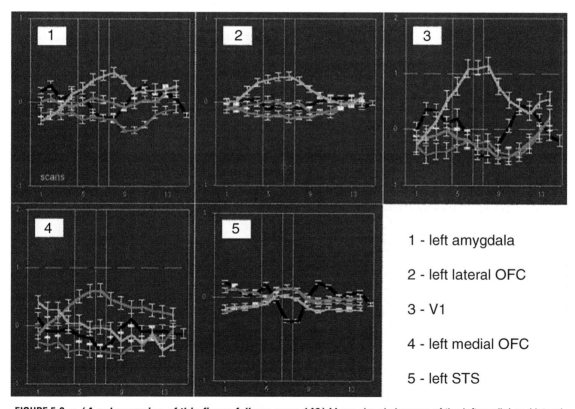

1 - left amygdala

2 - left lateral OFC

3 - V1

4 - left medial OFC

5 - left STS

FIGURE 5.2 ■ (*A color version of this figure follows page 146.*) Mean signal changes of the left medial and lateral OFC, left amygdala, primary visual cortex (V1), and the cortex of the left superior temporal sulcus (STS), obtained from averaged MR signal from all subjects. Curve colors correspond to experimental conditions as follows: yellow, unpleasant condition; light blue, moral condition; green, neutral condition; black, scrambled condition.

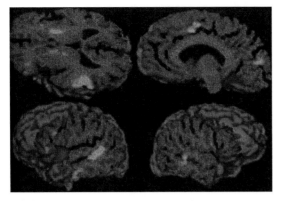

FIGURE 5.3 ■ (*A color version of this figure follows page 146.*) Brain regions activated by the neutral (NTR) as compared to scrambled (SCR) condition (both temporal lobes and frontal opercula, supplementary motor area, anterior cingulate, basal ganglia, and thalamus).

the left amygdala and medial OFC, and the number of statements judged as right vs wrong in the NM and M conditions, respectively. There was no relationship between the number of right vs wrong judgments and the magnitude of the hemodynamic response of the amygdala ($T = -0.20$, $P > 0.62$) or medial OFC ($T = 0.09$, $P > 0.74$), suggesting that activation in these brain regions was independent of the frequency of outcome of the categorical right vs wrong judgments.

When the NTR condition was contrasted to the SCR condition, a pattern of brain activation similar to that described in studies of sentence processing was observed (Bottini et al., 1994). Activated regions included the middle and posterior portions of the superior temporal gyrus and sulcus bilaterally (more extensively in the left hemisphere), the frontal opercula, the anterior cingulate and adjacent supplementary motor cortex, the thalamus and putamen, and additional foci in the anterior temporal lobes, fusiform gyrus, and cuneus (Figure 5.3).

Discussion

Our results provide new evidence that distinct neural networks are activated by different kinds of social judgment. In particular, moral judgments associated with unpleasant emotions induced activation in the anterior aspect of the medial OFC, whereas nonmoral social judgments associated with unpleasant emotions induced lateral OFC and amygdala activation. The amygdala has a major role in processing emotionally arousing stimuli, both pleasant and aversive, and it has been suggested that it may help allocate resources to processing different kinds of biologically salient stimuli (Adolphs et al., 1998; Golby et al., 2001).

Activation of the left amygdala by a cognitive-emotional elicitation procedure (e.g., through language) implies that top-down mechanisms may activate this brain region under these conditions, in accord with recent functional imaging studies employing threatening words (Isenberg et al., 1999) and the cognitive representation of fear (Phelps et al., 2001). This finding is also consistent with the suggestion that the left amygdala, rather than the right, is more closely related to linguistic affective processes (Markowitsch, 1998; Phelps et al., 2001). Contrary to our expectations, the amygdala was not activated in the moral judgment condition, even though those statements were rated as most emotionally evocative. A possible explanation is that the medial OFC, which is intimately linked to the processing of social rules and emotions related to moral processing, down-regulates the activity of the amygdala in certain circumstances (Baxter et al., 2000). The amygdala is densely interconnected with the visual cortex, which is strongly activated by aversive pictures or words (Reiman et al., 1997; Lane et al., 1999). Thus, the activation of the visual cortex in the NM condition is not surprising, and could have resulted from modulatory effects from the amygdala (Morris et al., 1998).

The amygdala is also massively interconnected with the OFC, especially with the caudal sector of its lateral subdivision (Baxter et al., 2000; Öngur and Price, 2000), which was activated in the NM condition. This region is activated in abstract reward/punishment acquisition in humans (O'Doherty et al., 2001) and, when damaged, is thought to impair social behavior (Anderson et al., 1999). The medial OFC activation in the M condition is compatible with evidence showing that humans sustaining lesions in this region frequently present with social disinhibition, lack of empathy and increased levels of aggression (Grafman et al.,

1996; Anderson et al., 1999; Pietrini et al., 2000; Raine et al., 2000). One explanation for these impairments is that patients are deficient in their ability to choose among behavioral alternatives based on inferences about positive or negative outcomes and changing reinforcement contingencies (Rolls et al., 1994; Bechara et al., 2000). The present findings suggest that the medial OFC may be even more critical for the integration of moral knowledge with the emotions that determine the reinforcing value of specific behavioral actions. It is also likely that the medial OFC, which receives projections from the STS region, integrates cues about the intentional and emotional states of others via signals from surface features of stimuli such as facial expression, body posture, and voice inflexions into decision-making (Adolphs, 1999; Hoffman and Haxby, 2000). The finding that the temporal pole was activated in the M vs NTR contrast, but not in the M vs NM or NM vs M comparisons, favors the view that it participates nonspecifically in both moral and nonmoral emotional processing. This result is consistent with the weaker activation of the right anterior temporal cortex when emotional impact was covaried in the design matrix in a previous study (Moll et al., 2001).

As reported above, different sectors of the OFC were activated when moral or nonmoral social judgments were being contemplated. Since RTs were equivalent for the M and NM conditions, we believe that these different patterns of activation are not attributable to task difficulty or effort. The dissociable networks we have identified probably work in an integrated fashion during many social interactions that combine moral, social, and emotional demands. One limitation of our findings regards agency. The judgments employed in our study did not require reference to the subjects' own behavior. On evolutionary grounds, it is likely that agency, or role-taking (Ruby and Decety, 2001), critically influences social and emotional-based reasoning and behavior and can have a direct impact on the outcomes of goal-directed behavior. Examining the brain activation patterns related to the differential effects of agency and emotion on moral and factual judgments is a logical next step for researchers interested in the brain representation of morality-influenced behavior.

REFERENCES

Adolphs, R. 1999. Social cognition and the human brain. *Trends Cogn. Sci.* 3: 469–479.

Adolphs, R., Tranel, D., and Damasio, A. R. 1998. The human amygdala in social judgment. *Nature* 393: 470–474.

Anderson, S. W., Bechara, A., Damasio, H., Tranel, D., and Damasio, A. R. 1999. Impairment of social and moral behavior related to early damage in human prefrontal cortex. *Nature Neurosci.* 2: 1032–1037.

Baxter, M. G., Parker, A., Lindner, C. C. C., Izquierdo, A. D., and Murray, A. E. 2000. Control of response selection by reinforcer value requires interaction of amygdala and orbital prefrontal cortex. *J. Neurosci.* 20: 4311–4319.

Bechara, A., Tranel, D., and Damasio, H. 2000. Characterization of the decision-making effect of patients with ventromedial prefrontal cortex lesions. *Brain* 123: 2189–2202.

Blair, R. J. R. 1995. A cognitive developmental approach to morality: Investigating the psychopath. *Cognition* 57: 1–29.

Blair, R. J. R. 1996. Brief report: Morality in the autistic child. *J. Autism Dev. Disord.* 26: 571–579.

Bottini, G., Corcoran, R., Sterzi, R., Paulesu, E., Schenone, P., Scarpa, P., Frackowiak, R. S., and Frith, C. D. 1994. The role of the right hemisphere in the interpretation of figurative aspects of language. A positron emission tomography activation study. *Brain* 117: 1241–1253.

Brothers, L. 1997. *Friday's Footprint. How Society Shapes The Human Mind.* Oxford, New York.

Brower, M. C., and Price, B. H. 2002. Neuropsychiatry of frontal lobe dysfunction in violent criminal behavior: A critical review. *J. Neurol. Neurosurg. Psychiatry* 71: 720–726.

Colby, A., Kohlberg, L., Speicher, B., Hewer, A., Candee, D., and Gibbs, J. 1990. *The Measurement of Moral Judgment.* Cambridge, New York.

Damasio, A. R., Grabowski, T. J., Bechara, A., Damasio, H., Ponto, L. L. B., Parvizi, J., and Hichwa, R. D. 2000. Subcortical and cortical brain activity during the feeling of self-generated emotions. *Nature Neurosci.* 3: 1049–1056.

de Zubicaray, G. I., Wilson, S. J., McMahon, K. L., and Muthiah, S. 2001. The semantic interference effect in the picture-word paradigm: An event-related fMRI study employing overt responses. *Hum. Brain Mapp.* 14: 218–227.

Eisenberg, L. 1995. The social construction of the human brain. *Am. J. Psychiatry* 152: 1563–1575.

Eslinger, P. J., and Damasio, A. R. 1985. Severe disturbance of higher cognition after bilateral frontal lobe ablation: Patient EVR. *Neurology* 35: 1731–1741.

Fisher L., and Blair R. J. 1998. Cognitive impairment and its relationship to psychopathic tendencies in children with emotional and behavioral difficulties. *J. Abnorm. Child Psychol.* 26: 511–519.

Fletcher, P. C., Happé, F., Frith, U., Baker, S. C., Dolan, R. J., Frackowiak, R. S., and Frith, C. D. 1995. Other minds in the brain: A functional imaging study of "theory of mind" in story comprehension. *Cognition* 57: 109–128.

Flynn, F., Cummings, J. L., and Tomiyasu, U. 1988. Altered behavior associated with damage to the ventromedial hypothalamus: A distinctive syndrome. *Behavioral Neurol.* 1: 49–58.

Forman, S. D., Cohen, J. D., Fitzgerald, M., Eddy, W. F., Mintun, M. A., and Noll, D. C. 1995. Improved assessment of significant activation in functional magnetic resonance imaging (fMRI): Use of a cluster-sized threshold. *Magn. Reson. Med.* 33: 636–647.

Friston, K. J., Holmes, A. P., Poline, J.-P., Grasby, P. J., Williams, S. C., Frackowiak, R. S., and Turner, R. 1995. Analysis of fMRI time-series revisited. *Neuroimage* 2: 45–53.

Frith, C. D., and Frith, U. 1999. Interacting minds—A biological basis. *Science* 286: 1692–1695.

Gilligan, C. 1993. *In a Different Voice*, 3rd ed. Harvard, Cambridge.

Golby, A. J., Gabrieli, J. D. L., Chiao, J. Y., and Eberhardt, J. L. 2001. Differential responses in the fusiform region to same-race and other-race faces. *Nature Neurosci.* 4: 845–850.

Gorman, D. G., and Cummings, J. L. 1992. Hypersexuality following septal injury. *Arch. Neurol.* 49: 308–310.

Grafman, J., Schwab, K., Warden, D., Pridgen, A., Brown, H. R., and Salazar, A. M. 1996. Frontal lobe injuries, violence, and aggression: A report of the Vietnam Head Injury Study. *Neurology* 46: 1231–1738.

Greene, J. D., Sommerville, R. B., Nystrom, L. E., Darley, J. M., and Cohen, J. D. 2001. An fMRI investigation of emotional engagement in moral judgment. *Science* 293: 2105–2108.

Haidt, J. The moral emotions. (in press) In *Handbook of Affective Sciences* (R. J. Davidson, K. Scherer, H. H. Goldsmith, Eds.) Oxford Univ. Press.

Hoffman, E. A., and Haxby, J. V. 2000. Distinct representations of eye gaze and identity in the distributed human neural system for face perception. *Nature Neurosci.* 3: 80–84.

Isenberg, N., Silbersweig, D., Engelien, A., Emmerich, S., Malavade, K., Beattie, B., Leon, A. C., and Stern, E. 1999. Linguistic threat activates the human amygdala. *Proc. Natl. Acad. Sci. USA* 96: 10456–10459.

Kandel, E., and Freed, D. 1989. Frontal-lobe dysfunction and anti-social behavior: a review. *J. Clin. Psychol.* 45: 404–413.

Kiehl, K. A., Smith, A. M., Hare, R. D., Mendrek, A., Forster, B. B., Brink, J., and Liddle, P. F. 2001. Limbic abnormalities in affective processing by criminal psychopaths as revealed by functional magnetic resonance imaging. *Biol. Psychiatry* 50: 677–684.

Lane, R., Chua, P., and Dolan, R. 1999. Common effects of emotional valence, arousal and attention on neural activation during visual processing of pictures. *Neuropsychologia* 37: 989–997.

Markowitsch, H. J. 1998. Differential contribution of right and left amygdala to affective information processing. *Behav. Neurol.* 11: 233–244.

Miller, B. L., Hou, C., Goldberg, M., and Mena, I. 1999. Anterior temporal lobes: Social brain. In *The Human Frontal Lobes: Functions and Disorders*. (B. L. Miller and J. L. Cummings, Eds.) Guilford Press.

Moll, J., Eslinger, P. J., and Oliveira-Souza, R. 2001. Frontopolar and anterior temporal cortex activation in a moral judgment task: Preliminary functional MRI results in normal subjects. *Arq. Neuropsiquiatr.* 59: 657–664.

Morris, J. S., Friston, K. J., Buchel, C., Frith, C. D., Young A. W., Calder A. J., and Dolan R. J. 1998. A neuromodulatory role for the human amygdala in processing emotional facial expressions. *Brain* 121: 47–57.

O'Doherty, J., Kringelbach, M. L., Rolls, E. T., Hornak, J., and Andrews, C. 2001. Abstract reward and punishment representations in the human orbitofrontal cortex. *Nature Neurosci.* 4: 95–102.

Oliveira-Souza, R., and Moll, J. 2000. The moral brain: Functional MRI correlates of moral judgment in normal adults. *Neurology* 54 (Suppl. 3): 252.

Öngür, D., and Price, J. L. 2000. The organization of networks within the orbital and medial prefrontal cortex of rats, monkeys and humans. *Cereb. Cortex* 10: 206–219.

Phelps, E. A., O'Connor, K. J., Gatenby, J. C., Gore, J. C., Grillon, C., and Davis, M. 2001. Activation of the left amygdala to a cognitive representation of fear. *Nature Neurosci.* 4: 437–441.

Pietrini, P., Guazzelli, M., Basso, G., Jaffe, K., and Grafman, J. 2000. Neural correlates of imaginal aggressive behavior assessed by positron emission tomography in healthy subjects. *Am. J. Psychiatry* 157: 1772–1781.

Raine, A., Lencz, T., Bihrle, S., LaCasse, L., and Colletti, P. 2000. Reduced prefrontal gray matter volume and reduced autonomic activity in antisocial personality disorder. *Arch. Gen. Psychiatry* 57: 119–127.

Reiman, E. M., Lane, R. D., Ahern, G. L., Schwartz, G. E., Davidson, R. J., Friston, K. J., Yun, L. S., and Chen, K. 1997. Neuroanatomical correlates of externally and internally generated human emotion. *Am. J. Psychiatry* 154: 918–925.

Rolls, E. T., Hornak, J., Wade, D., and McGrath, J. 1994. Emotion-related learning in patients with social and emotional changes associated with frontal lobe damage. *J. Neurol. Neurosurg. Psychiatry* 57: 1518–1524.

Ruby, P., and Decety, J. 2001. Effect of subjective perspective taking during simulation of action: A PET investigation of agency. *Nature Neurosci.* 4: 546–550.

Snarey, J. R. 1985. Cross-cultural universality of social-moral development: A critical review of Kohlbergian research. *Psychol. Bull.* 97: 202–232.

Talairach, J., and Tournoux, P. 1998. *Co-Planar Stereotaxic Atlas of the Human Brain*. Thieme Medical, New York.

Zahn, R., Huber, W., Drews, E., Erberich, S., Krings, T., Willmes, K., and Schwarz, M. 2000. Hemispheric lateralization at different levels of human auditory word processing: A functional magnetic resonance imaging study. *Neurosci. Lett.* 287: 195–198.

PART 4

Dissociable Systems for Face and Object Processing

Newborn babies prefer to look at pictures of faces compared to pictures of objects, and by childhood children are experts at recognizing faces. In contrast, individuals who suffer damage from a stroke in the ventral temporal cortex region, an approximately 20 cm square area of tissue on the bottom of the brain near the ears, are left with an inability to recognize familiar faces. Although these patients show no apparent difficulty differentiating among various objects, they cannot distinguish between their spouses and other individuals even though they show larger electrodermal (sweat) responses to their spouses! Are faces and objects processed differently by the brain, or does the region of the brain that appears important for processing faces also important for making detailed discriminations within a category of objects?

Early research suggested that the fusiform gyrus, which falls in the ventral temporal cortex, is selectively activated when viewing faces, and a nearby area of cortex typically medial to the face-sensitive area is activated when viewing places. This led to the suggestion that the fusiform gyrus was a face-specific processing module. However, subsequent research demonstrated that experts making fine-grain discriminations among objects in their expertise (e.g., automobiles) showed increased activity in the face-sensitive fusiform gyrus, as well.

Liu et al. (2002) employ a technique called magnetoencephalography (MEG) to explore the serial information processing stages that are involved when processing faces. Measurements using MEG provide high temporal and spatial resolution, although the sensitivity of MEG is limited to neural activity on or near the surface of the brain. Liu et al. (2002) found a stage of face processing earlier than previously thought possible—a response as early as 100 msec in the ventral temporal region that is associated with the successful categorization of a stimulus as a face. They additionally found a previously observed information processing stage that emerged around 170 msec (the N170 in the ventral temporal region, which tends to be larger in response to faces than other objects), which they found to be associated with the successful recognition of *individual* faces. Both MEG responses were more sensitive to face processing than object (house) processing. Finally, the authors found evidence that face processing involves a series of qualitatively different information processing operations. The neural response at 100 msec, for instance, was particularly sensitive to parts of the face (elemental information processing), whereas the neural response at 170 msec was especially sensitive to the configuration of a face (holistic information processing).

The Liu et al. (2002) study does not address whether participants who were as expert in recognizing houses as they were in recognizing faces would have displayed comparable MEG responses whether viewing houses or faces, but evidence is growing to suggest that these regions of the brain may be involved in the visual processing of nonface objects that elicit the same set of information processing operations. Haxby et al. (2001) address this latter possibility, providing compelling evidence that face and object processing both involve much more distributed information processing operations within the ventral temporal cortex than would be suggested by study of the brain region where the greatest activation is observed (e.g., fusiform gyrus). Work of the type illustrated by Haxby et al. (2001) is beginning to suggest that even if the evolutionary advantage of recognizing faces contributed to the emergence of a specialized neural substrate for face processing over evolutionary time, once evolved the information processing operations performed by this specialized neural substrate are exapted for use in nonsocial information processing, as well, and represent but one aspect of a representational system that is widely distributed and overlapping in the ventral temporal cortex. Alternatively, the readings in this section may reflect that as advanced general processing substrates emerge in evolution, their functions may be partially coopted for specialized processing (such as faces) that have particular adaptive significance for the species.

Stages of Processing in Face Perception: An MEG Study

Jia Liu[1], Alison Harris[1] and Nancy Kanwisher[1,2,3]

Here we used magnetoencephalography (MEG) to investigate stages of processing in face perception in humans. We found a face-selective MEG response occurring only 100 ms after stimulus onset (the 'M100'), 70 ms earlier than previously reported. Further, the amplitude of this M100 response was correlated with successful categorization of stimuli as faces, but not with successful recognition of individual faces, whereas the previously-described face-selective 'M170' response was correlated with both processes. These data suggest that face processing proceeds through two stages: an initial stage of face categorization, and a later stage at which the identity of the individual face is extracted.

Face recognition is one of the most important problems the human visual system must solve. Here we used MEG to characterize the sequence of cognitive and neural processes underlying this remarkable ability.

Two candidate stages of face processing are the categorization of a stimulus as a face, and the identification of a specific individual. Several studies of object recognition suggest that objects are first categorized at a 'basic level' (dog, bird) before a finer 'subordinate level' identification is achieved (poodle, sparrow)[1,2]. Evidence that a similar sequence may occur in face perception comes from single-unit recordings in macaques showing that the initial transient response of face-selective neurons in inferotemporal cortex reflects a rough categorization of face versus nonface, whereas subsequent firing of the same neural population represents finer information such as facial expression or individual identity[3]. It has been argued, however, that visual expertise in discriminating exemplars of a specific visual category may shift the point of initial contact

[1]Department of Brain and Cognitive Sciences, NE20–443, Massachusetts Institute of Technology, Cambridge, Massachusetts 02139, USA.
[2]The McGovern Institute for Brain Research, Massachusetts Institute of Technology, Cambridge, Massachusetts 02139, USA.

[3]MGH/MIT/HMS Athinoula A. Martinos Center for Biomedical Imaging, Charlestown, Massachusetts 02129, USA.

with memory representations from the basic level to the subordinate level[1,4]. Given that we are all experts at face recognition, this hypothesis predicts that people should be able to identify an individual face as fast as they can determine that it is a face at all. Although some behavioral evidence is consistent with this hypothesis[5], other evidence is not[6].

MEG is an ideal technique for addressing these questions, as its high temporal resolution enables us to tease apart processing stages that may occur within tens of milliseconds of each other. Prior work with MEG and event-related potentials (ERPs) has characterized a response component called the N170 (or M170 in MEG) that occurs around 170 ms after stimulus onset, and is about twice as large for face stimuli as for a variety of control nonface stimuli such as hands, houses or animals[7-10]. This response is thought to reflect the structural encoding of a face[7,11,12], that is, the extraction of a perceptual representation of the face. Although several reports of even earlier category-selective responses have been published[13-18], they are open to explanations invoking nonspecific repetition effects[19] or differences in the low-level features of the stimuli[20].

When do the first truly face-selective responses occur? We recorded MEG responses while subjects passively viewed a sequence of photographs of faces and a variety of control stimuli (experiments 1 and 2). These experiments found a new face-selective response occurring only 100 ms after stimulus onset (the M100), generated from extrastriate cortex (experiment 3). Further, we tested whether the M100 and M170 amplitudes are correlated with success in face categorization and/or face identification (experiment 4). Finally, we tested for further qualitative differences in the processes underlying the M100 and the M170 by measuring the responses of each component to face configurations and face parts (experiment 5).

Results

A Face-Selective Response at a Latency of 100 ms

An interpolated map of the t-value comparing the MEG response to faces versus houses for a typical subject (experiment 1) shows the previously-described[10] face-selective M170 response occurring at a latency of about 160 ms (Figure 6.1a). This response may correspond approximately to the N170 component in ERP studies[7] and/or the N200 in intracranial ERP studies[21], as discussed later.

In addition to the M170, we found a smaller response peaking at a mean latency of 105 ms (the 'M100'; range 84.5–130.5 ms, s.d. 16.1) that was significantly higher for faces than for houses. This result was seen with the same polarity in 13 of 15 subjects. The scalp distribution of the face-selective M100 response was slightly posterior to that of the M170, but the sensors showing the strongest face-selectivity for the M100 largely overlapped with those showing the strongest face-selectivity for the M170. The MEG response of a representative subject at a typical overlapping face-selective sensor in the right hemisphere is shown in Figure 6.1b.

For a stronger test of face selectivity, we measured the magnitude of the M100 response to a variety of control stimuli (experiment 2). Subjects were asked to press a button whenever two consecutive images were identical, obligating them to attend to all stimuli regardless of inherent interest. Target trials containing such repeated stimuli were excluded from the analysis. Accuracy on this one-back matching task was high for all categories (> 90% correct) except for hands (76%), which are visually very similar to each other. The MEG data from experiment 1 were first used to define sensors of interest (SOIs) in each subject— those sensors that produced significantly face-selective responses for both the M100 and the M170 (Methods). Both the amplitudes and latencies of peak responses to the new stimulus conditions in experiment 2 in these same SOIs were then quantified in the same subject in the same session. The M100 response to photographs of faces was greater (Figure 6.2) than that to photographs of animals ($F_{1,12} = 10.2$, $P < 0.01$), human hands ($F_{1,12} = 9.0$, $P < 0.02$), houses ($F_{1,12} = 8.1$, $P < 0.02$) and nonface objects ($F_{1,12} = 10.3$, $P < 0.01$). Therefore, the M100 is not generally selective for anything animate, or for any human body part; instead, it seems to be selective for faces. However, both the magnitude and selectivity of

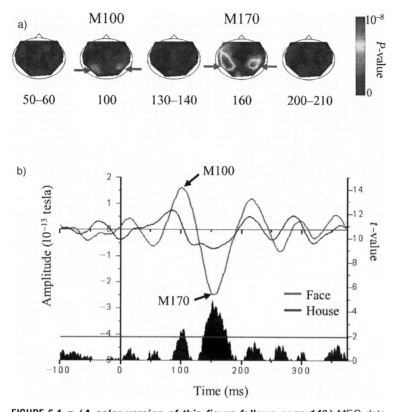

FIGURE 6.1 ■ **(*A color version of this figure follows page 146.*)** MEG data from a typical subject. (a) Pairwise *t*-tests between the responses at each sensor reveal early (M100) and late (M170) significant differences in the MEG response to faces versus houses over occipitotemporal cortex. (b) The MEG waveforms are averaged across all face and house trials at a typical sensor of interest in the right hemisphere. Red, faces; blue, houses; black, *t*-values. The left vertical scale indicates the amplitude of the MEG response (10^{-13} tesla) whereas the right one shows the *t*-value. A value $t = 1.99$ (horizontal green line) corresponds to $P < 0.05$ (uncorrected for comparisons at multiple time points).

the M100 response were weaker than those for the M170 response.

The earlier latency and somewhat more posterior scalp distribution of the M100 compared to the M170 suggest that the two components may not originate from the same anatomical source. To test whether the M100 might originate in retinotopically-organized visual cortex, we separately measured the amplitude of the M100 in each hemisphere to faces presented in the contralateral versus ipsilateral visual field (2.8° off fixation) in experiment 3. This manipulation is known to

affect responses in visual areas V1, V2, V3, VP, V3A and V4v in humans[22]. We found no difference in the amplitude of the M100 in each hemisphere for contralaterally versus ipsilaterally presented faces ($F_{1,10} < 1$), indicating that the source of this component must be beyond retinotopic cortex.

Decoupling Categorization and Identification

The results described so far implicate both the M100 and M170 in face processing, but do not

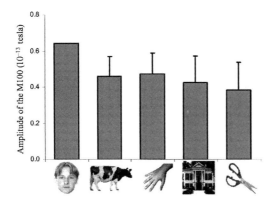

FIGURE 6.2 ■ Amplitudes of the peak M100 response, averaged across subjects, to faces and a variety of nonface objects at predefined sensors of interest. The error bars show the standard deviation across subjects of the difference of the M100 amplitudes between faces and each category of nonface object.

indicate what aspect of face processing each component reflects. In experiment 4, we asked whether each component is involved in the categorization of a stimulus as a face, in the extraction of the individual identity of a face, or both. Subjects were instructed to make two judgments about each stimulus, determining both its category (face or house) and its individual identity.

In this experiment, ten subjects matched front-view test images of faces and houses to profile views (faces) or three-quarter views (houses) of the same stimulus set presented earlier in the same trial (Figure 6.3a). There were three possible responses: 'different category' if the sample was a face and the test was a house or vice versa, 'different individual but same category' and 'same individual'. Correct categorization required discrimination between 'different category' trials and either 'different individual' or 'same individual' trials; correct identification required distinguishing between 'different individual' and 'same individual' trials.

A set of face and house stimuli (five exemplars each) were constructed, each of which had identical spatial frequency, luminance and contrast spectra. Subjects were first trained to match each face and house with its profile or three-quarter view, respectively, at 100% accuracy. Using a

technique similar to the recently proposed RISE technique[23,24] (Methods), each subject was then run on a psychophysical staircase procedure in which the percentage of phase coherence of each test stimulus was gradually reduced until the subject reached threshold performance on the matching task (75% correct, 20 steps by QUEST staircase[25]). In this way, five threshold face stimuli and five threshold house stimuli were constructed for each subject for each of the two tasks (categorization and identification). Across all stimuli and subjects, the resulting threshold face and house stimuli had a mean percent phase coherence of 14% (face) and 18% (house) for the categorization task and 38% (face) and 51% (house) for the identification task, indicating that more stimulus information was necessary for the identification task than for the categorization task, as expected.

Next, each subject performed the same matching task (different category, different individual, or same individual) in the MEG scanner, using face and house stimuli with phase coherence varied across four levels: 0%, 90%, and the two previously-derived sets of thresholds for that subject—one for the categorization task, and the other for the identification task (Figure 6.3b). In addition, the original version of each image with unmodified spatial frequencies was included to localize face-selective SOIs. By measuring both categorization and identification performance on each trial, the task allowed us to decouple the MEG correlates of successful categorization from those of successful identification. To obtain the MEG correlates of successful categorization, we compared the average MEG response to the same test image when the subject correctly categorized but failed to identify it, versus when they categorized it incorrectly. For identification, we compared the response to the same test image when the subject correctly identified it versus when they incorrectly identified it but categorized it successfully.

MEG waveforms averaged across each subject's face-selective SOIs from the face categorization and identification tasks are shown in Figure 6.4a. The magnitudes of both the M100 ($F_{1,9} = 9.5$, $P < 0.02$) and the M170 ($F_{1,9} = 5.8$, $P < 0.05$)

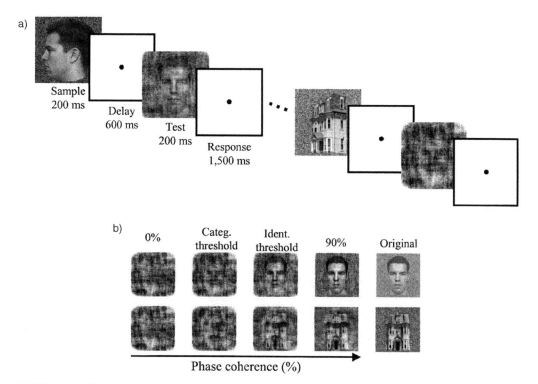

a)

Sample
200 ms

Delay
600 ms

Test
200 ms

Response
1,500 ms

b)

0%   Categ.   Ident.   90%   Original
       threshold threshold

Phase coherence (%)

FIGURE 6.3 ■ Stimulus and task for experiment 4. (a) In each trial, a sample stimulus was followed (after a delay) by a test stimulus. The sample images (5 exemplars for each category) were profile-view faces or three-quarter-view houses. (b) Test stimuli were frontal views of the sample stimuli. The phase coherence of the test stimuli was varied from 0% (visual noise) to 90% in four levels; original images with 100% coherence were also included. Here we show the data for the stimuli presented at categorization and identification thresholds only.

were larger for successful than for unsuccessful categorization of faces (Figure 6.4b, top left). However, only the M170 ($F_{1,9} = 43.3$, $P < 0.001$), but not the M100 ($F_{1,9} < 1$), was higher for correct than for incorrect identification of faces (interaction, $F_{1,9} = 8.7$, $P < 0.02$) (Figure 6.4b, bottom left). For house stimuli, neither the M100 nor the M170 differed for correct versus incorrect trials in either task ($F < 1$ in all cases; Figure 6.4b, top right and bottom right). The finding that the M170 is specific for face identification (not house identification) is further supported by a significant three-way interaction ($F_{1,9} = 6.73$, $P < 0.03$) of face versus house identification, success versus failure, and M100 versus M170 (Figure 6.4b, bottom left and right). In addition, neither the main effect of hemisphere nor the interaction of task by hemisphere was significant ($F < 1$ in both cases).

Accuracy on categorization and identification tasks at the two levels of phase coherence (derived from the previous psychophysical measurements) is shown in Table 6.1. Pairwise t-tests revealed no significant difference ($P > 0.2$ in all cases) in accuracy as a function of stimulus category (faces versus houses) for either task (categorization versus identification). Therefore, any difference between faces and houses seen in MEG responses cannot be

TABLE 6.1. Accuracy as a Function of Task and Stimulus Category (Experiment 4, Guessing Corrected)

	Categorization task		Identification task	
	Face	House	Face	House
Categorization threshold	74%	72%	26%	19%
Identification threshold	95%	95%	73%	65%

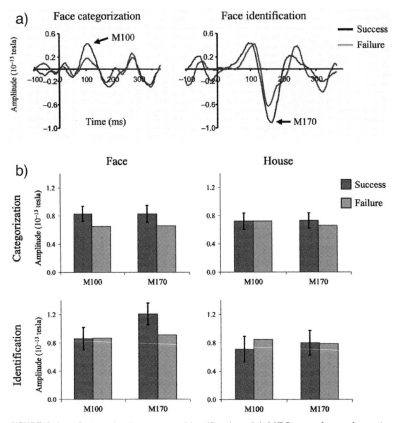

FIGURE 6.4 ■ Categorization versus identification. (a) MEG waveforms from the face categorization (left) and identification (right) tasks. Dark, success; light, failure. The waveforms were generated by averaging the selected raw data (Methods) from independently defined SOIs in ten subjects. (b) The amplitudes of the M100 and M170 at SOIs averaged across subjects. Successful categorization of faces elicited higher amplitudes at both M100 and M170 (top left), but no significant difference was found between successfully and unsuccessfully categorized houses at the predefined SOIs (top right). Correctly identified (compared to incorrectly identified) faces produced a significantly larger amplitude of the M170, but not of the M100 (bottom left). The amplitude elicited by houses was not affected by success or failure in the identification task (bottom right).

explained in terms of differences in behavioral performance. Note that even when the stimuli were degraded to 'categorization threshold level', the subjects' performances in the identification task was above chance ($P < 0.01$ in both cases).

In sum, both the M100 and M170 are correlated with successful face categorization, but only the later M170 component is correlated with successful face identification, indicating a dissociation between the two processes. One possible account of this dissociation is that the selectivity of the underlying neural population may continuously sharpen over time, permitting crude discriminations (for example, between a face and a house) earlier, and more fine-grained discriminations (for example, between two different faces) later. Indeed, the ratio of the response to faces versus houses was lower for the M100 (1.6) than for the

M170 (1.8, interaction $P < 0.03$), showing that selectivity does indeed sharpen over time. However, this fact alone does not indicate whether the selectivity changes only in degree, or whether qualitatively different representations underlie the M100 and the M170. This question was addressed in experiment 5, in which we measured the M100 and M170 responses to information about face configurations and face parts.

In experiment 5, two face-like stimulus categories were constructed from veridical human faces by orthogonally eliminating or disrupting either face configuration or face parts (eyes, nose and mouth; Figure 6.5a). Specifically, for 'configuration' stimuli, face parts in each stimulus were replaced by solid black ovals in their corresponding locations, preserving the face configuration but removing the contribution of face parts (Figure 6.5a, left). Conversely, for 'parts' stimuli, the face parts were kept intact but were rearranged into a novel nonface configuration (Figure 6.5a right). We measured MEG responses in 14 subjects who, while fixating, passively viewed these two sets of face-like stimuli (50 exemplars each) presented in a random order.

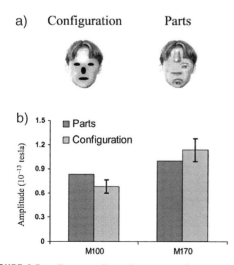

FIGURE 6.5 ■ Face configuration versus face parts. (a) Example stimuli. (b) Amplitudes of the M100 and the M170 response, averaged across subjects, to configuration and parts stimuli at predefined sensors of interest.

The responses to configuration and part stimuli recorded at independently defined face-selective sensors, averaged across subjects, are shown in Figure 6.5b. Critically, we found a significant two-way interaction of M100 versus M170 by configuration versus parts ($F_{1,13} = 13.4$, $P < 0.005$). This interaction reflects the fact that the amplitude of the M100 was significantly larger for parts stimuli than for configuration stimuli ($F_{1,13} = 11.5$, $P < 0.005$), whereas a trend in the opposite direction was found for the M170 ($F_{1,13} = 3.35$, $P = 0.09$). Thus it is not merely the degree of selectivity, but the qualitative nature of the selectivity, that differs between the M100 and the M170. Again, neither the main effect of hemisphere nor the interaction of stimulus type by hemisphere was significant ($F < 1$ in both cases).

Discussion

In experiments 1–3, we report an MEG response component, occurring over occipitotemporal cortex and peaking at a latency of ~100 ms, that is significantly larger for faces than for a variety of nonface objects. This result indicates that the categorization of a stimulus as a face begins within 100 ms after stimulus onset, substantially earlier than previously thought[7,20,26].

Unlike prior reports of very early category-selective ERP responses[13–18], the M100 reported here cannot be explained in terms of differences in the low-level features present in the stimuli. The M100 response was stronger when the same face stimulus was correctly perceived as a face than when it was wrongly categorized as a nonface. This result shows that the M100 reflects the subject's percept, not simply the low-level properties of the stimulus.

It is possible that a correlate of the face-selective M100 could be obtained with ERPs. However, because MEG is sensitive to only a subset of the neural activity that can be detected with scalp ERPs[27], there is no simple correspondence between MEG responses and scalp ERP responses, and selectivities that are clear in the MEG response may be diluted with ERPs. Similarly, the M170 response measured with MEG probably corresponds to only one of the two sources hypothesized to underlie the N170 response[7,28]. On the other hand, direct correspondences may exist between the M100 and M170 and the more focal intracranial P150 and N200 ERPs[21], respectively, assuming that the later latencies in the intracranial case arise from medication and/or histories of epilepsy typical of that subject population. Unfortunately, the limitations in current source localization techniques leave these correspondences only tentative at present.

The latency of the M100 response is not directly comparable to the category-selective response that occurs at a latency of 100 ms in inferotemporal (IT) neurons in macaques[29,30] because all cortical response latencies are shorter in macaques than humans. For example, V1 responses occur 40–60 ms after stimulus presentation in macaques[31]—about 20 ms earlier than they do in humans[26,32].

Given that at least 60–80 ms are thought to be necessary for visual information to reach primary visual cortex in humans[32], this leaves only an additional 20–40 ms for the first face-selective responses to be generated in cortex. Such latencies are hard to reconcile with models of visual categorization that rely heavily on iterative feedback loops and/or recurrent processing, and strengthen the claim that initial stimulus categorization is accomplished by largely feedforward mechanisms[33].

The second major finding of this study is that both the M100 and the M170 are correlated with successful face categorization, but only the later M170 component is correlated with successful face identification. This finding indicates that processes critical for the identification of a face begin at a substantially later latency than processes critical for the categorization of a stimulus as a face. Evidently, our expertise with faces has not led us to be able to identify individual faces as early as we can tell they are faces at all (as argued in ref. 5).

The dissociation we report here between the processes underlying face categorization and those underlying face identification do not simply reflect the greater difficulty of identification compared to categorization, because our results were obtained even when the stimuli were adjusted to produce identical performance in the categorization and identification tasks (experiment 4). Furthermore, the difference in the response for successful versus unsuccessful trials on face stimuli cannot be explained by general processes such as attention or association, because neither the M100 nor the M170 amplitude differed for correct versus incorrect trials on house stimuli. Thus, our data argue strongly that the categorization of a stimulus as a face begins substantially earlier than the identification of the particular face.

Are these two stages—categorization and identification—simply different points on a continuous spectrum of discrimination, with cruder discriminations occurring at earlier latencies and finer discriminations occurring later, perhaps as initially coarse neural population codes get sharpened over time[34,35]? Consistent with this hypothesis, the M170 shows stronger face selectivity than the M100. However, this hypothesis predicts that the rank ordering of preferred stimuli must be the same for the M100 and the M170. Contrary to this prediction, the M100 showed a stronger response to stimuli depicting face parts than face configurations, whereas the M170 showed the opposite response profile (experiment 5). If neural populations simply sharpened the selectivity of their response over time, this preference reversal would not be seen. Instead, our data suggest that qualitatively different information is extracted from faces at 100 ms versus 170 ms after stimulus onset. Finally, the observed change in response profile cannot be easily explained in terms of a progression from coarse/global information to fine/local information or in terms of a progression from less to more clear face features. Instead, information about relatively local face parts is more important in determining the M100 response, whereas information about relatively global face configurations is more important in the later M170 response. Thus the most natural account of our data is that the M100 and the M170 reflect qualitatively distinct stages of face perception: an earlier stage that is critical for categorizing a stimulus as a face, which relies more on information about face parts, and a later stage that is critical for identifying individual faces, which relies more on information about face configurations.

Will the findings reported here hold for stimulus classes other than faces? Given the numerous sources of evidence that faces are 'special'[36], we cannot simply assume that they will. Unfortunately, we cannot run experiments comparable to those reported here on other stimulus categories, because we have not found MEG markers selective for other categories. However, recent behavioral experiments suggest that the stages of processing reported here for face recognition will generalize to the visual recognition of nonface objects as well[6].

Methods

MEG recordings for experiments 1–3 were made using a 64-channel whole-head system with SQUID-based first-order gradiometer sensors (Kanazawa Institute of Technology MEG system at the KIT/MIT MEG Joint Research Lab at MIT); experiments 4 and 5 were run after the system was upgraded to 96 channels. Magnetic brain activity was digitized continuously at a sampling rate of 1,000 Hz (500 Hz for experiment 4) and was filtered with 1-Hz high pass and 200-Hz low-pass cutoff and a 60-Hz notch. Informed consent was obtained from all subjects, and the study was approved by the MIT Committee on the Use of Humans as Experimental Subjects (COUHES).

Experiments 1–3: The Face-Selective M100 Response

Fifteen subjects (age range 18–40) passively viewed 100 intermixed trials of faces and houses (50 exemplars each) in experiment 1; two additional subjects' data were discarded due to self-reported sleepiness. The thirteen subjects who showed the early face preference over occipitotemporal cortex also performed a one-back task on faces and a variety of nonface objects (50 exemplars each) in experiment 2. Each image subtended $5.7 \times 5.7°$ of visual angle and was presented at the center of gaze for 200 ms, followed by an ISI of 800 ms. The design for experiment 3 is described in Results.

For each subject in experiment 1, t-tests were conducted between the MEG responses to faces and houses at each time point (from -100 to 400 ms; 500 time points) and each sensor (64 channels) separately. SOIs were defined as those sensors where the magnetic fields evoked by faces were significantly larger than those by houses ($P < 0.05$) for at least five consecutive time points both within the time window centered at the latency of the M100 and within that of the M170. P-values for these SOI-defining statistics were not corrected for multiple sensors or multiple time point comparisons. All critical claims in this paper are based on analyses of the average responses over these sensors in independent data sets, and thus require no correction for multiple spatial hypotheses.

The peak amplitude of the M100 (maximum deflection) was determined for each stimulus type in each hemisphere within a specified time window (width > 40 ms) for each subject individually. Because there was no main effect of hemisphere ($P > 0.05$) and no interaction of condition by hemisphere ($F < 1$), in subsequent analyses the data from the left and right hemisphere were averaged within each subject (after flipping the sign of the data from the right hemisphere to match the polarities).

Experiment 4: Categorization Versus Identification

Ten subjects (age range 22–32) participated in experiment 4. The MEG recordings were preceded by a training session (< 10 min) and then a psychophysical staircase adjustment session conducted in the MEG room. MEG data from two additional subjects were discarded, one because of performance that was more than two standard deviations below the mean, the other because of polarities of both M100 and M170 that were reversed compared to all other subjects (although including the data from this subject did not change the pattern or significance of the results).

Noise images were generated by inverse Fourier transformation of the mean amplitude spectra with randomized phase spectra[23,24,37]. Intermediate images containing $x\%$ phase spectra of original images and $(100 - x)\%$ random phase spectra were generated using linear interpolation (phase spectra levels of 0% and 90% along with categorization and identification thresholds). This procedure ensured that all images were equated for spatial frequency, luminance and contrast.

Analyses were done on only the subset of data for which subjects responded both correctly and incorrectly to an identical stimulus. That is, for each stimulus, equal numbers of successful and unsuccessful trials were chosen, and the extra trials were omitted from the analysis from whichever condition had more trials. In particular, because there were more correct than incorrect trials, each incorrect trial was paired with the temporally closest correct trial. This analysis was conducted for each stimulus, guaranteeing that average MEG responses on successful and unsuccessful trials were derived from identical stimuli. Finally, the MEG recordings were averaged across stimuli separately for successful and unsuccessful trials. Note that the trials used to generate the waveform for face categorization were only selected from the MEG responses to those stimuli degraded to 'categorization thresholds', and the trials used to generate the waveform for face identification were only selected from the MEG responses to those stimuli degraded to 'identification thresholds'. The same held for house categorization and identification. The exact number of success and failure trials for each task varied across subjects, but ranged from 20 to 30 trials each for successful and unsuccessful categorization and from 15 to 20 trials for successful and unsuccessful identification.

Experiment 5: Face Configuration Versus Face Parts

Two stimulus categories were constructed from veridical faces. In 'configuration' stimuli, face parts in each veridical face were replaced by solid black ovals in their corresponding locations, whereas for 'parts' stimuli, the face parts were kept intact but were rearranged into a novel nonface configuration. The size of the black ovals in the configuration stimuli was matched to the actual size of corresponding face parts, and the arrangements of nonface configurations varied across all exemplars of parts stimuli. Photographs of these stimuli were presented at the center of gaze for 200 ms with an 800-ms ISI. Fourteen subjects (age range 18–41) passively viewed 100 intermixed trials of each stimulus category (50 exemplars each); three additional subjects' data were discarded due to lack of a face-selective MEG response in the independent localizer scan.

Acknowledgments

We thank J. Sadr and P. Sinha for helpful discussions on their RISE technique, M. Eimer, S. Hillyard, A. Marantz, M. Valdes-Sosa, P. Downing, W. Freiwald, K. Grill-Spector, Y. Jiang and the rest of the Kanwisher Lab for comments on the manuscript. Supported by the Reed Fund and National Eye Institute Grant (EY13455) to N.K.

REFERENCES

1. Rosch, E., Mervis, C. B., Gray, W. D., Johnson, D. M. & Boyes-Braem, P. Basic objects in natural categories. *Cognit. Psychol.* 8, 382–349 (1976).
2. Jolicoeur, P., Gluck, M. A. & Kosslyn, S. M. Pictures and names: making the connection. *Cognit. Psychol.* 16, 243–275 (1984).
3. Sugase, Y., Yamane, S., Ueno, S. & Kawano, K. Global and fine information coded by single neurons in the temporal visual cortex. *Nature* 400, 869–873 (1999).
4. Tanaka, J. W. & Taylor, M. Object categories and expertise: is the basic level in the eye of the beholder? *Cognit. Psychol.* 23, 457–482 (1991).
5. Tanaka, J. W. The entry point of face recognition: evidence for face expertise. *J. Exp. Psychol. Gen.* 130, 534–543 (2001).
6. Grill-Spector, K. & Kanwisher, N. Common cortical mechanisms for different components of visual object recognition: a combined behavioral and fMRI study. *J. Vision* 1, 474a (2001).
7. Bentin, S., Allison, T., Puce, A., Perez, E. & McCarthy, G. Electrophysiological studies of face perceptions in humans. *J. Cogn. Neurosci.* 8, 551–565 (1996).
8. Jeffreys, D. A. Evoked potential studies of face and object processing. *Vis. Cogn.* 3, 1–38 (1996).
9. Sams, M., Hietanen, J. K., Hari, R., Ilmoniemi, R. J. & Lounasmaa, O. V. Face-specific responses from the human inferior occipito-temporal cortex. *Neuroscience* 77, 49–55 (1997).

10. Liu, J., Higuchi, M., Marantz, A. & Kanwisher, N. The selectivity of the occipitotemporal M170 for faces. *Neuroreport* 11, 337–341 (2000).

11. Bruce, V. & Young, A. Understanding face recognition. *Br. J. Psychol.* 77 (Pt 3), 305–327 (1986).

12. Eimer, M. The face-specific N170 component reflects late stages in the structural encoding of faces. *Neuroreport* 11, 2319–2324 (2000).

13. Seeck, M. *et al.* Evidence for rapid face recognition from human scalp and intracranial electrodes. *Neuroreport* 8, 2749–2754 (1997).

14. Schendan, H. E., Ganis, G. & Kutas, M. Neurophysiological evidence for visual perceptual categorization of words and faces within 150 ms. *Psychophysiology* 35, 240–251 (1998).

15. Mouchetant-Rostaing, Y., Giard, M. H., Bentin, S., Aguera, P. E. & Pernier, J. Neurophysiological correlates of face gender processing in humans. *Eur. J. Neurosci.* 12, 303–310 (2000).

16. Kawasaki, H. *et al.* Single-neuron responses to emotional visual stimuli recorded in human ventral prefrontal cortex. *Nat. Neurosci.* 4, 15–16 (2001).

17. Braeutigam, S., Bailey, A. J. & Swithenby, S. J. Task-dependent early latency (30–60 ms) visual processing of human faces and other objects. *Neuroreport* 12, 1531–1536 (2001).

18. Streit, M., Wolwer, W., Brinkmeyer, J., Ihl, R. & Gaebel, W. Electrophysiological correlates of emotional and structural face processing in humans. *Neurosci. Lett.* 278, 13–16 (2000).

19. George, N., Jemel, B., Fiori, N. & Renault, B. Face and shape repetition effects in humans: a spatiotemporal ERP study. *Neuroreport* 8, 1417–1423 (1997).

20. VanRullen, R. & Thorpe, S. J. The time course of visual processing: from early perception to decision-making. *J. Cogn. Neurosci.* 13, 454–461 (2001).

21. Allison, T., Puce, A., Spencer, D. D. & McCarthy, G. Electrophysiological studies of human face perception. I: Potentials generated in occipitotemporal cortex by face and non-face stimuli. *Cereb. Cortex* 9, 415–430 (1999).

22. Tootell, R. B., Mendola, J. D., Hadjikhani, N. K., Liu, A. K. & Dale, A. M. The representation of the ipsilateral visual field in human cerebral cortex. *Proc. Natl. Acad. Sci. USA* 95, 818–824 (1998).

23. Sadr, J. & Sinha, P. Exploring object perception with Random Image Structure Evolution. *MIT Artif. Int. Lab. Memo,* 2001–6 (2001).

24. Sadr, J. & Sinha, P. Object recognition and random image structure evolution. *Cognit. Sci.* (in press).

25. Watson, A. B. & Pelli, D. G. Quest: a Bayesian adaptive psychometric method. *Percept. Psychophys.* 33, 113–120 (1983).

26. Thorpe, S., Fize, D. & Marlot, C. Speed of processing in the human visual system. *Nature* 381, 520–522 (1996).

27. Hämäläinen, M., Hari, R., Ilmoniemi, R. J., Knuutila, J. & Lounasmaa, O. V. Magnetoencephalography: theory, instrumentation and applications to noninvasive studies of the working human brain. *Rev. Mod. Phys.* 65, 413–497 (1993).

28. Bentin, S. in *Encyclopedia of Cognitive Science* (ed. Nadel, L.) Neural basis of face perception. (Macmillan, London, in press).

29. Oram, M. W. & Perrett, D. I. Time course of neural responses discriminating different views of the face and head. *J. Neurophysiol.* 68, 70–84 (1992).

30. Rolls, E. T. Neurons in the cortex of the temporal lobe and in the amygdala of the monkey with responses selective for faces. *Hum. Neurobiol.* 3, 209–222 (1984).

31. Thorpe, S. J. & Fabre-Thorpe, M. Seeking categories in the brain. *Science* 291, 260–263 (2001).

32. Gomez Gonzalez, C. M., Clark, V. P., Fan, S., Luck, S. J. & Hillyard, S. A. Sources of attention-sensitive visual event-related potentials. *Brain Topogr.* 7, 41–51 (1994).

33. Thorpe, S. & Imbert, M. *Connectionism in Perspective* (eds. Pfeifer, R., Schreter, Z., Fogelman-Soulie, F. & Steels, L.) 63–92 (Elsevier, Amsterdam, 1989).

34. Kovacs, G., Vogels, R. & Orban, G. A. Cortical correlate of pattern backward masking. *Proc. Natl. Acad. Sci. USA* 92, 5587–5591 (1995).

35. Keysers, C., Xiao, D. K., Foldiak, P. & Perrett, D. I. The speed of sight. *J. Cogn. Neurosci.* 13, 90–101 (2001).

36. Farah, M. J. *Visual Cognition* (eds. Kosslyn, S. M. & Osherson, D. N.) 101–119 (MIT Press, Cambridge, Massachusetts, 1995).

37. Rainer, G., Augath, M., Trinath, T. & Logothetis, N. K. Nonmonotonic noise tuning of BOLD fMRI signal to natural images in the visual cortex of the anesthetized monkey. *Curr. Biol.* 11, 846–854 (2001).

Distributed and Overlapping Representations of Faces and Objects in Ventral Temporal Cortex

James V. Haxby,[1] M. Ida Gobbini,[1,2] Maura L. Furey,[1,2] Alumit Ishai,[1] Jennifer L. Schouten,[1] and Pietro Pietrini[3]

The functional architecture of the object vision pathway in the human brain was investigated using functional magnetic resonance imaging to measure patterns of response in ventral temporal cortex while subjects viewed faces, cats, five categories of man-made objects, and nonsense pictures. A distinct pattern of response was found for each stimulus category. The distinctiveness of the response to a given category was not due simply to the regions that responded maximally to that category, because the category being viewed also could be identified on the basis of the pattern of response when those regions were excluded from the analysis. Patterns of response that discriminated among all categories were found even within cortical regions that responded maximally to only one category. These results indicate that the representations of faces and objects in ventral temporal cortex are widely distributed and overlapping.

The ventral object vision pathway in the human brain has the capacity to generate distinct representations for a virtually unlimited variety of individual faces and objects, but the functional architecture that embodies this capacity is a matter of intense debate. Single-cell recording studies in the nonhuman primate have demonstrated differential tuning of individual neurons in temporal cortex to faces, whole objects, and complex object form features (1–3). Although columns containing cells that respond selectively to faces or similar features tend to cluster together, these studies have not revealed any consistent larger scale organization for object representation. Numerous

[1]Laboratory of Brain and Cognition, National Institute of Mental Health, National Institutes of Health, Bethesda, MD 20892, USA. [2]Department of Human and Environmental Sciences and [3]Laboratory of Clinical Biochemistry, Department of Experimental Pathology, University of Pisa, 1-56126 Pisa, Italy.

computational models for object recognition have been developed (*4*), but the correspondence between these models and the neural architecture of the ventral object vision pathway is uncertain.

Unlike single-cell studies, functional brain imaging has revealed a large-scale spatial organization for specialization within the ventral object vision pathway, as demonstrated by differential patterns of response, i.e., increases in neural activity indicated by localized increases in blood oxygenation, to faces and other categories of objects in ventral temporal cortex (*5–17*). Models for this functional architecture fall into three classes. One model proposes that ventral temporal cortex contains a limited number of areas that are specialized for representing specific categories of stimuli (*5–8*). Thus far, two specialized areas have been described: the fusiform face area (FFA) and the parahippocampal place area (PPA) (Figure 7.1). A second model proposes that different areas in ventral temporal cortex are specialized for different types of perceptual processes (*9–11*). In particular, this model proposes that the FFA is specialized for expert visual recognition of individual exemplars from any object category, not just faces. The third model proposes that the representations of faces and different categories of objects are widely distributed and overlapping (*12–15*).

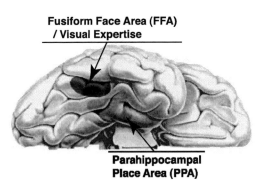

Fusiform Face Area (FFA) / Visual Expertise

Parahippocampal Place Area (PPA)

FIGURE 7.1 ■ Schematic diagram illustrating the locations of the fusiform face area (FFA), which also has been implicated in expert visual recognition, and the parahippocampal place area (PPA) on the ventral surface of the right temporal lobe. In most brains, these areas are bilateral.

According to this model, which we have named "object form topography," ventral temporal cortex has a topographically organized representation of attributes of form that underlie face and object recognition. The representation of a face or object is reflected by a distinct pattern of response across a wide expanse of cortex in which both large- and small-amplitude responses carry information about object appearance. Unlike the other models, object form topography predicts how all categories might evoke distinct patterns of response in ventral temporal cortex and, thereby, provides an explicit account for how this cortex can produce unique representations for a virtually unlimited number of categories.

We tested our model by investigating the patterns of response evoked in ventral temporal cortex by faces and multiple categories of objects. Our model predicts that each category elicits a distinct pattern of response in ventral temporal cortex that is also evident in the cortex that responds maximally to other categories.

Analysis of Patterns of Neural Response to Object Categories

Patterns of response were measured with functional magnetic resonance imaging (fMRI) in six subjects while they viewed pictures of faces, cats, five categories of man-made objects (houses, chairs, scissors, shoes, and bottles), and control, nonsense images (*18*) (Figure 7.2). The data were analyzed to determine whether each stimulus category evoked a pattern of response in the ventral object vision pathway that could be distinguished from the patterns of response evoked by all other individual categories. Patterns of response were examined in ventral temporal object-selective cortex, defined as those voxels with responses that differed significantly by category. The data for each subject were split into two sets, namely even and odd runs. We then determined whether the stimulus category that a subject was viewing could be identified by examining the similarity between the patterns of response evoked by each category on even and odd runs (*19*).

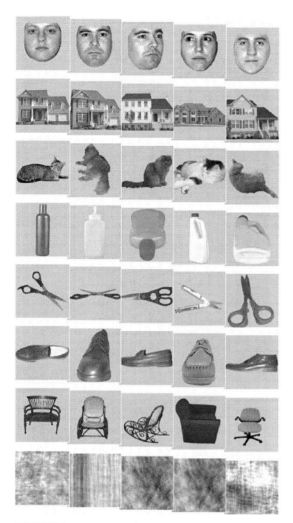

FIGURE 7.2 ■ Examples of stimuli. Subjects performed a one-back repetition detection task in which repetitions of meaningful pictures were different views of the same face or object.

Correlations between patterns of response served as indices of similarity (Figure 7.3). For example, to determine whether the pattern of response to one category, such as chairs, could be distinguished from the pattern of response to a different category, such as shoes, the correlation between the pattern of response to chairs on even runs and the response to chairs on odd runs (within-category correlation) was compared with the correlation between the response to chairs on even runs and the response to shoes on odd runs (between-category correlation).

Distinct Patterns of Neural Response for Multiple Categories of Objects

The pattern of response in object-selective ventral temporal cortex correctly identified the category being viewed in 96% of pairwise comparisons (20). The pattern of response indicated when subjects were viewing faces, houses, and scrambled pictures with no errors (Table 7.1). Identification accuracy for the small man-made objects (bottles, scissors, shoes, and chairs) was significantly better than chance for each category (21).

Category Identification Based on Patterns of Nonmaximal Responses

Although these results suggest that category-specific patterns of response are distributed and overlapping, higher within-category correlations could be due simply to the regions that reliably respond maximally to each category, with no information about a specific category carried by the pattern of response in cortex that responded maximally to other categories. To test whether the patterns of non-maximal responses carry category-related information, we analyzed whether each stimulus category evoked a distinct pattern of response in cortex that responded maximally to other categories. For each comparison between patterns of response evoked by two categories, all of the voxels that responded maximally to either category in either half of the data were excluded from the calculation of correlations (22). The specificity of the pattern of response to each category was barely diminished by thus restricting the analysis (Figure 7.4), with a mean accuracy of 94% for identifying the category being viewed (Table 7.1) (23).

Patterns of Response within Cortical Regions That Respond Maximally to One Category

These results indicate that the category specificity of responses in ventral temporal cortex is not restricted solely to regions that respond maximally

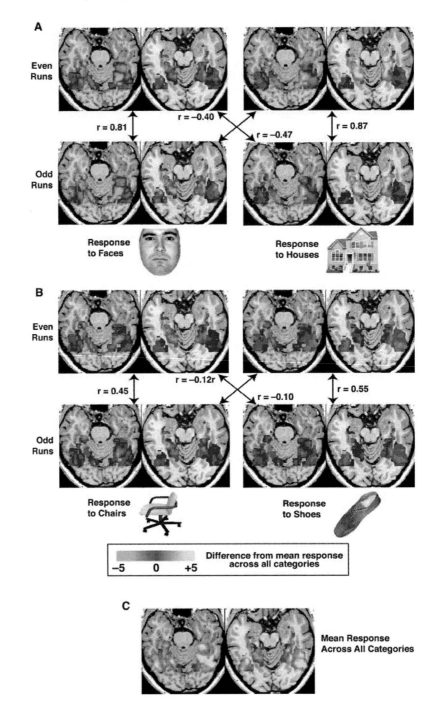

A

Even Runs

r = 0.81   r = −0.40

r = −0.47   r = 0.87

Odd Runs

Response to Faces

Response to Houses

B

Even Runs

r = 0.45   r = −0.12r

r = −0.10   r = 0.55

Odd Runs

Response to Chairs

Response to Shoes

Difference from mean response across all categories

−5   0   +5

C

Mean Response Across All Categories

TABLE 7.1. Accuracy of Identification of the Category being Viewed Based on the Patterns of Response Evoked in Ventral Temporal Cortex. Accuracies are the Percentage of Comparisons Between Two Categories that Correctly Identified which Category was being Viewed.

Region	Volume (cm³ ± SE)	Identification accuracy (%)							
		Faces	Houses	Cats	Bottles	Scissors	Shoes	Chairs	Scrambled
All ventral temporal object-selective cortex	22.9 ± 2.8	100***	100***	98 ± 2***	90 ± 6***	92 ± 6***	92 ± 7***	96 ± 2***	100***
Minus regions that were maximally responsive to categories being compared	15.4 ± 1.8	100***	100***	95 ± 2***	89 ± 6***	85 ± 9**	90 ± 8**	98 ± 1***	100***
Regions maximally responsive to:									
Faces	3.1 ± 0.9	94 ± 7***	99 ± 1***	76 ± 13*	81 ± 14*	77 ± 9*	70 ± 16	77 ± 11*	92 ± 7***
Houses	9.6 ± 1.8	100***	100***	88 ± 5***	85 ± 10**	81 ± 6**	96 ± 2***	94 ± 3***	100***
Cats	2.6 ± 0.4	96 ± 4***	96 ± 2***	82 ± 8**	65 ± 11	69 ± 5**	76 ± 9*	95 ± 4***	100***
Small objects	6.9 ± 1.1	100***	100***	95 ± 3***	83 ± 7**	92 ± 8**	94 ± 6***	90 ± 6***	96 ± 4***

Differs from chance (50%):*, $P < 0.05$;**, $P < 0.01$;***, $P < 0.001$.

to certain stimuli, thus raising the question of whether the representation of faces and objects in this cortex has a topographic organization that exists with a finer spatial resolution than that defined by such regions. To investigate whether the category specificity of response exists at this finer spatial resolution, we examined the patterns of response within regions that responded maximally to a single category or a small set of categories (22) (Table 7.1). Within only the cortex that responded maximally to houses, the pattern of response correctly identified the category being viewed with 93% accuracy. Within only the cortex that responded maximally to small, man-made objects, the pattern of response identified the category being viewed with 94% accuracy. Even within the much smaller region that responded maximally to faces, the pattern of response identified the category being viewed with 83% accuracy, and accuracies were significantly better than chance for all categories except shoes. Similarly, the pattern of response within the region that responded maximally to cats identified the category being viewed with 85% accuracy, with

←

FIGURE 7.3 ■ (*A color version of this figure follows page 146.*) The category specificity of patterns of response was analyzed with pairwise contrasts between within-category and between-category correlations. The pattern of response to each category was measured separately from data obtained on even-numbered and odd-numbered runs in each individual subject. These patterns were normalized to a mean of zero in each voxel across categories by subtracting the mean response across all categories. Brain images shown here are the normalized patterns of response in two axial slices in a single subject. The left side of the brain is on the left side of each image. Responses in all object-selective voxels in ventral temporal cortex are shown. For each pairwise comparison, the within-category correlation is compared with one between-category correlation. (A) Comparisons between the patterns of response to faces and houses in one subject. The within-category correlations for faces ($r = 0.81$) and houses ($r = 0.87$) are both markedly larger than the between-category correlations, yielding correct identifications of the category being viewed. (B) Comparisons between the patterns of response to chairs and shoes in the same subject. The category being viewed was identified correctly for all comparisons. (C) Mean response across all categories relative to a resting baseline.

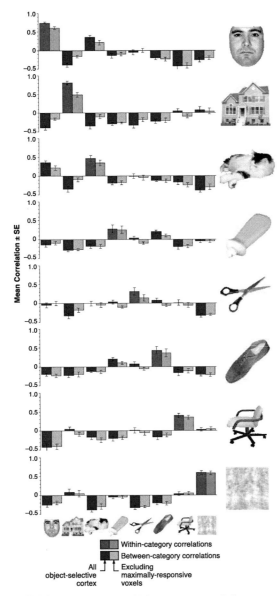

FIGURE 7.4 ■ Mean within-category and between-category correlations (±SE) between patterns of response across all subjects for all ventral temporal object-selective cortex and for ventral temporal cortex excluding the cortex that responded maximally to either of two categories being compared. The SE of within-category correlations after excluding maximally responsive cortex was based on the mean correlation across 14 pairwise comparisons for each subject.

accuracies that were better than chance for all categories except bottles.

These results demonstrate that the pattern of response in ventral temporal cortex carries information about the type of object being viewed, even in cortex that responds maximally to other categories, but the nature of this information is unknown. To examine whether this information concerns only low-level features of gray-scale photographs that are shared by a category, such as mean luminance, mean contrast, and spatial frequencies, we reanalyzed data from a previous study in which subjects viewed photographs and line drawings of three categories (faces, house, and chairs) (13). We examined whether the pattern of response to a category of line drawings can be identified on the basis of its similarity to responses to photographs of the same and different categories and, conversely, whether the pattern of response to a category of photographs can be identified on the basis of its similarity to responses to line drawings. The results of this reanalysis showed that similarities between patterns of response to photographs and line drawings of the same category correctly identified the category being viewed, even when the analysis was restricted to cortex that did not respond maximally to either of the categories being discriminated (96% correct pairwise discriminations) [for detailed results, see supplemental material (24)]. This result shows that patterns of nonmaximal responses do not represent low-level features that are specific to the type of stimuli, such as photographs, but, rather, appear to reflect information that is more definitive of object category.

Discussion

These findings demonstrate distinct patterns of response in ventral temporal cortex for multiple categories of objects, including different types of small man-made objects. This specificity is not restricted to categories for which dedicated systems might have evolved because of their biological significance. The specificity of the pattern of response for each category was a property of a much greater extent of object-selective cortex in the ventral temporal lobe than the sector that responded maximally to that category. The category being viewed still could be identified when the cortex that responded maximally to that category was excluded from the analysis. This result indicates that the representations of faces and objects in ventral temporal cortex are widely distributed and overlapping and that small or sub-maximal responses are an integral part of these representations. When the analysis was further restricted to regions that responded maximally to a single category (houses, faces, or cats) or a small number of categories (i.e., man-made objects—bottles, scissors, shoes, and chairs), the patterns of response to other categories within these regions were still significantly distinct. This result suggests that regions such as the "parahippocampal place area" or the "fusiform face area" are not dedicated to representing only spatial arrangements or human faces but, rather, are part of a more extended representation for all objects (25).

Object Form Topography

We have shown in previous studies that the maximally responsive regions for several of these categories—faces, houses, chairs, animals, and tools—have a consistent topography across individuals (12–14). Here, we show that the topographic arrangement of the full pattern of response is consistent within subjects, but we are not able to perform a similar correlational analysis across subjects because current methods for warping individual brains to a common shape are inadequate at this level of detail. The spatial resolution of this topography is smaller than that defined by category-selective areas (>1 cm), because category-related patterns can be discerned within these areas, and greater than that of randomaly arranged single columns or small clusters of columns (<1 mm), because of the spatial resolution of the fMRI images in this study (>3.5 mm). Single-unit recording studies in the monkey have suggested the existence of a columnar orgnization for representations of complex features of form but have not revealed any larger scale topographic arrangement (2).

We have proposed the term object form topography for the topographic organization of the distributed representation of faces and objects in ventral temporal cortex. Our results demonstrate a spatially organized functional architecture within subregions of ventral temporal cortex that are defined by a maximal response to a single object category. This architecture may be analogous to that found within early visual areas, such as V1, which contain spatially organized maps of simpler visual features, such as retinotopic location, edge orientation, and color. Object form topography presumably reflects how the more complex attributes of visual appearance that underlie object and face recognition are related visually, structurally, or semantically.

Population Encoding of Visual Appearance

The representation of a face or object involves the concerted neural activity in a widely distributed cortical space. Our analysis shows that the pattern of large and small responses, not just the location of large responses, carries category-related information, suggesting that small responses are an integral part of the representation. Population responses in simpler systems, such as color vision, similarly rely on both large and small responses to determine the quality of the integrated percept. In color vision, the perceptual quality of a hue that evokes a maximal red response in red-green neurons is also dependent on small responses in yellow-blue neurons that determine whether that hue is perceived as being more orange or violet (26–28).

What attributes of visual appearance could underlie a population encoding of objects and faces in which both large and small responses determine the quality of the integrated percept? Others have suggested that these attributes may be two-dimensional, view-dependent (2) or three-dimensional, structural (29) primitives that make up an alphabet for shape recognition. In a representation based on primitive features, however, a face or object would be specified by the strong responses that indicate the features that are present in the stimulus, not by a combination of large and small responses. Another possibility is suggested by models of face appearance and perception that describe a face on the basis of a small number of dimensions—operationalized as principal or independent components—that capture how configurations of features typically covary across faces (*30–32*). In a representation based on continuous dimensions, small and intermediate responses would be as important as large responses for specifying the location of a vector in feature space that best describes the appearance of a perceived face. Psychophysical evidence (*33, 34*) supports the proposal that the neural representation of faces may be based on such dimensions, represented as opponent processes referenced to the population mean. This opponent process model demonstrates how a limited number of channels can represent complex variations of form, such as those that distinguish one face from another, and suggests, further, how a limited cortical space could represent an unlimited variety of faces.

Our analysis did not reveal any sectors of ventral temporal cortex that did not convey information about discriminations among several stimulus categories, which leaves open the question of how lesions can cause selective impairments for recognizing individual faces (prosopagnosia) or discriminating between members of a single category of objects (*35–37*). Our results do not address the distribution or spatial scale of patterns of response that discriminate between exemplars within a category. Moreover, it is unclear whether any of these syndromes can be caused by a restricted lesion in a ventral temporal region that responds maximally to one category (*38*).

A population encoding based on the pattern of large and small responses in a wide expanse of cortex has the capacity to produce unique representations of a virtually unlimited number of object categories. Models of the functional architecture of ventral extrastriate cortex that analyze only mean responses in regions that are putatively specialized for restricted categories of stimuli (faces and places) (*5, 7*) or specific perceptual processes (visual expertise) (*9–11*) provide no explicit account for how neural representations of all object categories differ (*39*). By contrast, our results indicate how ventral extrastriate cortex can produce unique representations for all object categories. Fortuitously, these representations have a consistent topographic arrangement that may provide a key for decoding the information that underlies face and object recognition.

REFERENCES AND NOTES

1. C. G. Gross, C. E. Rocha-Miranda, D. B. Bender, *J. Neurophysiol.* 35, 96 (1972).
2. K. Tanaka, *Annu. Rev. Neurosci.* 19, 109 (1996).
3. N. K. Logothetis, D. L. Scheinberg, *Annu. Rev. Neurosci.* 19, 577 (1996).
4. S. Edelman, *Trends Cogn. Sci.* 1, 296 (1997).
5. N. Kanwisher, J. McDermott, M. Chun, *J. Neurosci.* 17, 4302 (1997).
6. G. McCarthy, A. Puce, J. C. Gore, T. Allison, *J. Cognit. Neurosci.* 9, 605 (1997).
7. R. Epstein, N. Kanwisher, *Nature* 392, 598 (1999).
8. G. K. Aguirre, E. Zarahn, M. D'Esposito, *Neuron* 21, 373 (1998).
9. I. Gauthier, M. J. Tarr, A. W. Anderson, P. Skudlarski, J. C. Gore, *Nature Neurosci.* 2, 568 (1999).
10. I. Gauthier, *Trends Cognit. Sci.* 4, 1 (2000).
11. ——, P. Skudlarski, J. C. Gore, A. W. Anderson, *Nature Neurosci.* 3, 191 (2000).
12. J. V. Haxby *et al., Neuron* 22, 189 (1999).
13. A. Ishai, L. G. Ungerleider, A. Martin, J. L. Schouten, J. V. Haxby, *Proc. Natl. Acad. Sci. U.S.A.* 96, 9379 (1999).
14. L. L. Chao, J. V. Haxby, A. Martin, *Nature Neurosci.* 2, 913 (1999).
15. J. V. Haxby, A. Ishai, L. L. Chao, L. G. Ungerleider, A. Martin, *Trends Cognit. Sci.* 4, 3 (2000).
16. S. Edelman, K. Grill-Spector, T. Kushnir, R. Malach, *Psychobiology* 26, 309 (1998).
17. K. Grill-Spector *et al., Neuron* 24, 187 (1999).
18. Neural responses, as reflected in hemodynamic changes, were measured in six subjects (five female and one male) with gradient echo echoplanar imaging on a GE 3T scanner (General Electric, Milwaukee, WI) [repetition time (TR) = 2500 ms, 40 3.5-mm-thick sagittal images, field of view (FOV) = 24 cm, echo time (TE) = 30 ms, flip angle = 90] while they performed a one-back repetition detection task. High-resolution T1-weighted spoiled gradient recall (SPGR) images were obtained for each subject to provide detailed anatomy (124 1.2-mm-thick sagittal images, FOV = 24 cm). Stimuli were gray-scale images of faces, houses, cats, bottles, scissors, shoes, chairs, and nonsense patterns. The categories were chosen so that all stimuli from a given category would have the same base level name. The specific categories were selected to allow comparison with our previous studies (faces, houses,

chairs, animals, and tools) or ongoing studies (shoes and bottles). Control nonsense patterns were phase-scrambled images of the intact objects. Twelve time series were obtained in each subject. Each time series began and ended with 12 s of rest and contained eight stimulus blocks of 24-s duration, one for each category, separated by 12-s intervals of rest. Stimuli were presented for 500 ms with an interstimulus interval of 1500 ms. Repetitions of meaningful stimuli were pictures of the same face or object photographed from different angles. Stimuli for each meaningful category were four images each of 12 different exemplars. Image data were analyzed with multiple regression with no spatial smoothing (40). To identify object-selective cortex, we used an eight-regressor model. The first regressor was the contrast between stimulus blocks and rest. The remaining seven regressors modeled the response to each meaningful category. The omnibus effect of these seven regressors was used as a test of the significance of differences among the responses to stimulus categories. To determine the patterns of response to each category on even-numbered and odd-numbered runs, we used a 16-regressor model—eight regressors to model the response to each category relative to rest on even runs and eight regressors to model the response to each category on odd runs with no regressor that contrasted all stimulus blocks to rest. The β weight for each regressor was used as an estimate of the strength of response relative to rest. Volumes of interest (VOI) were drawn on the high-resolution structural images to identify ventral temporal, lateral temporal, and ventrolateral occipital cortex. The VOI for ventral temporal cortex extended from 70 to 20 mm posterior to the anterior commissure in Talairach brain atlas coordinates (41) and consisted of the lingual, parahippocampal, fusiform, and inferior temporal gyri. The VOI for lateral temporal cortex also extended from 70 to 20 mm posterior to the anterior commissure and consisted of the middle temporal gyrus and both banks of the superior temporal sulcus. The VOI for ventrolateral occipital cortex extended from the occipital pole to 70 mm posterior to the anterior commissure and consisted of the lingual, fusiform, inferior occipital, and middle occipital gyri. Voxels within these VOIs that were significantly object-selective ($P < 10^{-6}$, uncorrected) were used for the analysis of within-category and between-category correlations.

19. Analysis of the accuracy with which the category being viewed could be identified focused on comparisons between patterns of response for pairs of categories, as illustrated in Figure 7.3. Mean response in each voxel across categories was subtracted from the response to each individual category in each half of the data before calculating correlations. If the within-category correlation (for example, response to category A on even and odd runs) was larger than the between-category correlation (correlation of the response to category A on even runs with the response to category B on odd runs), that comparison was counted as a correct identification. For each pair of categories, therefore, there were four such comparisons (within-category A versus category A on odd runs with category B on even runs, within-category A versus category A on even runs with category B on odd runs, and similar comparisons involving the within-category correlation for category B). The probability that the accuracy of identifying each individual category exceeded chance was determined with a simple test: The accuracy of identifying that category was determined for each subject as the proportion of pairwise comparisons that yielded correct identifications, and a t-test (df $= 5$) was used to test whether the mean accuracy across subjects exceeded chance (50%).

20. The category being viewed was correctly identified against all other categories in 83% of cases (within-category correlation for a given category was the greatest of all correlations between the response to that category in one half of the data and the responses to that and other categories in the other half of the data; chance accuracy would be 12.5%). Accuracies for identifying patterns for individual categories as compared with all other categories ranged from 100% (faces, houses, and scrambled pictures) to 67% (bottles and scissors). Detailed results are published as supplemental material (24).

21. Identification of the category being viewed when that category was one of the four, small, man-made categories (bottles, scissors, shoes, and chairs) was significantly better than chance even when only the comparisons among these categories were considered, both for all object-selective ventral temporal cortex (bottles: mean accuracy across subjects was 83% for pairwise comparisons among small man-made objects, differs from 50%, $P < 0.02$; scissors: 86%, $P < 0.01$; shoes: 86%, $P < 0.02$; chairs: 97%, $P < 0.001$) and for only cortex that responded maximally to other categories (bottles: 86%, $P < 0.01$; scissors: 83%, $P < 0.01$; shoes: 86%, $P < 0.02$; chairs: 100%). The analysis concentrated on patterns of response in ventral temporal cortex, where the category being viewed could be identified with greatest accuracy, but identification accuracies were nearly as great for lateral temporal (94%) and ventrolateral occipital cortices (92%). The ability to identify the category being viewed on the basis of the patterns of response within several subregions of ventral temporal cortex as well as in ventral occipital and lateral temporal cortex suggests the existence of multiple representations that encode different types of information about categories, such as visual form, typical patterns of motion, and internal spatial arrangements. We have suggested, for example, that the lateral temporal cortex represents different patterns of motion that are associated with faces and different categories of objects (42, 43).

22. For correlation analyses of subsets of object-selective cortex, the category that elicited the maximal response in each voxel was determined for even runs, odd runs, and all runs. To examine whether the pattern of response to a category could be discerned in cortex that responded maximally to other categories, we restricted comparisons of

responses to pairs of categories to voxels that did not respond maximally to either category on either even or odd runs. This was the most exacting test of this prediction that we could devise. To examine the response in regions that responded maximally to only a single category (faces, houses, or cats) or to only small man-made objects, we included only those voxels that had maximal responses averaged across all runs. Thus, there was no overlap between these regions.

23. The image data were not smoothed before analysis; nonetheless, it is possible that voxels outside of the regions showing maximal responses to a given category could still be influenced by the maximally responsive region because of spatial smoothness due to imaging techniques and partial volume effects. To address this issue, we also analyzed our data after excluding all voxels that responded maximally to the two categories being compared as well as all voxels that were adjacent to these regions. On average, this analysis excluded 58% of voxels from the calculation of correlations. Nonetheless, overall accuracy for identifying the category being viewed was 92%, demonstrating that the results are not attributable to the effect of maximally responsive regions on adjacent voxels.

24. Supplemental data are available on *Science* online at www.sciencemag.org/cgi/content/full/293/5539/2425/DC1.

25. Within the region that responds maximally to faces, sites may exist that respond exclusively to faces that are interdigitated with sites that respond maximally, but not exclusively, to faces, as suggested by studies of evoked potentials recorded with electrodes on the cortical surface (*44*). It is important to note, however, that most face-selective recording sites in these studies do show some response to other objects and even the sites that demonstrate an N200 response exclusively to faces appear to respond to other objects also but with different latencies.

26. E. Hering, *Outlines of a Theory of the Light Sense* (Harvard Univ. Press, Cambridge, MA, 1964).

27. L. M. Hurvich, D. Jameson, *Psychol. Rev.* 64, 384 (1957).

28. R. L. De Valois, *Cold Spring Harbor Symp. Quant. Biol.* 30, 567 (1965).

29. I. Biederman, *Psychol. Bull.* 94, 115 (1987).

30. A. J. O'Toole, H. Abdi, K. A. Deffenbacher, D. Valentin, *J. Opt. Soc. Am. A* 10, 405 (1993).

31. P. J. B. Hancock, A. M. Burton, V. Bruce, *Mem. Cognit.* 24, 26 (1996).

32. A. Lanitis, C. J. Taylor, T. F. Cootes, *IEEE Trans. Pattern Anal. Mach. Int.* 19, 743 (1997).

33. V. Blanz, A. J. O'Toole, T. Vetter, H. A. Wild, *Perception* 29, 885 (2000).

34. D. A. Leopold, A. J. O'Toole, T. Vetter, V. Blanz, *Nature Neurosci.* 4, 89 (2001).

35. H. Hecaen, R. Angelergues, *Arch. Neurol.* 7, 24 (1962).

36. A. Damasio *et al., Neurology* 32, 331 (1982).

37. E. K. Warrington, T. Shallice, *Brain* 107, 829 (1984).

38. Of the category-selective agnosias, only prosopagnosia is a purely visual agnosia, and controversy still exists over whether a pure prosopagnosia exists that has no effect on other aspects of visual object perception (*45*). Other category-selective agnosias also involve loss of nonvisual knowledge about the affected category and are associated with lesions in cortices other than those of the ventral temporal lobe (*37*). The literature on lesions that cause prosopagnosia is uninformative about what part of ventral temporal cortex is critical for face recognition. The lesions that cause prosopagnosia tend to be large (*37*). It has never been demonstrated that the critical part of lesions that cause prosopagnosia involves damage to the small region that responds maximally to faces. For a lesion to cause prosopagnosia, it may require damage in regions that show the most modulation of response to different individual faces, which may not be coextensive with the region that responds maximally to faces, or damaged connections to cortices in other parts of the brain that are critical for face recognition, such as the superior temporal sulcus or the anterior temporal cortex.

39. Models of the functional architecture of ventral extrastriate cortex that focus analysis on mean responses in regions that are putatively specialized for stimulus category (*5, 7*) or perceptual process (*9–11*) are not inconsistent with a coexisting functional architecture that embodies the distinct representations for all categories. Unlike the object form topography model proposed here, however, these specialized region models do not provide an explicit account for how such a coexisting functional architecture is organized or how the representations for an unlimited variety of categories could differ from each other within this architecture.

40. J. V. Haxby, J. M. Maisog, S. M. Courtney, in *Mapping and Modeling the Human Brain*, P. Fox, J. Lancaster, K. Friston, Eds. (Wiley, New York, in press).

41. J. Talairach, P. Tournoux, *Co-Planar Stereotoxic Atlas of the Human Brain* (Thieme, New York, 1988).

42. J. V. Haxby, E. A. Hoffman, M. I. Gobbini, *Trends Cognit. Sci.* 4, 223 (2000).

43. A. Martin, L. G. Ungerleider, J. V. Haxby, in *The New Cognitive Neurosciences*, M. S. Gazzaniga, Ed. (MIT Press, Cambridge, MA, 1999), pp. 1023–1036.

44. T. Allison, A. Puce, D. D. Spencer, G. McCarthy, *Cereb. Cortex* 9, 415 (1999).

45. I. Gauthier *et al., J. Cogn. Neurosci.* 12, 495 (2000).

46. We would like to thank R. Desimone, A. Martin, L. Pessoa, G. Ronca, and L. Ungerleider for discussion and comments on earlier versions of this reading.

PART 5

Dissociable Systems for the Perception of Biological Movement

The readings in the previous section, and again in this section, focus on early perceptual and attentional stages in social information processing. One might reasonably think that the influences of the social context would be reserved for later information processing stages—such as cultural prescriptions for what emotions are appropriate to display in different social contexts. However, there is compelling behavioral evidence that social factors (e.g., identifying and feeling cohesive with a group) affects perceptual processes. When a person views a circle surrounded by larger circles, it appears smaller than the identical circle surrounded by even larger circles. This visual illusion is called the Ebbinghaus effect. If the circles are replaced by faces, the illusion remains: when a person views a face surrounded by larger faces, it appears smaller than the identical face surrounded by even larger faces. According to social identity theory, members of highly entitative (e.g., cohesive) groups should represent natural comparison targets for each other, such that perceivers automatically and nonconsciously engage in greater intragroup comparison for members of highly entitative groups than members of nonentitative (e.g., noncohesive) groups. To test this hypothesis, sets of Ebbinghaus configurations were developed with faces used as the objects in the configurations. When these faces were given the label of a highly entitative group (sorority or fraternity members), the magnitude of the illusion was greater (indicating greater implicit social comparison) than when the faces were given the label of a nonentitative group (people born in the month of May). This work illustrates top-down influences of a social factor on perceptual processing.

Our perceptual world is not constituted solely by stationary objects but by a continuous flow of movement and transitions. A fundamental perceptual quality of other animals (including humans) in our habitat is the distinctive fashion in which these animals move. People have no difficulty distinguishing between the movement of an automobile and a pedestrian, and there appear to be a greater similarity in the movement of a walking person and a walking dog than there is between a walking person and a person in a moving automobile. In this section, we consider whether there are perceptual mechanisms specialized for detecting biological movement.

In the first of these readings, Grossman and Blake (2002) examine evidence that the visual perception of form and motion involve separable neural mechanisms. The readings thus far have pointed to the temporal lobe as being an important region for social perception. Grossman and Blake's research on the perception of biological motion again implicates this region, and the posterior part of the superior temporal sulcus in particular. Importantly, they link activity in this region with activity in brain regions found in the readings in the preceding section to be involved in face perception: the occipital and fusiform face areas. We again see that even very early features of social perception (in this case, biological motion) are subserved by a network of distributed neural processes distinguishable from

that which is involved in the perception of nonbiological motion.

Puce and Perrett (2003) focus more specifically on social perception. They discuss a variety of evidence from recordings of single-cell activity in the nonhuman primate brain to positron emission tomography (PET) and functional magnetic resonance imaging (fMRI) evidence in humans. Their research also points to the involvement of the superior temporal sulcus in the processing of moving faces and bodies. Interestingly, they report that movements of the mouth indicative of speaking and movements of the eyes indicative of changes in gaze—both of which carry information about social attention and communication—produce especially strong brain activation in the superior temporal sulcus. Like Grossman and Blake, Puce and Perrett conclude that the superior temporal sulcus is part of a more widely distributed system of neural processes that underlie social perception and cognition.

Parsimony refers to a preference for the simplest assumption in the formulation of theory or in the interpretation of data. It is simple to think of social perception and cognition as unfolding along a single serial set of information processing stages, with each stage forming an isomorphic (one-to-one) association with a familiar psychological construct. Parsimony, however, does not justify ignoring empirical anomalies that are inconsistent with simplistic formulations. The readings are challenging the simplicity of isomorphic thinking of this form. Evidence is accruing that even very early aspects of social information processing involve more distributed and overlapping information processing operations in the brain than suggested by simple, linear stage models of social perception and cognition, and by studies that focus exclusively on single loci based on where the greatest neural response is observed. Such challenges to simplistic theorizing are a sign of health. As the theoretical structures in social psychology grow in scope by drawing evidence from and providing new views of related domains, these theoretical structures acquire the property of consilience—the explanation of phenomena from different levels of organization that are connected and proven consistent with one another.

Brain Areas Active during Visual Perception of Biological Motion

Emily D. Grossman and Randolph Blake[*]

Theories of vision posit that form and motion are represented by neural mechanisms segregated into functionally and anatomically distinct pathways. Using point-light animations of biological motion, we examine the extent to which form and motion pathways are mutually involved in perceiving figures depicted by the spatio-temporal integration of local motion components. Previous work discloses that viewing biological motion selectively activates a region on the posterior superior temporal sulcus (STSp). Here we report that the occipital and fusiform face areas (OFA and FFA) also contain neural signals capable of differentiating biological from nonbiological motion. EBA and LOC, although involved in perception of human form, do not contain neural signals selective for biological motion. Our results suggest that a network of distributed neural areas in the form and motion pathways underlie the perception of biological motion.

Introduction

It is widely believed that primate vision comprises multiple visual areas organized into hierarchical pathways specialized for registering information about particular aspects of the visual scene (Felleman and Van Essen, 1991). Over the years, this overarching model has taken different forms, with some versions emphasizing distinctions between "sustained" and "transient" aspects of vision (Breitmeyer and Ganz, 1976; Kulikowski and Tolhurst, 1973), others distinguishing "color" and "broadband" channels (Schiller et al., 1990), and still others focusing on distinctions between perceiving objects and acting upon objects (Goodale and Humphrey, 1998). One currently popular version

[*]Both of Vanderbilt Vision Research Center/Department of Psychology, Vanderbilt University, Nashville, Tennessee 37203.

of this theory posits a so-called "motion" pathway extending into more dorsal aspects of extrastriate and posterior parietal cortex, specialized for registering information about the locations of objects and their movements within the visual scene, and an "object" stream pathway in ventral cortex involved in specifying information about the shapes and identities of visual objects (Ungerleider and Mishkin, 1982; Livingstone and Hubel, 1987). This particular version of the multiple pathway model has sparked a wealth of research aimed at testing the notion of object-grounded and motion-grounded neural systems (Haxby et al., 1991; Tanaka, 1996; Bradley et al., 1998; Kourtzi and Kanwisher, 2000).

While not disputing the notion of object-based and motion-based processing streams, several recent neural imaging studies have sought to determine the extent to which neural representations of objects are distributed throughout visual cortex. Sereno et al. (2002) found evidence for cue-invariant, 3D shape representations in multiple brain areas spanning object and motion pathways in anesthetized monkeys. Haxby et al. (2001) found that the distribution of brain activity associated with viewing faces and objects was widespread within ventral temporal cortex, leading these authors to downplay the importance of highly specialized neural areas in object recognition. We, too, have recently become interested in the question of distributed neural representations, in our case, representations associated with a particularly salient class of motion-defined forms, i.e., biological motion. In this paper, we report results from a brain imaging study that examines patterns of neural activity within multiple brain areas implicated in visual perception of bodies and body parts.

In these experiments, we have capitalized on a vivid, remarkable example of motion-defined shape: Johansson's "point-light" animation sequences (Johansson, 1973). These animations convey complex human activities using just a handful of dots placed on the joints of the human body. Single static frames resemble a meaningless cluster of dots portraying no hint of an object, human or otherwise, but when shown in rapid succession, these animated dots are grouped to create

the perception of a human form engaged in a readily identified activity (Cutting et al., 1978; Ahlström et al., 1997; Neri et al., 1998; Mather et al., 1992). The compelling sense of human form created by the spatio-temporal integration of these local dot motions would seem to imply that "object" and "motion" pathways are together creating perception of an active person.

Brain imaging studies in humans have pinpointed a region on the posterior superior temporal sulcus (STSp) that is active when observers perceive biological motion in point-light animations (Bonda et al., 1996; Howard et al., 1996; Grossman et al., 2000; Vaina et al., 2001). It seems reasonable to place STSp within the motion pathway, based on its proximity to motion-responsive areas MT and MST (Suneart et al., 1999); moreover, STSp is far removed from ventral temporal cortex and, by implication, brain areas involved in form perception. Nonetheless, point-light animations portraying biological motion create compelling impressions of a class of recognizable *objects*, namely humans, so it is natural to suppose that this unique type of structure from motion also activates "object-selective" ventral stream mechanisms. Thus while STSp may be selectively activated when viewing biological motion perception, the entire network of brain areas involved in registering all aspects of these salient animations may extend to the form pathway.

We have examined this supposition by isolating brain areas generally believed to be involved in the perception of objects, including human body parts, and then measuring BOLD signals in those areas produced by viewing biological motion sequences. These areas are: (1) the lateral occipital complex (LOC), which has been implicated in the perception of forms regardless of the visual cues used to define those forms (Grill-Spector et al., 1999); (2) the extrastriate body area (EBA), which has recently been implicated in the perception of images of bodies and body parts, but not faces (Downing et al., 2001); and (3) the occipital (OFA) and fusiform face areas (FFA), both of which have been implicated in the perception of faces (Kanwisher et al., 1997), as well as in the perception of other highly familiar objects (Gauthier et al., 1999). We used widely accepted stimuli and subtraction conditions to isolate these object-responsive brain areas, including pictures of headless bodies to activate the EBA, pictures of objects to activate the LOC, and pictures of faces to activate the FFA and OFA (Figure 8.1).

We also measured neural activity in STSp, the brain area implicated in perception of biological motion. In localizing STSp, observers viewed point-light actors performing a variety of human activities. However, these animations, composed of only 12 dots, are visually sparse in comparison to the pictures of headless bodies, faces, and objects. To evaluate the consequence of this sparseness on BOLD signal levels, we included animations in which the entire figure of the actor was visible. Also, to determine if neural responses were due to the presence of an object, or specifically because the object is biological, we included animations of a nonbiological object (a rotating, 3D globe) defined solely by dot motions.

Results

Our strategy entailed several steps: (1) use standard subtraction conditions to localize STSp, EBA, LOC, OFA, and FFA (Figure 8.2a), (2) assess patterns of activation across all of these areas by comparing evoked BOLD signals to a common baseline of fixation, and (3) determine whether neural signals within those regions are capable of discriminating between biological and scrambled point-light animations. To control for attention, which is known to modulate BOLD signals in many of the neural areas included in this study (Corbetta et al., 1991; Wojciulik et al., 1998), observers performed a 1-back task on the individual stimuli within each block.

Results from our measurements are discussed brain region by brain region in the following sections and are shown in Figures 8.2b–8.2e. Using some of the same data from Figure 8.2, Figures 8.3 and 8.4 highlight contrasts important for evaluating differences in selectivity among the areas.

The Posterior Superior Temporal Sulcus

STSp is located at the posterior end of the superior temporal sulcus, near the junction of the STS and the inferior temporal sulcus (ITS). This brain area responds more strongly to point-light animations portraying biological motion than it does to "scrambled" animations, created with the same motion vectors but whose starting positions are spatially randomized (Grossman and Blake, 2001). STSp does not respond well to coherent, translational motion, nor does it respond to the presence of kinetic boundaries (Grossman et al., 2000). In other words, this region is functionally and anatomically distinct from other motion-responsive areas in the human brain, including human MT+ (Watson et al., 1993; Tootell et al., 1995; Orban et al., 1995) and the kinetic occipital region (KO, or LO, as it is sometimes called; Van Oostende et al., 1997; Malach et al., 1995).

In the present study, observers viewed blocks of 1 s animations of point-light biological motion interleaved with blocks of 1 s animations of scrambled motion. In nine of the ten observers, a bilateral region on the posterior end of the STS, at the junction with the ITS, was more active during the biological epochs than during the scrambled epochs (p < .001). In the tenth observer, this region was only found in the left hemisphere (Table 8.1). Based on the anatomical location and the functional response during the localizer condition, these regions became the STSp region of interest (ROI) for each observer.

Within these ROIs, we compared BOLD signals during the four stimulus conditions depicting biological events (Figure 8.2b). Two of these conditions—whole body and point-light biological—were animated sequences depicting human activities, while the other two conditions—headless bodies and bodiless heads—were stationary images. BOLD activity levels were highest during the epochs of whole bodies, point-light bodies, and faces, and lowest during the epochs of headless bodies. Pairwise comparisons revealed that only the difference between whole bodies and headless bodies was significant (p < .001). It is noteworthy that bodies defined by only twelve points of light were as effective as whole body animations in activating STSp. This is the only brain area in which these two dynamic biological motion animations resulted in equivalent neural responses. This is testimony to the vividness of

a) Animated Stimuli

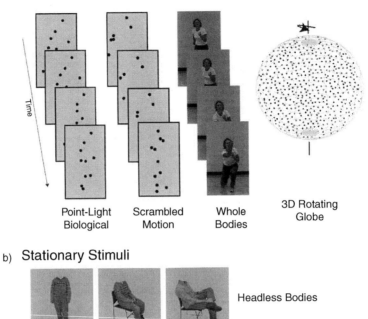

b) Stationary Stimuli

FIGURE 8.1 ■ Schematics of the stimuli. Dynamic human activity was portrayed by the motion twelve dots located on the joints and head of an actor performing various activities. Occlusions of some dots naturally occur as limbs pass behind the body. These occlusions help convey normal, three-dimensional body movement, and so were retained in the animations (i.e., not all dots were visible at all times). The scrambled animations contained the same motion vectors as the biological ones, but the initial starting positions of the dots are randomized within a region approximating the size of the body. The whole-body animations depicted an actor performing the same activities as the point-light animations. The rotating, structured globe was created by moving 200 dots sinusoidally within a circular aperture. The variable speed of the dots conveyed three-dimensional structure, but the direction of the rotation was ambiguous. The wire frame pictured above to denote three-dimensional structure was not visible in the experiment. The stationary, headless body condition consisted of images of bodies standing or sitting, with the heads erased. Observers also viewed images of faces and common household objects.

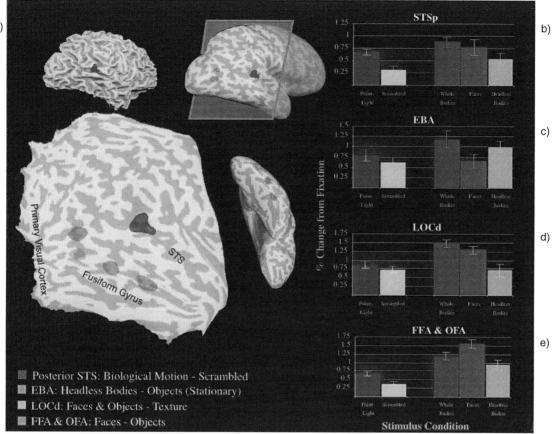

FIGURE 8.2 ■ *(A color version of this figure follows page 146.)* Summary of regions of interest (ROIs) and BOLD responses in biological related stimulus conditions. (a) The ROIs in the right hemisphere of observer D.L. are displayed on the lateral and ventral surfaces of the gray matter. A cut, as indicated by the green plane, was made and the posterior end of the cortex flattened. We examined BOLD signals in four regions of interest: STSp (red), EBA (purple), LOCd (blue), FFA and OFA (orange). (b–e) The average BOLD activity levels for these ROIs (with FFA and OFA averaged) during the stimulus conditions depicting some kind of biological object, or the scrambled biological motion vectors. These stimulus conditions included animations of point-light biological motion (pink), point-light scrambled motion (yellow), whole-bodies (dark purple), pictures of faces (magenta), and stationary images of headless bodies (green). The percent change activation levels are relative to a fixation baseline. Error bars indicate 1 standard error.

perception produced from these simple, sparsely sampled animations and to the importance of STSp in the perception of dynamically defined complex activity.

In contrast to BOLD signals evoked by biological motion, the rigidly rotating globe defined by moving dots evoked trivially small BOLD signals that were no different from those found during the scrambled motion epochs (Figure 8.3a). The weak, nonspecific neural response to the kinetic globe implies that STSp is not simply registering structure from motion but, instead, is specialized for the kinematics portraying biological motion. At the same time, motion is not absolutely crucial for activating STSp, for pictures of faces also produced reliable responses from this area. Face-responsive regions on the STS have been previously reported in the literature (Chao et al., 1999; Puce et al., 1998; Hoffman and Haxby, 2000), and it is possible that the face-responsive STS region

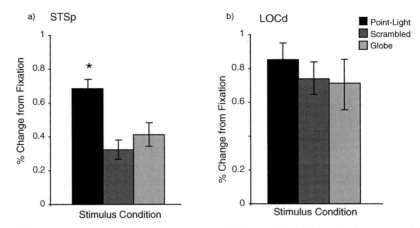

FIGURE 8.3 ■ Average percent change in the STSp and LOCd ROIs for the animated dot displays. Point-light biological, scrambled, and the rotating globe were the visually sparsest of all the stimuli used in these experiments. The biological and object identities were constructed by the movements of dots only, and could not be ascertained from a single, stationary frame. Even when animated, the scrambled animation looks like an incoherent cloud of dots. Asterisk indicates a significant difference for the biological motion condition over both the scrambled and rotating globe. All other contrasts were nonsignificant.

(STS-FA) and STSp overlap, resulting in strong BOLD responses to the images of faces. Using the FFA localizer (faces-objects), we attempted to determine the extent of overlap between STSp and STS-FA. However, we were able to localize STS-FA in only one observer, and there was no overlap between the two ROIs. Further testing is needed to determine conclusively the relationship between the face- and body-responsive regions on the STS.

The Extrastriate Body Area

Following the lead of Downing et al. (2001), we localized the EBA by subtracting activation evoked by pictures of stationary headless bodies from activity evoked by pictures of stationary household objects. Using this subtraction, we were able to localize a region in the anterior extent of occipital cortex, dorsal to the inferior occipital sulcus. This region was bilateral in five of the six observers tested, and only in the left hemisphere of the sixth (Talairach coordinates: left hemisphere: -39.3, -70.1, 13.5; right hemisphere: 40.6, -65.7, 10.6).

Results for EBA are summarized in Figure 8.2c. consistent with previous reports, this region

was most active during stimulus conditions in which pictures of the human body were shown ($p < .05$), which included the epochs of stationary headless bodies and animations of whole bodies (including the heads). We found that faces alone were slightly less effective (though not significantly different) in activating this region. Body shapes depicted by the point-light sequences were also slightly less effective than the explicit body images in activating the EBA.

Both STSp and EBA have been implicated in the perception of bodies, albeit using very different visual stimuli. How are these two areas different? To answer this question, it is interesting to compare the responses of EBA and STSp during the two localizers used to identify these regions (Figure 8.4). BOLD signal levels in STSp during point-light biological animations were significantly higher than during the scrambled intervals ($p < .01$), but this was not true for EBA ($p = .41$). Conversely, during the EBA localizer, the images of headless bodies produced significantly more activation in EBA than did images of objects ($p < .01$), but there was no significant difference between the two in STSp ($p = .53$). It is unlikely that the poor discrimination

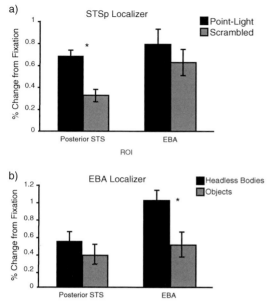

FIGURE 8.4 ■ Average percent BOLD signal change during the STSp and EBA localizer scans. (a) Subtracting BOLD signal levels during the point-light scrambled (light bars) from point-light biological (dark bars) motion intervals results in a significant contrast in STSp, but not in EBA. (b) However, subtracting activity levels elicited by pictures of household objects (light bars) from that elicited by pictures of stationary headless bodies (dark bars) results in higher percent signal change and more contrast in EBA.

between headless bodies and objects in STSp is due to the absence of a face in the headless bodies images. Quite the opposite, this region responded equally well to animated displays with no facial information (i.e., the point-light sequences) and to

images of faces. Instead, we believe it is the absence of dynamic signals, not the absence of a face, that is responsible for STSp's weak response to images of headless bodies.

The Lateral Occipital Complex (Dorsal)

The lateral occipital complex (LOC) is a large area of cortex starting most dorsally at the posterior end of the lateral occipital sulcus and extending through the ventral temporal cortex. We localized this region using the technique of Kourtzi and Kanwisher (2000), in which neural activity during periods of viewing texture patterns is subtracted from activity associated with viewing faces and objects. In our study, this subtraction revealed a large region of activation, the most posterior and dorsal extent of which we will refer to as LOCd (Talairach coordinates: left hemisphere: −28.4, −77.8, −2.5; right hemisphere: 33.9, −74.7, −1.0). The more anterior extent of the activated region lies on the ventral surface of the temporal lobe and encompasses other object- and face-responsive brain areas on the posterior fusiform gyrus, including the occipital face area (OFA). Based on previous work showing clear functional differences between anterior and posterior regions of LOC (Grill-Spector et al., 1999; Bar et al. 2001), we felt it important to analyze the BOLD signals separately for the LOCd (discussed in this section) and the OFA (discussed in the following section).

BOLD signal levels in the LOCd were significantly higher when observers viewed faces and

TABLE 8.1. Frequency of Activated Regions during the Point-Light Biological Motion Localizer

| | Talairach Coordinates | | | | | | | |
| | Num Observed Hemispheres | | Left | | | Right | | |
ROI	Left	Right	X	Y	Z	X	Y	Z
STSp	10/10	9/10	−41.3	−52.8	11.8	46.1	−48.5	12.4
ITS	6/10	5/10	−43.1	−58.5	11.2	48.8	−53.3	10.8
STSa	2/10	6/10	−46.9	−41.9	6.6	50.0	−33.0	4.3
FFA	3/10	4/10	−33.3	−40.5	−13.9	37.1	−36.0	−12.2

A total of ten observers viewed the biological and scrambled point-light animations. Simulations of false positive rates were used to determine the threshold for the activation maps. Table indicates the number of observers and Talairach coordinates for each hemisphere of the activated clusters. Abbreviations: STSp = superior temporal sulcus, the posterior end, ITS = inferior temporal sulcus, specifically the small region of the ITS between the STS and MT+, STSa = anterior region on the superior temporal sulcus, FFA = fusiform face area.

objects than when they viewed images of texture patterns created from scrambling the face and object pictures (p < .001). BOLD signals in LOCd were highest during the conditions showing whole-body animations and face images (no significant difference between the two conditions, p = .29), almost twice that for conditions when observers viewed stationary pictures of headless bodies or the point-light animations depicting biological motion (Figure 8.2d; p < .0001). There were no significant differences between BOLD signal levels while observers viewed point-light biological motion, scrambled motion, or the structured rotating globe animation (Figure 8.3b).

The Occipital and Fusiform Face Areas

Situated more anterior than LOC on the ventral surface of the temporal lobe is a cluster of foci related to object and face recognition. The most widely studied of these regions is the fusiform face area (FFA), located on the ventral medial aspect of the temporal lobe abutting the cerebellum. The FFA is functionally identified by its greater response to images of faces than to common household objects (Kanwisher et al., 1997). There is also another, more posterior region on the fusiform gyrus that responds strongly to faces and objects, and may lie within or just anterior to the LOC. This occipital face area (OFA), like the FFA, is often found by contrasting activation when observers view pictures of faces versus pictures of objects. We were able to localize the FFA in both hemispheres of all five observers tested using this contrast (Talairach coordinates: left hemisphere: −34.0, −39.7, −15.3; right hemisphere: 37.6, −38.9, −14.2); the OFA was localized in both hemispheres of three of these five observers, and only the left hemisphere of a fourth (Talairach coordinates: left hemisphere: −35.0, −55.0, −11.7, right hemisphere: 37.5, −54.2, −9.9). Across the stimulus conditions tested, we found no differences in the patterns of activity levels between the FFA and OFA, with the exception of overall slightly higher percent signals changes in the OFA. The results from these two regions, therefore, were averaged and are presented together.

Of all the stimulus conditions tested, the images of faces alone produced the highest responses in the fusiform areas (Figure 8.2e). This "face-only" activation was significantly higher than that produced when observers viewed pictures of objects (p < .001), headless bodies (p < .01), or whole bodies with the faces intact (p < .05).

Although faces also activated the fusiform face areas significantly more than the animations of point-light biological motion (p < .001), the contrast between point-light biological and point-light scrambled was also significant (p < .001). Critically, although activation levels are overall lower, the biological organization of the point-light animations is sufficient to activate this region, as evidenced by the contrast with scrambled animations. Incidentally, our failure to identify reliable FFA activation in an earlier study (Grossman et al., 2000) may be attributable, at least in part, to nonoptimal slice placement for capturing the ventral temporal cortex in all observers. It is also noteworthy that in the present study, unlike the earlier one, FFA was localized using the standard stimulus contrast (faces minus objects).

Discussion

People watch other people all the time, trying to deduce intentions and moods based on dynamic visual information. Indeed, recognizing what others are up to is one of the most important perceptual activities we engage in. It is not surprising, therefore, that people are remarkably adept at perceiving intentions and affect even when those personal characteristics are portrayed in point-light animations devoid of static form cues. Befitting such a crucial perceptual skill, neural representations of biological activity are widely distributed throughout visual cortex. Based on converging lines of evidence, Allison et al. (2000) propose that a major component in this distributed representation is a large expanse of cortex spread across the STS.

The results from our study, while confirming the importance of the STS in perception of biological activity, reveal that neural areas in the ventral stream are also activated when one views point-light biological motion animations. The fusiform and occipital face areas in ventral temporal cortex contain neural signals capable of discriminating between point-light animations that organize into biological motion and those that organize into scrambled motion. Our results also demonstrate that other neural areas previously found to be selectively involved in the perception of bodies and objects, specifically LOC and EBA, can not discriminate between biological and scrambled point-light animations. To determine the discriminability of the neural signals within these five regions—STSp, FFA, OFA, EBA, and LOC—we probed each with a variety of biological and non-biological visual stimuli. What conclusions can we draw from the patterns of activations in these distributed areas? To answer this question, we need to reconsider the response selectivity of these neural regions.

In the ventral stream, point-light bodies certainly produce weaker responses than those evoked by faces or, for that matter, by animated whole bodies in FFA and OFA. However, when observers view point-light bodies, the fusiform activations are significantly stronger than those resulting from the same point-lights scrambled to destroy the impression of a human body. In principle, then, neural activity in the fusiform region could form part of a distributed representation of human bodies, including bodies defined by motion. But how does this "object" pathway region—the FFA—acquire its selectivity for motion-defined bodies? After all, the human form in point-light animation sequences is portrayed exclusively by motion signals associated with hierarchical, pendular motions of the limbs: perception of a human form emerges only from the integration of motion signals over space and time. To the extent that the motion analyses underlying point-light animations are performed exclusively by neural mechanisms within the motion pathway, our results would imply that the outputs of those mechanisms project to the FFA; this idea, incidentally, is one component of a recently published model of face recognition (O'Toole et al.,

2002). Of course, it is possible that FFA itself contains neural machinery for registering the motion signals necessary for constructing the body representation in point-light animations. From our results, we cannot distinguish between these two hypotheses, and to do so may require using analytic techniques that reveal the strength of functional connectivity among areas (Friston et al., 1995).

In contrast to FFA and OFA, LOC has been characterized as a general object recognition area, responding invariantly to images that can be interpreted as shapes regardless of the visual cues creating the shapes' contours (Grill-Spector et al., 2001). Our results, however, place some limits on the generality of that characterization. In particular, point-light animations, although readily organized into a visible human form, produced no greater activation in LOCd than did scrambled animations which resembled a disorganized cloud of dots. Similarly, the rotating globe, also easily organized into a structured shape, did not increase brain activity beyond levels found during viewing of scrambled motion. Evidently, the cue invariance of LOC does not extend to all forms defined by motion.

Finally, biological and scrambled motion produced equivalent BOLD responses in EBA, implying that this brain region does not carry signals capable of registering the presence of human forms as depicted in point-light animations. This is not to say that EBA does not register the presence of a human form—indeed, this area is functionally defined by its stronger response to images of headless bodies than to nonhuman objects (Downing et al., 2001). Nor do our results imply that EBA is not involved in viewing bodies in motion, as evidenced by the equivalent BOLD responses to whole bodies in motion and to images of stationary, headless bodies. Instead, our results indicate that the BOLD signals in EBA are contingent upon the shape of the body being explicitly represented in the image.

It is interesting to note that STSp behaves in a fashion complementary to EBA. Unlike in EBA, the BOLD responses in STSp are selectively driven by the dynamics of the human form. This is evidenced by (1) the equivalent BOLD responses produced by stationary images of bodies and by nonhuman objects, and (2) the stronger BOLD responses produced by dynamic human bodies than by a moving, nonhuman object. Together, these results imply that STSp is specialized for a particular class of dynamic events, namely moving human bodies. Also, unlike in EBA, the BOLD responses in STSp do not depend on the explicit representation of the human body, for STSp responded just as strongly to point-light animation sequences as to animations showing whole bodies in motion.

To end on a speculative note, it is reasonable to wonder why the human brain would contain multiple areas (e.g., EBA and STSp) dedicated to the perception of human bodies. Perhaps identification of an individual constitutes a different perceptual task than perceiving an individual's mood or intentions. Intentions can be judged based on gestures, actions, and expressions independent of identity. Accurate identification, on the other hand, must generalize across gesture, mood, and activity. Given these divergent demands, extraction of the visual information subserving identification and perception of intention may require different neural operations, perhaps most efficiently embodied in separate neural architectures (EBA and STSp, respectively).

Experimental Procedures

Participants

Ten individuals (6 men, 4 women) with normal or corrected to normal vision participated in this study. All observers had experience viewing point-light animations and easily recognized all the biological motion sequences as human activities. The observers gave informed consent as approved by Vanderbilt University Institutional Review Board.

Stimuli

Visual stimuli were displayed using Matlab (Mathworks, Inc.) together with routines from the Psychophysics Toolbox (Brainard, 1997; Pelli,

1997). Point-light biological motion sequences were created by videotaping an actor performing various activities, including running, jumping, throwing, and kicking. The segments were digitized, and the joint positions in each frame were encoded as motion vectors with initial starting positions. Scrambled biological motion animations were created by randomizing the starting positions of each joint within a region approximating that covered by the biological sequences. The motion vectors were left intact so that the joints moved naturally as they would in the biological animations. This manipulation ensured the individual motion components were identical in both the biological and scrambled animations; only the hierarchical relations among the dots in the scrambled displays were destroyed. For both kinds of animations, the joints were displayed as small, black dots subtending approximately 9 arc min of visual angle against a gray background. Each biological activity sequence consisted of 20 frames displayed in a 1 s interval (33 ms interframe interval, 60 Hz). At this display rate, the biological animations generated smooth apparent motion, depicting natural body movement.

Whole body animations depicted the same activities as the point-light sequences, with the entire body of the actor being visible. These animations sequences were recorded with a digital video camera, edited into 1 s clips that were then converted to Quicktime files displayed with Matlab QT routines.

Random dot cinematograms depicting a structured "globe" and coherent planar motion were created with 200 dots horizontally displaced within a circular aperture. Approximately half the dots moved leftwards within the aperture while the other half moved rightwards. To create the structured globe, the speed of the dots was sinusoidally modulated such that the dots moved fastest on the outer edges of the aperture and slowest in the center. These animations create the vivid impression of a 3D transparent globe rotating about its vertical axis (Doner et al., 1984). Two coherent planes of transparent motion were created by moving half the dots leftward and half rightward, with the constant speed throughout the animation. The average speed of the dots was 4.8°/s (48 ms interframe interval, 60Hz), and the aperture subtended 7.2° × 7.2° of visual angle.

Some observers also viewed grayscale images of faces, headless bodies, and common household objects. These images were static, not animated, and they subtended 7.5° × 7.5° of visual angle. Texture patterns were created by breaking the images into small pieces that were then spatially shuffled to yield scrambled images lacking coherent spatial structure.

All individuals participated in the STSp localizer experiment in which point-light biological and scrambled motion animations were presented alternately in a block design. The resulting images from this scan were used to determine biological motion responsive ROI. All individuals also viewed alternating blocks of biological, scrambled, and whole-body motion, and in a separate scan the structured rotating globe and planar transparent motion. For five individuals, epochs of point-light biological motion were included within the structured globe and planar motion scan to eliminate any effect of neural adaptation to the coherent dots and still maintain the attention of the observers. We found no difference in BOLD signal levels for the structured globe or planar motion in the two condition or three condition scans. Six of the ten observers (D.L., D.R., F.R., J.L., K.B., M.R.) participated in additional scans designed to localize the EBA (alternating blocks of stationary headless bodies and objects). Five observers (D.L., D.R., F.R., K.B., M.R.) were also scanned to localize LOC and the FFA (alternating blocks of faces, objects, and texture patterns).

Imaging

All brain images were collected on a 3 Tesla GE Signa scanner located within Vanderbilt University Medical School. Observers participated in scanning sessions that lasted approximately 1.5 hr. During this time, we acquired high resolution T1 anatomical images of the observer's head (124 slices, 1.4 × 1.4 × 9375 mm), T2 functional images in the axial plane (single-shot EPI, TR = 1500 ms, TE = 25 ms, flip = 90°, 21 axial slices,

3.75 × 3.75 mm inplane, 5 mm, no gap), and T1 high resolution images of the slice positions. Slices positions were chosen to cover the entire occipital pole, the ventral surface of the temporal lobe, and the posterior extent of the superior temporal sulcus. Because the high resolution slice anatomy images were collected in alignment with the T2 functional images, the high and low resolution images were naturally co-registered with each other. The slice anatomy images were manually aligned with the T1 whole-brain images, subsequently allowing us to register the functional images into the whole-brain coordinate space. Using this alignment method, we were able to have some individuals return to the scanner on different days, align the data into common space, and treat the images as if they had been acquired on the same day.

Functional scans lasted 172.5 s, the initial 6 s (4 volumes) of which were discarded prior to analysis to allow for MR stabilization. The images and animations were blocked into 10.5 s epochs consisting of seven stimuli (1 s each, 500 ms interstimulus interval). The exemplars within the block were chosen randomly on each trial, but with a 50% chance of repeating on successive trials. Observers were instructed to monitor the stimuli carefully, and indicate sequential repetitions with a button press (1-back task), and the task was made more taxing by requiring observers to respond within the short 500 ms interval between the animations. This kind of challenging task maintains the observer's level of attention through a block of trials, an important consideration in view of evidence that attention can modulate BOLD signal in early and extrastriate visual areas (Somers et al., 1999; Watanabe et al., 1998). During the intervals involving the structured globe and planar motion, the near and far surfaces of the flowfield were inherently ambiguous, resulting in spontaneous reversals of depth ordering. Consequently, a 1-back task would have had no objective measure of correctness. To promote attention in these epochs, observers were instructed to monitor the motion direction of the dots in the nearest plane of depth. For all conditions, the order of the blocks was counterbalanced across subjects. Following each stimulus block was a 3 s (2 volume) interval of fixation during which only a small cross in the center of the screen was visible.

Visual displays were back-projected with a DLP projector onto a screen located at the observer's feet. A periscope mirror attached to the birdcage headcoil was adjusted prior to the onset of the scans to maximize viewing angle of the screen.

Analysis

Images were corrected for in- and out-of-plane motion using AIR 3.08 (Woods et al., 1998). All subsequent analyses were done using Brain Voyager (Brain Innovations, Inc.) and Matlab. The re-aligned images were corrected for linear trend over time then spatially filtered with a 5 mm FWHM Gaussian filter. The filtered and unfiltered images were averaged together to create "multifiltered" images, as described by Skudlarski et al. (1999). Multifiltering minimizes sites of single voxel false positive activations while maximizing signal change that may be lost by spatial smoothing alone.

All observers viewed alternating blocks of point-light biological and scrambled motion, allowing us to localize STSp as described in our earlier work (Grossman et al., 2000). Because of spatial and temporal correlations naturally occurring in the data, the actual r-cutoff value for determining regions of interest (ROIs) was empirically derived through repeated simulations of false positive rates occurring in the voxels within the brain. This was done in the following manner: (1) the BOLD signal values within each voxel were randomly shuffled in time, (2) the correlation between the randomized time series and the localizer boxcar was computed for each voxel, (3) the value corresponding to the upper .01% cutoff of the distribution of r values across the brain (corresponds to a 1% Type I error rate) was selected. These steps were repeated 1000 times, and the final r value threshold for determining the activation maps was taken as the mean value of the distribution of cutoff values.

In localizing the ROIs, we used previously published and widely accepted "subtraction" conditions.

However, to compare the activity levels during a variety of visual tasks, the raw MR signal from each scan was converted into percent change of the mean BOLD signal activation level during the fixation intervals in the scan. Further, we found that because of the short time between volume acquisitions (1.5), and the relatively short block duration (10.5 s), the MR signal barely reached saturation before the end of the epoch, and was more appropriately fit by a sinusoidal model (i.e., Boynton et al., 1996) than by an on-off boxcar function. Thus in calculating percent change values, we calculated the peak-to-peak differences between the stimulus and fixation intervals.

Acknowledgments

This work was supported by a Vanderbilt University Discovery Grant, NSF BCS0079579 and NSF BCS0121962. We thank Nancy Kanwisher and Paul Downing for their headless bodies and object stimuli, and we thank Marvin Chun, David Lyon, and Duje Tadin for comments on an earlier version of the manuscript.

REFERENCES

Ahlström, V., Blake, R., and Ahlström, U. (1997). Perception of biological motion. Perception 26, 1539–1548.

Allison, T., Puce, A., and McCarthy, G. (2000). Social perception from visual cues: Role of the STS region. Trends Cogn. Sci. 4, 267–278.

Bar, M., Tootell, R.B.H., Schacter, D.L., Greve, D.N., Fischl, B., Mendola, J.D., Rosen, B.R., and Dale, A.M. (2001). Cortical mechanisms specific to explicit visual object recognition. Neuron 29, 529–535.

Bonda, E., Petrides, M., Ostry, D., and Evans, A. (1996). Specific involvement of human parietal systems and the amygdala in the perception of biological motion. J. Neurosci. 16, 3737–3744.

Boynton, G.M., Engel, S.A., Glover, G.H., and Heeger, D.J. (1996). Linear systems analysis of functional magnetic resonance imaging in human V1. J. Neurosci. 16, 4207–4221.

Bradley, D.C., Chang, G.C., and Andersen, R.A. (1998). Encoding of three-dimensional structure-from-motion by primate area MT neurons. Nature 392, 714–717.

Brainard, D.H. (1997). The psychophysics toolbox. Spat. Vis. 10, 443–446.

Breitmeyer, B.G., and Ganz, L. (1976). Implications of sustained and transient channels for theories of visual pattern matching, saccadic suppression, and information processing. Psychol. Rev. 8, 1–36.

Chao, L.L., Martin, A., and Haxby, J.V. (1999). Are face-responsive regions selective only for faces? Neuroreport *10*, 2945–2950.

Corbetta, M., Miezin, F.M., Dobmeyer, S., Shulman, G.L., and Petersen, S.E. (1991). Selective and divided attention during visual discriminations of shape, color, and speed: functional anatomy by positron emission tomography. J. Neurosci. *11*, 2383–2402.

Cutting, J.E., Proffitt, D.R., and Kozlowski, L.T. (1978). A biomechanical invariant for gait perception. J. Exp. Psychol. Hum. Percept. Perform. *4*, 357–372.

Doner, J., Lappin, J.S., and Perfetto, G. (1984). Detection of three-dimensional structure in moving optical patterns. J. Exp. Psychol. Hum. Percept. Perform. *10*, 1–11.

Downing, P., Jiang, Y., Shuman, M., and Kanwisher, N. (2001). A cortical area selective for visual processing of the human body. Science *293*, 2470–2473.

Felleman, D.J., and Van Essen, D.C. (1991). Distributed hierarchical processing in the primate cerebral cortex. Cereb. Cortex *1*, 1–47.

Friston, K.J., Ungerleider, L.G., Jezzard, P., and Turner, R. (1995). Characterizing modulatory interactions between areas V1 and V2 in human cortex: A new treatment of functional MRI data. Hum. Brain Mapp. *2*, 211–224.

Gauthier, I., Skudlarski, P., Gore, J.C., and Anderson, A.W. (1999). Activation of the middle fusiform 'face area' increases with expertise in recognizing novel objects. Nat. Neurosci. *2*, 568–573.

Goodale, M.A., and Humphrey, G.K. (1998). The objects of action and perception. Cognition *67*, 181–207.

Grill-Spector, K., Kushnir, T., Edelman, S., Avidan, G., Itzchak, Y., and Malach, R. (1999). Differential processing of objects under various viewing conditions in the human lateral occipital complex. Neuron *24*, 187–203.

Grill-Spector, K., Kourtzi, Z., and Kanwisher, N. (2001). The lateral occipital complex and its role in object recognition. Vision Res. *41*, 1409–1422.

Grossman, E.D., and Blake, R. (2001). Brain activity evoked by inverted and imagined biological motion. Vis. Res. *41*, 1475–1482.

Grossman, E., Donnelly, M., Price, R., Pickens, D., Morgan, V., Neighbor, G., and Blake, R. (2000). Brain areas involved in perception of biological motion. *J. Cogn. Neurosci. 12*, 711–720.

Haxby, J.V., Grady, C.L., Horwitz, B., Ungerleider, L.G., Mishkin, M., Carson, R.E., Herscovitch, P., Schapiro, M.B., and Rapoport, S.I. (1991). Dissociation of object and spatial visual processing pathways in human extrastriate cortex. Proc. Natl. Acad. Sci. USA *88*, 1621–1625.

Haxby, J.V., Gobbini, M.I., Furey, M.L., Ishai, A., Schouten, J.L., and Pietrini, P. (2001). Distributed and overlapping representations of faces and objects in ventral temporal cortex. Science *293*, 2425–2430.

Hoffman, E., and Haxby, J. (2000). Distinct representations of eye gaze and identity in the distributed human neural system for face perception. Nat. Neurosci. *2*, 574–580.

Howard, R.J., Brammer, M., Wright, I., Woodruff, P.W., Bullmore, E.T., and Zeki, S. (1996). A direct demonstration of functional specialization within motion-related visual and auditory cortex of the human brain. Curr. Biol. *6*, 1015–1019.

Johansson, G. (1973). Visual perception of biological motion and a model for its analysis. Percept. Psychophys. *14*, 201–211.

Kanwisher, N., McDermott, J., and Chun, M.M. (1997). The fusiform face area: a module in human extrastriate visual cortex specialized for face perception. J. Neurosci. *17*, 4302–4311.

Kourtzi, Z., and Kanwisher, N. (2000). Cortical regions involved in processing object shape. J. Neurosci. *20*, 3310–3318.

Kulikowski, J.J., and Tolhurst, D.J. (1973). Psychophysical evidence for sustained and transient detectors in human vision. J. Physiol. *232*, 149–162.

Livingstone, M.S., and Hubel, D.H. (1987). Segregation of form, color, movement, and depth: Anatomy, physiology, and perception. Science *240*, 740–749.

Malach, R., Reppas, J.B., Benson, R.R., Kwong, K.K., Jiang, H., Kennedy, W.A., Ledden, P.J., Brady, T.J., Rosen, B.R., and Tootell, R.B. (1995). Object-related activity revealed by functional magnetic resonance imaging in the human occipital cortex. Proc. Natl. Acad. Sci. USA *92*, 8135–8139.

Mather, G., Radford, K., and West, S. (1992). Low-level visual processing of biological motion. Proc. R. Soc. Lond. B Biol. Sci. *249*, 149–155.

Neri, P., Morrone, M.C., and Burr, D.C. (1998). Seeing biological motion. Nature *395*, 894–896.

Orban, G.A., Dupont, P., De Bruyn, B., Vogels, R., Vandenberghe, R., and Mortelmans, L. (1995). A motion area in human visual cortex. Proc. Natl. Acad. Sci. USA *92*, 993–997.

O'Toole, A.J., Roark, D.A., and Abdi, H. (2002). Recognizing moving faces: A psychological and neural synthesis. Trends Cogn. Sci. *6*, 261–266.

Pelli, D.G. (1997). The Video Toolbox software for visual psychophysics: Transforming numbers into movies. Spat. Vis. *10*, 437–442.

Puce, A., Allison, T., Bentin, S., Gore, J.C., and McCarthy, G. (1998). Temporal cortex activations in viewing eye and mouth movements. J. Neurosci. *18*, 2188–2199.

Schiller, P.H., Logothetis, N.K., and Charles, E.R. (1990). Functions of the colour-opponent and broad-band channels of the visual system. Nature *343*, 68–70.

Sereno, M.E., Trinath, T., Augath, M., and Logothethis, N.K. (2002). Three-dimensional shape representation in monkey cortex. Neuron *33*, 635–652.

Skudlarski, P., Constable, R.T., and Gore, J.C. (1999). ROC analysis of statistical methods used in functional MRI: Individual subjects. Neuroimage *9*, 311–329.

Somers, D.C., Dale, A.M., Seiffert, A.E., and Tootell, R.B. (1999). Functional MRI reveals spatially specific attentional modulation in human primary visual cortex. Proc. Natl. Acad. Sci. USA *96*, 1663–1668.

Suneart, S., Van Hecke, P., Marchal, G., and Orban, G.A. (1999). Motion responsive regions of the human brain. Exp. Brain Res. *127*, 355–370.

Tanaka, K. (1996). Inferotemporal cortex and object vision. Annu. Rev. Neurosci. *19*, 109–139.

Tootell, R.B.H., Reppas, J.B., Kwong, K.K., Malach, R., Born, R.T., Brady, T.J., Rosen, B.R., and Belliveau, J.W. (1995). Functional analysis of human MT and related visual cortical areas using magnetic resonance imaging. J. Neurosci. *15*, 3215–3230.

Ungerleider, L., and Mishkin, M. (1982). Two cortical visual systems. In Analysis of Visual Behavior, D. Ingle, M. Goodale, and R. Mansfield, eds. (Cambridge, MA: MIT Press), pp. 549–586.

Vaina, L.M., Solomon, J., Chowdhury, S., Sinha, P., and Belliveau, J.W. (2001). Functional neuroanatomy of biological motion perception in humans. Proc. Natl. Acad. Sci. USA *98*, 11656–11661.

Van Oostende, S., Sunaert, S., Van Hecke, P., Marchal, G., and Orban, G.A. (1997). The kinetic occipital (KO) region in man: An fMRI study. Cereb. Cortex *7*, 690–701.

Watanabe, T., Hamer, A.M., Miyauchi, S., Sasaki, Y., Nielsen, M., Palomo, D., and Mukai, I. (1998). Task-dependent influences of attention on the activation of human primary visual cortex. Proc. Natl. Acad. Sci. USA *95*, 11489–11492.

Watson, J.D.G., Myers, R., Frackowiak, R.S., Hajnal, J.V., Woods, R.P., Mazziotta, J.C., Shipp, S., and Zeki, S. (1993). Area V5 of the human brain: Evidence from a combined study using positron emission tomography and magnetic resonance imaging. Cereb. Cortex *3*, 79–94.

Wojciulik, E., Kanwisher, N., and Driver, J. (1998). Covert visual attention modulates face-specific activity in the human fusiform gyrus: fMRI study. J. Neurophys. *79*, 1574–1578.

Woods, R.P., Grafton, S.T., Watson, J.D., Sicotte, N.L., and Mazziotta, J.C. (1998). Automated image registration: II. Intersubject validation of linear and nonlinear models. J. Comput. Assist. Tomogr. *22*, 155–165.

Electrophysiology and Brain Imaging of Biological Motion

Aina Puce[1] and David Perrett[2]

The movements of the faces and bodies of other conspecifics provide stimuli of considerable interest to the social primate. Studies of single cells, field potential recordings and functional neuroimaging data indicate that specialized visual mechanisms exist in the superior temporal sulcus (STS) of both human and non-human primates that produce selective neural responses to moving natural images of faces and bodies. STS mechanisms also process simplified displays of biological motion involving point lights marking the limb articulations of animate bodies and geometrical shapes whose motion simulates purposeful behaviour. Facial movements such as deviations in eye gaze, important for gauging an individual's social attention, and mouth movements, indicative of potential utterances, generate particularly robust neural responses that differentiate between movement types. Collectively such visual processing can enable the decoding of complex social signals and through its outputs to limbic, frontal and parietal systems the STS may play a part in enabling appropriate affective responses and social behaviour.

Keywords: biological motion; event related potentials; functional magnetic resonance imaging; humans; single-unit electrophysiology; animals.

1. Introduction

Primates, being social animals, continually observe one another's behaviour so as to be able to integrate effectively within their social living structure. At a non-social level, successful predator evasion also necessitates being able to 'read' the actions of other species in one's vicinity. The

[1]Centre for Advanced Imaging, Department of Radiology, West Virginia University, PO Box 9236, Morgantown, WV 26506–9236, USA.

[2]School of Psychology, University of St Andrews, St Andrews, Fife KY16 9JU, UK.

ability to interpret the motion and action of others in human primates goes beyond basic survival and successful interactions with important conspecifics. Many of our recreational and cultural pursuits would not be possible without this ability. Excellent symphony orchestras exist not only owing to the exceptional musicians, but also their ability to interpret their conductors' non-verbal instructions. Conductors convey unambiguously not only the technical way that the orchestra should execute the piece of music, but modulate the mood and emotional tone of the music measure by measure. The motion picture industry owes much of its success today to its silent movie pioneers, who could entertain with their non-verbal antics. The world's elite athletes rely on the interpretation of other's movements to achieve their team's goals successfully and foil opponents.

2. Human Behavioural Studies of Biological Motion Perception

The perception of moving biological forms can rely on the ability to integrate form and motion but it can also rely on the ability to define form from motion (Oram & Perrett 1994, 1996). The latter is evident in the ingenious work of Johansson who filmed actors dressed in black with white dots attached to their joints on a completely black set (Johansson 1973). With these moving dots human observers could reliably identify the walking or running motions, for example, of another human or an animal (Figure 9.1). This type of stimulus is known as a Johansson, point light or biological motion display.

A number of important observations have emerged from the human behavioural biological motion perception literature. First, the perceptual effect of observing an individual walking or running is severely compromised when the display is inverted (Dittrich 1993; Pavlova & Sokolov 2000). Second, while biological motion representing locomotory movements is recognized the most efficiently, social and instrumental actions can also be recognized from these impoverished displays (Dittrich 1993). Third, biological motion can be perceived even within masks of dots (Perrett

FIGURE 9.1 ■ An example of a biological motion stimulus. (Adapted from Johansson (1973), with permission from *Percept. Psychophys.*)

et al. 1990a; Thornton *et al.* 1998). Fourth, the gender of the walker (and even the identity of specific individuals) can be recognized from pattern of gait and idiosyncratic body movements in these impoverished displays (Cutting & Kozlowski 1977; Kozlowski & Cutting 1977). Fifth, there is a bias to perceive forward locomotion, at the expense of misinterpreting the underlying form in time-reversed biological motion films (Pavlova *et al.* 2002). Finally, observers can discern various emotional expressions from viewing Johansson faces (Bassili 1978).

In very low light conditions many animals are efficient at catching prey or evading predators. In such conditions the patterns of articulation (typical of biological motion) may be more discernible than the form of stationary animals. Indeed, in behavioural experiments it is evident that point light displays are sufficient for cats to discriminate the pattern of locomotion of conspecifics (Blake 1993). In an ingenious behavioural study in cats, a forced choice task where selection of a biological motion display (of a cat walking or running) was rewarded with food resulted in the animals performing significantly above chance. A series of foil stimuli showing dots changing their spatial location provided a set of tight controls in this experiment (Blake 1993).

Evidence for the existence of specialized brain systems that analyse biological motion (and the motion of humans and non-humans) comes from neuropsychological lesion studies. Dissociations between the ability to perceive biological motion and other types of motion have been demonstrated. Several patients who are to all intents and purposes 'motion blind' can discriminate biological motion stimuli (Vaina *et al.* 1990; McLeod *et al.* 1996). The opposite pattern, i.e., an inability to perceive biological motion yet have relatively normal motion perception in general, has also been reported (Schenk & Zihl 1997).

3. Biological Motion Perception in Non-Humans

One brain region known as the STP area in the cortex surrounding the STS has been the subject of considerable scrutiny ever since cells selective for the sight of faces were characterized in this region in monkeys (Perrett *et al.* 1982; Desimone 1991). This STS brain region is known to be a convergence point for the dorsal and ventral visual streams. The STP area derives its input from the MST area in the dorsal pathway and the anterior inferior-temporal area in the ventral pathway (Boussaoud *et al.* 1990; Felleman & Van Essen 1991). The cortex of the STS has connections with the amygdala (Aggleton *et al.* 1980) and also with the orbitofrontal cortex (Barbas 1988), regions implicated in the processing of stimuli of social and emotional significance in both human and non-human primates (reviewed in Baron-Cohen 1995; Brothers 1997; Adolphs 1999).

In addition to having face-specific cells, the cortex of the STS has other complex response properties. It has emerged that visual information about the shape and posture of the fingers, hands, arms, legs and torso all impact on STS cell tuning in addition to facial details such as the shape of the mouth and direction of gaze (Desimone *et al.* 1984; Wachsmuth *et al.* 1994; Perrett *et al.* 1984, 1985a; Jellema *et al.* 2000). Motion information presumed to arrive from the dorsal stream projections arrives in the STS some 20 ms ahead of form information from the ventral stream (Figure 9.2a);

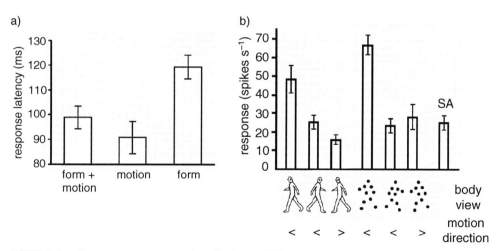

FIGURE 9.2 ■ Some response properties of primate STP area neurons elicited by biological motion stimuli. (Adapted from Oram & Perrett (1994, 1996), with permission.) (*a*) Average response latencies for neurons with different response properties. (*b*) An example of a neuron that does not differentiate between real human motion and biological motion. Also, the strongest response is in the motion direction compatible with direction of the body.

but despite this asynchrony, STS processing overcomes the 'binding problem' and only form and motion arising from the same biological object are integrated within 100 ms of the moving form becoming visible (Oram & Perrett 1996). Indeed, STS cell integration of form and motion is widespread and there are numerous cell types specializing in the processing of different types of face, limb and whole body motion (Perrett *et al.* 1985*b*; Carey *et al.* 1997; Jellema *et al.* 2000, 2002; Jellema & Perrett 2002).

While most STS cells derive sensitivity to body movement by combining signals about the net translation or rotation of the body with the face and body form visible at any moment in time, a smaller proportion (20%) of cells are able to respond selectively to the form of the body defined through patterns of articulation in point light displays (Perrett *et al.* 1990*a,b*; Oram & Perrett 1994, 1996; Figure 9.1). These cells tuned to biological motion are selective for the sight of the same action visible in full light and when depicted in point light displays.

Cells responding to whole body motion exhibit selectivity for direction of motion and view of the body: most respond preferentially to compatible motion with the body moving forward in the direction it faces, though some are tuned to backward locomotion with the body moving in the opposite direction to the way it faces (Perrett *et al.* 1985*b*, 1989; Oram & Perrett 1996; Figure 9.2b). This cellular tuning bias for forward locomotion may underlie the forward bias found in perceptual interpretation of locomotion depicted in point light displays (Pavlova *et al.* 2002).

Responses to purposeful hand object actions such as reaching for, picking, tearing and manipulating objects have also been characterized in the STS (Perrett *et al.* 1989, 1990*c*; Jellema *et al.* 2000). These STS cells are sensitive to the form of the hand performing the action, and are unresponsive to the sight of tools manipulating objects in the same manner as hands. Furthermore, the cells code the spatio-temporal interaction between the agent performing the action and the object of the action. For example, cells tuned to hands manipulating an object cease to respond if the hands and

object move appropriately but are spatially separated. This selectivity ensures that the cells are more responsive in situations where the agent's motion is causally related to the object's motion. The STS cell populations coding body and hand actions appear to be exclusively visual, although information from the motor system does affect other STS cell populations (Hietanen & Perrett 1996) and modulates STS activity in humans (Iacoboni *et al.* 2001; Nishitani & Hari 2001).

Information defined by the visual characterization of actions in the STS appears to be relayed via parietal systems (Gallese *et al.* 2002) to frontal motor planning systems. In frontal and parietal areas a neural system has recently been found to respond selectively both during the execution of hand actions, and (like STS cells) during the observation of corresponding actions performed by others. The frontal region of primate cortex had long been known to be somatotopically organized for the representation and control of movements of the mouth and arm (Rizzolatti *et al.* 1988). Neurons within area F5 of the monkey premotor cortex have now been labelled 'mirror' neurons, because they discharge when monkeys perform or observe the same hand actions (di Pellegrino *et al.* 1992; Rizzolatti *et al.* 1996*a,b*; Gallese *et al.* 1996). An F5 cell selective for the action of grasping would respond for example when the monkey grasps an object in sight or in the dark (thereby demonstrating motoric properties). The visual properties of such an F5 cell are strikingly similar to those described in the STS: both F5 and STS cells will respond when the monkey observes the experimenter reaching and grasping an object, but not to the sight of the experimenter's hand motion alone or the sight of the object alone. These conjoint properties have led Rizzolatti *et al.* (1996*a,b*) and Gallese *et al.* (1996) to postulate that the F5 neurons form a system for matching observation and executing actions for the grasping, manipulation and placement of objects. Because the cells additionally respond selectively to the sound of actions (Kohler *et al.* 2002), the mirror system may provide a supra-modal conceptual representation of actions and their consequences in the world.

Crucially the properties of the frontal mirror system indicate that we may understand actions performed by others because we can match the actions we sense through vision (and audition) to our ability to produce the same actions ourselves.

The actions of others are not always fully visible, for example someone may become hidden from our sight as they move behind a tree, or their hands may not remain fully in view as they reach to retrieve an object. The similarity of STS and F5 systems in processing of actions has become more apparent in experiments investigating the nature of processing during these moments when actions are partially or totally occluded from sight. Within the STS it is now apparent that specific cell populations are activated when the presence of a hidden person can be inferred from the preceding visual events (i.e., they were witnessed passing out of sight behind a screen and have not yet been witnessed re-emerging into sight, so they are likely to remain behind the screen; Baker *et al.* 2001). In an analogous manner, F5 cells may respond to the sight of the experimenter reaching to grasp an object. The same cells are active when the experimenter places an object behind a screen and then reaches as if to grasp it (even though the object and hand are hidden from view (Umilta *et al.* 2001)). The sight of equivalent reaching when there is no reason to believe an object is hidden from sight fails to activate the F5 cells. Thus F5 and STS cells code the sight of actions on the basis of what is currently visible and on the basis of the recent perceptual history (Jellema & Perrett 2002; Jellema *et al.* 2002).

The manner in which temporal STS and frontal F5 systems interact is not fully clear, but appears to involve intermediate processing steps mediated by parietal areas (Nishitani & Hari 2000, 2001; Gallese *et al.* 2002). While STS and F5 cells have similar visual properties they may subserve distinct functions; the frontal system perhaps serves to control the behaviour of the self particularly in dealing with objects (Rizzolatti *et al.* 1996*a,b*), whereas the STS system is specialized for the detection and recognition of the behaviour of others (Perrett *et al.* 1990*c*; Mistlin & Perrett 1990; Hietanen & Perrett 1996).

4. Human Neuroimaging and Electrophysiological Studies of Biological Motion Perception

The first suggestion that humans may possess specialized biological motion perception mechanisms came from a point light display depicting a moving body designed to investigate the response properties of medial temporal/V5, a region of occipito-temporal cortex known to respond to motion. In this fMRI study activation was observed in MT/V5 as well as areas of superior temporal cortex. This was regarded at that time as surprising, as the activation appeared to lie in brain regions traditionally regarded as participating in auditory speech processing (Howard *et al.* 1996). Localization of primary auditory cortex was not performed in this visual stimulation study. In a PET study published in the same year Johansson displays of body motion (depicting a person dancing), hand motion (depicting a hand reaching for a glass and bringing it to a mouth), object motion (depicting a three-dimensional structure rotating and pitching) and control conditions, consisting of either random dot motion or a static display of randomly placed dots, were shown to a group of healthy subjects (Bonda *et al.* 1996). The human motion conditions selectively activated the inferior parietal region and the STS. Specifically, the body motion condition selectively activated the right posterior STS, whereas the hand motion condition activated the left intraparietal sulcus and the posterior STS (Bonda *et al.* 1996). In a more recent fMRI study, a Johansson display depicting a walker was used and the activation contrasted to control conditions that included a dot display with non-random motion and a gender discrimination task with real images of faces (Vaina *et al.* 2001). Biological motion differentially activated a large number of dorsal and ventral regions, most notably the lateral occipital complex, but the STS was not preferentially activated in this study.

Grossman and colleagues found that biological motion stimuli depicting jumping, kicking, running and throwing movements produced more right STS activation than control motion irrespective of the visual field in which the biological motion display was presented. Conversely, the control motion, including scrambled biological motion displays, activated MT/MST areas and the lateral-occipital complex (Grossman *et al.* 2000). Moreover, the STS region could also be activated by *imagining* Johansson stimuli, although the size of the activation was small (Grossman *et al.* 2000). While the most robust STS activation was elicited by viewing upright Johansson displays, a smaller STS activation signal was also seen to viewing inverted Johansson displays.

While biological motion clearly activates the STS region in humans, the function of the region may be more general in performing a visual analysis of bodies based on either the characteristic patterns of articulation that comprise biological motion or information about bodies that can be derived from static images (Downing *et al.* 2001); hence the term 'extrastriate body area' has been applied to one cortical region within the STS complex.

5. Biological Motion Perception Versus Human Motion Perception

As in non-human primates, responsiveness to Johansson-like displays of facial motion is present in STS regions that also respond to real images of facial motion, e.g., non-linguistic mouth movements (Puce *et al.* 2001), although the percent magnetic resonance signal change to the Johansson-like face was smaller than that observed to the natural facial images. In parallel to the neuroimaging data, direct measures of neural activity in humans, in the form of scalp ERPs, are elicited to Johansson-like and real images of faces (Thompson *et al.* 2002*b*), with a prominent negativity occurring at *ca.* 170 ms post-motion onset (N170) over the bilateral temporal scalp. This activity is significantly greater than that seen to motion controls.

Over the latter half of the 1990s, a series of PET and fMRI studies examining activation to viewing the motion and actions of others have pointed to the existence of cortical networks that

preferentially process certain attributes of these high-level visual displays (reviewed by Allison *et al.* 2000; Blakemore & Decety 2001). Figure 9.3 displays activation observed in these studies, lying along the posterior extent of the STS and its ascending limb in inferior parietal cortex in response to observing movements of the body, hands, eye and mouth. Activation in these regions can also be elicited to imagining the motion of others (Grossman *et al.* 2000), and additionally to viewing static images of implied motion (Kourtzi & Kanwisher 2000).

Interestingly, differences in activation patterns can occur when subjects view compatible versus incompatible motion of the head or body (Thompson *et al.* 2002*a*). Specifically, the bilateral posterior lateral temporal cortex is active when viewing compatible motion. By contrast, viewing incompatible motion activates the right posterior lateral temporal cortex, left anterior temporal cortex, left temporoparietal junction and left precentral gyrus. This extended network of activation might be due to the novelty or salience of the incongruent body and head motion stimuli (Downar *et al.* 2002). The differential experience with compatible and incompatible motion may explain STS cell sensitivity to the compatibility of motion direction and body view during the locomotion described above.

What is unique about the motion of animate beings? Animals and humans possess articulated joints, enabling the movement of body parts without having to maintain a constant spatial relationship in space relative to each other. This results in the ability to produce a limitless set of movements. Man-made objects, such as utensils and tools, in general do not have this capability. Beauchamp *et al.* (2002) investigated the differences in brain activation to these different types of high-level motion stimuli. Interestingly, observing human motion stimuli activated the STS and observing the motion of tools/utensils activated cortex ventral to the STS, on the MTG. In another fMRI experiment in this same study, stimuli depicting articulated and non-articulated human motion were presented. The STS responded to the articulated human motion and the MTG to non-articulated

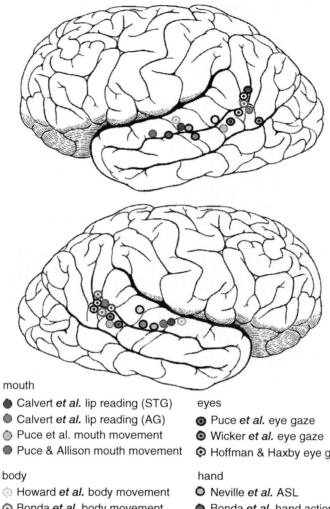

mouth

● Calvert *et al.* lip reading (STG)
◐ Calvert *et al.* lip reading (AG)
○ Puce et al. mouth movement
● Puce & Allison mouth movement

eyes

◉ Puce *et al.* eye gaze
◉ Wicker *et al.* eye gaze
◉ Hoffman & Haxby eye gaze

body

◉ Howard *et al.* body movement
◉ Bonda *et al.* body movement
◉ Senior *et al.* body movement
◉ Kourtzi & Kanwisher
    body movement
◉ Grossman *et al.* body movement

hand

○ Neville *et al.* ASL
◕ Bonda *et al.* hand action
○ Grezes *et al.* hand action
◐ Grezes *et al.* hand movement
◑ Grafton *et al.* hand grasp
◑ Rizzolatti *et al.* hand grasp

FIGURE 9.3 ■ (*A color version of this figure follows page 146.*) Centers of activation to viewing the face, hand and body movements of others obtained from a series of PET and fMRI studies. (Adapted from Allison *et al.* (2000), with permission.)

motion, indicating that these high-order processing mechanisms process selectively the higher-order motion type (Beauchamp *et al.* 2002).

Grezes *et al.* (2001) also reported activation differences between observing rigid and non-rigid motion. Specifically, they observed an anterior-posterior gradient of activation in the STS regions, with non-rigid motion producing the most anterior activation. Additionally, they observed activation in left intraparietal cortex to non-rigid biological motion (Grezes *et al.* 2001). The magnitude of the activation in the STS to biological motion, and indeed in other cortical regions, can be coloured by the task requirements and the attention that the observer places on the 'human' quality of the motion (Vaina *et al.* 2001). Additionally, attention to the displayed emotion enhances fMRI activation in the STS, whereas increased activation to facial attributes *per se*, such as identity or isolated features, increased activation in all known face-sensitive cortical regions (Narumoto *et al.* 2001).

A. Social Cognition

The limbic system, in conjunction with the orbitofrontal cortex and the STS, is thought to form a network that is involved in social cognition (Baron-Cohen 1995; Brothers 1997; Adolphs 1999). One important aspect of social cognition is the identification of the direction of another's attention from their direction of gaze or head view (Perrett *et al.* 1985a, 1992; Kleinke 1986; Allison *et al.* 2000; Emery 2000). Indeed, the existence of an eye direction detector has been postulated in this hierarchical system of social cognition, which at its top level allows us to 'mind-read' and infer the intentions of others (Baron-Cohen 1995; Baron-Cohen *et al.* 1997). While there is evidence for cell populations coding for eye and attention direction within STS (Perrett *et al.* 1985a, 1992), the populations are not anatomically grouped in such a way that scalp evoked potentials are necessarily linked to a given eye direction (Bentin *et al.* 1996; Eimer 1998; Taylor *et al.* 2001). Our attention and behaviour can be modified when confronted with a face with averted gaze. A peripheral target stimulus is detected by normal subjects more efficiently when it lies in the direction of gaze of a central stimulus face (Friesen & Kingstone 1998; Driver *et al.* 1999; Hietanen 1999, 2002; Langton & Bruce 2000). Moreover, patients with unilateral neglect are less likely to extinguish a contralesional target stimulus when it lies in the gaze path of a stimulus face (Vuilleumier 2002). Following the attention direction of someone's gaze may be such an over-learned response that it needs little conscious awareness.

B. Gaze Perception

Neuroimaging studies involving gaze perception indicate that there is an active cortical network involving occipito-temporal cortex (fusiform gyrus, inferior temporal gyrus, parietal lobule and bilateral middle temporal gyri) when subjects passively view gaze aversion movements (Wicker *et al.* 1998). One prominently active region to viewing eye movements (gaze aversion and also eyes looking at the observer) is the cortex around the STS, particularly in the right hemisphere, and this same region is active also to viewing opening and closing movements of the mouth (Puce *et al.* 1998). Thus, as is evident from the single cell responses, the STS region contains neural populations representing multiple aspects of the appearance of the face (including gaze) and body and their motion; the STS should not be considered exclusively an 'eye detector' or 'eye processor'. The STS is more activated during judgements of gaze direction than during judgements of identity, whereas the fusiform and inferior occipito-temporal activation is stronger during judgements of identity than gaze direction (Hoffman & Haxby 2000). Intracranial ERP recordings from these structures indicate that the STS responds to facial motion, whereas the ventral-temporal cortex responds more strongly to static facial images (Puce & Allison 1999). This is not surprising if one considers that eye gaze direction changes are transient and their detection might require motion processing systems, whereas identity judgements can be made independently of facial movements. Indeed, the processing of dynamic information about facial expression and the processing of static information about facial identity appear neuropsychologically dissociable (Campbell 1992; Humphreys *et al.* 1993).

C. Lip Reading

Lip reading, an important function for both hearing and deaf individuals, can be neuropsychologically dissociated from face recognition (Campbell *et al.* 1986), in a somewhat similar manner to gaze perception. Normal lip reading uses cortex of the STG in addition to other brain regions such as the angular gyrus, posterior cingulate, medial frontal cortex and frontal pole (Calvert *et al.* 1997). The STG and surrounding cortex activate bilaterally when subjects view face actions that could be interpreted as speech (Puce *et al.* 1998; Campbell *et al.* 2001), while some regions of the posterior right STS activate for the sight of speech and non-speech mouth movements (Campbell *et al.* 2001). Centres of activation to visual speech appear to overlap those associated with hearing speech (Calvert *et al.* 1997), indicating that these regions receive multimodal inputs during speech analysis (Kawashima *et al.* 1999; Calvert *et al.* 2000). Further evidence for this multimodal integration is a phenomenon known as the McGurk effect (McGurk & MacDonald 1976), where what observers hear when listening to speech sounds is altered by simultaneously viewing mouth movements appropriate to a different speech utterance. Indeed, magnetoencephalographic recordings of neural activity to speech stimuli show sensitivity to auditory-visual mismatch (Sams *et al.* 1991) with activity 200 ms poststimulus augmented when the visual speech does not correspond to the accompanying auditory speech.

D. The Mirror Neuron System and Action Observation/Execution

The existence of a mirror neuron system in humans has been investigated during the manipulation of objects (Rizzolatti *et al.* 1996a,b; Binkofski *et al.* 1999a,b). The activation in fronto-central regions, seen when subjects observe and/or execute grasping behaviours, is accompanied by activity in the parietal cortex and STS (Jeannerod *et al.* 1995; Iacoboni *et al.* 1999, 2001; Rizzolatti *et al.* 2001; Gallese *et al.* 2002), paralleling the mirror neuron system in non-human primates.

Additionally, the secondary somatosensory cortex, SII, located in the temporal operculum is postulated to analyse the intrinsic properties of the graspable object while activation observed in the cortex in the intraparietal sulcus was thought to be related to kineasthetic processes (Binkofski *et al.* 1999b), although strictly speaking it is not part of the mirror neuron system.

The neuroimaging data mesh well with reported disturbances in executing grasping movements in the neuropsychological lesion literature. For example, Jeannerod and colleagues have reported a case with bilateral posterior parietal lesions of vascular origin where there was no difficulty in reaching toward the location of the object; however, a profound deficit in executing the anticipatory grasping movement with the fingers occurred to nondescript objects (cylindrical dowels). Interestingly, there was no deficit in grasping behaviour when well-known recognizable objects were used in the same test (Jeannerod *et al.* 1994). Mental imagery of hand and finger movements was found to be impaired in patients with unilateral parietal lesions, who had difficulties in producing movements with their hands and fingers (Sirigu *et al.* 1996). It has been reported that patients with unilateral parietal lesions have more difficulty in imitating gestures involving their own bodies relative to movements involving external objects, particularly if the lesion is in the left hemisphere (Halsband *et al.* 2001).

The human STS in its posterior extent has been found to be active not only to the hand and body movements of others (see Figure 9.3; Allison *et al.* 2000), but also to faces (Puce *et al.* 1998). Interestingly, ERP recordings indicate that neural activity can differentiate between types of facial movements (Puce *et al.* 2000). Viewing mouth opening movements produces larger N170 responses relative to viewing mouth closing movements. A similar N170 response gradient is seen for observing eyes averting their gaze away from the observer relative to eyes focusing their gaze on the observer. Augmented neural responses to eye aversion movements may be a powerful signal that the observer is no longer the focus of another's attention. Similarly, larger N170s to mouth opening movements might be important for recognizing the beginning of an utterance (Puce *et al.* 2000). With recording electrodes sited in the STS of epilepsy surgery patients, selective responses to mouth opening have been elicited (see Allison *et al.* 2000, box 1). No responses were observed to mouth closing movements or eye deviations, indicating that these regions might be responsive during lip reading (or the sight of gestures and emotional expressions in which the mouth opens, e.g., during eating and surprise). The Talairach coordinates of these electrode positions are comparable to sites of fMRI activation in lip reading (Calvert *et al.* 1997).

If eye aversion movements are given a context, late ERPs that differ as a function of the social significance of the aversion movement can be elicited (Figure 9.4; A. Cooper and A. Puce, unpublished data). This was demonstrated in a visual task where two permanently gaze-averted flanker faces were presented with a central face that changed its gaze direction. The central face could look in the same direction as both flanker faces, setting up an apparently common focus of attention off to the side ('group attention').

Alternatively, if the central face looked away from the observer in the opposite direction to the other two faces, a mutual gaze exchange between the central face and one of the flankers became apparent ('mutual gaze exchange'). Finally, the central face could look away from the observer and the other two flanker faces by looking up ('control'). An N170 ERP to the gaze aversion of the central face was elicited, and its characteristics did not change as a function of condition (see also Puce *et al.* 2000). A later positive ERP, elicited between 300 and 500 ms post-motion onset (P400) was seen to differentiate in latency as a function of viewing condition: group attention produced the shortest latency response, followed by the mutual gaze exchange condition and then the control condition.

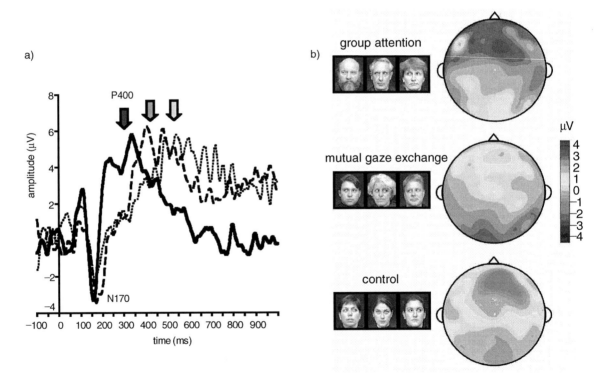

FIGURE 9.4 ■ (*A color version of part b of this figure follows page 146.*) ERPs elicited to a social attention task. (a) ERP waveforms elicited to three conditions: solid line, group attention; dashed line, mutual gaze exchange; dotted line, control. The arrows indicate a late peak of ERP activity that follows the N170 ERP (P400), which changes its latency as a function of viewing condition. (b) Voltage maps for the three viewing conditions generated at the peak of P400 activity for the group attention condition (black arrow in (a)). The group attention condition shows fronto-temporal positivity, whereas the other two conditions show small posterior positivities.

Our non-verbal and verbal facial movements usually do occur in an affective context, and preliminary ERP data indicate that our brains are very sensitive to these gesture-affect blends. If facial movements (either non-verbal or verbal) are combined with different types of affect, temporal scalp N170 peak latency and the amplitude of later ERP activity can be altered as a function of affect type (Wheaton *et al.* 2002*b*). If gesture-affect combinations are incongruous, as shown by increased reaction time to classify affect in behavioural data, late ERP activity from 300 to 975 ms post-motion onset is modulated as a function of not only affect or gesture but also their combination (Wheaton *et al.*

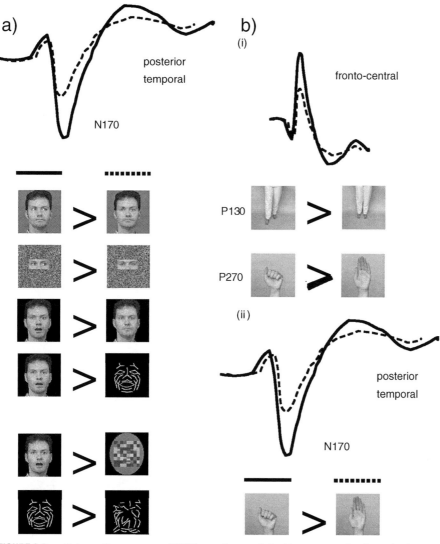

FIGURE 9.5 ■ Schematic summary of ERP waveforms elicited in response to observing human motion. (*a*) Posterior temporal N170 (solid line) to conditions listed in the left column is larger relative to N170 (dashed line) elicited to conditions listed in the right column. *b*(i) Frontocentral ERPs show larger P130 and P270 components across body and hand motion conditions shown in the left and right columns (solid versus dashed line). *b*(ii) Posterior temporal N170 (solid line) is larger to hand closure relative to hand opening (dashed line).

2002*a*). These preliminary data indicate that the processing of inconsistencies in others' behaviour can be detected physiologically.

ERPs, in the form of N170 negativities occurring over bilateral temporal scalp regions, have been elicited not only to facial movements but also to hand and body movements (Wheaton *et al.* 2001). The N170 activity was larger for observing hand clenching movements relative to hand opening movements. In addition, ERP activity was also observed to hand and body motion over the central scalp. Interestingly, ERP activity was larger to observing a body stepping forward than to a body stepping back (paralleling the cellular bias for forward or compatible direction of locomotion; Perrett *et al.* 1985*b*; Oram & Perrett 1994). Taken together, the ERP differentiation in the hand and body movements might indicate a stronger neural signal for potentially threatening movements (Wheaton *et al.* 2001). When fMRI activation to these movement types is compared, there is a robust signal within the temporoparietal cortex to all of these motion types (Wheaton *et al.* 2002*c*). Figure 9.5 summarizes the main findings from the ERP studies (Puce *et al.* 2000; Wheaton *et al.* 2001; Thompson *et al.* 2002*b*), and indicates that processing between movement types begins before 200 ms postmotion onset not only in the posterior temporal cortex but also in the frontocentral regions, which would be expected from the distribution of action processing evident in fMRI and cell recording.

E. Gesture and Action Processing: Implications for Disorders of Social Communication

The processing of non-verbally presented messages, in the form of face and hand gestures, is crucial for social primates to be able to interact with one another—and there are considerable similarities in the high-level biological motion processing systems in human and non-human primates. The importance of comprehending actions of others may also be evident when such comprehension is impaired in clinical conditions. Disorders such as autism, Asperger syndrome, and schizophrenia are characterized by the inability to form or maintain social relationships. This can be difficult if the sufferer cannot process incoming social messages communicated by the bodily and facial actions of others, or sends inappropriate social reactions to such signals (e.g., Williams *et al.* 2001). Further neuroimaging and neurophysiological studies of healthy subjects and those with impairments of human motion processing may shed light on the interactions between the various components of these high-level biological motion processing systems.

Acknowledgments

A.P.'s research has been supported by the National Health and Medical Research Council (Australia) and the Australia Research Council.

REFERENCES

Adolphs, R. 1999 Social cognition and the human brain. *Trends Cogn. Sci.* 3, 469–479.

Aggleton, J.P., Burton, M.J. & Passingham, R.E. 1980 Cortical and subcortical afferents to the amygdala of the rhesus monkey (*Macaca mulatta*). *Brain Res.* 190, 347–368.

Allison, T., Puce, A. & McCarthy, G. 2000 Social perception from visual cues: role of the STS region. *Trends Cogn. Sci.* 4, 267–278.

Baker, C.I., Keysers, C., Jellema, T., Wicker, B. & Perrett, D.I. 2001 Neuronal representation of disappearing and hidden objects in temporal cortex of the macaque. *Exp. Brain Res.* 140, 375–381.

Barbas, H. 1988 Anatomic organization of basoventral and mediodorsal visual recipient prefrontal regions in the rhesus monkey. *J. Comp. Neurol.* 276, 313–342.

Baron-Cohen, S. 1995 *Mindblindness: an essay on autism and theory of mind*. Cambridge, MA: MIT Press.

Baron-Cohen, S., Wheelwright, S. & Joliffe, T. 1997 Is there a 'language of the eyes'? Evidence from normal adults, and adults with autism or Asperger syndrome *Vis. Cogn* 4, 311–331.

Bassili, J. N. 1978 Facial motion in the perception of faces and of emotional expression. *J. Exp. Psychol. Hum. Percept. Perf.* 4, 373–379.

Beauchamp, M. S., Lee, K. E., Haxby, J. V. & Martin, A. 2002 Parallel visual motion processing streams for manipulable objects and human movements. *Neuron* 34, 149–159.

Bentin, S., Allison, T., Puce, A., Perez, A. & McCarthy, G. 1996 Electrophysiological studies of face perception in humans. *J. Cogn. Neurosci.* 8, 551–565.

Binkofski, F., Buccino, G., Posse, S., Seitz, R. J., Rizzolatti, G. & Freund, H. J. 1999*a* A fronto-parietal circuit for object manipulation in man: evidence from an fMRI study. *Eur. J. Neurosci.* 11, 3276–3286.

Binkofski, F., Buccino, G., Stephan, K. M., Rizzolatti, G., Seitz, R. J. & Freund, H. J. 1999*b* A parieto-premotor network for object manipulation: evidence from neuroimaging. *Exp. Brain Res.* 128, 210–213.

Blake, R. 1993 Cats perceive biological motion. *Psychol. Sci.* 4, 54–57.

Blakemore, S.-J. & Decety, J. 2001 From the perception of action to the understanding of intention. *Nature Rev. Neurosci.* 2, 561–567.

Bonda, E., Petrides, M., Ostry, D. & Evans, A. 1996 Specific involvement of human parietal systems and the amygdala in the perception of biological motion. *J. Neurosci.* 16, 3737–3744.

Boussaoud, D., Ungerleider, L. G. & Desimone, R. 1990 Pathways for motion analysis: cortical connections of the medial superior temporal and fundus of the superior temporal visual areas in the macaque. *J. Comp. Neurol.* 296, 462–495.

Brothers, L. 1997 *Friday's footprint: how society shapes the human mind.* New York: Oxford University Press.

Calvert, G. A., Bullmore, E. T., Brammer, M. J., Campbell, R., Williams, S. C., McGuire, P. K., Woodruff, P. W., Iversen, S. D. & David, A. S. 1997 Activation of auditory cortex during silent lipreading. *Science* 276, 593–595.

Calvert, G. A., Campbell, R. & Brammer, M. J. 2000 Evidence from functional magnetic resonance imaging of crossmodal binding in the human heteromodal cortex. *Curr. Biol.* 10, 649–657.

Campbell, R. 1992 The neuropsychology of lipreading. *Phil. Trans. R. Soc. Lond.* B 335, 39–45.

Campbell, R., Landis, T. & Regard, M. 1986 Face recognition and lipreading. *Brain* 109, 509–521.

Campbell, R., MacSweeney, M., Surguladze, S., Calvert, G., McGuire, P., Suckling, J., Brammer, M. J. & David, A. S. 2001 Cortical substrates for the perception of face actions: an fMRI study of the specificity of activation for seen speech and for meaningless lower-face acts (gurning). *Brain Res. Cogn. Brain Res.* 12, 233–243.

Carey, D. P., Perrett, D. I. & Oram, M. W. 1997 Recognizing, understanding and reproducing action. In *Handbook of neuropsychology*, vol. 11. *Action and cognition* (ed. M. Jeannerod), pp. 111–129. Amsterdam: Elsevier.

Cutting, J. E. & Kozlowski, L. T. 1977 Recognizing friends by their walk: gait perception without familiarity cues. *Bull. Psychonomic. Soc.* 9, 353–356.

Desimone, R. 1991 Face-selective cells in the temporal cortex of monkeys. *J. Cogn. Neurosci.* 3, 1–8.

Desimone, R., Albright, T. D., Gross, C. G. & Bruce, C. 1984 Stimulus-selective properties of inferior temporal neurons in the macaque. *J. Neurosci.* 4, 2051–2062.

di Pellegrino, G., Fadiga, L., Fogassi, V., Gallese, V. & Rizzolatti, G. 1992 Understanding motor events: a neurophysiological study. *Exp. Brain Res.* 91, 176–180.

Dittrich, W. H. 1993 Action categories and the perception of biological motion. *Perception* 22, 15–22.

Downar, J., Crawley, A. P., Mikulis, D. J. & Davis, K. D. 2002 A cortical network sensitive to stimulus salience in a neutral behavioral context across multiple sensory modalities. *J. Neurophysiol.* 87, 615–620.

Downing, P. E., Jiang, Y. H., Shuman, M. & Kanwisher, N. 2001 A cortical area selective for visual processing of the human body. *Science* 293, 2470–2473.

Driver, J., Davis, G., Ricciardelli, P., Kidd, P., Maxwell, E. & Baron-Cohen, S. 1999 Gaze perception triggers reflexive visuospatial orienting. *Vis. Cogn.* 6, 509–540.

Eimer, M. 1998 Does the face-specific N170 component reflect the activity of a specialized eye processor? *Neuroreport* 9, 2945–2948.

Emery, N. J. 2000 The eyes have it: the neuroethology, function and evolution of social gaze. *Neurosci. Biobehav. Rev.* 24, 581–604.

Felleman, D. J. & Van Essen, D. C. 1991 Distributed hierarchical processing in the primate cerebral cortex. *Cerebr. Cortex* 1, 1–47.

Friesen, C. K. & Kingstone, A. 1998 The eyes have it! Reflexive orienting is triggered by nonpredictive gaze. *Psychol. Bull. Rev.* 5, 490–495.

Gallese, V., Fadiga, L., Fogassi, L. & Rizzolatti, G. 1996 Action recognition in the premotor cortex. *Brain* 119, 593–609.

Gallese, V., Fadiga, L., Fogassi, L. & Rizzolatti, G. 2002 Action representation and the inferior parietal lobule. *Attention Perform.* 19, 247–266.

Grezes, J., Fonlupt, P., Bertenthal, B., Delon-Martin, C., Segebarth, C. & Decety, J. 2001 Does perception of biological motion rely on specific brain regions? *Neuroimage* 13, 775–785.

Grossman, E., Donnelly, M., Price, R., Pickens, D., Morgan, V., Neighbor, G. & Blake, R. 2000 Brain areas involved in perception of biological motion. *J. Cogn. Neurosci.* 12, 711–720.

Halsband, U., Schmitt, J., Weyers, M., Binkofski, F., Grützner, G. & Freund, H. J. 2001 Recognition and imitation of pantomimed motor acts after unilateral parietal and premotor lesions: a perspective on apraxia. *Neuropsychologia* 39, 200–216.

Hietanen, J. K. 1999 Does your gaze direction and head orientation shift my visual attention? *Neuroreport* 10, 3443–3447.

Hietanen, J. K. 2002 Social attention orienting integrates visual information from head and body orientation. *Psychol. Res.* 66, 174–179.

Hietanen, J. K. & Perrett, D. I. 1996 Motion sensitive cells in the macaque superior temporal polysensory area: response discrimination between self- and externally generated pattern motion. *Behav. Brain Res.* 76, 155–167.

Hoffman, E. A. & Haxby, J. V. 2000 Distinct representations of eye gaze and identity in the distributed human neural system for face perception. *Nature Neurosci.* 3, 80–84.

Howard, R. J., Brammer, M., Wright, I., Woodruff, P. W., Bullmore, E. T. & Zeki, S. 1996 A direct demonstration of functional specialization within motion-related visual and auditory cortex of the human brain. *Curr. Biol.* 6, 1015–1019.

Humphreys, G. W., Donnelly, N. & Riddoch, M. J. 1993 Expression is computed separately from facial identity, and it is computed separately for moving and static faces: neuropsychological evidence. *Neuropsychologia* 31, 173–181.

Iacoboni, M., Woods, R. P., Brass, M., Bekkering, H., Mazziotta, J. C. & Rizzolatti, G. 1999 Cortical mechanisms of human imitation. *Science* 286, 2526–2528.

Iacoboni, M., Koski, L. M., Brass, M., Bekkering, H., Woods, R. P., Dubeau, M. C., Mazziotta, J. C. & Rizzolatti, G. 2001 Reafferent copies of imitated actions in the right superior temporal cortex. *Proc. Natl Acad. Sci. USA* 98, 13 995–13 999.

Jeannerod, M., Decety, J. & Michel, F. 1994 Impairment of grasping movements following a bilateral posterior parietal lesion. *Neuropsychologia* 32, 369–380.

Jeannerod, M., Arbib, M. A., Rizzolatti, G. & Sakata, H. 1995 Grasping objects: the cortical mechanisms of visuomotor transformation. *Trends Neurosci.* 18, 314–320.

Jellema, T. & Perrett, D. I. 2002 Coding of visible and hidden actions. *Attention Perform.* 19, 356–380.

Jellema, T., Baker, C. I., Wicker, B. & Perrett, D. I. 2000 Neural representation for the perception of the intentionality of hand actions. *Brain Cogn.* 44, 280–302.

Jellema, T., Oram, M. W., Baker, C. I. & Perrett, D. I. 2002 Cell populations in the banks of the superior temporal sulcus of the macaque and imitation. In *The imitative mind: development, evolution, and brain bases* (ed. A. Meltzoff & W. Prinz), pp. 267–290. Cambridge University Press.

Johansson, G. 1973 Visual perception of biological motion and a model of its analysis. *Percept. Psychophys.* 14, 202–211.

Kawashima, R., Imaizumi, S., Mori, K., Okada, K., Goto, R., Kiritani, S., Ogawa, A. & Fukuda, H. 1999 Selective visual and auditory attention toward utterances: a PET study. *Neuroimage* 10, 209–215.

Kleinke, C. L. 1986 Gaze and eye contact: a research review. *Psychol. Bull.* 100, 78–100.

Kohler, E., Keysers, C., Umilta, M. A., Fogassi, L., Gallese, V. & Rizzolatti, G. 2002 Hearing sounds, understanding actions: action representation in mirror neurons. *Science* 297, 846–848.

Kourtzi, Z. & Kanwisher, N. 2000 Activation in human MT/MST by static images with implied motion. *J. Cogn. Neurosci.* 12, 48–55.

Kozlowski, L. T. & Cutting, J. E. 1977 Recognizing the sex of a walker from a dynamic point-light display. *Percept. Psychophys.* 21, 575–580.

Langton, S. R. H. & Bruce, V. 2000 You must see the point: automatic processing of cues to the direction of social attention. *J. Exp. Psychol. Hum. Percep. Perf.* 26, 747–757.

McGurk, H. & MacDonald, J. 1976 Hearing lips and seeing voices. *Nature* 264, 746–748.

McLeod, P., Dittrich, W., Driver, J., Perrett, D. I. & Zihl, J. 1996 Preserved and impaired detection of structure from motion in a 'motion-blind' patient. *Vis. Cogn.* 3, 363–391.

Mistlin, A. J. & Perrett, D. I. 1990 Visual and somatosensory processing in the macaque temporal cortex: the role of 'expectation'. *Exp. Brain Res.* 82, 437–450.

Narumoto, J., Okada, T., Sadato, N., Fukui, K. & Yonekura, Y. 2001 Attention to emotion modulates fMRI activity in human right superior temporal sulcus. *Cogn. Brain Res.* 12, 225–231.

Nishitani, N. & Hari, R. 2000 Temporal dynamics of cortical representation for action. *Proc. Natl Acad. Sci. USA* 97, 913–918.

Nishitani, N. & Hari, R. 2001 Sign language and mirror neuron system. *Neuroimage* 12(6), S452.

Oram, M. W. & Perrett, D. I. 1994 Responses of anterior superior temporal polysensory (STPa) neurons to 'biological motion' stimuli. *J. Cogn. Neurosci.* 6, 99–116.

Oram, M. W. & Perrett, D. I. 1996 Integration of form and motion in the anterior superior temporal polysensory area (STPa) of the macaque monkey. *J. Neurophysiol.* 76, 109–129.

Pavlova, M. & Sokolov, A. 2000 Orientation specificity in biological motion perception. *Percept. Psychophys.* 62, 889–899.

Pavlova, M., Krägeloh-Mann, I., Birbaumer, N. & Sokolov, A. 2002 Biological motion shown backwards: the apparent-facing effect. *Perception* 31, 435–443.

Perrett, D. I., Rolls, E. T. & Caan, W. 1982 Visual neurons responsive to faces in the monkey temporal cortex. *Exp. Brain Res.* 47, 329–342.

Perrett, D. I., Smith, P. A. J., Potter, D. D., Mistlin, A. J., Head, A. S., Milner, A. D. & Jeeves, M. A. 1984 Neurones responsive to faces in the temporal cortex: studies of functional organization, sensitivity to identity and relation to perception. *Hum. Neurobiol.* 3, 197–208.

Perrett, D. I., Smith, P. A. J., Potter, D. D., Mistlin, A. J., Head, A. S., Milner, A. D. & Jeeves, M. A. 1985a Visual cells in the temporal cortex sensitive to face view and gaze direction. *Proc. R. Soc. Lond.* B 223, 293–317.

Perrett, D. I., Smith, P. A. J., Mistlin, A. J., Chitty, A. J., Head, A. S., Potter, D. D., Broennimann, R., Milner, A. D. & Jeeves, M. A. 1985b Visual analysis of body movements by neurones in the temporal cortex of the macaque monkey: a preliminary report. *Behav. Brain Res.* 16, 153–170.

Perrett, D. I., Harries, M. H., Bevan, R., Thomas, S., Benson, P. J., Mistlin, A. J., Chitty, A. J., Hietanen, J. K. & Ortega, J. E. 1989 Frameworks of analysis for the neural representation of animate objects and actions. *J. Exp. Biol.* 146, 87–113.

Perrett, D. I., Harries, M. H., Benson, P. J., Chitty, A. J. & Mistlin, A. J. 1990a Retrieval of structure from rigid and biological motion; an analysis of the visual response of neurons in the macaque temporal cortex. In *AI and the eye* (ed. T. Troscianko & A. Blake), pp. 181–201. Chichester, UK: Wiley.

Perrett, D. I., Harries, M., Chitty, A. J. & Mistlin, A. J. 1990b Three stages in the classification of body movements by visual neurones. In *Images and understanding* (ed. H. B.

Barlow, C. Blakemore & M. Weston-Smith), pp. 94–108. Cambridge University Press.

Perrett, D. I., Mistlin, A. J., Harries, M. H. & Chitty, A. J. 1990c Understanding the visual appearance and consequence of hand actions. In *Vision and action: the control of grasping* (ed. M. A. Goodale), pp. 163–180. Norwood, NJ: Ablex Publishing.

Perrett, D. I., Hietanen, J. K., Oram, M. W. & Benson, P. J. 1992 Organization and functions of cells responsive to faces in the temporal cortex. *Phil. Trans. R. Soc. Lond.* B 335, 23–30.

Puce, A. & Allison, T. 1999 Differential processing of mobile and static faces by temporal cortex. *Neuroimage* 9(6), S801.

Puce, A., Allison, T., Bentin, S., Gore, J. C. & McCarthy, G. 1998 Temporal cortex activation in humans viewing eye and mouth movements. *J. Neurosci.* 18, 2188–2199.

Puce, A., Smith, A. & Allison, T. 2000 ERPs evoked by viewing moving eyes and mouths. *Cogn. Neuropsychol.* 17, 221–239.

Puce, A., Castiello, U., Syngeniotis, A. & Abbott, D. 2001 The human STS region integrates form and motion. *Neuroimage* 13(6), S931.

Rizzolatti, G., Camarda, R., Fogassi, L., Gentilucci, M., Luppino, G. & Matelli, M. 1988 Functional organization of inferior area 6 in the macaque monkey. II. Area F5 and the control of distal movements. *Exp. Brain Res.* 71, 491–507.

Rizzolatti, G., Fadiga, L., Gallese, V. & Fogassi, L. 1996a Premotor cortex and the recognition of motor actions. *Brain Res. Cogn. Brain Res.* 3, 131–141.

Rizzolatti, G., Fadiga, L., Matelli, M., Bettinardi, V., Paulesu, E., Perani, D. & Fazio, F. 1996b Localization of grasp representations in humans by PET. 1. Observation versus execution. *Exp. Brain Res.* 111, 246–252.

Rizzolatti, G., Fogassi, L. & Gallese, V. 2001 Neurophysiological mechanisms underlying the understanding and imitation of action. *Nature Rev. Neurosci.* 2, 661–670.

Sams, M., Aulanko, R., Hämäläinen, M., Hari, R., Lounasmaa, O. V., Lu, S. T. & Simola, J. 1991 Seeing speech: visual information from lip movements modifies activity in the human auditory cortex. *Neurosci. Lett.* 127, 141–145.

Schenk, T. & Zihl, J. 1997 Visual motion perception after brain damage: II. Deficits in form-from-motion perception. *Neuropsychologia* 35, 1299–1310.

Sirigu, A., Duhamel, J. R., Cohen, L., Pillon, B., Dubois, B. & Agid, Y. 1996 The mental representation of hand movements after parietal cortex damage. *Science* 273, 1564–1568.

Taylor, M. J., Edmonds, G. E., McCarthy, G. & Allison, T. 2001 Eyes first! Eye processing develops before face processing in children. *Neuroreport* 12, 1671–1676.

Thompson, J. C., Wheaton, K., Berkovic, S. F., Jackson, G. & Puce, A. 2002a Hemodynamic responses in humans to the perception of compatible and incompatible body motion. In *The fMRI Experience IV Proc.* NIH, Maryland, 2002, 93.

Thompson, J. C., Wheaton, K., Castiello, U. & Puce, A. 2002b ERPs differentiate between facial motion and motion in

general. Abstract no. 14221. Academic Press OHBM Annual Scientific Meeting 2002.

Thornton, I. M., Pinto, J. & Shiffrar, M. 1998 The visual perception of human locomotion. *Cogn. Neuropsychol.* 15, 535–552.

Umilta, M. A., Kohler, E., Gallese, V., Fogassi, L., Fadiga, L., Keysers, C. & Rizzolatti, G. 2001 I know what you are doing: a neurophysiological study. *Neuron* 31, 155–165.

Vaina, L. M., LeMay, M., Bienfang, D. C., Choi, A. Y. & Nakayama, K. 1990 Intact 'biological motion' and 'structure from motion' perception in a patient with impaired motion mechanisms: a case study. *Vis. Neurosci.* 5, 353–369.

Vaina, L. M., Solomon, J., Chowdhury, S., Sinha, P. & Belliveau, J. W. 2001 Functional neuroanatomy of biological motion perception in humans. *Proc. Natl Acad. Sci. USA* 98, 11 656–11 661.

Vuilleumier, P. 2002 Perceived gaze direction in faces and spatial attention: a study in patients with parietal damage and unilateral neglect. *Neuropsychologia* 40, 1013–1026.

Wachsmuth, E., Oram, M. W. & Perrett, D. I. 1994 Recognition of objects and their component parts: responses of single units in the temporal cortex of the macaque. *Cerebr. Cortex* 4, 509–522.

Wheaton, K. J., Pipingas, A., Silberstein, R. & Puce, A. 2001 Neuronal responses elicited to viewing the actions of others. *Vis. Neurosci.* 18, 401–406.

Wheaton, K. J., Aranda, G. & Puce, A. 2002a ERPs elicited to combined emotional and gestural movements of the face as a function of congruency. Abstract no. 14186. Academic Press OHBM Annual Scientific Meeting 2002.

Wheaton K. J., Aranda, G. & Puce, A. 2002b Affective modulation of gestural and visual speech stimuli: an ERP study. Abstract no. 14215. Academic Press OHBM Annual Scientific Meeting 2002.

Wheaton, K. J., Thompson, J. C., Berkovic, S. F., Jackson, G. & Puce, A. 2002c Brain regions responsive to the perception of human motion. *The fMRI Experience IV Proc.* NIH, Maryland 2002, p. 103.

Wicker, B., Michel, F., Henaff, M.-A. & Decety, J. 1998 Brain regions involved in the perception of gaze: a PET study. *Neuroimage* 8, 221–227.

Williams, J. H., Whiten, A., Suddendorf, T. & Perrett, D. I., 2001 Imitation, mirror neurons and autism. *Neurosci. Biobehav. Rev.* 25, 287–295.

GLOSSARY

ERP: event-related potential
fMRI: functional magnetic resonance imaging
MST: medial superior temporal
MTG: mid-temporal gyrus
PET: positron emission tomography
STG: superior temporal gyrus
STP: superior temporal polysensory
STS: superior temporal sulcus

PART 6

Biological Movement: From Perception to Imitation to Emotion

In 1909, one of the fathers of psychology, Edward Tichner, argued that people could never know what another felt by reasoning, that they could only know by *feeling themselves* into the other's feelings. Since that time, a voluminous literature in human and nonhuman animals has accrued demonstrating mimicry and contagion effects—typically without any conscious awareness or control by the individuals involved. In the preceding section, we learned that the perception of biological movement involved a distributed neural system separable from the system involved in the perception of nonbiological movement, and we saw that the perception of particularly powerful social cues in biological movement (e.g., changes in gaze direction, articulatory movements of the mouth) produced especially robust activation of related brain regions. In this section, evidence is reviewed that illuminates the neural substrates of imitative and emotional contagion effects and raises the notion of a mirror system—a system of neurons that subserve an individual's capacity to recognize actions made by others and in so doing to mirror the observed actions.

The human premotor cortex, which is involved in voluntary movements of the body, is organized somatotopically. Using functional magnetic resonance imaging (fMRI), Buccino et al. (2001) localized areas of the brain that were active during the observation of movement by another individual. They found that regions of the premotor cortex were activated when individuals observed the actions of another and, more specifically, that the areas activated in the premotor cortex corresponded to the regions that would be active were the individual to have executed the observed actions. The findings of Buccino et al. (2001) are in accord with the hypothesis that there is a brain circuit that extracts and neurologically represents the motor commands of another individual's observed actions—the so-called direct matching hypothesis. Imitative actions of the sort investigated by Buccino et al. do not require voluntary control, however. Evidence from other researchers indicates that imitative reactions are faster than simple visual reaction times, and that people's awareness of their own imitative reactions occur significantly later than their imitative reactions.

The regions of the brain important for imitation are not the regions important in emotion, but instead there is substantial overlap in the brain regions important in imitation and observation. By mimicking the observed action, however, individuals are in a better position to know by feeling themselves what another person is feeling. This reasoning implies a mechanism through which imitation produces *emotional* contagion. Evidence for this reasoning is provided by Carr et al. (2003) in the second reading in this section. Using fMRI, Carr and colleagues found that the brain regions important for action representation and imitation, such as the superior temporal sulcus, are connected to the insula and amygdala—regions in the limbic lobe that are involved in emotions.

Action Observation Activates Premotor and Parietal Areas in a Somatotopic Manner: An fMRI Study

G. Buccino, F. Binkofski,[1] G. R. Fink,[1,2] L. Fadiga, L. Fogassi,
V. Gallese, R. J. Seitz,[1] K. Zilles,[2] G. Rizzolatti and H.-J. Freund[1]

Functional magnetic resonance imaging (fMRI) was used to localize brain areas that were active during the observation of actions made by another individual. Object- and non-object-related actions made with different effectors (mouth, hand and foot) were presented. Observation of both object- and non-object-related actions determined a somatotopically organized activation of premotor cortex. The somatotopic pattern was similar to that of the classical motor cortex homunculus. During the observation of object-related actions, an activation, also somatotopically organized, was additionally found in the posterior parietal lobe. Thus, when individuals observe an action, an internal replica of that action is automatically generated in their premotor cortex. In the case of object-related actions, a further object-related analysis is performed in the parietal lobe, as if the subjects were indeed using those objects. These results bring the previous concept of an action observation/execution matching system (mirror system) into a broader perspective: this system is not restricted to the ventral premotor cortex, but involves several somatotopically organized motor circuits.

Keywords: action observation, humans, mirror system, parietal lobe, premotor cortex.

Istituto di Fisiologia Umana, Università di Parma, Via Volturno 39, I-43100 Parma, Italy.
[1]Department of Neurology, Heinrich Heine University of Duesseldorf, 5 Moorenstrasse, D-40225, Duesseldorf, Germany.

[2]Institute of Medicine, Research Center Juelich GmbH, Germany.

Introduction

In the monkey premotor cortex (area F5) there are neurons that discharge both when the monkey performs specific hand actions (e.g., grasping an object) and when it observes another individual performing the same or a similar action (Gallese *et al.*, 1996; Rizzolatti *et al.*, 1996a). The hypothesis was forwarded that these neurons, called 'mirror neurons', subserve the capacity of individuals to recognise actions made by others.

There is growing evidence that a 'mirror' system, similar to that described in the monkey, also exists in humans. Electrophysiological studies (Hari *et al.*, 1998; Cochin et al., 1999) showed that when a human subject observes hand actions there is a desynchronization of the motor cortex similar, although weaker, to that occurring during active movements. In agreement with these findings, transcranial magnetic stimulation (TMS) experiments showed that motor-evoked potentials recorded from hand muscles increase during the observation of hand movements (Fadiga *et al.*, 1995; Strafella & Paus, 2000).

Because the motor cortex of primates does not receive a significant visual input, its activation, during observation of actions made by others, ought to be mediated by the premotor areas that are connected with it. This conclusion has been supported by brain imaging studies showing that during observation of hand/arm actions there is an activation of the ventral premotor cortex centred to the Broca's region (Grafton et al., 1996; Rizzolatti *et al.*, 1996b; Decety *et al.*, 1997; Grezes *et al.*, 1998; Iacoboni *et al.*, 1999). Considering, however, that Broca's area is the cortical motor speech centre, the possibility cannot be excluded that Broca's area activation, during action observation, were due to an internal verbalisation of the observed actions rather than to a 'mirror' mechanism.

The main aim of the present study was to assess whether the observation of actions made with different effectors would activate specific parts of the premotor cortex in accord with the somatotopic motor organization of the region. This activation specificity, if proved, would show on one side, that the mirror system is not limited to hand action and on the other, would allow one to rule out the hypothesis that the activation of Broca's area, reported during hand action observation, was due to verbalization. If the verbalization hypothesis were true, Broca's area should be the major activation focus during action observation, regardless of the effector used.

The second aim was to determine to what extent the presence of an object influences the analysis of an observed action. When an individual acts on an object, a specific, pragmatic analysis of the object is carried out in the parietal lobe. This analysis is distinct from the semantic processing performed in the temporal lobe (Jeannerod, 1994; Milner & Goodale, 1995). Would the observation of object-related actions evoke this pragmatic analysis? An activation of pragmatic representations would be evidence, that during action observation, individuals internally 're-act' the observed action in terms of both action and the object acted upon.

Materials and Methods

Subjects

Twelve healthy, right-handed subjects, aged 25–38 years old, took part in the experiment. All subjects (except two) were naive as to the purpose of the experiment. They all gave their written consent to the experimental procedure. The study was approved by the Ethical Committee of the Heinrich Heine University, Duesseldorf.

MRI Scanner and Scanning Sequences

Functional magnetic resonance imaging (fMRI) measurements were performed on a 1.5 Tesla Siemens Vision scanning system using standard echo-planar imaging (EPI) and a standard radio frequency head coil for signal transmission and reception. Thirty consecutive slices orientated parallel to the anterior-posterior commissure plane and covering the whole brain were acquired. The following EPI sequences were used: repetition time, 5 s; signal-gathering time (echo-time), 66 ms; α, 90°; voxel size, 3×3×4 mm.

Experimental Protocol

While being scanned, subjects were asked to carefully observe different videotaped object- and non-object-related actions, performed by another individual with different effectors (mouth, arm/hand and foot). These videotaped actions were presented on a screen, situated outside the scanner. Subjects could see them through a mirror (10×15 cm) which was positioned in the scanner in front of them. Videotaped actions were presented in sequences 25 s long. During each sequence the same action was presented 3–4 times. Each sequence was presented twice during the experimental session. The observed actions were: biting an apple and chewing (mouth actions); reaching and grasping a ball or a little cup with the hand and mimicking these actions without the object (hand actions) or kicking a ball or pushing a brake and mimicking these actions without the object (foot actions). Observation of both object- and non-object-related mouth, hand and foot actions (active condition) was contrasted with the observation of a static face, a static hand and a static foot, respectively, as a control condition. Static stimuli were presented for 25 s continuously. At the end of the experimental session, subjects had to report the actions they were presented with. All subjects reported them correctly.

Image Analysis

Image analysis was performed on a SPARC II workstation (Sun Microsystems) using MATLAB (Mathworks Inc., Natick, MA, USA) and statistical parametric mapping package SPM97d (Friston *et al.*, 1995, 1997). First, functional images of each condition were realigned to the tenth image to correct for head movements between scans. Then the images were coregistered and transformed into a standard stereotactic space, using the intercommissural line as the reference plane for transformation (Friston *et al.*, 1997). Active and control conditions were modelled using a delayed box-car reference vector, accounting for the delayed cerebral blood flow change after stimulus presentation. Significantly activated pixels were searched for by using the general linear model approach for time series proposed by Friston *et al.* (1995). Group activation maps were calculated by pooling the data for each condition across all subjects. Pixels were identified as

significantly activated if they passed the highest threshold of Z-score (3.09) and belonged to a cluster of at least 10 activated pixels ($P < 0.05$, corrected for multiple comparisons). The activated pixels surviving this procedure were superimposed on high-resolution magnetic resonance (MR) scans of a standard brain (Montreal Neurological Institute, MNI). Clusters of activated foci were assigned to the regions of interest according to their centres of mass activity with the aid of Talairach coordinates (1988) and prominent sulcal landmarks. Furthermore, as far as Broca's region is concerned, Talairach coordinates were also compared with the coordinates of cytoarchitectonically defined probability maps (Amunts *et al.*, 1999).

Results

The results of the experiment are shown in Figures 10.1–10.3. Frontal and parietal activations related to action observation are presented in colour. Other activations (mostly occipital) are shown in grey. These latter activations (probably due to stronger activation of visual areas with moving stimuli) will not be discussed here.

Activations during mouth action observation are shown in Figure 10.1. During the observation of non-object-related mouth actions (chewing, a), activation foci were present in areas 6 and 44 on both sides and in area 45 in the right hemisphere. Right hemisphere activation was larger and stronger than left hemisphere activation. During the observation of object-related mouth actions (biting an apple, b), the pattern of premotor activation was similar, although weaker, to that found during non-object-related actions. In addition, two activation foci were present in the parietal lobe. These foci were larger in the left than in the right hemisphere. The rostral focus was located in area 40 (area PF of von Economo, 1929), the caudal focus in area 39 (area PG).

Figure 10.2 shows activation foci relative to observation of arm/hand actions. During the observation of non-object-related hand actions (mimicking reaching to grasp, a) there was a bilateral activation of area 6 that was located dorsal

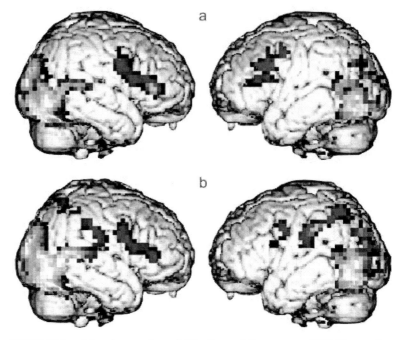

FIGURE 10.1 ■ (*A color version of this figure follows page 146.*) Observation of mouth actions. Projections of the activation foci on the lateral surface of a standard brain [Montreal Neurological Institute (MNI)] during the observation of non-object-related (chewing: a) and object-related (biting an apple: b) mouth actions.

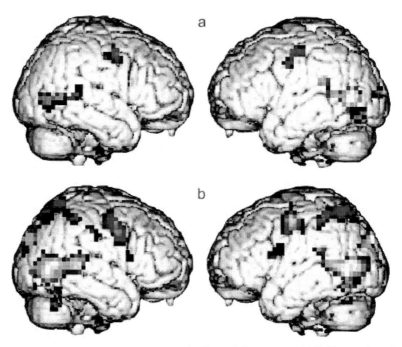

FIGURE 10.2 ■ (*A color version of this figure follows page 146.*) Observation of hand actions. Projections of the activation foci on the lateral surface of a standard brain (MNI) during the observation of non-object-related (mimicking grasping of a cup or a ball, without object: a) and object-related (grasping a cup or a ball: b) hand actions.

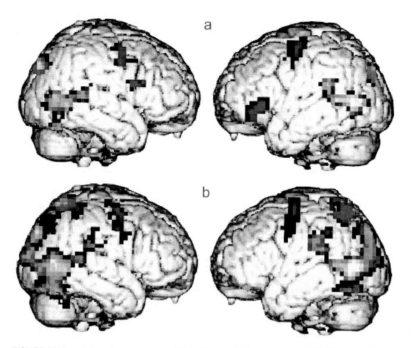

FIGURE 10.3 ■ **(*A color version of this figure follows page 146.*)** Observation of foot actions. Projections of the activation foci on the lateral surface of a standard brain (MNI) during the observation of non-object-related (mimicking kicking a ball or pushing a brake, without the object: a) and during the observation of object-related foot actions (kicking a ball or pushing a brake: b) foot actions.

to that found during mouth movement observation. During the observation of object-related arm/hand actions (reaching-to-grasp movements, b) there was a bilateral activation of premotor cortex plus an activation site in area 44. Most interestingly, as in the case of the observation of mouth movements, two activation foci were present in the parietal lobe. The rostral one was located inside the intraparietal sulcus, in an area caudal and dorsal to that found in the mouth movement observation condition. This area probably corresponds to the anterior intraparietal area of the monkey. The caudal focus was in area 39 (area PG). This last focus considerably overlapped that found during mouth movement observation.

Figure 10.3 shows activation foci elicited by observation of foot actions. During the observation of non-object-related foot actions (mimicking ball kicking or brake pushing, a), there was an activation of a dorsal sector of area 6. There also was an

activation of the frontal lobe (rostrally located). Because we have no explanation for this activation (found only in this condition), we will not comment on it further. During the observation of object-related foot actions (kicking a ball or pushing a brake, b), there was, as in the previous condition, an activation of a dorsal sector of area 6. In addition, there was an activation of the posterior part of the parietal lobe. The parietal activation was in part located in Brodmann's area 7 [(PE)], in part it overlapped the activation seen during mouth and hand actions (Brodmann's area 39/PG).

Figure 10.4 gives a global picture of the activations found during observation of mouth, hand and foot actions. It is evident that both the premotor cortex and the parietal lobe activation foci are somatotopically organized. The premotor somatotopy follows a pattern similar to that of the classical motor homunculus (Penfield & Rasmussen,

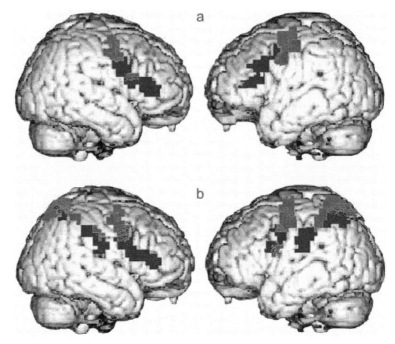

FIGURE 10.4 ■ (*A color version of this figure follows page 146.*) Somatotopy of premotor and parietal cortices as revealed by action observation. (a) Observation of non-object-related actions. (b) Observation of object-related actions. Activation foci, shown in detail in the three previous figures, are projected on the lateral surface of a standard brain (MNI). Red, activation during the observation of mouth movements; green, activation during the observation of hand movements; blue, activation during the observation of foot movements. Overlap of colours indicates activation foci present during observation of actions made by different effectors.

1952). In the parietal lobe, the mouth is represented rostrally while the foot is located caudally.

Table 10.1 shows the Talairach coordinates and Z scores of the activated foci during the observation of object- and non-object-related mouth, hand, and foot actions.

Discussion

The results of the present experiment show that when an individual observes actions (made by another individual) performed with different effectors, different sectors of the premotor cortex are activated. During mouth actions, there is a bilateral activation of ventral area 6 and area 44 plus an activation of the right area 45. During hand actions, a more dorsal part of ventral area 6 plus a dorsal sector of area 44 are recruited in both hemispheres. Finally, the observation of foot actions elicits an activation of a dorsal sector of area 6, bilaterally. There is, therefore, a clear topographic shift in the premotor cortex activation from ventral to dorsal when the effector used in the observed action moves from mouth to arm/hand and to foot, respectively. This shift is congruent with the classical motor organization of the region (see Penfield & Rasmussen, 1952).

These results are important for two reasons. First, the effector related somatotopic activation pattern in the premotor cortex during the mere observation of actions proves that, in humans, the mirror system is not restricted to hand actions, but includes a rich repertoire of body actions. It therefore constitutes the neural substrate for a matching mechanism

TABLE 10.1. Talairach Coordinates and Z-Scores of the Activated Foci During Observation of Object- and Non-Object-Related Mouth, Hand, and Foot Actions

| | Activated foci during the observation of | | | | | | | |
| | Object-related actions | | | | Non-object-related actions | | | |
Actions/Brain area	x	y	z	Z-score	x	y	z	Z-score
Mouth actions								
Brodmann's area 6								
R	48	0	32	4.38	52	0	32	3.28
L	−56	0	36	4.18	−52	4	44	3.55
Brodmann's area 44								
R	60	8	24	3.76	56	12	16	3.79
L	−64	12	20	3.01	−60	16	16	3.07
Brodmann's area 45								
R	60	16	20	4.13	60	28	20	4.31
Inferior parietal lobule								
R	52	−24	20	3.31				
	52	−32	44	3.39				
L	−36	−52	56	5.16				
	−60	−24	36	4.21				
Arm/hand actions								
Brodmann's area 6								
R	48	0	44	4.66	52	0	48	3.64
L	−56	−4	44	5.84	−60	−4	40	3.72
Brodmann's area 44								
R	56	12	12	3.01				
L	−64	4	24	3.72				
Anterior intraparietal area								
R	40	−40	52	4.55				
L	−36	−40	52	4.63				
Foot actions								
Brodmann's area 6								
R	40	−4	60	3.38	44	−4	56	3.93
L	−32	−8	64	3.30	−40	−4	60	4.05
Superior parietal lobule								
R	24	−60	68	5.69				
L	−32	−64	60	5.05				

R, right hemisphere; L, left hemisphere; *x, y, z,* Talairach coordinates.

mapping the observed actions on the observer's motor representations. Second, these results definitively rule out the interpretation that cortical activation during action observation is due to verbalization.

A further important result of the present experiment is the demonstration of a marked difference between the activation during the observation of object-related and non-object-related actions. Any time an object is the target of an action, the parietal lobe is strongly activated. This object-related activation is also somatotopically organized and depends on the effector used. During the observation of mouth actions, there is an activation

of the rostral part of the inferior parietal lobule (area 40). During the observation of hand actions, a more posterior sector of area 40, inside the intraparietal sulcus, becomes active. This sector closely corresponds to that shown to be active during object manipulation (Binkofski *et al.,* 1999). It has been suggested that this sector is the human homologue of monkey anterior intraparietal area. The observation of foot actions activates predominantly the posterior part of the superior parietal lobule. Finally, in all conditions there is activation of area 39 (area PG).

Although the motor organization of the parietal lobe is not fully established, an organization similar to that described here for action observation in humans can be recognized for active movements in nonhuman primates. In the monkey, mouth movements are represented in the rostral part of PF (Leinonen & Nyman, 1979; Fogassi et al., 1998), distal hand movements in the anterior intraparietal area (Sakata et al., 1995) and arm reaching movements, posteriorly on the medial bank of the intraparietal sulcus (Colby & Duhamel, 1991; Snyder et al., 1997). Furthermore, clinical and brain imaging studies strongly suggest that a segregated pattern of effector representations in the parietal lobe is also present in humans (De Renzi, 1982; Jeannerod, 1986; Pause et al., 1989; Seitz et al., 1991).

It is generally accepted that a fundamental role of the parietal lobe is to describe objects for action (Jeannerod, 1994; Jeannerod et al., 1995; Milner & Goodale, 1995). This 'pragmatic', action-orientated object description has been contrasted with the 'semantic' description coded in the infero-temporal lobe (Milner & Goodale, 1995; Jeannerod et al., 1995). The results of the present experiment indicate that a 'pragmatic' analysis is also carried out when an individual observes an object-directed action made by another individual. If action understanding were based on higher cognitive functions, this parietal analysis would be unnecessary.

Taken together, the results of the present experiment strongly support the view that during action observation there is a recruitment of the same neural structures which would be normally involved in the actual execution of the observed action. When individuals observe an action, they code that action in terms of the related voluntary movements. The 'seen' actions are mapped onto the corresponding motor representations of the frontal lobe and, in the case of object-related actions, the 'seen' objects on the effector-related, pragmatic representations, in the parietal lobe.

Acknowledgments

This study was supported by the Deutsche Forschungsgemeinschaft, MURST and by Human Frontier Science Program.

Abbreviations

EPI, echo planar imaging; fMRI, functional magnetic resonance imaging; MNI, Montreal Neurological Institute; TE, signal- (echo-) gathering time; TR, sequence repetition time.

REFERENCES

Amunts, K., Schleicher, A., Buergel, U., Mohlberg, H., Uylings, H.B.M. & Zilles, K. (1999) Broca's region re-visited: cytoarchitecture and intersubject variability. *J. Comp. Neurol.*, 412, 319–341.

Binkofski, F., Buccino, G., Posse, S., Seitz, R.J., Rizzolatti, G. & Freund, H.-J. (1999) A fronto-parietal circuit for object manipulation in man: evidence from an fMRI study. *Eur. J. Neurosci.*, 11, 3276–3286.

Cochin, S., Barthelemy, C., Roux, S. & Martineau, J. (1999) Observation and execution of movement: similarities demonstrated by quantified electroencephalography. *Eur. J. Neurosci.*, 11, 1839–1842.

Colby, C.L. & Duhamel, J.R. (1991) Heterogeneity of extrastriate visual areas and multiple parietal areas in the macaque monkeys. *Neuropsychologia*, 29, 517–537.

De Renzi, E. (1982) *Disorders of Space Exploration and Cognition*. Wiley, New York.

Decety, J., Grezes, J., Costes, N., Perani, D., Jeannerod, M., Procyk, E., Grassi, F. & Fazio, F. (1997) Brain activity during observation of actions. Influence of action content and subject's strategy. *Brain*, 120, 1763–1777.

von Economo, C., (1929) *The Cytoarchitectonics of the Human Cerebral Cortex*. Oxford University Press, London.

Fadiga, L., Fogassi, L., Pavesi, G. & Rizzolatti, G. (1995) Motor facilitation during action observation: a magnetic stimulation study. *J. Neurophysiol.*, 73, 2608–2611.

Fogassi, L., Gallese, V., Fadiga, L. & Rizzolatti, G. (1998) Neurons responding to the sight of goal-directed hand/arm actions in the parietal area PF (7b) of the macaque monkey. *Soc. Neurosci. Abstr.*, 24, 154.

Friston, K.J., Ashburner, J., Poline, J.B., Firth, C.D., Heather, J.D. & Frackowiak, R.S.J. (1997) Spatial realignment and normalization of images. *Hum. Brain Mapp.*, 2, 165–189.

Friston, K.J., Holmes, A.P., Poline, J.B., Grasby, P.J., Williams, S.C.R., Frackowiak, R.S.J. & Turner, R. (1995) Analysis of fMRI time-series revisited. *Neuroimage*, 2, 5–53.

Gallese, V., Fadiga, L., Fogassi, L. & Rizzolatti, G. (1996) Action recognition in the premotor cortex. *Brain*, 119, 593–609.

Grafton, S.T., Arbib, M.A., Fadiga, L. & Rizzolatti, G. (1996) Localization of grasp representations in humans by PET: 2. Observation compared with imagination. *Exp. Brain Res.*, 112, 103–111.

Grezes, J., Costes, N. & Decety, J. (1998) Top-down effect of strategy on the perception of human biological motion: a PET investigation. *Cogn. Neuropsychol.*, 15, 553–582.

Hari, R., Forss, N., Avikainen, S., Kirveskari, E., Salenius, S. & Rizzolatti, G. (1998) Activation of human primary motor cortex during action observation: a neuromagnetic study. *Proc. Natl Acad. Sci. USA*, 95, 15061–15065.

Iacoboni, M., Woods, R.P., Brass, M., Bekkering, H., Mazziotta, J.C. & Rizzolatti, G. (1999) Cortical mechanisms of human imitation. *Science*, 286, 2526–2528.

Jeannerod, M. (1986) The formation of finger grip during prehension. A cortically mediated visuomotor pattern. *Behav. Brain Res.*, 19, 99–116.

Jeannerod, M. (1994) The representing brain: neural correlates of motor intention and imagery. *Behav. Brain Sci.*, 17, 187–245.

Jeannerod, M., Arbib, M.A., Rizzolatti, G. & Sakata, H. (1995) Grasping objects: the cortical mechanisms of visuomotor transformation. *Trends Neurosci.*, 18, 314–320.

Leinonen, L. & Nyman, G. (1979) Functional properties of cells in anterolateral part of area 7 associative face area of awake monkeys. *Exp. Brain Res.*, 34, 321–333.

Milner, A.D. & Goodale, M.A. (1995) *The Visual Brain in Action*. Oxford University Press, Oxford.

Pause, M., Kunesch, E., Binkofski, F. & Freund, H.-J. (1989) Sensorimotor disturbances in patients with lesions of the parietal cortex. *Brain*, 112, 1599–1625.

Penfield, W. & Rasmussen, T. (1952) *The Cerebral Cortex of Man*. MacMillan. New York.

Rizzolatti, G., Fadiga, L., Gallese, V. & Fogassi, L. (1996a) Premotor cortex and the recognition of motor actions. *Cognitive Brain Res.*, 3, 131–141.

Rizzolatti, G., Fadiga, L., Matelli, M., Bettinardi, V., Paulesu, E., Perani, D. & Fazio, F. (1996b) Localization of grasp representations in humans by PET: 1. Observation versus execution. *Exp. Brain Res.*, 111, 246–252.

Sakata, H., Taira, M., Murata, A. & Mine, S. (1995) Neural mechanisms of visual guidance of hand action in the parietal cortex of the monkey. *Cerebral Cortex*, 5, 429–438.

Seitz, R.J., Roland, P.E., Bohm, C., Greitz, T. & Stone-Elander, S. (1991) Somatosensory discrimination of shape: tactile exploration and cerebral activation. *Eur. J. Neurosci.*, 3, 481–492.

Snyder, L.H., Batista, A.P. & Andersen, R.A. (1997) Coding of intention in the posterior parietal cortex. *Nature*, 386, 167–169.

Strafella, A.P. & Paus, T. (2000) Modulation of cortical excitability during action observation: a transcranial magnetic stimulation study. *Exp. Brain Res.*, 11, 2289–2292.

Talairach, J. & Tournoux, P. (1988) *Co-Planar Stereotactic Atlas of the Human Brain*. Thieme Medical Publishers, New York.

Neural Mechanisms of Empathy in Humans: A Relay from Neural Systems for Imitation to Limbic Areas

Laurie Carr[†], Marco Iacoboni[†‡§], Marie-Charlotte Dubeau[†],
John C. Mazziotta[†§‖ **††], and Gian Luigi Lenzi[‡‡]

How do we empathize with others? A mechanism according to which action representation modulates emotional activity may provide an essential functional architecture for empathy. The superior temporal and inferior frontal cortices are critical areas for action representation and are connected to the limbic system via the insula. Thus, the insula may be a critical relay from action representation to emotion. We used functional MRI while subjects were either imitating or simply observing emotional facial expressions. Imitation and observation of emotions activated a largely similar network of brain areas. Within this network, there was greater activity during imitation, compared with observation of emotions, in premotor areas including the inferior frontal cortex, as well as in the superior temporal cortex, insula, and amygdala. We understand what others feel by a mechanism of action representation that allows empathy and modulates our emotional content. The insula plays a fundamental role in this mechanism.

Empathy plays a fundamental social role, allowing the sharing of experiences, needs, and goals across individuals. Its functional aspects and corresponding neural mechanisms, however, are poorly understood. When Theodore Lipps (as cited in ref. 1) introduced the concept of empathy

†Ahmanson-Lovelace Brain Mapping Center, Neuropsychiatric Institute, Departments of ‡Psychiatry and Biobehavioral Sciences, ‖ Neurology, **Pharmacology, and ††Radiological Sciences, and §Brain Research Institute, David Geffen School of Medicine, University of California, Los Angeles, CA 90095; and ‡‡Department of Neurological Sciences, University "La Sapienza," Rome, Italy 00185.

(Einfühlung), he theorized the critical role of *inner imitation* of the actions of others in generating empathy. In keeping with this concept, empathic individuals exhibit nonconscious mimicry of the postures, mannerisms, and facial expressions of others (the *chameleon effect*) to a greater extent than nonempathic individuals (2). Thus, empathy may occur via a mechanism of action representation that modulates and shapes emotional contents.

In the primate brain, relatively well-defined and separate neural systems are associated with emotions (3) and action representation (4–7). The limbic system is critical for emotional processing and behavior, and the circuit of frontoparietal networks interacting with the superior temporal cortex is critical for action representation. This latter circuit is composed of inferior frontal and posterior parietal neurons that discharge during the execution and also the observation of an action (*mirror* neurons; ref. 7), and of superior temporal neurons that discharge only during the observation of an action (6, 8, 9). Anatomical and neurophysiological data in the nonhuman primate brain (see review in ref. 7) and imaging human data (10–13) suggest that this circuit is critical for imitation and that within this circuit, information processing would flow as follows. (*i*) The superior temporal cortex codes an early visual description of the action (6, 8, 9) and sends this information to posterior parietal *mirror* neurons (this privileged flow of information from superior temporal to posterior parietal is supported by the robust anatomical connections between superior temporal and posterior parietal cortex) (14). (*ii*) The posterior parietal cortex codes the precise kinesthetic aspect of the movement (15–18) and sends this information to inferior frontal mirror neurons (anatomical connections between these two regions are well documented in the monkey) (19). (*iii*) The inferior frontal cortex codes the goal of the action [both neurophysiological (5, 20, 21) and imaging data (22) support this role for inferior frontal mirror neurons]. (*iv*) Efferent copies of motor plans are sent from parietal and frontal mirror areas back to the superior temporal cortex (12), such that a matching mechanism between the visual description of the observed

action and the predicted sensory consequences of the planned imitative action can occur. (*v*) Once the visual description of the observed action and the predicted sensory consequences of the planned imitative action are matched, imitation can be initiated.

How is this moderately recursive circuit connected to the limbic system? Anatomical data suggest that a sector of the insular lobe, the dysgranular field, is connected with the limbic system as well as with posterior parietal, inferior frontal, and superior temporal cortex (23). This connectivity pattern makes the insula a plausible candidate for relaying action representation information to limbic areas processing emotional content.

To test this model, we used functional MRI (fMRI) while subjects were either observing or imitating emotional facial expressions. The predictions were straightforward: If action representation mediation is critical to empathy and the understanding of the emotions of others, then even the mere observation of emotional facial expression should activate the same brain regions of motor significance that are activated during the imitation of the emotional face expressions. Moreover, a modulation of the action representation circuit onto limbic areas via the insula predicts greater activity during imitation, compared with observation of emotion, throughout the whole network outlined above. In fact, *mirror* areas would be more active during imitation than observation because of the simultaneous encoding of sensory input and planning of motor output (13). Within *mirror* areas, the inferior frontal cortex seems particularly important here, given that understanding goals is an important component of empathy. The superior temporal cortex would be more active during imitation than observation, as it receives efferent copies of motor commands from *mirror* areas (12). The insula would be more active during imitation because its relay role would become more important during imitation, compared with mere observation. Finally, limbic areas would also increase their activity because of the modulatory role of motor areas with increased activity. Thus, observation and imitation of emotions should yield substantially similar patterns of activated brain areas, with greater activity during imitation in premotor areas, in inferior frontal cortex, in superior temporal cortex, insula, and limbic areas.

Materials and Methods

Subjects

Eleven healthy, right-handed subjects participated in the experiment (seven males and four females). The mean age of the subject group was 29, and ranged from 21 to 39 years. All subjects were evaluated with a brief neurological examination and questionnaire to screen for any medical/behavioral disorders. Handedness was evaluated by using a modified version of the Edinburgh Handedness Inventory (24). The study was approved by the University of California at Los Angeles Institutional Review Board and was performed in accordance with the ethical standards laid down in the 1964 Declaration of Helsinki. Written informed consent was obtained from all subjects before inclusion in the study.

Stimuli

Stimuli were presented to subjects through magnet-compatible goggles. Using as stimulus a widely known set of facial expressions (25), three stimulus picture sets were assembled, each containing randomly ordered depictions of six emotions (happy, sad, angry, surprise, disgust, and afraid). Of the three stimulus sets, one contained whole faces, and the other two sets contained only eyes or only mouths, which were cropped from the same set of whole faces. All pictures, whether whole face, only mouth, or only eyes, consisted of different individuals, with males and females in equal proportion. The rationale for showing only parts of faces was suggested by the cortical representation of body parts in inferior frontal cortex, where the mouth is represented but the eyes are not (26). In principle, if eye emotional expressions can be dissociated from the emotional expression of the rest of the face, one might see the predicted pattern of activity in inferior frontal cortex during imitation of the whole face or of the mouth, but not during imitation of eye emotional expressions. However, our imaging data (see below) do not support such dissociation.

Behavioral Tasks

Subjects were presented three runs of stimuli. One run consisted of six blocks of 24 s each. Each block contained six pictures (of the six emotion types), and each picture was presented for 4 s. Blocks were homogenous for stimulus type (i.e., all faces, or all eyes, or all mouths). Subjects were asked to imitate and internally generate the target emotion on the computer screen, or to simply observe. Imitate/observe conditions were counterbalanced across runs, and task blocks were separated by seven rest periods of 24 s (blank screen). The first rest period actually lasted 36 s, the additional 12 s being related to the first three brain volumes, which were discarded from the analysis due to signal instabilities.

Imaging

Structural and fMRI measurements were performed on a General Electric 3.0 Tesla MRI scanner with advanced nuclear magnetic resonance echo-planar imaging (EPI) up-grade located in the Ahmanson-Lovelace Brain Mapping Center. Structural and functional scanning sequences performed in each subject included: one structural scan (coplanar high-resolution EPI volumes: repetition time (TR) = 4,000 ms; echo time (TE) = 54 ms; flip angle = 90°; 128 × 128 matrix; 26 axial slices; 3.125-mm in-plane resolution; 4-mm thickness; skip 1 mm) for anatomical data, and three functional scans (echo planar T_2*-weighted gradient echo sequence; TR = 4,000 ms; TE = 25 ms; flip angle = 90°; 64 × 64 matrix; 26 axial slices; 3.125-mm in-plane resolution; 4-mm thickness; skip 1 mm). Each of the functional acquisitions covered the whole brain.

Individual subjects' functional images were aligned and registered to their respective coplanar structural images by using a rigid body linear registration algorithm (27). Intersubject image registration was performed with fifth-order polynomial nonlinear warping (28) of each subject's images into a Talairach-compatible brain magnetic resonance atlas (29). Data were smoothed by using an in-plane Gaussian filter for a final image resolution of 8.7 × 8.7 × 8.6 mm.

Image Statistics

Image statistics was performed with analyses of variance (ANOVAs), allowing to factor out run-to-run variability within subjects as well as intersubject overall signal variability (12, 13, 30–33). Given the time-course of the blood oxygen level-dependent (BOLD) fMRI response, which takes several seconds to return to baseline (34), contiguous brain volumes cannot be considered independent observations (35, 36). Thus, the sum of signal intensity at each voxel throughout each task was used as the dependent variable (12, 13, 22). Significance level was set at $P = 0.001$ uncorrected at each voxel. To avoid false positives, only clusters bigger than 20 significantly activated voxels were considered (37). Factors included in the ANOVAs were subjects ($n = 11$), functional scans ($n = 3$), state ($n = 2$, task/rest), task ($n = 2$, imitation/observation), and stimuli ($n = 3$, whole face, eyes, and mouth).

Results

Preliminary ANOVAs revealed no differences in activation among the three imitation tasks, and no differences in activations among the three observation tasks. Thus, main effects of imitation, observation, and imitation minus observation are reported here. As Table 11.1 shows, there was a substantially similar network of activated areas for both imitation and observation of emotion. Among the areas commonly activated by imitation and observation of facial emotional expressions, the premotor face area, the dorsal sector of pars opercularis of the inferior frontal gyrus, the superior temporal sulcus, the insula, and the amygdala had greater activity during imitation than observation of emotion. To give a sense of the good overlap between the network described in this study and previously reported peaks of activation, Table 11.2 compares peak of activations in the right hemisphere observed in this study

with previously published peaks in meta-analyses or individual studies in regions relevant to the hypothesis tested in this study.

Figures 11.1 and 11.2 show, respectively, the location and time-series of the right primary motor face area and of the premotor face area. The peaks of these activations correspond well with published data, as discussed below. Task-related activity is seen not only during imitation, but also during observation. This observation-related activity is very clear in premotor cortex but also visible in primary motor cortex (although not reaching significance in primary motor cortex).

Figure 11.3 shows the activations in inferior frontal cortex and anterior insula, with their corresponding time-series. The activity of these three regions is evidently correlated.

Figure 11.4 shows the significantly increased activity in the right amygdala during imitation, compared with observation of emotional facial expressions

Discussion

The results of this study support our hypothesis on the role of action representation for understanding the emotions of others. Largely overlapping networks were activated by both observation and imitation of facial emotional expressions. Moreover, the observation of emotional expressions robustly activated premotor areas. Further, fronto-temporal areas relevant to action representation, the amygdala, and the anterior insula had significant signal increase during imitation compared with observation of facial emotional expression.

The peak of activation reported here in primary motor cortex during imitation of facial emotional expressions corresponds well with the location of the primary motor mouth area as determined by a meta-analysis of published positron-emission tomography (PET) studies, by a meta-analysis of original data in 30 subjects studied with PET, and by a consensus probabilistic description of the location of the primary motor mouth area obtained merging the results of the two previously described meta-analyses (38). This convergence confirms the robustness and reliability of the

Color Plates

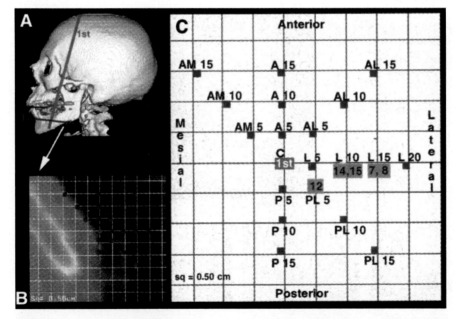

FIGURE 1.2 ■ View of the entry-level area with the *a priori* most likely first trajectory. (A) Skull with this first vector and the level (red) at which entry points were marked. (B) View of a segment of section 1. On the left is the mandibular ramus, and on the right is the array of entry points. (C) Enlargement of the array of entry points. One additional point was added (L20) to ensure that every viable entry point was surrounded by nonviable points. Nonviable vectors are shown in red, and viable vectors with labels identifying their exit points are shown in green. Abbreviations: A, anterior; L, lateral; P, posterior; AM, anteromesial; AL, anterolateral; PL, posterolateral; C, central.

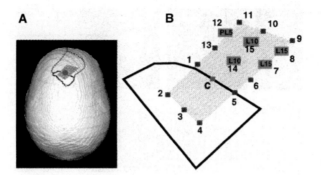

FIGURE 1.3 ■ (A) View from above the deformed skull with the exit hole and the anterior bone flap traced in black. The blue circle represents the first vector tested, and the gray surface represents the area where exit points were tested. (B) Schematic enlargement of the exit hole and of the area tested for exit points. The letter C marks the first tested vector (blue). The numbers 1 through 15 mark the other exit points tested. Red indicates nonviable vectors, green indicates viable vectors, and the label identifies the entry point. Note that the *a priori* best fit C was not viable.

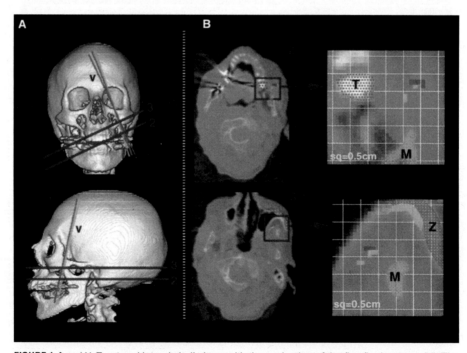

FIGURE 1.4 ■ (A) Front and lateral skull views with the projection of the five final vectors (V). The two red lines show the position of the two sections seen in (B). (B) Skull sections 2 and 3: examples of two bottleneck levels at which the viability of vectors was checked. Next to each section is an enlargement of the critical area. Abbreviations: T, missing tooth; M, intact mandible; Z, intact zygoma with a chipped area (light blue).

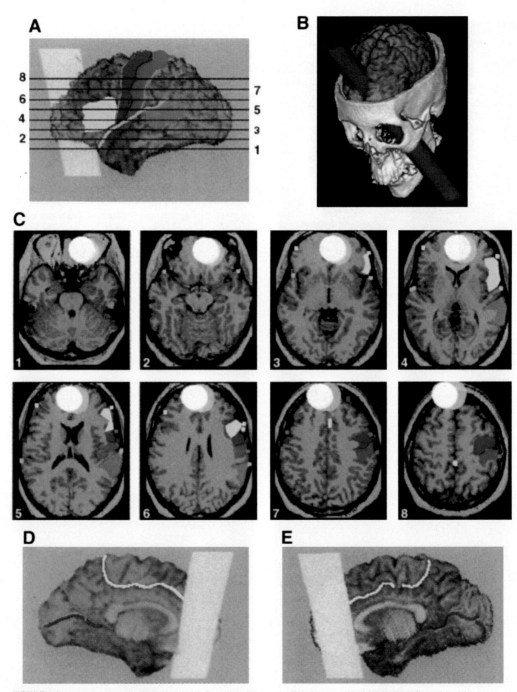

FIGURE 1.5 ■ Normal brain fitted with the five possible rods. The best rod is highlighted in solid white [except for (B), where it is shown in red]. The areas spared by the iron are highlighted in color: Broca, yellow; motor, red; somatosensory, green; Wernicke, blue. (A) Lateral view of the brain. Numbered black lines correspond to levels of the brain section shown in (C). (D and E) Medical view of left and right hemispheres, respectively, with the rod shown in white.

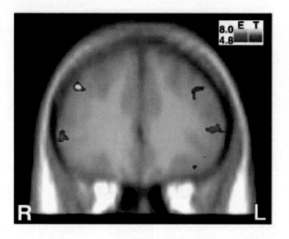

FIGURE 3.1 ■ Anterior-posterior (A-P) distribution of prefrontal cortex activation. (e) Group-averaged *t* test results (*P* < 0.001 uncorrected) for the contrast between emotional distracters (plotted in blue spectrum) and attentional targets (plotted in red spectrum). Attentional target activity was observed in left MFG (BA 9/46; Talairach coordinates -36, 35, 30) and right MFG (BA 9/46; 44, 35, 31). Emotional distracter activity was observed in left IFG (BA 45/47; -51, 33, 4) and right IFG (BA 45/47; 55, 33, 0). The coronal section in *E* shows the single prefrontal slice where differential activation between attentional targets and emotional distracters was most remarkable. However, peak activation to emotional distracters was located ≈1 cm more posteriorly within IFG. R, right hemisphere; L, left hemisphere.

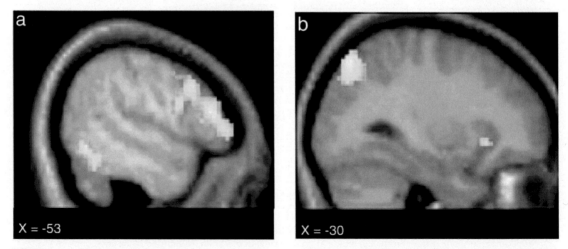

FIGURE 4.1 ■ Activation maps show brain areas to be more active during Object trials than during Person trials. Regions of modulation included the left inferior prefrontal cortex and the left IT cortex (a), as well as the left posterior parietal and the left insula cortex (b). See Table 4.1 for the Talairach and Tournoux (49) atlas coordinates.

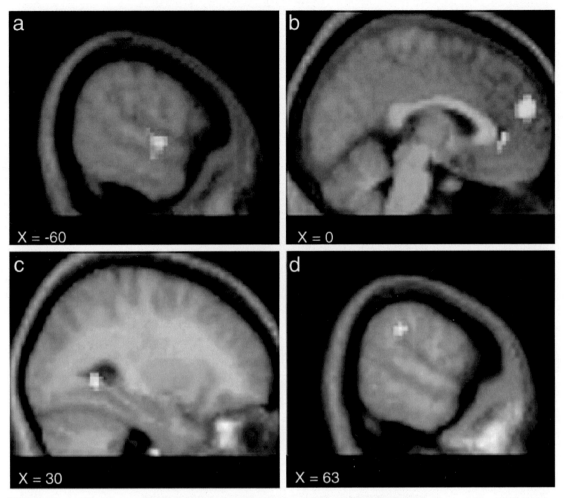

FIGURE 4.2 ■ Activation maps show brain areas to be more active during Person trials than during Object trials. Regions of modulation included the left temporal sulcus (a), the dorsal and ventral MPFC (b), the right FuG (c), and the right parietal temporal-occipital junction (d). See Table 4.2 for the Talairach and Tournoux (49) atlas coordinates.

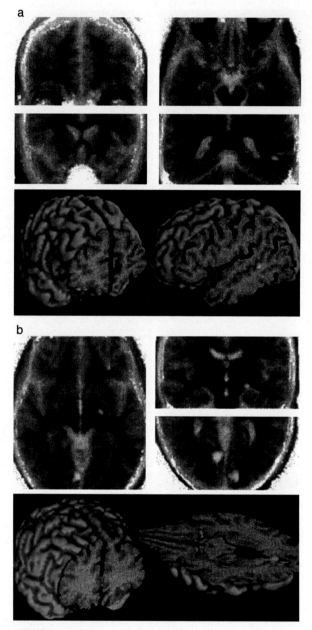

FIGURE 5.1 ■ Brain regions activated by emotionally evocative moral (M) and nonmoral (NM) judgments compared to neutral (NTR) ones. Activations were overlaid on sections through an averaged brain from all subjects with inverted grayscale and on 3-D renderings of a reference brain. (a) M vs NTR condition. Activated regions were in the left orbitofrontal cortex (OFC) and in the superior temporal sulcus and the left temporal pole. (b) NM vs NTR condition. Activated regions were in the left amygdala and lateral OFC, and bilaterally in the visual cortex.

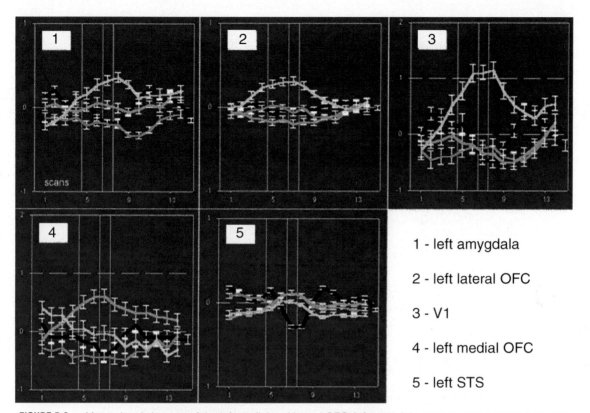

1 - left amygdala

2 - left lateral OFC

3 - V1

4 - left medial OFC

5 - left STS

FIGURE 5.2 ■ Mean signal changes of the left medial and lateral OFC, left amygdala, primary visual cortex (V1), and the cortex of the left superior temporal sulcus (STS), obtained from averaged MR signal from all subjects. Curve colors correspond to experimental conditions as follows: yellow, unpleasant condition; light blue, moral condition; green, neutral condition; black, scrambled condition.

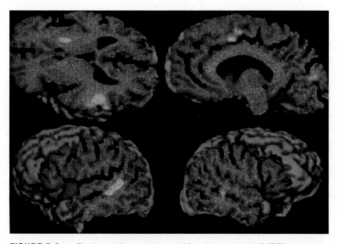

FIGURE 5.3 ■ Brain regions activated by the neutral (NTR) as compared to scrambled (SCR) condition (both temporal lobes and frontal opercula, supplementary motor area, anterior cingulate, basal ganglia, and thalamus).

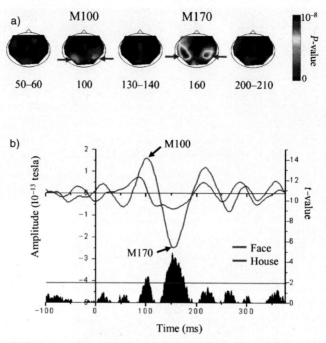

FIGURE 6.1 ■ MEG data from a typical subject. (a) Pairwise *t*-tests between the responses at each sensor reveal early (M100) and late (M170) significant differences in the MEG response to faces versus houses over occipitotemporal cortex. (b) The MEG waveforms are averaged across all face and house trials at a typical sensor of interest in the right hemisphere. Red, faces; blue, houses; black, *t*-values. The left vertical scale indicates the amplitude of the MEG response (10^{-13} tesla) whereas the right one shows the *t*-value. A value $t = 1.99$ (horizontal green line) corresponds to $p < 0.05$ (uncorrected for comparisons at multiple time points).

FIGURE 7.3 ■ The category specificity of patterns of response was analyzed with pairwise contrasts between within-category and between-category correlations. The pattern of response to each category was measured separately from data obtained on even-numbered and odd-numbered runs in each individual subject. These patterns were normalized to a mean of zero in each voxel across categories by subtracting the mean response across all categories. Brain images shown here are the normalized patterns of response in two axial slices in a single subject. The left side of the brain is on the left side of each image. Responses in all object-selective voxels in ventral temporal cortex are shown. For each pairwise comparison, the within-category correlation is compared with one between-category correlation. (A) Comparisons between the patterns of response to faces and houses in one subject. The within-category correlations for faces ($r = 0.81$) and houses ($r = 0.87$) are both markedly larger than the between-category correlations, yielding correct identifications of the category being viewed. (B) Comparisons between the patterns of response to chairs and shoes in the same subject. The category being viewed was identified correctly for all comparisons. (C) Mean response across all categories relative to a resting baseline.

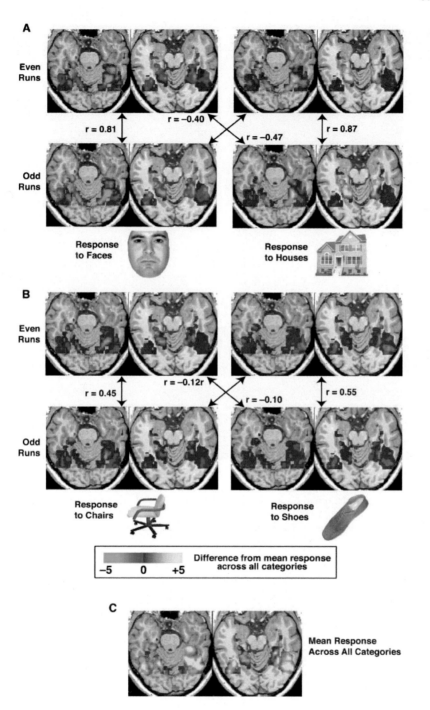

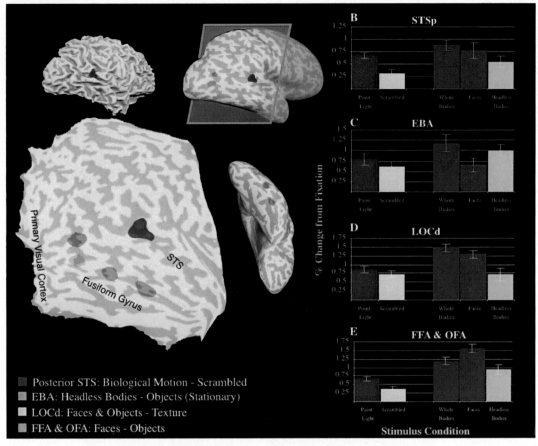

FIGURE 8.2 ■ Summary of regions of interest (ROIs) and BOLD responses in biological related stimulus conditions. (A) The ROIs in the right hemisphere of observer D.L. are displayed on the lateral and ventral surfaces of the gray matter. A cut, as indicated by the green plane, was made and the posterior end of the cortex flattened. We examined BOLD signals in four regions of interest: STSp (red), EBA (purple), LOCd (blue), FFA and OFA (orange). (B–E) The average BOLD activity levels for these ROIs (with FFA and OFA averaged) during the stimulus conditions depicting some kind of biological object, or the scrambled biological motion vectors. These stimulus conditions included animations of point-light biological motion (pink), point-light scrambled motion (yellow), whole-bodies (dark purple), pictures of faces (magenta), and stationary images of headless bodies (green). The percent change activation levels are relative to a fixation baseline. Error bars indicate 1 standard error.

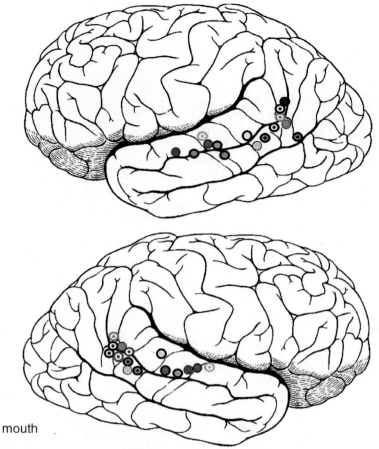

mouth

● Calvert *et al.* lip reading (STG)
● Calvert *et al.* lip reading (AG)
○ Puce et al. mouth movement
● Puce & Allison mouth movement

eyes

◉ Puce *et al.* eye gaze
◉ Wicker *et al.* eye gaze
◉ Hoffman & Haxby eye gaze

body

◉ Howard *et al.* body movement
◉ Bonda *et al.* body movement
◉ Senior *et al.* body movement
◉ Kourtzi & Kanwisher
              body movement
◉ Grossman *et al.* body movement

hand

● Neville *et al.* ASL
● Bonda *et al.* hand action
○ Grezes *et al.* hand action
● Grezes *et al.* hand movement
● Grafton *et al.* hand grasp
● Rizzolatti *et al.* hand grasp

FIGURE 9.3 ■ Centers of activation to viewing the face, hand and body movements of others obtained from a series of PET and fMRI studies. (Adapted from Allison *et al.* (2000), with permission.)

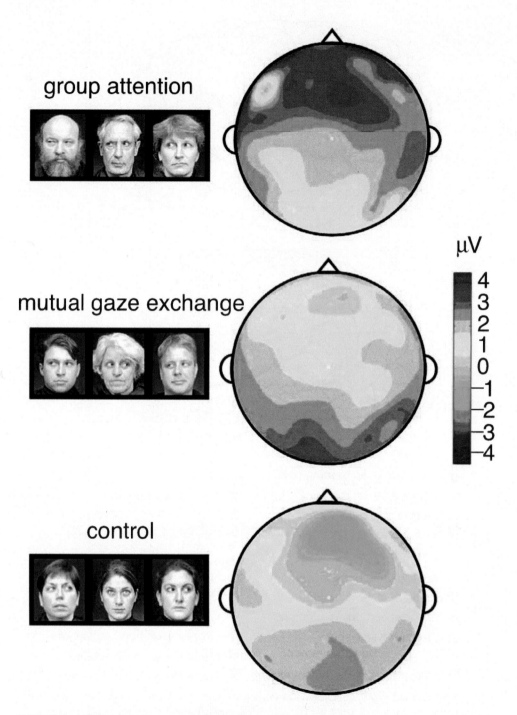

FIGURE 9.4 ■ ERPs elicited to a social attention task. (b) Voltage maps for the three viewing conditions generated at the peak of P400 activity for the group attention condition (black arrow in (a)). The group attention condition shows fronto-temporal positivity, whereas the other two conditions show small posterior positivities.

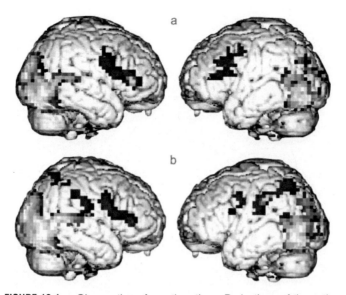

FIGURE 10.1 ■ Observation of mouth actions. Projections of the activation foci on the lateral surface of a standard brain [Montreal Neurological Institute (MNI)] during the observation of non-object-related (chewing: a) and object-related (biting an apple: b) mouth actions.

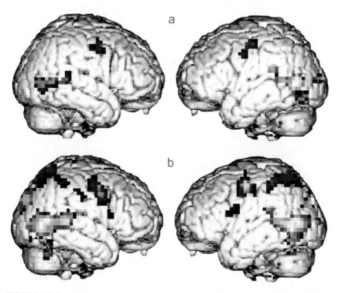

FIGURE 10.2 ■ Observation of hand actions. Projections of the activation foci on the lateral surface of a standard brain (MNI) during the observation of non-object-related (mimicking grasping of a cup or a ball, without object: a) and object-related (grasping a cup or a ball: b) hand actions.

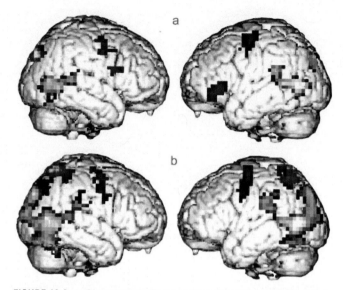

FIGURE 10.3 ■ Observation of foot actions. Projections of the activation foci on the lateral surface of a standard brain (MNI) during the observation of non-object-related (mimicking kicking a ball or pushing a brake, without the object: a) and during the observation of object-related foot actions (kicking a ball or pushing a brake: b) foot actions.

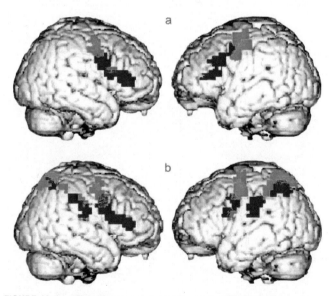

FIGURE 10.4 ■ Somatotopy of premotor and parietal cortices as revealed by action observation. (a) Observation of non-object-related actions. (b) Observation of object-related actions. Activation foci, shown in detail in the three previous figures, are projected on the lateral surface of a standard brain (MNI). Red, activation during the observation of mouth movements; green, activation during the observation of hand movements; blue, activation during the observation of foot movements. Overlap of colours indicates activation foci present during observation of actions made by different effectors.

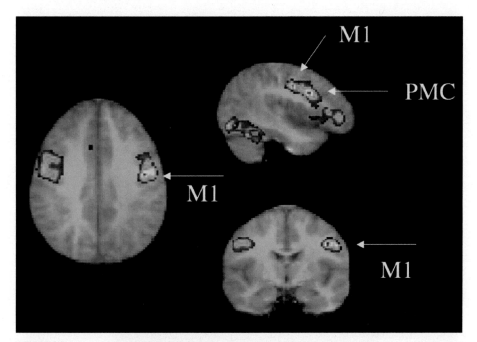

FIGURE 11.1 ■ Peaks of activations in the right central (labeled M1) and precentral (labeled PMC) sulcus. The peak labeled M1 ($x = 44$, $y = -10$, $z = 36$) corresponds entirely (considering spatial resolution and variability factors) with meta-analytic PET data ($x = 48 \pm 5.2$, $y = -9 \pm 5.6$, $z = 35 \pm 5.5$) for the mouth region of human primary motor cortex. The peak labeled PMC ($x = 48$, $y = 8$, $z = 28$) corresponds well with previously reported premotor mouth ($x = 48$, $y = 0$, $z = 32$) peaks.

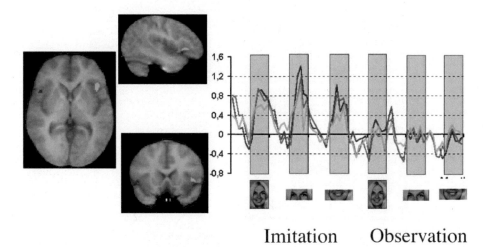

Imitation   Observation

FIGURE 11.3 ■ Activations in the right insula (green) and right (blue) and left (red) inferior frontal cortex. Relative time-series are coded with the corresponding colors. The time-series have been normalized to the overall activity of each region. The activity profile of these three regions is extremely similar throughout the whole series of tasks.

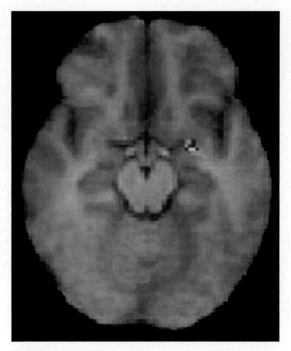

FIGURE 11.4 ■ Significantly increased activity in the right amygdala during imitation of emotional facial expressions compared with simple observation.

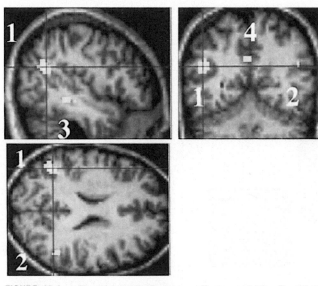

FIGURE 13.1 ■ Experiment 1. Random effects analysis, $P < 0.05$, corrected, $n = 25$. Theory of mind > mechanical inference stories. Crosshair marks the most significant voxel in the left TPJ (1). Also visible are activations in right TPJ (2), left aSTS (3), and precuneus (4). TPJ, temporo-parietal junction; aSTS, anterior superior temporal sulcus.

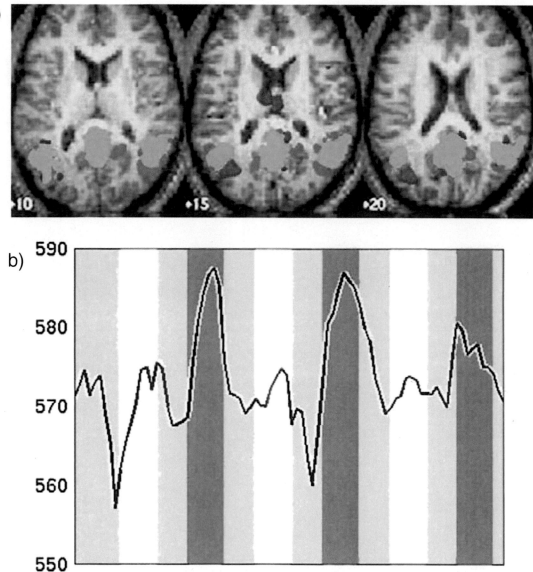

FIGURE 13.3 ■ (a) Experiments 1 and 2. Activation overlap within an individual subject showing bilateral temporo-parietal junction (bilateral TPJ) and precuneus regions (fixed effects, $P < 0.001$). Red = theory of mind > mechanical inference (Exp. 1). Blue = false belief > false photo (Exp. 2). Green = both. (b) Single subject time course of response during Experiment 2 to false belief (dark gray) and false photograph (white) stories in the same subject's TPJ-M, independently defined by a greater response to theory of mind than to mechanical inference stories in Experiment 1; $P < 0.0001$, uncorrected. Medium gray indicates fixation. Time course averaged over four runs.

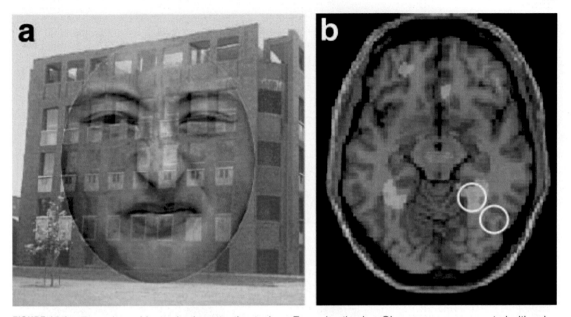

FIGURE 14.1 ■ Face-place object selection attention task, *a*, Example stimulus. Observers were presented with color-coded superimposed faces (disgusted, fearful, and neutral expressions in red) and places (inside and outside of buildings in green). Before each test stimulus, observers were presented with a color-coded prompt indicating which task they were to perform on that trial: indicate the gender of the face (attend trials) or indicate the location of the place (un-attend trials). *b*, A representative subject demonstrated a greater response when attending to places (in green) in a bilateral region along the collateral sulcus, consistent with the PPA and a greater response when attending to faces (in red) in the right middle fusiform gyrus, consistent with the FFA.

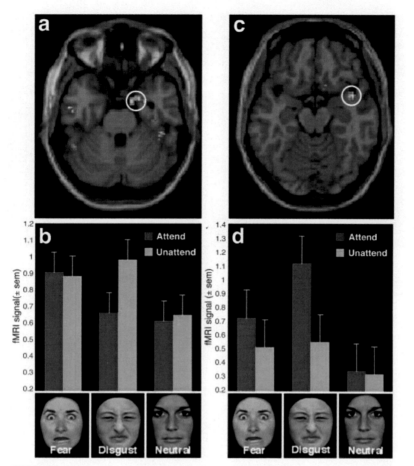

FIGURE 14.2 ■ Attentional dependence of amygdala and anterior insular responses to facial expressions. a, The amygdala was functionally defined by the group level contrast of fear relative to neutral trials when faces were attended. This resulted in a prominent activation in the right amygdala (at a peak height x,22;y,1;z,-28;$F_{(1,11)}$ = 20.52;p < 0.0001). b, Effect of stimulus and attention on amygdala response. Peak amygdala response is displayed for each facial stimulus type during attended (red) and unattended (green) conditions. Attention did not significantly reduce the magnitude of amygdala response to fear, but the enhanced response to disgust during reduced attention suggests attention influenced the specificity of amygdala response. c, The insula was functionally defined by contrasting activation on disgust trials compared with neutral trials when faces were attended. This resulted in a prominent activation in the right anterior insula (at a peak height x,44;y,5;z, -14;$F_{(1,11)}$ = 32.72,p < 0.0001). d, Effect of stimulus and attention on anterior insular response. Peak anterior insular response is displayed for each facial stimulus type during attended (red) and unattended (green) conditions. Reduced attention significantly reduced the magnitude of anterior insular response to disgust.

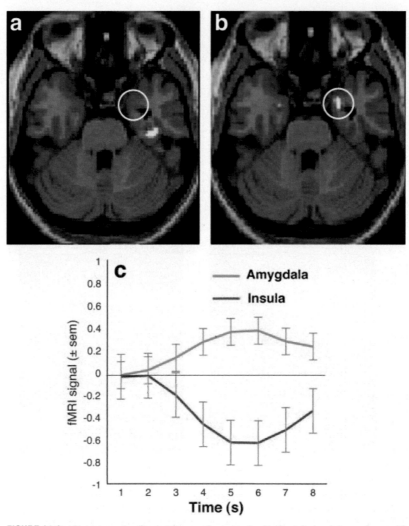

FIGURE 14.3 ■ Response to disgust faces when unattended. a, Amygdala response to disgust relative to neutral faces when observers were attending to faces. No significant activation was found when faces were attended. b, Amygdala response to disgust relative to neutral faces when observers were attending to places. Activation was present when disgust faces were unattended. c, Time course of the disgust response difference score (unattended minus attended). A negative deflection of time course represents a decreased response when faces were attended. A positive deflection represents an increased response when faces were unattended. An inverse effect of attention on anterior insula and amygdala response to disgust faces peaked ~6 sec after the stimulus onset.

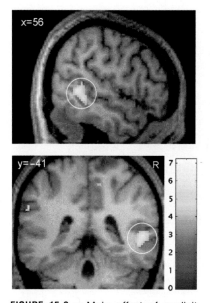

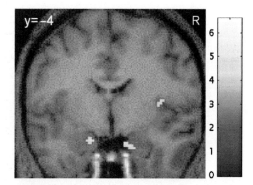

FIGURE 15.3 ■ Main effect of trustworthiness in amygdala and insula. (a) Significant increases in BOLD signal to untrustworthy faces in the right and left amygdalae and right insula (right amygdala, −18, 0, −24; $Z = 4.29$; $p < 0.01$ corrected; left amygdala, −16, −4, −20; $Z = 3.92$; $p < 0.025$ corrected; right insula, 42, −4, 12; $Z = 3.48$; $p < 0.001$ uncorrected).

FIGURE 15.2 ■ Main effect of explicit social judgments. (a) Random-effects SPM overlaid on a normalized structural scan from a single subject showing activation in right superior temporal sulcus region (x, y, $z = 56$, −44, 4; $Z = 4.27$; $p < 0.05$ small volume corrected) when making judgments about trustworthiness compared to age. For illustration, using threshold $p < 0.001$ uncorrected, extent threshold of 5 voxels.

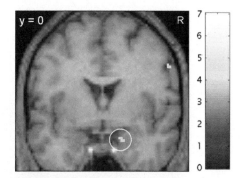

FIGURE 15.5 ■ Main effect of trustworthiness in amygdala independent of facial emotion. Significant increases in BOLD signal in response to untrustworthy faces in right amygdala even when scores for four basic facial emotions are additionally used as parametric covariates in the analysis. This activation is significant at $p < 0.05$, corrected for multiple comparisons across the volume of bilateral amygdala. Activation peak at 18, 2, −22 ($Z = 4.06$), but overlaps with right amygdala activation focus shown in Figure 15.2. At lower threshold of $p < 0.005$ uncorrected, activation is evident in left amygdala.

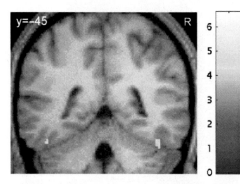

FIGURE 15.4 ■ Main effect of trustworthiness in fusiform gyrus. (a) Significant increases in BOLD signal to untrustworthy faces in the fusiform gyrus bilaterally (right, 44, −46, −22; $Z = 3.58$; $p < 0.05$, small volume corrected; left, −48, −48, −24; $Z = 3.60$; $p < 0.05$, small volume corrected).

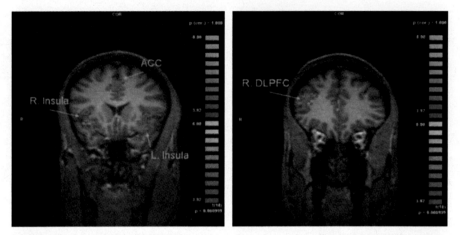

FIGURE 16.2 ■ Activation related to the presentation of an unfair offer. (a) Map of the *t* statistic for the contrast [unfair human offer – fair human offer] showing activation of bilateral anterior insula and anterior cingulate cortex. Areas in orange showed greater activation following unfair as compared with fair offers (p < 0.001). (b) Map of the *t* statistic for the contrast [unfair human offer – fair human offer] showing activation of right dorsolateral prefrontal cortex.

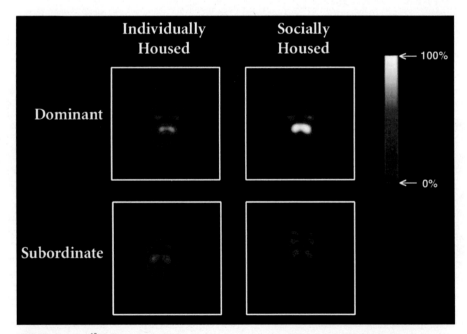

FIGURE 18.3 ■ [^{18}F]FCP binding potential increases in dominant monkeys. Normalized, co-registered PET images (percent injected dose per ml) of [^{18}F]FCP binding in the basal ganglia of a dominant and a subordinate monkey, while individually housed and socially housed.

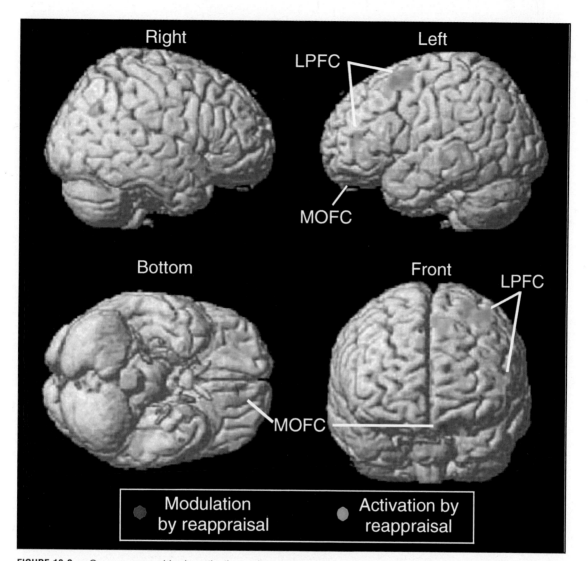

FIGURE 19.2 ■ Group-averaged brain activations when reappraising or attending to feelings in response to the most negative photos. Two contrasts are shown: The Attend > Reappraise (shown in red) contrast shows regions important for emotion processing that are significantly modulated by reappraisal and the Reappraise > Attend (shown in green) contrast shows regions significantly activated when exerting cognitive control over emotion activated by reappraisal. Top and bottom brain images on the right show regions of the left dorsal and ventral LPFC associated with cognitive control that were activated by reappraisal. Right side and bottom left brain images show reappraisal-related modulation of a region of left MOFC associated with representing the affective properties of stimuli.

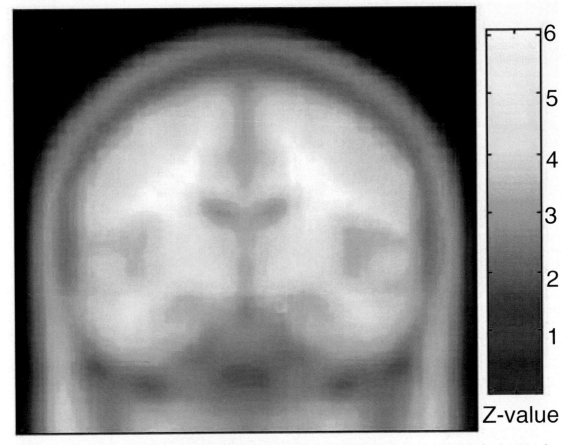

FIGURE 19.4 ■ Coronal image showing the group-averaged cluster of activation in right amygdala for the Attend > Reappraise contrast for trials with the most negative photos ($p <$ .005). The focus is centered on MNI coordinates (16, −12, −20). Activation is shown on group-averaged anatomy.

TABLE 11.1. Peaks of Activation in Talairach Coordinates

Hemisphere	Region	BA	Talairach coordinates			t values		
			x	y	z	Imitation	Observation	Imi-obs
L	M1	4	−52	−4	32	9.63	NS	7.44
R	M1	4	44	−10	36	10.93	NS	7.3
L	S1	2	−40	−38	40	4.42	NS	NS
R	S1	3	56	−22	36	4.14	NS	4.74
L	PPC	7	−24	−60	40	4.42	5.77	NS
L	PPC	40	−40	−46	50	4.51	3.72	NS
R	PPC	39	30	−54	38	4.98	5.3	NS
L	PMC	6	−30	−2	50	6.14	NS	4.93
L	**PMC**	**6**	**−40**	**2**	**32**	**10.98**	**3.91**	**4.84**
L	**PMC**	**6**	**−52**	**10**	**26**	**10.28**	**3.81**	**5.63**
R	**PMC**	**6**	**48**	**8**	**28**	**11.4**	**6.14**	**6.7**
R	**PMC**	**6**	**40**	**6**	**30**	**10.23**	**5.86**	**4.84**
L	Pre-SMA	6	8	6	58	8.84	NS	8.05
R	Pre-SMA	6	0	4	52	9.26	NS	8.42
L	RCZp	32	−4	14	44	7.72	NS	6.74
L	RCZa	32	−8	30	26	4.98	NS	3.54
R	ACC	32	8	16	52	NS	4.28	NS
R	MPFC	9	6	54	34	NS	4.7	NS
L	LPFC	10	−36	50	12	11.86	NS	11.26
R	**LPFC**	**10**	**44**	**38**	**4**	**7.81**	**4.65**	**6.19**
R	LPFC	10	34	42	6	8.61	NS	6.37
L	**IFG**	**44**	**−40**	**14**	**24**	**7.58**	**6.56**	**3.53**
R	**IFG**	**44**	**50**	**14**	**16**	**9.16**	**4.74**	**6.51**
L	IFG	44	−50	12	2	7.02	NS	9.26
R	IFG	44	50	12	2	8.98	NS	9.91
L	IFG	45	−46	36	12	NS	5.67	NS
R	**IFG**	**45**	**46**	**26**	**8**	**8.14**	**3.4**	**5.4**
L	Insula	45	−36	18	4	2.6	NS	4.65
R	**Insula**	**45**	**36**	**30**	**6**	**7.91**	**3.02**	**6.09**
L	**STS**	**22**	**−46**	**−48**	**12**	**4.33**	**2.37**	**3.53**
R	STS	22	46	−44	12	NS	3.72	NS
R	FFA	19	39	−64	−14	11.86	11.86	NS
L	Temp. pole	38	−24	20	−32	4.74	NS	5.49
R	Temp. pole	38	36	26	−28	8.47	NS	8.09
L	Temp. pole	38	−42	20	−20	NS	4.28	NS
R	Temp. pole	38	26	8	−26	NS	3.95	NS
R	Striatum		24	8	6	4.88	NS	3.67
L	Amygdala		−22	0	−16	NS	3.91	NS
R	**Amygdala**		**22**	**0**	**−10**	**4.7**	**3.16**	**3.77**

In bold are peaks that follow the pattern predicted by the hypothesis of action representation route to empathy (i.e., activation during imitation and observation, and greater activity during imitation compared to observation). The majority of these peaks were predicted *a priori*, the only exception being the right dorsolateral prefrontal cortex, BA10. In italics are statistical levels approaching significance in predicted areas. NS, not significant.

TABLE 11.2. Comparison of Observed Peaks of Activation in Predicted Regions with Previously Reported Peaks of Activation in Imaging Meta-Analyses and Individual Studies of Action Observation, Imitation, and Emotion

Region	x	y	z	Ref.	x	y	z
M1	44	−10	36	38	48	−9	35
PMC	48	8	28	40	48	0	32
IFG	50	14	16	22	57	14	12
Insula	36	30	6	60	35	31	9
STS	−46	−48	12	50	−49	−50	9
Amygdala	22	0	−10	59	24	−2	−22

findings, despite the presence of facial motion during imitation. In fact, residual motion artifacts that were still present at individual level after motion correction were eliminated by the group analysis. This result is likely due to the fact that each subject had different kinds of motion artifacts and, when all of the data were considered, only common patterns of activity emerged.

The data also clearly show peaks of activity in the presupplementary motor area (pre-SMA) face

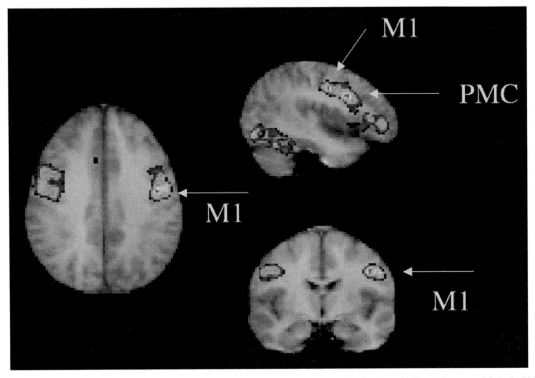

FIGURE 11.1 ■ **(A color version of this figure follows page 146.)** Peaks of activations in the right central (labeled M1) and precentral (labeled PMC) sulcus. The peak labeled M1 ($x = 44$, $y = -10$, $z = 36$) corresponds entirely (considering spatial resolution and variability factors) with meta-analytic PET data ($x = 48 \pm 5.2$, $y = -9 \pm 5.6$, $z = 35 \pm 5.5$) for the mouth region of human primary motor cortex. The peak labeled PMC ($x = 48$, $y = 8$, $z = 28$) corresponds well with previously reported premotor mouth ($x = 48$, $y = 0$, $z = 32$) peaks.

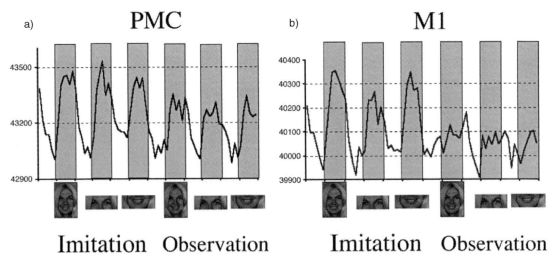

FIGURE 11.2 ■ Time-series of peaks of activity in right central (M1) and precentral (PMC) sulcus shown in Figure 11.1. Task-related activity is observable not only during imitation but also during observation of emotional facial expressions, especially in PMC.

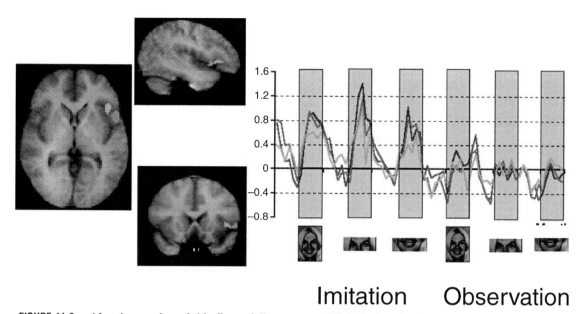

Imitation   Observation

FIGURE 11.3 ■ (*A color version of this figure follows page 146.*) Activations in the right insula (green) and right (blue) and left (red) inferior frontal cortex. Relative time-series are coded with the corresponding colors. The time-series have been normalized to the overall activity of each region. The activity profile of these three regions is extremely similar throughout the whole series of tasks.

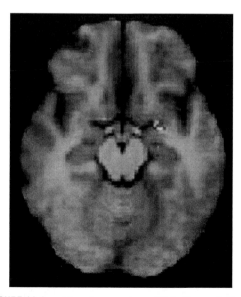

FIGURE 11.4 ■ (*A color version of this figure follows page 146.*) Significantly increased activity in the right amygdala during imitation of emotional facial expressions compared with simple observation.

area and the face area of the posterior portion of the rostral cingulate zone (RCZp) that correspond well with the pre-SMA and RCZp face locations as determined by a separate meta-analysis of PET studies focusing on motor areas in the medial wall of the frontal lobe (39). Thus, our dataset represents an fMRI demonstration of human primary motor and rostral cingulate face area. With regard to premotor regions, the peaks that we observe correspond well with premotor mouth peaks described by action observation studies (40). As Figure 11.2 shows, robust pre-motor responses during observation of facial emotional expressions were observed, in line with the hypothesis that action representation mediates the recognition of emotions in others even during simple observation.

The activity in pars opercularis shows two separate foci during imitation, a ventral and a dorsal peak. Only the dorsal peak remained activated, although at significantly lower intensity, during observation of emotion (Table 11.1).

This pattern, with very similar peaks of activation, was also observed in a recent fMRI meta-analysis comprising more than 50 subjects performing hand action imitation and observation in our lab.[*] Pars opercularis maps probabilistically onto Brodmann area 44 (41, 42), which is considered the human homologue of monkey area F5 (43–46) in which mirror neurons were described. In the monkey, F5 neurons coding arm and mouth movements are not spatially segregated, and the human imaging data are consistent with this observation. The imaging data suggest that the dorsal sector represents the *mirror* sector of pars opercularis, whereas the ventral sector may be simply a premotor area for hand and face movements.

The superior temporal sulcus (STS) area shows greater activity for imitation than for observation of emotional facial expressions, as predicted by the action representation mediation to empathy hypothesis. This area also corresponds anatomically well with an STS area specifically responding to the observation of mouth movements observed in different studies from different labs (47–50).

The anterior sector of the insula was active during both imitation and observation of emotion, but more so during imitation (Figure 11.3), fulfilling one of the predictions of our hypothesis that action representation is a cognitive step toward empathy. This finding is in line with two kinds of evidence available on this sector of the insular lobe. First, the anterior insula receives slow-conducting unmyelinated fibers that respond to light, caress-like touch and may be important for emotional and affiliative behavior between individuals (51). Second, imaging data suggest that the anterior insular sector is important for the monitoring of agency (52), that is, the sense of ownership of actions, which is a fundamental aspect of action

representation. This finding confirms a strong input onto the anterior insular sector from areas of motor significance.

The increased activity in the amygdala during imitation compared with observation of emotional facial expression (Figure 11.4) reflects the modulation of the action representation circuit onto limbic activity. It has been long hypothesized (dating back to Darwin; refs. 53–55) that facial muscular activity influences people's affective responses. We demonstrate here that activity in the amygdala, a critical structure in emotional behaviors and in the recognition of facial emotional expressions of others (56–59), increases while subjects imitate the facial emotional expressions of others, compared with mere observation.

Previous and current literature on observing and processing facial emotional expression provides a rich context in which to consider the nature of the empathic resonance induced by our imitation paradigm. In general, our findings fit well with previously published imaging data on observation of facial expressions that report activation in both amygdala and anterior insula for emotional facial expressions (for a review, see ref. 57 and references therein). A study on conscious and unconscious processing of emotional facial expression (58) has suggested that the left but not the right amygdala is associated with explicit representational content of the observed emotion. Our data, showing a right lateralized activation of the amygdala during imitation of facial emotional expression, suggest that the type of empathic resonance induced by imitation does not require explicit representational content and may be a form of "mirroring" that grounds empathy via an experiential mechanism.

In this study, we treated emotion as a single, unified entity. Recent literature has clearly shown that different emotions seem related to different neural systems. For instance, disgust seems to activate preferentially the anterior insula (60), whereas fear seems to activate preferentially the amygdala (56, 57). We adopted this approach

---

[*] Molnar-Szakacs, I., Iacoboni, M., Koski, L., Maeda, F., Dubeau, M. C., Aziz-Zadeh, L. & Mazziotta, J. C. (2002) *J. Cogn. Neurosci.*, Suppl. S, F118 (abstr.).

because our main goal was to investigate the relationships between action representation and emotion via an imitation paradigm. Future studies may successfully employ imitative paradigm to further explore the differential neural correlates of emotions.

Taken together, these data suggest that we understand the feelings of others via a mechanism of action representation shaping emotional content, such that we ground our empathic resonance in the experience of our acting body and the emotions associated with specific movements. As Lipps noted, "When I observe a circus performer on a hanging wire, I feel I am inside him" (1). To empathize, we need to invoke the representation of the actions associated with the emotions we are witnessing. In the human brain, this empathic resonance occurs via communication between action representation networks and limbic areas provided by the insula. Lesions in this circuit may determine an impairment in understanding the emotions of others and the inability to "empathize" with them.[**]

Acknowledgments

This work was supported, in part, by the Brain Mapping Medical Research Organization, the Brain Mapping Support Foundation, the Pierson-Lovelace Foundation, the Ahmanson Foundation, the Tamkin Foundation, the Jennifer Jones-Simon Foundation, the Capital Group Companies Charitable Foundation, the Robson Family, the Northstar Fund, and grants from the National Center for Research Resources (RR12169 and RR08655).

Abbreviations

fMRI, functional MRI; PET, positron-emission tomography.

[**] Vicenzini, E., Bodini, B., Gasparini, M., Di Piero, V., Mazziotta, J. C., Iacoboni, M. & Lenzi, G. L. (2002) *Cerebrovasc. Dis.* **13**, Suppl. 3, 52 (abstr.).

REFERENCES

1. Gallese, V. (2001) *J. Conscious. Stud.* 8, 33–50.
2. Chartrand, T. L. & Bargh, J. A. (1999) *J. Pers. Soc. Psychol.* 76, 893–910.
3. LeDoux, J. E. (2000) *Annu. Rev. Neurosci.* 23, 155–184.
4. diPellegrino, G., Fadiga, L., Fogassi, L., Gallese, V. & Rizzolatti, G. (1992) *Exp. Brain Res.* 91, 176–180.
5. Gallese, V., Fadiga, L., Fogassi, L. & Rizzolatti, G. (1996) *Brain* 119, 593–609.
6. Perrett, D. I., Harries, M. H., Bevan, R., Thomas, S., Benson, P. J., Mistlin, A. J., Chitty, A. J., Hietanen, J. K. & Ortega, J. E. (1989) *J. Exp. Biol.* 146, 87–113.
7. Rizzolatti, G., Fogassi, L. & Gallese, V. (2001) *Nat. Rev. Neurosci.* 2, 661–670.
8. Perrett, D. I. & Emery, N. J. (1994) *Curr. Psychol. Cogn.* 13, 683–694.
9. Perrett, D. I., Harries, M. H., Mistlin, A. J., Hietanen, J. K., Benson, P. J., Bevan, R., Thomas, S., Oram, M. W., Ortega, J. & Brierly, K. (1990) *Int. J. Comp. Psychol.* 4, 25–55.
10. Decety, J., Grezes, J., Costes, N., Perani, D., Jeannerod, M., Procyk, E., Grassi, F. & Fazio, F. (1997) *Brain* 120, 1763–1777.
11. Grezes, J. & Decety, J. (2001) *Hum. Brain Mapp.* 12, 1–19.
12. Iacoboni, M., Koski, L. M., Brass, M., Bekkering, H., Woods, R. P., Dubeau, M. C., Mazziotta, J. C. & Rizzolatti, G. (2001) *Proc. Natl. Acad. Sci. USA* 98, 13995–13999.
13. Iacoboni, M., Woods, R. P., Brass, M., Bekkering, H., Mazziotta, J. C. & Rizzolatti, G. (1999) *Science* 286, 2526–2528.
14. Seltzer, B. & Pandya, D. N. (1994) *J. Comp. Neurol.* 343, 445–463.
15. Kalaska, J. F., Caminiti, R. & Georgopoulos, A. P. (1983) *Exp. Brain Res.* 51, 247–260.
16. Lacquaniti, F., Guigon, E., Bianchi, L., Ferraina, S. & Caminiti, R. (1995) *Cereb. Cortex.* 5, 391–409.
17. Mountcastle, V., Lynch, J., Georgopoulos, A., Sakata, H. & Acuna, C. (1975) *J. Neurophysiol.* 38, 871–908.
18. Sakata, H., Takaoka, Y., Kawarasaki, A. & Shibutani, H. (1973) *Brain Res.* 64, 85–102.
19. Rizzolatti, G. & Luppino, G. (2001) *Neuron* 31, 889–901.
20. Kohler, E., Keysers, C., Umilta, M. A., Fogassi, L., Gallese, V. & Rizzolatti, G. (2002) *Science* 297, 846–848.
21. Umilta, M. A., Kohler, E., Gallese, V., Fogassi, L., Fadiga, L., Keysers, C. & Rizzolatti, G. (2001) *Neuron* 31, 155–165.
22. Koski, L., Wohlschlager, A., Bekkering, H., Woods, R. P., Dubeau, M. C., Mazziotta, J. C. & Iacoboni, M. (2002) *Cereb. Cortex* 12, 847–855.
23. Augustine, J. R. (1996) *Brain Res. Rev.* 2, 229–294.
24. Oldfield, R. C. (1971) *Neuropsychologia* 9, 97–113.
25. Ekman, P. & Friesen, W. V. (1976) *Pictures of Facial Affect* (Consulting Psychologist Press, Palo Alto, CA).
26. Gentilucci, M., Fogassi, L., Luppino, G., Matelli, M., Camarda, R. & Rizzolatti, G. (1988) *Exp. Brain Res.* 71, 475–490.

27. Woods, R. P., Grafton, S. T., Holmes, C. J., Cherry, S. R. & Mazziotta, J. C. (1998) *J. Comput. Assist. Tomogr.* 22, 139–152.
28. Woods, R. P., Grafton, S. T., Watson, J. D. G., Sicotte, N.L. & Mazziotta, J. C. (1998) *J. Comput. Assist. Tomogr.* 22, 153–165.
29. Woods, R. P., Dapretto, M., Sicotte, N. L., Toga, A. W. & Mazziotta, J. C. (1999) *Hum. Brain Mapp.* 8, 73–79.
30. Iacoboni, M., Woods, R. P. & Mazziotta, J. C. (1996) *J. Neurophysiol.* 76, 321–331.
31. Iacoboni, M., Woods, R. P., Lenzi, G. L. & Mazziotta, J. C. (1997) *Brain* 120, 1635–1645.
32. Iacoboni, M., Woods, R. P. & Mazziotta, J. C. (1998) *Brain* 121, 2135–2143.
33. Woods, R. P., Iacoboni, M., Grafton, S. T. & Mazziotta, J. C. (1996) in *Quantification of Brain Function Using PET*, eds. Myers, R., Cunningham, V., Bailey, D. & Jones, T. (Academic, San Diego), pp. 353–358.
34. Aguirre, G. K., Zarahn, E. & D'Esposito, M. (1998) *Neuroimage* 8, 360–369.
35. Zarahn, E., Aguirre, G. K. & D'Esposito, M. (1997) *Neuroimage* 5, 179–197.
36. Aguirre, G. K., Zarahn, E. & D'Esposito, M. (1997) *Neuroimage* 5, 199–212.
37. Forman, S. D., Cohen, J. D., Fitzgerald, M., Eddy, W. F., Mintun, M. A. & Noll, D. C. (1995) *Magn. Reson. Med.* 33, 636–647.
38. Fox, P. T., Huang, A., Parsons, L. M., Xiong, J. H., Zamarippa, F., Rainey, L. & Lancaster, J. L. (2001) *Neuroimage* 13, 196–209.
39. Picard, N. & Strick, P. L. (1996) *Cereb. Cortex* 6, 342–353.
40. Buccino, G., Binkofski, F., Fink, G. R., Fadiga, L., Fogassi, L., Gallese, V., Seitz, R. J., Zilles, K., Rizzolatti, G. & Freund, H. J. (2001) *Eur. J. Neurosci.* 13, 400–404.
41. Mazziotta, J., Toga, A., Evans, A., Fox, P., Lancaster, J., Zilles, K., Woods, R., Paus, T., Simpson, G., Pike, B., *et al.* (2001) *Philos. Trans. R. Soc. London B Biol. Sci.* 356, 1293–1322.
42. Mazziotta, J., Toga, A., Evans, A., Fox, P., Lancaster, J., Zilles, K., Woods, R., Paus, T., Simpson, G., Pike, B., *et al.* (2001) *J. Am. Med. Inform. Assoc.* 8, 401–430.
43. Geyer, S., Matelli, M., Luppino, G. & Zilles, K. (2000) *Anat. Embryol.* 202, 443–474.
44. Petrides, M. & Pandya, D. N. (1994) in *Handbook of Neuropsychology*, eds. Boller, F. & Grafman, J. (Elsevier, Amsterdam), Vol. 9, pp. 17–58.
45. Rizzolatti, G. & Arbib, M. (1998) *Trends Neurosci.* 21, 188–194.
46. vonBonin, G. & Bailey, P. (1947) *The Neocortex of Macaca Mulatta* (Univ. of Illinois Press, Urbana).
47. Campbell, R., MacSweeney, M., Surguladze, S., Calvert, G., McGuire, P., Suckling, J., Brammer, M. J. & David, A. S. (2001) *Brain Res. Cogn. Brain Res.* 12, 233–243.
48. Puce, A., Allison, T., Bentin, S., Gore, J. C. & McCarthy, G. (1998) *J. Neurosci.* 18, 2188–2199.
49. Allison, T., Puce, A. & McCarthy, G. (2000) *Trends Cogn. Sci.* 4, 267–278.
50. Calvert, G. A., Campbell, R. & Brammer, M. J. (2000) *Curr. Biol.* 10, 649–657.
51. Olausson, H., Lamarre, Y., Backlund, H., Morin, C., Wallin, B. G., Starck, G., Ekholm, S., Strigo, I., Worsley, K., Vallbo, A. B. & Bushnell, M. C. (2002) *Nat. Neurosci.* 5, 900–904.
52. Farrer, C. & Frith, C. D. (2002) *Neuroimage* 15, 596–603.
53. Buck, R. (1980) *J. Pers. Soc. Psychol.* 38, 811–824.
54. Ekman, P. (1973) *Darwin and Facial Expression: A Century of Research in Review* (Academic, New York).
55. Ekman, P. (1999) *Handbook of Cognition and Emotion* (Wiley, Chichester, England), pp. 301–320.
56. Phillips, M. L., Young, A. W., Scott, S. K., Calder, A. J., Andrew, C., Giampietro, V., Williams, S. C., Bullmore, E. T., Brammer, M. & Gray, J. A. (1998) *Proc. R. Soc. London Ser. B Biol. Sci.* 265, 1809–1817.
57. Phan, K. L., Wager, T., Taylor, S. F. & Liberzon, I. (2002) *Neuroimage* 16, 331–348.
58. Morris, J. S., Ohman, A. & Dolan, R. J. (1998) *Nature* 393, 467–470.
59. Hariri, A. R., Bookheimer, S. Y. & Mazziotta, J. C. (2000) *NeuroReport* 11, 43–48.
60. Phillips, M. L., Young, A. W., Senior, C., Brammer, M., Andrew, C., Calder, A. J., Bullmore, E. T., Perrett, D. I., Rowland, D., Williams, S. C., *et al.* (1997) *Nature* 389, 495–498.

PART 7

Animacy, Causality, and Theory of Mind

More than a half century ago, social psychologist Fritz Heider and Mary-Ann Simmel constructed a simple film animation of three geometric shapes—a small yellow circle, a small blue triangle, and a larger gray triangle—set in motion. The relative distances among these three shapes, and their positions in and about a large rectangle, varied during the film. Heider and Simmel simply asked observers to describe what they saw in the film. Most observers told elaborate stories, such as the circle and the little triangle being in love, the gray triangle trying to steal away the circle, the blue triangle fighting back, the circle and little triangle escaping into the house, and once inside safely embracing. So prevalent is this tendency that it may seem unremarkable that people imbue simple moving geometric shapes with individual identities, motives, and emotions. Some individuals missing a limbic structure called the amygdala, however, simply see geometric objects moving about the screen.

You enter a new car showroom, intent on purchasing the automobile you long dreamed of owning. A salesperson greets you politely, shows you the car, answers your questions patiently, and even gives you the keys to test-drive the car. When you return, the salesperson invites you into a private office and asks what you would like to pay for the car. Despite the fact that the salesperson has shown you extraordinary courtesy to this point, you have little trust in the individual, and you guard your words at each point in the negotiation that unfolds. You watch the salesperson intently, trying to glean a hint regarding the lowest price the salesperson is willing to accept. In so doing, you realize that the salesperson has knowledge, beliefs, and motives behind the behaviors you are allowed to see, and you develop a theory of these aspects of the salesperson's mind, which you use to predict the salesperson's actions. Indeed, you make ample use of your theory of mind in almost all your social interactions. You may not recall, but you were not born with this capacity; in most children a theory of mind does not develop until about age 5.

In the preceding sections, we learned that people often subtly mimic the behaviors they observe and empathize with the emotions they see displayed. The readings in this section build on these observations to address how the brain is a *social* information processing organ. Castelli et al. (2000) used positron emission tomography (PET) to image the brain of six individuals while they watched short animated films similar to the one constructed by Fritz and Simmel six decades ago. The attribution of mental states (beliefs, motives, emotions) was associated with increased activity in the medial prefrontal cortex, superior temporal sulcus, fusiform gyrus, temporal poles near the amygdala, and occipital gyrus. By now, many of these are becoming familiar areas to readers, for they have been implicated in other studies in self-referent processing and in the perception of faces and biological motion.

In the second reading, Saxe and Kanwisher (2003) explore the possible neural substrates of people's theory of mind. Functional magnetic resonance imaging (fMRI) was performed on individuals as they read short stories. In their first study, participants were instructed to read each story silently and to make sure they understood what was happening. They then read stories from each of four categories: false belief, mechanical inference, human action, and nonhuman descriptions. Only the stories that featured false beliefs invoked reasoning about others' beliefs, reasoning, and feelings—that is, theory of mind reasoning. In their second study, participants read another series of studies that varied in the extent to which theory of mind was required to answer questions about the story. The results of this research revealed greater bilateral activation in the temporo-parietal junction (a region near the superior temporal sulcus) in tasks that required reasoning about another person's mental state. Importantly, the difficulty of the task was unrelated to activity in this region, suggesting it may be selectively involved in tasks that require reasoning about another person's mental states. Together, the two readings in this section suggest that the human brain is not just an isolated information processing machine, but a social brain, for with little encouragement or information, it appears capable of calculating the mental states of others.

Movement and Mind: A Functional Imaging Study of Perception and Interpretation of Complex Intentional Movement Patterns

Fulvia Castelli,[*] Francesca Happé,[†] Uta Frith,[*] and Chris Frith[‡]

We report a functional neuroimaging study with positron emission tomography (PET) in which six healthy adult volunteers were scanned while watching silent computer-presented animations. The characters in the animations were simple geometrical shapes whose movement patterns selectively evoked mental state attribution or simple action description. Results showed increased activation in association with mental state attribution in four main regions: medial prefrontal cortex, temporoparietal junction (superior temporal sulcus), basal temporal regions (fusiform gyrus and temporal poles adjacent to the amygdala), and extrastriate cortex (occipital gyrus). Previous imaging studies have implicated these regions in self-monitoring, in the perception of biological motion, and in the attribution of mental states using verbal stimuli or visual depictions of the human form. We suggest that these regions form a network for processing information about intentions, and speculate that the ability to make inferences about other people's mental states evolved from the ability to make inferences about other creatures' actions.

Keywords: brain imaging; theory of mind; mentalizing; biological motion; autism.

*Institute of Cognitive Neuroscience, University College London, Alexandra House, 17 Queen Square, London WCIN 3AR, United Kingdom; †Institute of Psychiatry, Kings College London; and ‡Wellcome Department of Cognitive Neurology, Institute of Neurology, University College London.

Introduction

Recent interest in the evolution, development, and breakdown of social cognition has focused on Theory of Mind, the ability to attribute independent mental states to self and others in order to explain and predict behaviour (Carruthers and Smith, 1996; Baron-Cohen *et al.*, 2000). Fodor (1992), Leslie and Thaiss (1992), Scholl and Leslie (1999), and others have suggested that our ability to attribute mental states, or "mentalize," results from a dedicated, domain-specific, and possibly modular cognitive mechanism. This proposal gains particular support from studies of autism, a biologically based developmental disorder, which appears to be characterized by a selective impairment in Theory of Mind (Baron-Cohen *et al.*, 1985; Frith *et al.*, 1991; Happé and Frith, 1996). Interest in the brain basis of normal Theory of Mind is fired by the hope of a better understanding of the neural systems affected in people with autism, who are (in the main) unable to "mind-read" (Baron-Cohen, 1995).

There is a growing number of published reports of functional brain imaging studies of Theory of Mind (ToM). Most of these studies implicate activation in medial frontal and temporoparietal regions. For example, Fletcher *et al.* (1995), in a PET study, scanned volunteers reading and answering questions about stories involving complex mental states (ToM stories) and those involving inferences of physical cause and effect ("physical" stories). Comparison of activation during ToM versus "physical" stories revealed increased activation in the medial frontal gyrus on the left (BA 8/9), as well as in the posterior cingulate cortex and the right inferior parietal cortex (BA 40) at the temporoparietal junction. Gallagher *et al.* (2000) used the same set of stories in an fMRI study with normal volunteers. In addition to the written stories, subjects were shown figurative drawings (humorous cartoons) which also prompted attribution of mental states. With the greater resolution of fMRI it was possible to distinguish a number of peaks in Brodmann areas 8/9 and the border of 10 and 32, associated with both ToM cartoons and stories. The location of these

areas of activity was close to those previously reported by Fletcher *et al.* (1995) and by Goel *et al.* (1998), and relates to the paracingulate sulcus. Activity was also observed in the temporoparietal junction bilaterally.

Previous brain imaging studies of mental state attribution have tended to use high-level verbal stimuli (Baron-Cohen *et al.*, 1994; Fletcher *et al.*, 1995; Happé *et al.*, 1996; Goel *et al.*, 1998) or visual depictions of humans (Gallagher *et al.*, 2000; Baron-Cohen *et al.*, 1999). Mentalizing, however, involves processes at a number of levels, from perceptual to conceptual. If mentalizing relies on a dedicated cognitive mechanism, or module, then one interesting question concerns the nature of its obligatory triggering inputs. The aim of the present study was to examine brain activation during exposure to simple, nonverbal stimuli designed to evoke mental state attribution by their kinetic properties alone. Inspiration for appropriate stimuli came from the classic work of Heider and Simmel (1944), who demonstrated that even simple geometric shapes could elicit by their pattern of contingent movement the attribution of complex internal states, such as intentions and beliefs. Subsequent work by Berry and colleagues (Berry *et al.*, 1992; Berry and Springer, 1993) has shown that properties of the movement, rather than of the stimuli/characters, are fundamental to the complex attributions made by adults and children from the late preschool years onwards.

To explore brain activation during such movement-provoked mental state attribution we used silent animations of three types. In our Theory of Mind (ToM) condition, interaction between two shapes (big and small triangle) was scripted to imply complex mental states, such as intention to deceive. Thus, in these animations one character's actions were readily seen as determined by what the other character "thought." In the second animation type, "Goal-directed" (GD), the characters interacted on a simple, purposeful level. That is, in these animations, one character's actions were seen as determined by what the other character "did." In the third animation type, "Random action" (R), the two characters did not interact, and their behavior was not contingent—in effect they were merely floating or bouncing around. Stimuli in all three animation types moved in a self-propelled fashion. Our stimuli could therefore be graded in terms of complexity of predominantly evoked descriptions, from random movements, to goal-directed actions, and finally to complex intentional states. Conversely, people's descriptions could be graded in terms of their degree of mentalizing regardless of the animation sequences they were describing.

The present animations were first used in a behavioral study that collected descriptions from children with autism, children with developmental delays, normally developing children, and adults (Abell *et al.*, 2000). Results from this study supported the validity of the three types of animations. Children with autism proved to be less accurate in their descriptions of ToM animations than children without autism. The 14 adults taking part in this study attributed precise mental states, matching the underlying script in 89% of their responses to the ToM animations, with descriptions of purposeful movements for the remaining responses. They attributed precise purposeful interactions in 93% of their responses to the Goal-directed animations with the remaining responses all involving mental state attribution. Description of simple movement without a purposeful component were given in 64% of responses to the Random sequences while purposeful movement was described for the remainder. Even though the vast majority of descriptions of the three types of animations fell into an orderly pattern, the animations were ambiguous enough for interpretations to occur that were either simpler or richer than intended by the designers. Our prediction for the present study was that the ToM animations, but not the Random animations, would evoke mental state attributions and show activation patterns similar to those found in previous functional imaging studies of Theory of Mind (Goel *et al.*, 1998; Fletcher *et al.*, 1995; Baron-Cohen *et al.*, 1999; Gallagher *et al.*, 2000). We expected the GD animations to have an intermediate status. Going one step further, we predicted activation in ToM-related areas for all sequences that provoked mental state interpretations, regardless of the animation condition.

Method

Subjects

Six right-handed male volunteers (aged 20 to 31, mean 24.5 years) took part in this study. All subjects were healthy, with no history of significant medical, psychiatric, or neurological illness. All gave written, informed consent to take part in the study, which was approved by the ethics committee of the National Hospital for Neurology and Neurosurgery and the Administration of Radioactive Substances Advisory Committee (ARSAC), UK.

Data Acquisition

All subjects underwent both PET and MRI scanning on the same day. A Siemens VISION (Siemens, Erlangen) operating at 2.0T was used to acquire axial T1 weighted structural MRI images for anatomical coregistration. PET scans were performed with an ECAT EXACT HR+ scanning system (CTI Siemens, Knoxville, TN) in high sensitivity 3-D mode with septa retracted (Townsend *et al.*, 1991). A venous cannula to administer the tracer was inserted in the antecubital fossa vein. Approximately 350 Mbq of H_2 ^{15}O in 3 ml of normal saline were loaded into intravenous tubing and flushed into subjects over 20 s at a rate of 10 ml/min by an automatic pump. After a delay of approximately 35 s, a rise in counts could be detected in the head that peaked 30–40 s later (depending on individual circulation time). The interval between successive administrations was 8 min. The data were acquired in one 90 s frame, beginning 5 s before the rising phase of the head curve. After correcting for background activity, the true counts accumulated during this period were taken as an index of cerebral blood flow (Fox and Mintun, 1989). Images were reconstructed by filtered back projection (Hanning filter, cut off frequency 0.5 cycles per pixel) into 63 image planes (separation 2.4 mm) and into a 128×128 pixel image matrix (pixel size 2.1 mm). Twelve scans were acquired per subject.

Statistical Analysis

Functional imaging analysis used the technique of Statistical Parametric Mapping implemented in

SPM97 (Wellcome Department of Cognitive Neurology, London, UK) (http://www.fil.ion.ucl.ac.uk/spm). For each subject, a set of 12 PET scans was automatically realigned and then stereotactically normalized (Friston *et al.*, 1995b) into the space of Talairach and Tournoux (1988). The scans were then smoothed using a Gaussian kernel of 12 mm full-width half maximum.

The analysis of functional imaging data entails the creation of statistical parametric maps that represent a statistical assessment of condition-specific effects hypothesised by the experimenter (Friston *et al.*, 1995a). The effects of global changes in blood flow were modelled as a confound using a subject-specific ANCOVA (Friston *et al.*, 1990). Areas of significant change in brain activity were specified by appropriately weighted linear contrasts of the condition-specific effects and determined using the *t*-statistic on a voxel by voxel basis. We created the relevant SPM [*t*] for each comparison of conditions, which was then transformed into an SPM [Z] and thresholded at a Z score of 3.09 ($P < 0.001$ uncorrected). Clusters of activated voxels were characterized in terms of their peak height and spatial extent conjointly.

Design

A 3×2 repeated measures within subjects design was used. Four different examples of each of three types of animation. ToM, Goal-directed, and Random were displayed over the course of 12 scans, divided into two consecutive counterbalanced blocks: cued animation and uncued animation. In a previous study (Fletcher *et al.*, 1995) subjects were cued before the scan. They were told in advance which kind of stimuli they were going to see (see Appendix 1). In the present study we counterbalanced cued with uncued animations in order to control for the effect of prior knowledge.

Animation Materials

Twelve animations were used during the scanning, and an additional three were shown for practice. All the animations featured two characters, a big red triangle and a small blue triangle, moving about on a framed white background. Each sequence lasted

between 34 and 45 s, and the three types of animations were matched for length. The "scripts" for the ToM sequences involved the two triangles persuading, bluffing, mocking, and surprising one another. The Goal-directed "scripts" involved the two triangles dancing together, one chasing, one imitating, and one leading the other. The Random movement showed the two triangles bouncing off the walls resembling the movement of billiard balls, or merely drifting about. While the type of movement was by definition different between the three conditions, the basic visual characteristics in terms of shape, overall speed, and orientation changes were as similar as possible.

Procedure

Subjects were instructed before scanning (see Appendix 1) and were given practice examples of the three types of animations. The animations were presented on the screen of a Power Macintosh computer suspended on an adjustable cradle at a suitable distance for each subject. Prior to scanning, it was ascertained that the subject could watch the animations comfortably.

There was a cued and an uncued condition. Before the cued condition subjects were told either that they were going to see an animation showing "an interaction with feelings and thoughts" (ToM), or "a random movement" (R), or "a simple interaction" (GD). Before the uncued condition, subjects were simply told that they were about to see the next animation. Order of cued and uncued blocks was counterbalanced across subjects, so that half the subjects obtained cued animations first, and half uncued animations first.

After each scan subjects were asked to tell the experimenter what they thought the triangles were doing. The experimenter always asked the same neutral question: "What was happening in this animation?" Answers were recorded for later scoring. On no occasion was feedback given, but subjects were generally praised for their descriptions.

Scoring

The verbal descriptions given after each presentation (in between scans) were coded along four different dimensions. The aim of the scores was to distinguish in each answer (1) the implied "intentionality," that is, the degree of appreciation of mental states, (2) their appropriateness, that is, how well the underlying script was captured, (3) the certainty of the explanation, and (4) the length of each answer. The Intentionality score reflected the use of mental state terms, with scores ranging from 0 (nondeliberate action), to 5 (deliberate action aimed at affecting another's mental state; see Appendix 2 for examples). Two raters gave the identical score 65% of the time, and had an average discrepancy of only 1.4 points in the remaining 35% of the cases. The Appropriateness score measured the understanding of the event depicted in the animations, as intended by the designers (0 to 3). The Certainty score graded the degree of hesitation present in the verbal description (0 to 3). The Length score classified the number of clauses in each answer (0 to 4). Details of scoring are given in Appendix 2.

Results

Behavioral Data

Table 12.1 shows the ratings of the descriptions of each type of animation. As can be seen, the three animation types differed significantly in the degree of mental state attribution they evoked ($F(2, 10) = 154.75$, $P < 0.001$). As expected on the basis of Abell et $al.$'s results (2000) subjects attributed more intentionality to the characters' behavior during ToM animations than during GD (t value $= 5.89$, $P = 0.002$) and R animations (t value $= 16.04$, $P < 0.001$). Random animations evoked significantly fewer mental state attributions than Goal-directed animations (t value $= 17.43$, $P < 0.001$).

The length of the descriptions differed significantly ($F(2,10) = 19.49$, $P < 0.001$), with the ToM animations eliciting longer explanations than Goal-directed ($t = 5.48$, $P = 0.003$) or Random animations ($t = 5.11$, $P = 0.004$), which did not differ from each other ($t = 1.05$, $P = 0.341$). There was no difference, however, in the "appropriateness" or "certainty" of the explanations given to the three animation types ($F(2,10) = 0.49$, $P = 0.628$ and $F(2, 10) = 3.33$, $P = 0.078$, respectively). Absence or presence of cueing revealed neither a main effect nor interaction with the animation type in any of the four scores.

Regional Cerebral Blood Flow: Subtraction Analysis

There were no significant differences between cued and uncued presentations, nor were there any order effects, or any significant interactions. Data for cued and uncued sequences were therefore combined. There were significant differences between the three types of animation. ToM animations elicited more activity than Random animations in four regions: temporalparietal junction (at the end of the superior temporal sulcus), basal temporal region (fusiform gyrus and temporal poles, immediately adjacent to the amygdala), extrastriate cortex (occipital gyrus), and medial prefrontal cortex (see Table 12.2). All these differences were observed in both hemispheres, but were more significant in the right hemisphere, except for the medial prefrontal cortex. For all these regions differences occurred between the ToM and the Random condition, with the Goal-directed condition showing intermediate

TABLE 12.1. Verbal Descriptions Given by the Six Subjects for ToM, Goal-Directed, and Random Animations Rated on Four Dimensions

	Total score maximum	ToM mean (s.d.)	Goal-Directed mean (s.d.)	Random mean (s.d.)
Intentionality	20	15.8 (1.5)	9.7 (1.5)	0.7 (1.2)
Appropriateness	12	11.2 (1.6)	10.5 (1.4)	11.2 (1.2)
Certainty	12	10.7 (0.8)	10 (1.9)	11.3 (1.2)
Length	16	12.5 (3)	8.5 (3)	7.7 (3.6)

Note: Differences between the three conditions were significant at $P < 0.01$ for Intentionality. Differences between ToM animations vs GD and R animations were significant at $P < 0.01$ for Length. All other differences were not significant.

TABLE 12.2. Subtraction Analysis: Regions Where ToM Animations Elicited More Activity Than Random Animations

Foci of activation	BA	Coordinates						
		Left (x, y, z)		Z score	P<	Right (x, y, z)		Z score	P<
Temporal-parietal junction								
STS	22/39	−58, −48, 4		4.3	0.06	60, −56, 12		6.2	0.001
Basal temporal								
FuG	37	−38, −44, −22		3.8		36, −56, −20		5.1	0.01
TmP/Am	38	−38, −4, −32		3.2		34, 6, −26		4.0	0.05
Occipital lobe								
OcG	19/18	−30, −94, −12		4.6	0.02	38, −96, −10		5.0	0.01
OcG	19/18	−32, −82, −24		4.1					
Medial prefrontal								
SFG	9	−4, 60, 32		4.1					

Note: The coordinates are given in the stereotactic space of Talairach and Tournoux (1988). Numbers in bold type indicate regions where differences in activity were significant when corrected for multiple comparisons. Numbers in plain type indicate regions where differences in activity were significant at P < 0.0001, uncorrected. Brain regions are identified by name and by putative Brodmann Area (BA) on the basis of the atlas of H. M. Duvernoy (1999) *The Human Brain: Surface, Three-Dimensional Sectional Anatomy with MRL and Blood Supply*. Springer, Wien, New York. STS, superior temporal sulcus; TmP/Am, temporal pole adjacent to amygdala; FuG, fusiform gyrus; OcG, occipital gyrus; SFG, superior frontal gyrus.

activity (see Figure 12.1). Direct comparison of ToM with GD confirmed that the differences apparent in Figure 12.1 were significant in the case of temporoparietal regions and the temporal pole at a level of $P < 0.0001$ uncorrected and for occipital gyrus and fusiform gyrus at $P < 0.01$. Random movement when compared to ToM movement, elicited more activity in one region of

medial occipital cortex ($-2x$, $-94y$, 14z). The locations of the activations are shown superimposed on a standard brain in Figure 12.2.

Regional Cerebral Blood Flow: Correlational Analysis

A further analysis was performed in which Intentionality scores, regardless of condition, were

CASTELLI ET AL.

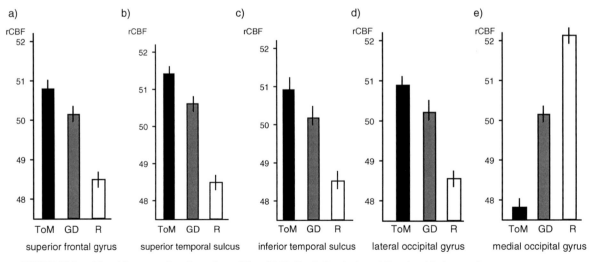

FIGURE 12.1 ■ Blood flow as a function of condition (ToM, Goal-directed, and Random) in key regions.

a)

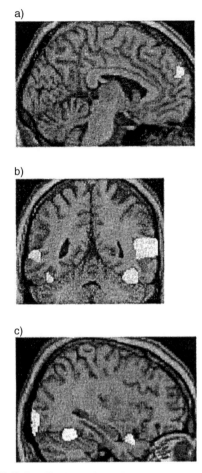

b)

c)

FIGURE 12.2 ■ Regions of significant cerebral blood flow (rCBF) change associated with the perception of ToM animations vs Random animations. (a) Saggital view of activation in superior frontal gyrus. (b) Coronal view of activation in superior temporal sulcus and fusiform gyrus. (c) Saggital view of activation in temporal pole adjacent to the amygdala, fusiform gyrus, and occipital gyrus.

correlated with blood flow response. This analysis was carried out within subjects, thus avoiding the assumption that different individuals use the same range of descriptions. An assumption inherent in this analysis is a linear relationship between intentionality scores and blood flow response. However, further analysis which allowed for a nonlinear relationship did not produce a significant increase in variance accounted for.

The results of the correlational analysis were clearcut. The same four areas were identified as

more active as in the comparison of the three conditions (see Table 12.3). These results were not affected when the length of the descriptions given by the subjects was entered as a confounding covariate.

Discussion

The present experiment took as its starting point the pervasive tendency to perceive intentions in complex movement patterns even when no human forms are depicted. We showed that different types of silent animations selectively evoked descriptions of what the characters were thinking or descriptions of what the characters were doing. The different types of descriptions occurred spontaneously, since alerting subjects in advance to the nature of a particular sequence had no effect.

The main aim of this study was to locate a brain system associated with the attribution of mental states evoked by kinetic stimulus properties. At the same time we wished to relate the findings to earlier studies of mentalizing with different kinds of stimuli. Subtraction analysis (contrasting the ToM sequences with Random or Goal-directed sequences) gave the same picture as correlational analysis (correlating blood flow with degree of mental state description across all animations). The results showed increased activation in four main areas bilaterally. These areas include medial prefrontal cortex, temporoparietal junction (superior temporal sulcus), basal temporal region (fusiform gyrus and temporal poles adjacent to the amygdala), and occipital cortex. All of these areas have been implicated in prior studies of mentalizing. This suggests that a system can be delineated which is to some extent independent of the mode of stimulus input, visual or verbal.

The results of this study do not enable us to identify the functions of these four regions, but clues to their significance can be gained by considering previous studies involving different paradigms.

The Medial Prefrontal Region

An as yet unpublished fMRI study using Heider and Simmel type silent animations has recently been summarized by Klin *et al.* (2000). The results

TABLE 12.3. Correlation Analysis: Regions with Significant Correlations between Blood Flow Response and Intentionality Score

Foci of activation	BA	Coordinates					
		Left (x, y, z)	Z score	P<	Right (x, y, z)	Z score	P<
Temporal-parietal junction							
MTG	21/37	−60, −48, 4	4.6	0.02			
STS	39				62, −58, 12	6.6	0.001
Basal temporal							
FuG	37	−36, −42, −22	3.7		38, −54, −22	4.9	0.01
TmP/Am	34/38				30, 4, −24	2.9	
					22, 0, −16	3.05	0.08
Occipital lobe							
OcG	18				40, −96, −10	4.8	0.01
OcG	17	−16, −100, −8	4.2	0.05			
Medial prefrontal							
SFG	8/9	−6, 58, 32	3.0				

Note: Conventions as in Table 12.2. MTG, middle temporal gyrus; STS, superior temporal sulcus; FuG, inferior temporal gyrus; TmP/Am, temporal pole adjacent to amygdala; OcG, occipital gyrus; SFG, superior frontal gyrus.

appear to be highly consistent with our findings. In particular, these authors mention strong activation in medial prefrontal cortex. The medial prefrontal region activated during the attribution of mental states to animated triangles has also been shown to be activated by other stimuli evoking attribution of beliefs and intentions. These studies are summarized in Table 12.4.

For example, Goel *et al.* (1998) found left medial prefrontal gyrus activation associated with reasoning about other people's thoughts regarding a novel object. Fletcher *et al.*'s (1995) story comprehension task, requiring inferences about a character's intentions, showed peak activation in a dorsal region of medial frontal cortex. This region was not activated in individuals with Asperger syndrome, who show delays and deficits in Theory of Mind (Happé *et al.*, 1996). Gallagher *et al.* (2000) have compared the same story task with a nonverbal comprehension task, using static single frame cartoons. They found a convergence between activations in response to verbal and visual stimuli that prompt mental state attribution (reading a text and viewing a cartoon, respectively), with bilateral activation in a ventral area of the medial prefrontal cortex.

In addition, medial prefrontal areas have been shown to be activated during a rather different task that may, nonetheless, require attribution of mental states. In a task of metaphor comprehension, which, according to some theorists (Sperber and Wilson, 1986; Happé, 1993), requires recognition of the speaker's intentions, Bottini *et al.* (1994) found activation in several loci, including left rostral anterior cingulate cortex, very close to the area implicated in the studies of mentalizing mentioned above. It appears, therefore, that a number of very different mentalizing tasks across several modalities (e.g., verbal, nonverbal) and with differing stimulus qualities (e.g., static, moving), activate regions of medial frontal cortex (see Table 12.4 for coordinates). Prefrontal cortex is implicated in a number of cognitive processes that might have a role in mentalizing tasks such as working memory and retrieval from episodic memory. However, these processes usually engage lateral regions of prefrontal cortex rather than medial regions as observed in the present experiment (Grady, 1999).

Studies of *self-monitoring* have also shown increased activity in areas including medial prefrontal and cingulate cortex. This suggests that when subjects have to reflect on their *own* mental states, they may use neural pathways similar to those underlying attribution of mental states to others. For example, subjects required to monitor their intended speech, in order to judge whether distorted feedback was their own or another

TABLE 12.4. Coordinates for Activation of Medial Frontal Regions in Present and Related Studies

Task	Cognitive process	Study	Coordinates Left (x, y, z)	Right (x, y, z)
Observing complex intentional movement (vs random movement)	Mental state attribution	Present study	−4, 60, 32	
Judge others' knowledge	Mental state attribution	Goel et al. (1998)	−12, 38, 32	
Story comprehension	Mental state attribution	Fletcher et al. (1995)	−12, 42, 40	
Story comprehension (Asperger syndromes)	Mental state attribution	Happé et al. (1996)	−12, 36, 36	
Story and cartoon comprehension	Mental state attribution	Gallagher et al. (2000)	−10, 48, 12	8, 22, 46
Metaphor comprehension	Attribution of speaker's communicative intention	Bottini et al. (1994)	−2, 42, 8	
Intended speech monitoring	Monitoring own mental states	McGuire et al. (1996a)	−2, 36, 36 −10, 32, 24	2, 52, −4
Self-generated thoughts	Monitoring own mental states	McGuire et al. (1996b)	−8, 38, 24 0, 38, 36	
Perceiving pain	Monitoring own mental states	Rainville et al. (1997)		3, 20, 30
Perceiving tickle	Monitoring own mental states	Blakemore et al. (1998)		2, 42, 6
Reporting emotions	Monitoring own mental states	Lane et al. (1997)		0, 50, 16
Intended response monitoring	Monitoring own mental states	Carter et al. (1998)		4, 25, 43
Observing human body movement	Perception of biological motion	Bonda et al. (1996)	−7, 58, 26	

person's voice (McGuire et al., 1996a), showed activation of bilateral medial frontal cortex and anterior cingulate gyrus/medial prefrontal cortex as well as temporoparietal junction bilaterally. The prefrontal region was also activated in a study where subjects reported self-generated thoughts independent from stimuli in the immediate environment (McGuire et al., 1996b). A quite different type of self-monitoring task investigated the neural substrates of perceived pain (Rainville et al., 1997). The anterior cingulate cortex showed increased activity when subjects perceived (under hypnosis) the increasing unpleasantness of hot water on their hand. Blakemore et al. (1998) found anterior cingulate activity associated with reporting a tickling sensation from self-produced tactile stimulation. Activity in anterior cingulate, extending into the medial prefrontal region, was also observed when subjects reported their own emotional responses to pleasant, unpleasant and neutral pictures (Lane et al., 1997).

A more complex self-monitoring task elicited activity in anterior cingulate cortex when subjects were required to choose between competing responses (Carter et al., 1998). Taken together, these results seem to indicate that online monitoring of inner states—own or others'—may engage the anterior cingulate cortex and neighbouring medial frontal regions, regardless of the specific source of information.

The medial frontal region activated by our ToM animations also overlaps with regions activated by point-light displays of biological motion. Bonda et al. (1996) used two biological movement conditions, a dancing figure (human body movement) and a grasping hand simulating the act of reaching out for a glass and bringing it to the mouth (goal-directed action). The comparison of activation during the two conditions showed that perception of a dancing figure versus a grasping hand elicited a network of activation, including left medial prefrontal cortex, close to that activated by our ToM animations.

Grady (1999) provides an exhaustive list of activations observed in prefrontal cortex classified in terms of putative Brodmann areas. The vast majority of these are lateral. However, some medial activations have been observed in the vicinity of the area reported in the present study. The only study observing a relevant activation in Brodmann area 10 was that of Bottini *et al.* (1994) on metaphor comprehension. Activation in relevant regions of Brodmann area 9 have been observed in motor learning tasks and working memory tasks, but the majority of the activations observed during such tasks are more lateral and more posterior. Activations are also reported in medial Brodmann area 8 for some language tasks and for some object processing tasks, but here again all the activations are more posterior than the one observed in the present study.

In previous studies of mentalizing, the activity in medial frontal cortex lies at the border of anterior cingulate cortex and medial frontal cortex in the paracingulate sulcus (Gallagher *et al.*, 2000). In an exhaustive examination of studies that have activated anterior cingulate cortex, Paus *et al.* (1998) conclude that this region has distinct functions. The posterior part of ACC is primarily engaged by motor tasks while the more anterior portions are particularly engaged when emotions are involved. The areas associated with mentalizing are clearly anterior to the motor region of anterior cingulate cortex.

Temporoparietal Region

Increased activation in the junction between parietal and temporal lobes has been observed using a story comprehension task and static cartoons (Gallagher *et al.*, 2000). Again this area was highly active in response to stimuli that share properties of biological motion. Bonda *et al.* (1996), for example, reported activity in the left caudal-most part of the superior temporal sulcus when viewing grasping hand movement compared to random movement. Puce *et al.* (1998) found increased superior temporal sulcus activation when viewing faces in which eye gaze repeatedly changed direction, and faces in which the mouth opened and closed. Similarly Calvert *et al.* (1997) observed increased activation in a region of the superior

temporal gyrus during silent lip-reading of numbers versus still lips, and Grezes *et al.* (1998) reported activation of the superior/middle temporal region during viewing of meaningful hand gestures with tools and objects compared to stationary hands. Taken together these studies implicate the superior temporal sulcus and adjacent cortex in the perception of a variety of human body movements. This region is anterior and superior to the visual motion area MT/V5 (Puce *et al.*, 1998), indicating that these activations are not attributable to movement *per se*. It is notable, too, that all our animations (including Random) displayed self-propelled movement as might be expected of animate agents. Our triangles, when described as moving purposefully and intentionally, activated the key brain regions that have been activated by viewing biological motion. Human-like face or body characteristics thus do not appear to be necessary to trigger the attribution of mental states. Future investigations are needed to clarify what particular properties of biological motion are functionally associated with temporoparietal activation, and whether distinct regions respond preferentially to specific visual attributes of biological stimuli.

Basal Temporal Cortex

The ToM animations also elicited bilateral activation in the basal temporal region, with peak components in the caudal part of the fusiform gyrus and in the temporal poles adjacent to the amygdala. Baron-Cohen *et al.* (1999) reported increased activation in the amygdala region during a mentalizing task involving judgement of a person's eyes, as well as activation in medial prefrontal cortex and the temporoparietal region. Connections between these areas are known to be strong (Amaral *et al.*, 1992). Temporal pole activation has previously been associated with narratives (Mazoyer *et al.*, 1993; Fletcher *et al.*, 1995) and this fits with the idea that subjects inferred the scripts underlying ToM animations. These animations had certainly more narrative content compared to the other sequences.

The studies of biological movement perception discussed above, also reported peak activations in left fusiform gyrus and left temporal pole in response to observing meaningful hand gestures compared to stationary hands (Grezes *et al.*, 1998). Left fusiform gyrus activation was found during observation of a dancing human figure compared to random movement (Bonda *et al.*, 1996). The ventral temporal area has also been implicated in visual processing of static stimuli: while reading words and naming pictures (e.g., Vandenberghe *et al.*, 1996) and while reading Braille words, versus letter-strings (Buchel *et al.*, 1998). Several imaging studies have reported specific regions of the fusiform gyrus to be more active during face viewing compared to assorted pictures, hands, scrambled faces, and houses (e.g., Kanwisher *et al.*, 1997), and more active during face than letter-string and texture perception (e.g., Puce *et al.*, 1996). Gorno-Tempini *et al.* (1998) reported increased activity in bilateral temporal poles associated with famous and non-famous face and proper name processing. Activity in bilateral fusiform gyri was increased while processing faces relative to names and scrambled faces. Thus different areas of the fusiform gyrus appear to be specialised for recognition of different kinds of objects, including animate agents.

Occipital Cortex

In the present study, the ToM animations (relative to Random) elicited increased bilateral occipital activation in a lateral area, as was also found in Gallagher *et al.*'s (2000) study using a mentalizing task involving static cartoons. In contrast, the reverse comparison (Random versus ToM) activated a medial region of occipital cortex. This result indicates a task specific effect, not found in other studies of mentalizing, that deserves further exploration. These areas were implicated in recent studies of global and local processing of complex visual stimuli (Fink *et al.*, 1997). In the Fink *et al.* study (1997a) subjects were presented with large letters made out of small letters, and required to switch attention between global and local perceptual levels. Attentional modulation between local and global processing was associated with differential activity in prestriate cortex along the mediolateral axis. Local processing elicited increased left lateral activation, whereas global processing elicited increased right medial activation. This distinction between lateral and medial occipital regions was replicated in a second study using

objects rather than letters (Fink *et al.*, 1997b): local processing elicited increased lateral activation, while global processing elicited increased medial activation. It is notable that the comparisons between our ToM and Random animations showed similar differential activations: lateral during ToM stimuli, and medial during Random stimuli. An important difference between the method used in the present study and in Fink *et al.*'s studies is that the latter reported activations associated with global and local processing resulting from a "top-down" (endogenous) process. Subjects were specifically instructed to attend to the stimuli at either the global or the local level, whereas in our study subjects were not instructed how to view the stimuli. It makes some intuitive sense, however, that participants may have attended to global patterns of movement in the, effectively meaningless, Random condition (floating, bouncing), and paid more attention to the specifics of movement, interaction, and character details (e.g., which way a triangle is pointing) in the ToM scenarios. Taken together, these studies suggest that occipital sites may be implicated in the perception of movement patterns that engage attention at different (local-global) levels relevant to the attribution of animacy and intention. Although this speculation is unsupported with regard to the present animations, it is amenable to empirical testing.

Of necessity, the movements in the ToM animations were more complex in terms of greater variation of speed and direction of movement. It may be this greater complexity that results in increased activity in extrastriate regions. Thus, it remains possible that the pattern of activation we attribute to mentalising reflects in part extraneous tasks differences in, for example, psychophysical properties of the stimuli or resulting eye-movement differences. Future tests in which psychophysical properties are systematically varied, are clearly needed.

In conclusion, the present study has shown that abstract movement patterns activate regions previously associated with mentalizing in stories and static pictures. Our ToM animations revealed increased activation in a network of brain regions, including the medial prefrontal cortex, the temporal pole adjacent to the amygdala region and the temporoparietal junction. All these regions have been repeatedly implicated in previous studies of mental state attribution and might reflect different components of this process. Two particularly important components, paracingulate sulcus and temporoparietal junction, show overlap with previous mentalizing studies as well as studies of self-monitoring and perception of biological motion. We tentatively suggest that the ability to make inferences about other people's mental states evolved from the ability to make inferences about other creatures' actions and movements. This fits with the observation that we commonly infer intentions on the basis of observed action outcomes. The activity of the prefrontal cortex and temporoparietal junction in our study is combined with activity in a ventral visual pathway, from the extrastriate cortex to the inferior and middle temporal gyri. Thus the regions activated by viewing artfully animated triangles appear to reveal a network for processing visual-kinetic information about intention in action.

Appendix 1

Instructions Given to Participants

The aim of this experiment is to understand which parts of your brain are active while watching a short animated film sequence.

All you have to do is relax, and watch the animations shown on the monitor in front of you. Each animation lasts approximately 40 seconds. The sequences are similar to one another (two triangular shapes moving about) but different in their content. The triangles act as characters performing different movements, for example, dancing, drifting or courting each other.

There are different types of content: In some animations the behaviour of both triangles will appear disconnected from each other. They just move about, with random movement.

By contrast, other animations will show the two triangles moving about doing something together, interacting. Their actions are somehow connected to each other, for example, they are imitating each other, or one is feeding the other.

Still other animations show the two triangles doing something more complex together, as if they are taking into account their reciprocal feelings and thoughts. By just watching them you will probably imagine they are interacting, for example, courting each other.

In this experiment there is no "right" or "wrong" answer. Sometimes I will tell you in advance what kind of animation you are going to see, for example, a random movement, a simple interaction or an interaction involving thoughts and feelings. While you are watching the animations, be relaxed, and … enjoy them! After each cartoon is over, I will ask you what you think the triangles were doing, whether they were randomly moving about, or whether they were doing something more specific.

Appendix 2

Scoring Criteria and Examples for Verbal Descriptions of Animations

Score (0–5) for Intentionality:

0 = action, nondeliberate
(e.g., "Bouncing," "Moving around," "Rotating")
1 = deliberate action with no other
(e.g., "Ice-skating")
2 = deliberate action with another
(e.g., "Blue and red are fighting," "Parent is followed by child")
3 = deliberate action in response to other's action
(e.g., "Big is chasing little," "Red is allowing the Blue to get close to him," "Big is guarding little who was trying to escape")
4 = deliberate action in response to other's mental state
(e.g., "The little one is mocking the big one," "Two people are arguing," "A parent is encouraging a child to go outside")
5 = deliberate action with goal of affecting other's mental state
(e.g., "The blue triangle wanted to surprise the red one," "Child pretending not to be doing anything")

Score (0–3) for Appropriateness:

0 = no answer, "I don't know"
1 = inappropriate answer: reference to the wrong type of interaction between triangles

2 = partially correct answer: reference to correct type of interaction but confused overall description

3 = appropriate, clear answer

Score (0–3) for Certainty (Based on Voice Tone):

0 = long hesitation or silence

1 = hesitation, few words, sentences unfinished, need to be prompted to say more

2 = hesitation between words, alternative answers

3 = no hesitation at all, quick answer, description correctly reflects the script underlying the animation

Score (0–4) for Length:

0 = no response

1 = one clause

2 = two clauses

3 = four clauses

4 = more than four clauses

Appendix 3

The stills in Figure 12.3 illustrate a "Theory of Mind" animation. The animation was designed following a script in which Big Triangle is coaxing the reluctant Little Triangle to come out of an enclosure. Subjects were presented with the animations

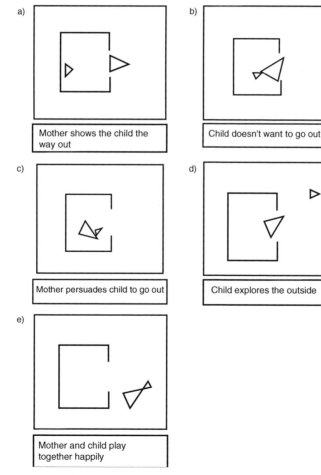

a) Mother shows the child the way out

b) Child doesn't want to go out

c) Mother persuades child to go out

d) Child explores the outside

e) Mother and child play together happily

FIGURE 12.3

without any suggestion relative to a story or characters' roles. The captions have been added here for clarification.

Acknowledgments

Support from The Wellcome Trust and the MRC is gratefully acknowledged. F. Castelli is supported by the European TMR Marie Curie Research Training Grant ERBFMBICT972667.

REFERENCES

Abell, F., Happé, F., and Frith, U. 2000. Do triangles play tricks? Attribution of mental states to animated shapes in normal and abnormal development. *J. Cogn. Dev.*, 15:1–20.

Amaral, D., Price, J. L., Pitkanen, A., and Carmichael, S. T. 1992. Anatomical organisation of the primate amygdaloid cortex. In *The Amygdala: Neurobiological Aspects of Emotion, Memory and Mental Dysfunction* (J. Aggleton, Ed.), pp. 1–66. Wiley, NY.

Baron-Cohen, S., Leslie, A. M., and Frith, U. 1985. Does the autistic child have a "theory of mind?" *Cognition* 21:37–46.

Baron-Cohen, S. 1995. *Mindblindness: An Essay on Autism and Theory of Mind.* MIT Press, Cambridge, MA.

Baron-Cohen, S., Ring, H., Moriarty, J., and Schmitz, B. 1994. Recognition of mental state terms: Clinical findings in children with autism and a functional neuro-imaging study of normal adults. *Br. J. Psychiatry* 165:640–649.

Baron-Cohen, S., Ring, H., Williams, S., Weelwright, S., Bullmore, E., Brammer, M., and Andrew, C. 1999. Social intelligence in the normal and autistic brain: An fMRI study. *Eur. J. Psychiatry* 11:1891–1898.

Baron-Cohen, S., Tager-Flusberg, H., and Cohen, D.J. (Eds.) 2000. *Understanding Other Minds: Perspectives from Autism*, 2nd ed. Oxford Univ. Press, Oxford.

Berry, D. S., Misovich, S. J., Kean, K. J., and Baron, R. M. 1992. Effects of disruption of structure and motion on perceptions of social causality. *Personal. Soc. Psychol. Bull.* 18:237–244.

Berry, D. S., and Springer, K. 1993. Structure, motion, and pre-schoolers' perceptions of social causality. *Ecol. Psychol.* 5:273–283.

Blakemore, S. J., Wolpert, D. M., and Frith, C. D. 1998. Central cancellation of self-produced tickle sensation. *Nat. Neurosci.* 1:635–639.

Bonda, E., Petrides, M., Ostry, D., and Evans, A. 1996. Specific involvement of human parietal systems and the amygdala in the perception of biological motion. *J. Neurosci.* 16:3737–3744.

Bottini, G., Corcoran, R., Sterzi, R., Paulesu, E., Schenone, P., Scarpa, P., Frackowiak, R. S., and Frith, C. D. 1994. The role of the right hemisphere in the interpretation of figurative aspects of language. A positron emission tomography activation study. *Brain* 117:1241–1253.

Buchel, C., Price, C., and Friston, K. 1998. A multimodal language region in the central visual pathway. *Nature* 394:274–277.

Calvert, G. A., Bullmore, E. T., Brammer, M. J., Campbell, R., Williams, S. C., McGuire, P. K., Woodruff, P. W., Iversen, S. D., and David, A. S. 1997. Activation of auditory cortex during silent lipreading. *Science* 276:593–596.

Carruthers, P., and Smith, P. K. (Eds.) 1996. *Theories of Theories of Mind.* Cambridge Univ. Press, Cambridge.

Carter, C. S., Braver, T. S., Barch, D. M., Botvinick, M. M., Noll, D., and Cohen, J. D. 1998. Anterior cingulate cortex, error detection, and the online monitoring of performance. *Science* 280:747–749.

Duvernoy, H. M. 1999. *The Human Brain: Surface, Three-Dimensional Sectional Anatomy with MRI, and Blood Supply.* Springer-Wien, New York.

Fink, G. R., Halligan, P. W., Marshall, J. C., Frith, C. D., Frackowiak, R. S., and Dolan, R. J. 1997. Neural mechanisms involved in the processing of global and local aspects of hierarchically organized visual stimuli. *Brain* 120:1779–1791.

Fletcher, P. C., Happé, F., Frith, U., Baker, S. C., Dolan, R. J., Frackowiak, R. S. J., and Frith, C. D. 1995. Other minds in the brain: A functional imaging study of "theory of mind" in story comprehension. *Cognition* 57:109–128.

Fodor, J. A. 1992. A theory of the child's theory of mind. *Cognition* 44:283–296.

Fox, P. T., and Mintun, M. A. 1989. Non-invasive functional brain mapping by change-distribution analysis of averaged PET images of H_2 ^{15}O issue activity. *J. Nuclear Med.* 30:141–149.

Friston, K. J., Worsley, K., Frackowiak, R. S. J., Mazziotta, J. C., and Evans, A. C. 1994. Assessing the significance of focal activations using their spatial extent. *Hum. Brain Mapp.* 1:214–220.

Friston, K. J., Ashburner, J., Frith, C. D., Poline, J. B., Heather, J. D., and Frackowiak, R. S. J. 1996. Spatial registration and normalization of images. *Hum. Brain Mapp.* 2:165–189.

Friston, K. J., Frith, C. D., Liddle, P. F., Dolan, R. J., Lammertsma, A. A., and Frackowiak, R. S. J. 1990. The relationship between global and local changes in PET scans. *J. Cereb. Blood Flow Metab.* 10:458–466.

Friston, K. J., Holmes, A. P., Worsley, K. J., Poline, J. B., Frith, C. D., and Frackowiak, R. S. J. 1995. Statistical parametric maps in functional imaging: A General Linear approach. *Hum. Brain Mapp.* 2:189–210.

Frith, U., Morton, J., and Leslie, A. M. 1991. The cognitive basis of a biological disorder: autism. *Trends Neurosci.* 14:433–438.

Gallagher, H. L., Happé, F., Brunswick, N., Fletcher, P. C., Frith, U., and Frith, C. D. 2000. Reading the mind in cartoons and stories: An fMRI study of Theory of Mind in verbal and nonverbal tasks. *Neuropsychologia* 38:11–21.

Goel, V., Grafman, J., Tajik, J., Gana, S., and Danto, D. 1998. Modelling other minds. *Brain* 120:1805–1822.

Gorno-Tempini, M. L., Price, C. J., Josephs, O., Vandenberghe, R., Cappa, S. F., Kapur, N., and Frackowiak, R. S. J. 1998. The neural systems sustaining face and proper-name processing. *Brain* 121: 2103–2118.

Grady, C. L. 1999. Neuroimaging and activation of the frontal lobes. In *The Human Frontal Lobes: Functions and Disorders* (B. L. Miller and J. L. Cummings, Eds.), pp. 196–230. Guilford Press, NY.

Grezes, J., Costes, N., and Decety, J. 1998. Top-down effect of strategy on the perception of human biological motion: A PET investigation. *Cogn. Neuropsychol.* 15:553–582.

Happé, F. 1993. Communicative competence and theory of mind in autism: A test of Relevance theory. *Cognition* 48:101–119.

Happé, F., Ehlers, S., Fletcher, P., Frith, U., Johansson, M., Gillberg, C., Dolan, R., Frackowiak, R., and Frith, C. D. 1996. Theory of Mind in the brain: Evidence from a PET scan study of Asperger syndrome. *NeuroReport* 8:197–201.

Happé, F., and Frith, U. 1996. The neuropsychology of autism. *Brain* 119:1377–1400.

Heider, F., and Simmel, M. 1944. An experimental study of apparent behavior. *Am. J. Psychol.* 57:243–259.

Kanwisher, N., McDermott, J., and Chun, M. M. 1997. The fusiform face area: A module in human extrastriate cortex specialized for face perception. *J. Neurosci.* 17:4302–4311.

Klin, A., Schultz, R., and Cohen, D. J. 2000. Theory of Mind in action: Developmental perspectives on social neuroscience. In *Understanding Other Minds. Perspectives from Developmental Cognitive Neuroscience* (S. Baron-Cohen, H. Tager-Flusberg, and D. J. Cohen, Eds.), 2nd ed., pp. 357–388. Oxford Univ. Press, Oxford.

Lane, R. D., Fink, G. R., Chau, P. M., and Dolan, R. J. 1997. Neural activation during selective attention to subjective emotional responses. *Neuroreport* 8:3969–3972.

Leslie, A. M., and Thaiss, L. 1992. Domain specificity in conceptual development: Neuropsychological evidence from autism. *Cognition* 43:225–251.

Mazoyer, B. M., Tzourio, N., Frak, V., Syrota, A., Murayama, N., Levrier, O., Salamon, G., Dehaene, S., Cohen, L., and Mehler, J. 1993. The cortical representation of speech. *J. Cogn. Neurosci.* 5:467–479.

McGuire, P. K., Silbersweig, D. A., and Frith, C. D. 1996a. Functional neuroanatomy of verbal self-monitoring. *Brain* 119:907–917.

McGuire, P. K., Paulesu, E., Frackowiak, R. S., and Frith, C. D. 1996b. Brain activity during stimulus independent thought. *Neuroreport* 7:2095–2099.

Nobre, A. C., Allison, T., and McCarthy, G. 1994. Word recognition in the human inferior temporal lobe. *Nature* 372:260–263.

Paus, T., Koski, L., Caramanos, Z., and Westbury, C. 1998. Regional differences in the effects of task difficulty and motor output on blood flow response in the human anterior cingulate cortex. *NeuroReport* 9:35–45.

Price, C. J., Moore, C. J., Humphreys, G. W., and Wise, R. J. S. 1997. Segregating semantic from phonological processes during reading. *J. Cogn. Neurosci.* 9:727–733.

Puce, A., Allison, T., Asgari, M., Gore, J. C., and McCarthy, G. 1996. Differential sensitivity of human visual cortex to faces, letter strings, and textures: A functional magnetic resonance imaging study. *J. Neurosci.* 16:5205–5215.

Puce, A., Allison, T., Bentin, S., Gore, J. C., and McCarthy, G. 1998. Temporal cortex activation in humans viewing eye and mouth movements. *J. Neurosci.* 18:2188–2199.

Rainville, P., Duncan, G. H., Price, D. D., Carrier, B., and Bushnell, M. C. 1997. Pain affect encoded in human anterior cingulate but not somatosensory cortex. *Science* 277: 968–971.

Scholl, B. J., and Leslie, A. M. 1999. Modularity, development and "theory of mind." *Mind Lang.* 14:131–153.

Sperber, D., and Wilson, D. 1986. *Relevance: Communication and Cognition*. Blackwell, Oxford.

Talairach, J., and Tournoux, P. 1988. *A Co-planar Stereotaxic Atlas of a Human Brain*. Thieme-Verlag, Stuttgart.

Townsend, D. W., Geissbuller, A., Defrise, M., Hoffman, E. J., Spinks, T. J., Bailey, D. L. *et al.* 1991. Fully three-dimensional reconstruction for a PET camera with retractable septa. *IEEE Trans. Med. Eng.* 10:505–512.

Vandenberghe, R., Price, C., Wise R., Josephs, O., and Frackowiak, R. S. J. 1996. Functional anatomy of a common semantic system for words and pictures. *Nature* 383: 254–256.

READING 13

People Thinking about Thinking People: The Role of the Temporo-Parietal Junction in "Theory of Mind"

R. Saxe[a] and N. Kanwisher[a,b]

Humans powerfully and flexibly interpret the behaviour of other people based on an understanding of their minds: that is, we use a "theory of mind." In this study we distinguish theory of mind, which represents another person's mental states, from a representation of the simple presence of another person per se. The studies reported here establish for the first time that a region in the human temporo-parietal junction (here called the TPJ-M) is involved specifically in reasoning about the contents of another person's mind. First, the TPJ-M was doubly dissociated from the nearby extrastriate body area (EBA; Downing et al., 2001). Second, the TPJ-M does not respond to false representations in non-social control stories. Third, the BOLD response in the TPJ-M bilaterally was higher when subjects read stories about a character's mental states, compared with stories that described people in physical detail, which did not differ from stories about nonhuman objects. Thus, the role of the TPJ-M in understanding other people appears to be specific to reasoning about the content of mental states.

Keywords: fMRI; Social cognitive neuroscience; False belief; Mentalising; Superior temporal sulcus; EBA.

The remarkable human facility with social cognition depends on a fundamental ability to reason about other people. Specifically, we predict and interpret the behaviour of people based on an understanding of their minds: that is, we use a "theory of mind."[1] In this study we show that a

[a]Department of Brain and Cognitive Sciences, Massachusetts Institute of Technology, Cambridge, MA, USA
[b]McGovern Institute for Brain Research, Massachusetts Institute of Technology, Cambridge, MA, USA

[1]The term "theory of mind" has a more restricted sense, referring to the suggestion that the structure of knowledge in the mind is analogous to a scientific theory (e.g., Carey, 1985; Wellman and Gelman, 1992). For discussions about the so-called theory-theory, see Carruthers and Smith, 1996, and Malle et al., 2001. In this study, we use the term theory of mind in a broader sense, to refer to any reasoning about another person's representational mental states (also called "belief-desire psychology," e.g., Bartsch and Wellman, 1995).

region of human temporo-parietal junction is selectively involved in reasoning about the contents of other people's minds.

Brain regions near the temporo-parietal junction (TPJ) have been implicated in a broad range of social cognition tasks (Allison et al., 2000; Gallagher and Frith, 2003; Greene and Haidt, 2003). Regions near the TPJ have preferential responses to human faces (e.g., Hoffman and Haxby, 2000), bodies (e.g., Downing et al., 2001) and biological motion (e.g., Grossman et al., 2000). There is also some evidence that regions within human TPJ are involved in theory of mind (ToM). A number of studies have reported increased responses in the TPJ when subjects read verbal stories or see pictorial cartoons that require inferences about a character's (false) beliefs, compared with physical control stimuli (Fletcher et al. 1995; Brunet et al. 2000; Gallagher et al. 2000; Castelli et al. 2000; Vogeley et al. 2001. A number of other brain regions have also been implicated in theory of mind; see reviews by Gallagher and Frith, 2003, and Greene and Haidt, 2003).

What is the role of the TPJ in these tasks? ToM reasoning depends upon at least two kinds of representation: a representation of another person per se and a representation of that other person's mental states (see Leslie, 1999). While a representation of a person per se is a likely prerequisite for ToM, achieving a representation of others' mental states is the core responsibility of a ToM. Some authors suggest that the TPJ is involved only in the preliminary stages of social cognition that "aid" ToM, not in ToM reasoning itself (e.g., Gallagher and Frith, 2003). We provide here evidence against this suggestion, and argue on the contrary that a region of the TPJ is selectively involved in representation of other peoples' mental states.

Neuroimaging studies have followed developmental psychology in using "false belief" stories as the prototypical problem for ToM reasoning (Fletcher et al., 1995; Gallagher et al., 2000; see also Vogeley et al., 2001). In these scenarios, a character's action is based on the character's false belief (Wimmer and Perner, 1983). False beliefs provide a useful behavioural test of a ToM, because when the belief is false, the action predicted by the belief is different from the action that would be predicted by the true state of affairs (Dennett, 1978). Note, though, that everyday reasoning about other minds, by adults and children, depends on attributions of mostly true beliefs (e.g., Dennett, 1996; Bartsch and Wellman, 1995).

Previous investigations of the neural correlates of ToM (Fletcher et al., 1995; Gallagher et al., 2000) have compared false belief ("theory of mind") stories with two control conditions: "non-theory of mind stories," which describe actions based on the character's true beliefs, and "control" stories, consisting of unrelated sentences. These authors found that the TPJ response was high during theory of mind stories, but was also high during non-theory of mind stories. They concluded (see also Gallagher and Frith, 2003) that the TPJ is not selectively involved in ToM. This conclusion does not follow. Because the non-theory of mind stories invite inferences about the character's (true) beliefs, a region involved in reasoning about other minds should show a high response to these stories, as well as to the so-called theory of mind stories. (For an argument against the use of unrelated sentences as the baseline condition, see Ferstl and von Cramon, 2002.)

We propose two basic tests for a region selectively involved in ToM reasoning. First, it must show increased response to tasks/stimuli that invite ToM reasoning (about true or false beliefs) compared with logically similar non-social controls. Second, the region must respond not just when a person is present in the stimulus, but specifically when subjects reason about the person's mental states. Below, we provide evidence that a subregion of the TPJ, here called the TPJ-M, passes both these criteria for a selective role in ToM.

Experiment 1

We devised a new version of the false belief stories task (Fletcher et al., 1995) to compare reasoning about true and false beliefs to reasoning about non-social control situations. ToM stories described a character's action caused by his/her false belief. Descriptions of human actions required analysis of mental causes, in the absence of false beliefs. We compared these conditions to two non-social control conditions, (1) mechanical inference control stories, which required the subject to infer a hidden physical (as opposed to mental) process, such as melting or rusting (for examples, see Appendix 1), and (2) descriptions of nonhuman objects.

Unlike previous studies, we did not cue or instruct subjects to attend specifically to mental states. With this design we were able to look for regions of cortex in individual subjects that are selectively and spontaneously involved in understanding the mental (as opposed to physical) causes of events.

To test whether the response to ToM stories was a response to the presence of a person in the stimulus, we presented still photographs of people, and nonhuman objects. Downing et al. (2001) reported a bilateral region near the posterior superior temporal cortex that responds preferentially to the visual appearance of human bodies, compared with a range of control objects (the extrastriate body area, EBA). We tested directly the functional and anatomical relationship between the EBA and the (proposed) TPJ-M.

Methods

Twenty-five healthy right-handed adults (12 women) volunteered or participated for payment. All subjects had normal or corrected-to-normal vision and gave informed consent to participate in the study.

Subjects were scanned in the Siemens 1.5- (9 subjects) and 3.0-T (16 subjects) scanners at the MGH-NMR center in Charlestown, MA, using a head coil. Standard echoplanar imaging procedures were used [TR = 2 s, TE = 40 (3 T) or 30 (1.5 T) ms, flip angle 90°]. Twenty 5-mm-thick near-coronal slices (parallel to the brainstem) covered the occipital lobe and the posterior portion of the temporal and parietal lobes.

Stimuli consisted of short center-justified stories, presented in 24-point white text on a black background (average number of words = 36).

Stories were constructed to fit four categories: false belief, mechanical inference, human action, and nonhuman descriptions (Appendix 1). Each story was presented for 9500 ms, followed by a 500-ms interstimulus interval. Each scan lasted 260 s: four 40-s epochs, each containing four stories (one from each condition), and 20 s of fixation between epochs. The order of conditions was counterbalanced within and across runs. Subjects were asked to press a button to indicate when they had finished reading each story. Subjects read a total of 8 (4 subjects) or 12 (21 subjects) stories per condition.

Fourteen of the subjects from Experiment 1 (7 women) were also scanned on an EBA localizer in the same scan session, all at 3.0 T. Stimuli consisted of 20 grayscale photographs of whole human bodies (including faces) in a range of postures, standing and sitting, and 20 photographs of easily recognizable inanimate objects (e.g., car, drum, tulip). (Two other conditions, cropped faces and scrambled objects, were included in the scan but were not analyzed here.)

Image presentation followed the blocked design described in Tong et al. (2000; Experiment 1) except that images were presented at a rate of one every 800 ms (stimulus duration = 500 ms, interstimulus interval = 300 ms), and each scan lasted 336 s. Subjects performed a one-back matching task (Tong et al., 2000).

MRI data were analyzed using SPM 99, FSfast, and in-house software.

Results

Average reading times for theory of mind and mechanical inference stories did not differ significantly (ToM = 6.4 s, MI = 6.5 s, $P > 0.2$).

Random effects analyses of 25 subjects revealed five loci of greater activation during the theory of mind compared with mechanical inference stories ($P < 0.05$ corrected for multiple spatial hypotheses): left and right TPJ-M, left and right anterior superior temporal sulcus (aSTS), and precuneus (Table 13.1, Figure 13.1). [Consistent with many previous studies (e.g., Gusnard and Raichle, 2001; Raichle et al., 2000) the precuneus was deactivated (BOLD signal less than

TABLE 13.1. Experiment 1[a]

Region	MNI coordinate (max voxel)	Z	No. of voxels (P < 0.05, corrected)
LTPJ-M	[−54 −60 21]	5.88	63
LaSTS	[−57 −27 −12]	5.40	55
Prec	[−9 −51 33]	5.20	41
R TPJ-M	[51 −54 27]	5.10	10
R aSTS	[66 −18 −15]	4.91	2

[a]Five regions showed increased signal during theory of mind, compared with mechanical inference, stories (random effects, $n = 25$, $P < 0.05$): left and right temporo-parietal junction (TPJ-M), left and right anterior superior temporal sulcus (aSTS), and precuneus (Prec). All coordinates are according to the Montreal Neurological Institute standard brain.

fixation baseline) during all of our story conditions. The ToM stories deactivated the precuneus less than mechanical inference stories. It was therefore unclear whether this effect should be considered a response to ToM or to mechanical inference stories, and the precuneus response was not analyzed further.]

The same pattern of results was apparent in individual subjects (fixed effects $P < 0.0001$, uncorrected for all results reported here). Voxels more responsive during ToM than mechanical inference stories were observed at the TPJ in 22 of 25 subjects (bilaterally in 14, left in 5, and right in 3 subjects). The aSTS activation was significant at this level in 10 of 25 subjects. Because the TPJ-M was most consistent across subjects and was the focus of our prior hypotheses, we concentrated on this region in the subsequent analyses.

We defined TPJ-M regions of interest (ROI) in the left and right TPJ in each individual subject as contiguous voxels in each hemisphere that were more active ($P < 0.0001$) during false belief than mechanical inference stories. The TPJ-M bilaterally generalized beyond false beliefs, responding significantly more to human action (HA) stories than to nonhuman descriptions [N-H D; paired samples t tests, right: HA average percent signal change from fixation (PSC): 0.22, N-H D average

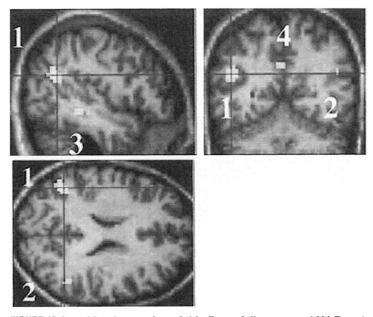

FIGURE 13.1. ■ (*A color version of this figure follows page 146.*) Experiment 1. Random effects analysis, $P < 0.05$, corrected, $n = 25$. Theory of mind > mechanical inference stories. Crosshair marks the most significant voxel in the left TPJ (1). Also visible are activations in right TPJ (2), left aSTS (3), and precuneus (4). TPJ, temporo-parietal junction; aSTS, anterior superior temporal sulcus.

PSC: 0.02, $P < 0.0001$; left: HA average PSC: 0.35, N-H D average PSC: 0.10, $P < 0.0001$].

In the 14 subjects who also had an EBA localizer scan, EBA ROIs were defined as the cluster of contiguous voxels in extrastriate cortex (bilaterally in 13 subjects and right-only in 1 subject) that was more active ($P < 0.0001$) during pictures of human bodies than during pictures of nonhuman objects in each individual subject (following Downing et al., 2001). Both right and left EBA ROIs failed to discriminate between any story conditions (paired samples t tests, all $P > 0.4$, all story PSCs below 0.01; Figure 13.2).

TPJ-M response to photographs was lateralized. The left TPJ-M did not discriminate between photographs of people (PSC: −0.04) and of objects (PSC: −0.09, paired samples t test, $P > 0.4$). The right TPJ-M showed a trend toward a greater

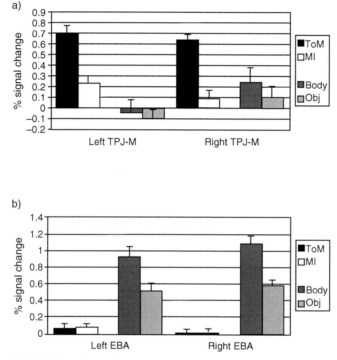

FIGURE 13.2 ■ Experiment 1. Average percent signal change from fixation in (a) left and right TPJ-M and (b) left and right EBA, defined in individual subjects ($n = 14$). The EBA consisted of contiguous voxels in bilateral extrastriate cortex that responded significantly more to pictures of human bodies than pictures of nonhuman objects ($P < 0.0001$, uncorrected). The TPJ-M consisted of contiguous voxels near the temporo-parietal junction that responded significantly more to theory of mind (ToM) stories than to mechanical inference (MI) stories ($P < 0.0001$, uncorrected). (Response magnitudes for the conditions that were used to define the regions of interest are illustrative only.) The EBA did not respond to story stimuli. The right TPJ-M differentiated between pictures of bodies and of objects ($P < 0.05$, paired samples t test), but the left TPJ-M did not. ToM = theory of mind (false belief) stories; MI = mechanical inference stories, Body = photographs of human bodies, Obj = photographs of nonhuman objects; EBA, extrastriate body area.

response to photographs of people (PSC: 0.24) than of objects (PSC: 0.10, paired samples *t* test, $P < 0.10$). A repeated-measures ANOVA of content (person versus object) by stimulus modality (stories versus photograph) by hemisphere (right versus left) revealed a main effect of person > object ($P < 0.001$) and of stories > photographs ($P < 0.05$) modulated by an interaction between stimulus modality and hemisphere (response to photographs only on the right, $P < 0.005$) and a trend toward a three-way interaction (the right TPJ-M response distinguishes photographs of bodies and objects more than the left TPJ-M, $P < 0.1$; Figure 13.2).

Discussion

Experiment 1 thus shows an increased BOLD response in a region of the TPJ bilaterally, here called the TPJ-M, during ToM compared with mechanical inference stories. This activation is robust and reliable across individual subjects. This finding replicates the earlier reports with a new set of stimuli, a less biased task (no cues), and with more stringent statistical tests (both individual subject analyses and random effects group analyses). Our results confirm that the TPJ-M response to verbal descriptions generalizes to human actions based on true beliefs.

Importantly, we distinguished the TPJ-M from its neighbour, the EBA, which did not respond to any verbal story conditions. However, the TPJ-M response to nonverbal social stimuli appeared to be lateralized. The left TPJ-M response was selective for verbal descriptions, while the right TPJ-M activation may generalize to nonverbal stimuli, such as photographs.

Experiment 2

The results of Experiment 1 established that bilateral regions near the TPJ show a greater increase in BOLD signal when subjects reason about others' mental states, than when they reason about nonhuman objects. However, in Experiment 1, stories involving people and mental states were compared with stories that involve neither people

nor mental states. In Experiment 2, we asked which of these two components was responsible for the observed activation. We directly compared the response of the TPJ-M to stories about people that did (desires) or did not (physical people) require inferences based on mental states.

Also, while they were controlled for difficulty and causal structure, the logical structure of the ToM stories used in Experiment 1 (and previous studies) differed systematically from the control stories: only the false belief stories require the notion of a false representation, in this case a false belief. This confounding factor was perceived by developmental psychologists, who invented its solution: "false photograph" stories (Zaitchik, 1990), which require subjects to represent the (false) content of a physical representation such as a photograph or map.

For Experiment 2, we therefore created five new sets of stories (for examples, see Appendix 2): (1) false belief stories, (2) false photograph stories, (3) desires, (4) inanimate descriptions, and (5) physical people. Desire stories described a character's goals or intentions and thus rely on ToM. Nonhuman description stories consisted of short descriptions of nonhuman objects such as plants, cars, or planets. Physical people stories were short descriptions of people from a purely physical perspective: clothing, hair colour, facial markings, and so on.

We predicted that regions specifically involved in ToM should have an equally low response in the nonhuman description and (critically) physical people conditions, and a higher BOLD response in the desire condition. By contrast, regions involved in processing any other representation of other people would show a high BOLD signal for the physical people condition.

Methods

Twenty-one naive right-handed subjects (11 women) were scanned at 1.5 T, using twenty 5-mm-thick axial slices that covered the whole brain. An additional 7 subjects from Experiment 1 (4 women) also participated in part of Experiment 2. All were scanned at 3.0 T using twenty 5-mm-thick near-coronal slices (parallel to the brainstem) covering most of the occipital lobe and the posterior portion of the temporal and parietal lobes.

Story stimuli consisted of 70 stories (12 each of false belief, false photograph, desire, physical description, and nonhuman description, average number of words = 32; see Appendix 2). After each story a two-alternative forced choice "fill-in-the-blank" question was presented for 4 s. The question consisted of a single sentence with a word missing, presented above two alternative completions on the left and right side of the screen. Subjects pressed the left-hand response button if the word on the left completed the sentence to fit the story, and the right-hand button to choose the word on the right. Fifty percent of the false belief, false photograph, and desire story questions probed the character's mental states; the other 50% probed the actual outcome, to prevent formulaic response preparation. Subjects were given three practice trials before going into the scanner: two false belief trials, and one false photograph trial.

Fourteen subjects (including the 7 from Experiment 1) were tested on only false belief and false photograph stories. For these subjects, each run lasted 204 s and consisted of six blocks [each containing 1 story (10 s) and 1 question (4 s)], alternating between the two conditions; there were three blocks per condition per run. The remaining 14 subjects were tested on all five conditions. Each run lasted 272 and consisted of 10 blocks [each containing 1 story (10 s) and 1 question (4 s)]. There were two blocks per condition per run.

Fixations of 12 s were interleaved between blocks. The order of conditions was counterbalanced across runs. Behavioural data were collected during the scan.

Results

Subjects were slower when responding to questions about false photograph than false belief stories (FB: 2.6 vs. FP: 2.8 s, $P < 0.01$), making it unlikely that false belief inferences were simply more difficult.

As predicted, a random effects analysis on the 21 subjects who underwent whole brain scanning revealed regions of increased BOLD signal to false belief compared with false photograph stories ($P < 0.0001$, uncorrected) at the TPJ bilaterally [right: (54 −51 **18**), left: (−48 −63 33)], precuneus/posterior cingulate [(3 −54 30)], right anterior superior temporal sulcus [(54 −18 −15)], and in medial superior frontal gyrus [(6 57 18)] in the frontal pole (Figure 13.2). Medial prefrontal cortex has repeatedly been implicated in ToM processing, both in neuroimaging and in lesion studies (e.g., Rowe et al., 2001; Stuss et al., 2001).

For the 7 subjects who were scanned in both Experiments 1 and 2, two additional analyses were conducted to confirm that the TPJ-M was consistent across experiments. First, in all 7 subjects the TPJ-M defined in Experiment 1 overlapped strikingly with TPJ-M defined by the contrast of false belief (FB) versus false photograph (FP) stories in Experiment 2. Figure 13.3a shows the overlap in a typical individual subject of the TPJ-M defined by these two tasks. Second, this overlap was confirmed with a functional ROI analysis. Voxels near the TPJ are more active during ToM than mechanical inference stories in these individual subjects in Experiment 1 ($P < 0.0001$, uncorrected) were probed for their response during Experiment 2. This independent ROI showed a much greater response to false belief than false photograph stories in Experiment 2 (mean FB PSC = 1.6, mean FP PSC = 0.7, t test $P < 0.02$; Figure 13.3b). The reliability of the TPJ-M across experiments makes it unlikely that the results of Experiment 1 were the result of stimulus confounds or logical differences between conditions.

For the 14 subjects who saw all five conditions, the fMRI data were further analyzed within individually defined functional regions of interest (ROI) that included all voxels that met two criteria, i.e., they were significantly more active in at least half of the individual subjects during false belief than false photograph stories ($P < 0.0001$, uncorrected), and they fell within a sphere of 15-mm radius centered on the most significant voxel of clusters identified in the random effects group analysis ($P < 0.0001$, uncorrected) of the same contrast. Using these criteria, we identified ROIs in the TPJ-M bilaterally and right aSTS.

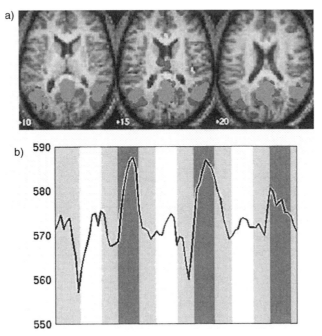

FIGURE 13.3 ■ (*A color version of this figure follows page 146.*) (a) Experiments 1 and 2. Activation overlap within an individual subject showing bilateral temporo-parietal junction (bilateral TPJ) and precuneus regions (fixed effects, $P < 0.001$). Red = theory of mind > mechanical inference (Exp. 1). Blue = false belief > false photo (Exp. 2). Green = both. (b) Single subject time course of response during Experiment 2 to false belief (dark gray) and false photograph (white) stories in the same subject's TPJ-M, independently defined by a greater response to theory of mind than to mechanical inference stories in Experiment 1; $P < 0.0001$, uncorrected. Medium gray indicates fixation. Time course averaged over four runs.

In the TPJ-M and the right aSTS, the BOLD signal change during desire stories was significantly greater than during either physical people or nonhuman description stories (both paired samples t tests $P < 0.05$), which did not differ from each other (Figure 13.4). The left and right TPJ-M did not differ. Thus, these regions are not involved in the detection of any person in verbal stories, but respond selectively to stories in which describe (or imply) characters' mental states. Did any regions show the predicted profile of a response to a person per se? At a lower threshold, a separate whole brain analysis ($P < 0.001$, uncorrected) of physical people > nonhuman descriptions revealed regions of frontal cortex [dorsal

medial prefrontal (-3 57 39), and right lateral frontal cortex (39 15 54)].

Discussion

The results of Experiment 2 confirm that the TPJ-M shows an increased response to stimuli that invite ToM reasoning compared with logically similar nonsocial controls (false photograph stories). Second, the TPJ-M does not show an increased response to the mere presence of a person in the stimulus (physical people stories). The right and left TPJ-M responses to physical people stories did not differ, thus resolving the ambiguity of the apparently lateralized response to photographs of bodies in Experiment 1.

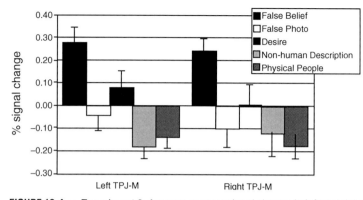

FIGURE 13.4 ■ Experiment 2. Average percent signal change in left and right TPJ-M, defined in individual subjects ($n = 14$) as voxels that respond significantly more to false belief (FB) than to false photo (FP) stories ($P < 0.0001$, uncorrected. Response magnitude for these two conditions is illustrative only, since these data were used to determine the region of interest). In the TPJ-M bilaterally the BOLD response to physical people stories was significantly lower than to desire stories ($P < 0.05$), and not significantly different from nonhuman description stories ($P < 0.1$, repeated-analysis of variance). Response decreases are commonly observed in the TPJ vicinity during demanding nonsocial tasks (Shulman et al., 1997; Gusnard and Raichle, 2001).

General Discussion

In two experiments we found greater BOLD response in a region within the TPJ bilaterally (here called TPJ-M) while subjects read stories that describe or imply a character's goals and beliefs than during stories about nonhuman objects. This pattern is robust across subjects, tasks, and stimuli, and is not merely an effect of the difficulty or logical structure of false belief stories, since the TPJ-M did not respond to the more difficult and logically similar false photograph stories.

We asked whether the TPJ-M represents the simple presence of another person (possibly via detecting a human body and/or biological motion) or is involved specifically in ToM. We found that the TPJ-M was anatomically and functionally distinct from the nearby EBA (Downing et al., 2001), which responded preferentially to the visual appearance of human bodies, suggesting the presence of at least two distinct regions involved in social information processing.

A key innovation of this study over previous studies was the inclusion in Experiment 2 of physical people stories, which described the physical appearance of human bodies. Previous studies (Fletcher et al., 1995; Gallagher et al., 2000) have included "physical" stories describing acting people, which produced greater activation in the TPJ than a scrambled sentence control. Our data show that the TPJ-M response was no greater to stories that described other people in physical detail than that to stories describing the physical details of non-human objects—and was significantly lower than to stories that did invite a mental state interpretation (desire stories).

Could the TPJ-M activation reflect mental imagery of the biological motion or goal-directed action described in the false belief, human action, and desire stories? We think this is unlikely. Saxe, R., Xiao, D.K., Kovacs, G., Perrett, D., and Kanwisher, N. (unpublished data) found that the TPJ-M response to a movie of a walking person was much lower than its response to false belief stories. If the response of the TPJ-M to verbal stories was merely a consequence of subjects' imagining biological motion, we would predict the opposite. Also the TPJ-M was doubly dissociated from its neighbour, the pSTS-VA (visual analysis of action), which responded more to the movies than to verbal stories.

In all, our results show that a region of the TPJ[2] is involved in reasoning about other minds, not just in understanding stories involving people per se (Gallagher and Frith, 2003; p 80). But critically, neighbouring subregions of cortex have different functional profiles, highlighting the necessity of careful within-subject comparisons. The TPJ-M, identified here by responses to (false) belief stories, may play a broad role in social and even moral cognition (Moll et al., 2002; Greene and Haidt, 2003).

Acknowledgments

This work was funded by grants NEI 13455 and NIHM 66696. Our thanks especially to Yuhong Jiang for comments and conversation, and to Ben Balas, Robb Rutledge, Miles Shuman, and Amal Dorai for help with data collection and analysis.

Appendix

Experiment 1

Instructions: "Read each story silently to yourself. Please make sure you understand what is happening; it is more important that you understand the story, than that you go as fast as possible. When you are done reading the story, press the button."

Theory of mind (ToM) sample story

A boy is making a paper mache project for his art class. He spends hours ripping newspaper into even strips. Then he goes out to buy flour. His mother comes home and throws all the newspaper strips away.

Mechanical inference (MI) sample story

A pot of water was left on low heat yesterday in case anybody wanted tea. The pot stayed on the heat all night. Nobody did drink tea, but this morning, the water was gone.

Human action sample story

Jane is walking to work this morning through a very industrial area. In one place the crane is taking up the whole sidewalk. To get to her building, she has to take a detour.

Experiment 2

Instructions: "Please read each story carefully. After each story, you will be given one fill-in-the-blanks question about the story. Underneath will be two words that could fill in the blank. Choose the correct word (to make the sentence true in the story) by pressing the left button to choose the left-hand word, and the right button to choose the right-hand word."

False belief (FB) sample story

John told Emily that he had a Porsche. Actually, his car is a Ford. Emily doesn't know anything about cars though, so she believed John.

—

When Emily sees John's car she thinks it is a
Porsche   Ford

False photograph (FP) sample story

A photograph was taken of an apple hanging on a tree branch. The film took half an hour to develop. In the meantime, a strong wind blew the apple to the ground.

—

The developed photograph shows the apple on the
ground   branch

Desire sample story

For Susie's birthday, her parents decided to have a picnic in the park. They wanted ponies and games

---

[2]What is the relationship between the TPJ-M and attention? Selective attention leads to increases in regions of the TPJ during social perception tasks (e.g., Narumoto et al., 2001; Winston et al., 2002), and to decreases in regions of the TPJ during visual attention tasks (Shulman et al., 1997; Gusnard and Raichle, 2001; Jiang Y., Kanwisher, N., unpublished data). Downar et al. (2001) proposed "a role for the TPJ in detecting behaviourally relevant events in the sensory environment" (p. 1256) that is interfered with by demanding visual attention. One possibility is that the mental states of other people constitute a particular category of such "behaviourally relevant" stimuli. Alternatively, these results may reflect functionally and anatomically distinct subregions within the TPJ. Direct testing of the relationship between the TPJ-M and selective attention is an important avenue for future work.

on the lawn. If it rained, the children would have to play inside.

—

Susie's parents wanted to have her birthday
inside   outside

Physical people sample story

Emily was always the tallest kid in her class. In kindergarten she was already over 4 feet tall. Now that she is in college she is 6´4." She is a head taller than the others.

—

In kindergarten Emily was over
4 ft   6ft
… tall.

Non-human description sample story

Nine planets and their moons, plus various lumps of debris called asteroids and comets, make up the sun's solar system. The earth is one of four rocky planets in the inner solar system.

—

The solar system has
four   nine
… planets.

REFERENCES

Allison, T., Puce, A., et al. 2000. Social perception from visual cues: role of the STS region. Trends Cogn. Sci. 4, 267–278.

Bartsch, K., Wellman, H., 1995. Children Talk about the Mind. Oxford University Press, New York.

Brunet, E., Sarfati, Y., et al., 2000. A PET investigation of the attribution of intentions with a nonverbal task. Neuroimage 11, 157–166.

Carey, S., 1985. Conceptual Change in Childhood. MIT Press, Cambridge, MA.

Carruthers, P., Smith, P., 1996. Theories of Theories of Mind. Cambridge University Press, New York.

Castelli, F., Happe, F., et al., 2000. Movement and mind: a functional imaging study of perception and interpretation of complex intentional movement patterns. Neuroimage 12, 314–325.

Dennett, D., 1978. Beliefs about beliefs. Behav. Brain Sci. 1, 568–570.

Dennett, D., 1996. Kinds of Minds: Toward an Understanding of Consciousness. Basic Books, New York, NY.

Downar, J., Crawley, A.P., et al., 2001. The effect of task relevance on the cortical response to changes in visual and auditory stimuli: an event-related fMRI study. Neuroimage 14, 1256–1267.

Downing, P.E., Jiang, Y., et al., 2001. A cortical area selective for visual processing of the human body. Science 293, 2470–2473.

Ferstl, E.C., von Cramon, D.Y., 2002. What does the fronto-median cortex contribute to language processing: coherence or theory of mind? Neuroimage 17, 1599–1612.

Fletcher, P.C., Happe, F., et al., 1995. Other minds in the brain: a functional imaging study of "theory of mind" in story comprehension. Cognition 57, 109–128.

Frith, C.D., Frith, U., 1999. Interacting minds—a biological basis. Science 286, 1692–1695.

Gallagher, H.L., Frith, C.D., 2003. Functional imaging of "theory of mind." Trends Cogn. Sci. 7, 77–83.

Gallagher, H.L., Happe, F., et al., 2000. Reading the mind in cartoons and stories: an fMRI study of "theory of mind" in verbal and nonverbal tasks. Neuropsychologia 38, 11–21.

Greene, J., Haidt, J., 2003. How (and where) does moral judgement work? Trends Cogn. Sci. 6, 517–523.

Grossman, E., Donnelly, M., et al., 2000. Brain areas involved in perception of biological motion. J. Cogn. Neurosci 12, 711–720.

Gusnard, D.A., Raichle, M.E., 2001. Searching for a baseline: functional imaging and the resting human brain. Nat. Rey. Neurosci. 2, 685–694.

Hoffman, E.A., Haxby, J.V., 2000. Distinct representations of eye gaze and identity in the distributed human neural system for face perception. Nat. Neurosci. 3, 80–84.

Leslie, A., 1999. "Theory of mind" as a mechanism of selective attention, in: Gazzanigal, M. (Ed.), The New Cognitive Neurosciences. MIT Press, Cambridge, MA.

Malle, B.F., Moses, L.J., Baldwin, D.A. (Eds.), 2001. Intentions and Intentionality: foundations of Social Cognition. MIT Press, Cambridge, MA.

Moll, J., et al., 2002. The neural correlates of moral sensitivity: a functional magnetic resonance imaging investigation of basic and moral emotions. J. Neurosci 22, 2730–2736.

Narumoto, J., Okada, T., et al., 2001. Attention to emotion modulates fMRI activity in human right superior temporal sulcus. Brain Res. Cogn. Brain Res. 12, 225–231.

Rowe, A.D., Bullock, P.R., et al., 2001. "Theory of mind" impairments and their relationship to executive functioning following frontal lobe excisions. Brain 124 (Pt 3), 600–616.

Saxe, R., Xiao, D.K., et al., 2003. Distinct representations of bodies, actions and thoughts in posterior superior temporal sulcus, submitted.

Shulman, G.L., Corbetta, M., et al., 1997. Top-down modulation of early sensory cortex. Cereb Cortex 7, 193–206.

Stuss, D.T., Gallup Jr., G.G., et al., 2001. The frontal lobes are necessary for "theory of mind." Brain 124 (Pt 2), 279–286.

Tong, F., Nakayama, N., et al., 2000. Response properties of the human fusiform face area. Cogn. Neuropsychol. 17, 257–279.

Vogeley, K., Bussfeld, P., et al., 2001. Mind reading: neural mechanisms of theory of mind and self-perspective. Neuroimage 14 (1 Pt 1), 170–181.

Wellman, H.M., Gelman, S., 1992. Cognitive development: foundational theories of core domains. Annu. Rev. Psychol. 43, 337–375.

Wimmer, H., Perner, J., 1983. Beliefs about beliefs: representation and constraining function of wrong beliefs in young children's understanding of deception. Cognition 13, 103–128.

Winston, J.S., Strange, B.A., et al., 2002. Automatic and intentional brain responses during evaluation of trustworthiness of faces. Nat. Neurosci. 5, 277–283.

Zaitchik, D., 1990. When representations conflict with reality: the pre-schooler's problem with false beliefs and "false" photographs. Cognition 35, 41–68.

PART 8

Social Perception and Cognition: Multiple Routes

During most of the past century, the nuances of social cognition and social processes, including unconscious processes, were plumbed through the clever experimental designs and measures of verbal reports, judgments, and reaction time. It has also long been recognized that self-reports and overt behavior provide incomplete information on the human mind. Although chronotropic measures provided a means of exploring possible differences in the components of a series of cognitive operations as they unfold over time, they, too, could be insensitive to the extent of parallel processing that might be ongoing. When one adds a desire for parsimony, or an economy of explanation, it is simple to see how theories in social psychology tended to take the form of a series of information processing steps or stages.

The 19th century neurologist John Hughlings Jackson, who cared more about understanding his patients' symptomatologies than parsimony, came to appreciate the redundancy and complexity of the brain and mind. He further suggested that the central nervous system was structured hierarchically such that there was a rerepresentation of functions at multiple levels within this neural hierarchy. Primitive protective responses to aversive stimuli are organized at the level of the spinal cord, as is apparent in flexor (pain) withdrawal reflexes that can be seen even after spinal transection. These primitive protective reactions are expanded and embellished at higher levels of the nervous system. The evolutionary development of higher neural systems, such as the limbic system, endowed organisms with an expanded behavioral repertoire, including escape reactions, aggressive responses, and even the ability to anticipate and avoid aversive encounters. Evolution not only endowed humans with primitive, lower-level adaptive reactions, but also sculpted the remarkable information processing capacities of the highest levels of the brain. The implication is that neurobehavioral mechanisms are not localized to a single level of organization within the brain, but rather are represented at multiple levels of the nervous system. Indeed, at progressively higher (more rostral) levels of organization (spinal, brain stem, limbic, cortical regions) there is a general expansion in the range and relational complexity of contextual controls and in the breadth and flexibility of discriminative and adaptive responses.

In the first reading in this section, Anderson et al. (2003) revisit the neural correlates of face processing, but show that facial displays (neutral, fear, disgust) communicated different emotional circumstances. Displays indicating threats in particular have been suggested to trigger increased vigilance and preparatory responses in the observer largely independent of the observer's awareness. Anderson et al. (2003) employed functional magnetic resonance imaging (fMRI) to examine whether displays of disgust as well as fear would trigger the automatic processing of threat and to examine in more detail the role of the amygdala in the processing of threat. Their results indicated that

under conditions of reduced attention, the amygdala responded to expressions of fear and disgust in a fashion suggesting coarse automatic processing of social signals which may communicate a threat, but under conditions of normal attention amygdala responds specifically to expressions of fear.

The findings of Anderson et al. (2003) are consistent with the suggestion that there are two parallel pathways to the amygdala—one that provides fast but coarse processing and is subcortically mediated, and one that provides slower, more refined processing and is cortically mediated. It further follows from this model that the amygdala should be involved in processing the potential threat whether social judgments are performed explicitly or implicitly, whereas cortical streams of social information processing should be especially likely to emerge when social judgments are performed explicitly. The study by Winston et al. (2002) speaks directly to this question. Participants were told to judge either the trustworthiness of faces they saw (explicit judgment) or the age of the faces they saw. Results of the fMRI scans during the task indicated that activity in the amygdala increased to untrustworthy facial displays whether participants were judging trustworthiness or age. Brain activation in, for instance, the superior temporal sulcus, by contrast, was greater when participants made explicit rather than implicit trustworthiness judgments, and this activation was unrelated to the level of trustworthiness of the facial display. Together these studies suggest that there are multiple processes that may be invoked when processing social signals.

Neural Correlates of the Automatic Processing of Threat Facial Signals

Adam K. Anderson,[1] Kalina Christoff,[1] David Panitz,[1]
Eve De Rosa,[2] and John D.E. Gabrieli[1,3]

The present study examined whether automaticity, defined here as independence from attentional modulation, is a fundamental principle of the neural systems specialized for processing social signals of environmental threat. Attention was focused on either scenes or faces presented in a single overlapping display. Facial expressions were neutral, fearful, or disgusted. Amygdala responses to facial expressions of fear, a signifier of potential physical attack, were not reduced with reduced attention to faces. In contrast, anterior insular responses to facial expressions of disgust, a signifier of potential physical contamination, were reduced with reduced attention. However, reduced attention enhanced the amygdala response to disgust expressions; this enhanced amygdala response to disgust correlated with the magnitude of attentional reduction in the anterior insular response to disgust. These results suggest that automaticity is not fundamental to the processing of all facial signals of threat, but is unique to amygdala processing of fear. Furthermore, amygdala processing of fear was not entirely automatic, coming at the expense of specificity of response. Amygdala processing is thus specific to fear only during attended processing, when cortical processing is undiminished, and more broadly tuned to threat during unattended processing, when cortical processing is diminished.

Keywords: amygdala; insula; fear; disgust; attention; emotion; faces; fMRI.

Departments of Psychology,[1] Psychiatry,[2] and Neuroscience,[3]
Stanford University, Stanford, California 94305.

Introduction

Facial expressions serve as important social signals of imminent environmental conditions. It is now known that distinct expressions signaling environmental threat draw on distinct neural substrates specialized for their evaluation. Patient and neuroimaging studies suggest that the amygdala is critical for evaluating fearful facial expressions (Adolphs et al., 1994; Breiter et al., 1996; Morris et al., 1996; Whalen et al., 1998). Similar evidence indicates that the anterior insula, a region of primary gustatory cortex substantially connected with the amygdala (Mesulam and Mufson, 1982), is specialized for evaluating facial expressions of disgust (Phillips et al., 1997, 1998; Calder et al., 2000). The evidence that expressions of fear, a form of threat related to physical attack (Gray, 1987), and expressions of disgust, a form of threat related to physical contamination and disease (Rozin and Fallon, 1987), draw on specialized brain substrates is one measure of the special informational status the human brain places on social signals of potential environmental threats. Another measure of the special status of social signals of threat is the proposal that their processing occurs automatically, proceeding largely independently of attention (Ohman et al., 2001) and awareness (Esteves et al., 1994). Evidence for such automaticity has been shown by how the amygdala responds to fearful faces during diminished attention (Vuilleumier et al., 2001, 2002) and awareness (Whalen et al., 1998). Amygdala activation to fearful faces has also been shown in patients with visual neglect (Vuilleumier et al., 2002) and in patients with cortical blindness (Morris et al., 2001).

However, it is unknown whether automaticity is unique to amygdala fear processing or whether it is a fundamental principle of neural systems dedicated to threat signals. There is little, if any, evidence about the attentional properties of the neural processing of disgust, or any facial expression other than fear. Furthermore, recent challenges to the preattentive nature of amygdala processing (Pessoa et al., 2002a,b) suggest that the precise nature of automatic processing in the amygdala is unknown. For instance, it has been proposed that fear responses draw on two distinct pathways to the amygdala: one pathway cortically and another subcortically mediated (LeDoux, 1996; Morris et al., 1999, 2001). By circumventing the cortex, the subcortical pathway may be more rapid and automatic, but should be at the expense of a more detailed cortical analysis of the stimulus (Jarrell et al., 1987; LeDoux, 1995). Thus, amygdala automatic processing may be qualitatively distinct from processing under conditions of full awareness, occurring at the expense of its specificity for fear.

To address these issues, the present study used event-related functional magnetic resonance imaging (fMRI) to examine how attention influences amygdala and anterior insular processing of fear and disgust. Manipulations of visual attention result in a pronounced modulation of extrastriate responses (Corbetta et al., 1990; Haxby et al., 1994; Wojciulik et al., 1998; O'Craven et al., 1999). If automaticity, defined here as the lack of reduction in activation with reduced attention, is a fundamental principle of the neural processing of social signals of environmental threat, then lack of attentional modulation should extend to both amygdala processing of fear and anterior insular processing of disgust. Furthermore, if automatic processing is qualitatively similar to processing taking place during full attention, then reduced attention should not influence the response specificity in the amygdala and/or anterior insula.

Materials and Methods

Participants

Informed consent to take part in a study approved by the Stanford University Panel on Human Subjects in Medical Research was obtained from each subject (three men, nine women; mean age, 22.1 years; range, 18–29).

Stimuli

Stimuli consisted of photographs either of fearful, disgusted, or neutral faces superimposed on pictures of places (see Figure 14.1a). For the purposes of decreasing stimulus repetition, which is thought to relate to pronounced amygdala habituation

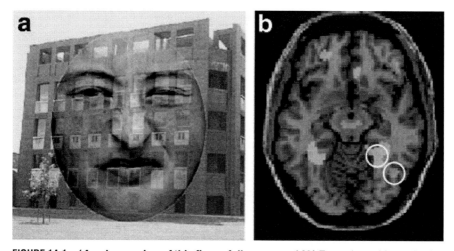

FIGURE 14.1 ■ (*A color version of this figure follows page 146.*) Face-place object selection attention task, *a*, Example stimulus. Observers were presented with color-coded superimposed faces (disgusted, fearful, and neutral expressions in red) and places (inside and outside of buildings in green). Before each test stimulus, observers were presented with a color-coded prompt indicating which task they were to perform on that trial: indicate the gender of the face (attend trials) or indicate the location of the place (unattend trials). *b*, A representative subject demonstrated a greater response when attending to places (in green) in a bilateral region along the collateral sulcus, consistent with the PPA and a greater response when attending to faces (in red) in the right middle fusiform gyrus, consistent with the FFA.

(Breiter et al., 1996), increasing the number of unique facial exemplars was emphasized. Facial expression stimuli were taken from the Facial Affect Series and supplemented by additional appropriately normed exemplars, resulting in three facial expression types for 18 distinct individuals (9 male, 9 female). Place stimuli consisted of photos of 18 interiors and 18 exteriors of buildings. Superimposition was achieved by rendering each of the faces and places semi-transparent. All stimuli were standardized for luminosity, contrast, and transparency. All background place stimuli were 300 × 300 pixels in size (at 72 dpi) with faces presented in an oval aperture ~200 × 250 in size, which occluded gender stereotypic features such as hair and facial shape. Stimuli were created such that face gender, expression, and underlying place (interior and exterior) were completely crossed, yielding 108 independent stimuli. Across the course of scanning, each of these stimuli were presented once during attended and once during unattended conditions for a total of 216 trials. Stimuli were presented using a magnet-compatible back-projector (Resonance Technology, Van Nuys, CA).

Task Design

We used an intermixed trial event-related design. On each trial, participants were first presented with central fixation (1 sec), which was replaced by a color-coded prompt (750 msec) that indicated whether to make a male/female judgment (attend to the face) or an inside/outside judgment (attend to the place) of a subsequently presented stimulus. After 250 msec, the superimposed face/place stimulus was presented for 750 msec. Participants were asked to indicate, as quickly and as accurately as possible, either the gender of the face (attend condition) or to indicate whether the place was the inside or outside of a building (unattend condition). We opted to use such an object attentional selection task to limit the role of eye movements, which would be a larger concern in spatial-selection tasks. To ensure appropriate averaging of the overlapping hemodynamic responses from distinct trial types, trials were presented in a fixed randomized order that counterbalanced trial type history.

After the test scans, participants took part in a fusiform face area (FFA) and parahippocampal place area (PPA) localizer scan. On each trial, subjects were first presented with central fixation (1 sec) and then an image of a neutral face (12 male, 12 female) or a building (1 sec). Images were presented in a fixed random intermixed order and participants were asked to simply indicate whether a picture of a face or a place was presented. All stimuli were distinct from those used in the previous test scans.

Image Acquisition and Analysis

Participants were scanned with a 3 tesla Signa (General Electric, Milwaukee, WI) scanner with a prototype head coil. Foam padding placed around the head was used to minimize movement. Every second we acquired seventeen 4 mm slices ranging from the body of the corpus callosum to the ventral surface of the anterior temporal lobe using a T_2*-weighted spiral pulse sequence (in-plane resolution, 3.755 mm; repetition time, 1000 msec; echo time, 30 msec; 60° flip angle, 24 cm field of view; 64 × 64 matrix acquisition). The intertrial interval (ITI) was 8 sec. Four separate scans collected 1728 frames (288 per condition), with 36 repetitions for each of the six trial types. Two dummy trials were added at the beginning of each session to avoid scanner equilibration effects. The same slice prescription and scanning parameters were used in the subsequent localizer scan, with the exception of an increased ITI of 20 sec. One session collected 960 frames (480 place, 480 face), resulting in 24 repetitions of each trial type. T_1-weighted spin echo images were acquired for all slices that received functional scans as well as an additional T_1-weighted whole-brain anatomy for the purposes of normalization of functional data into common stereotactic space.

Statistical analysis was performed using statistical parametric mapping software (SPM99; Wellcome Department of Cognitive Neurology, London, UK). After image reconstruction, motion estimation, realignment, slice-time correction, normalization, and spatial smoothing (full width at half-maximum, 6 mm) were performed. During normalization, voxels were resampled to 2 × 2 × 4 mm. The presentation of each face/place stimulus was modeled by a canonical hemodynamic response function (hrf). For each individual, contrast images were calculated by applying appropriate weights to the parameter estimates for the regressor of each event type. Group analysis for identification of the amygdala and anterior insular regions of interest (ROIs) was performed on these contrast images, which were submitted to a one-sample t test across the 12 subjects, with subjects entered as a random effect. Group contrast images were overlaid onto the SPM99 high-resolution T_1 individual template image for viewing. Coordinates of activation were converted from Montreal Neurological Institute to Talairach space.

ROI Delineation

The first phase of analysis was to replicate four separate findings for purposes of ROI delineation: (1) amygdala activation to fear faces, (2) anterior insular activation to disgust faces, (3) FFA activation to faces, and (4) PPA activation to places. Accordingly, the ROIs were localized with relatively liberal uncorrected criterion ($p < 0.01$); subsequently, signals from these regions were submitted for examination of the main hypotheses. The amygdala ROI was defined by the contrast of fear relative to neutral faces when subjects were attending to faces (cluster extent threshold, 10 voxels). The anterior insular ROI was defined by disgust relative to neutral faces when subjects were attending to faces (extent threshold, 10 voxels). Post-test localizer data were used to identify the FFA and PPA for each subject (extent threshold, 5 voxels). Each subject's FFA and PPA were defined by a combination of functional and structural features. Right-hemisphere voxels confined to the middle fusi-form gyrus that were more active while viewing faces compared with places were considered to be the FFA. In addition, voxels lateral to the occipital temporal sulcus and confined to the inferior and middle temporal gyri that were more active while viewing faces compared with places were considered to be face-responsive regions within the lateral occipital complex, referred to here as the LOCf. Bilateral voxels confined to the parahippocampal gyrus that were more active while viewing places compared with faces were considered to be the PPA.

ROI Signal Analyses

For each subject, signal change indexed by the fit of canonical hrf was extracted for each of the eight data frames for each of the six trial types averaged across 36 trial repetitions and then submitted to statistical analysis. The α value for analysis of ROI signal was set at $p < 0.01$.

Results

Behavioral Performance

Observers were less accurate in making gender judgments on faces than location judgments on places (87.3 ± 1.1 vs $79.3 \pm 1.4\%$; $F_{(1,11)} = 14.07$; $p < 0.003$). Gender judgments were influenced by emotional expression (neutral, $75.7 \pm 1.7\%$; disgust, $81.9 \pm 2.7\%$; fear, $80.3 \pm 2.3\%$; $F_{(2,22)} = 3.62$; $p < 0.05$). Accuracy in making place judgments was not influenced by the stimulus content of the to-be-ignored faces (neutral, $87.5 \pm 2.2\%$; disgust, $86.6 \pm 1.6\%$; fear, $87.7 \pm 2.2\%$; $F_{(2,22)} = 0.24$; $p > 0.79$). Analysis of response latency revealed no significant difference in the times taken to make face and place judgments (820 ± 49 vs 754 ± 46 msec; $F_{(1,11)} = 2.58$; $p > 0.14$). The response latency for gender judgments was influenced by emotional expression (neutral, 786 ± 81 msec; disgust, 755 ± 69 msec; fear, 811 ± 89 msec; $F_{(2,22)} = 4.46$; $p < 0.03$). The response latency for making place judgments was not influenced by the stimulus content of the to-be-ignored faces (neutral, 732 ± 81 msec; disgust, 727 ± 77 msec; fear, 753 ± 86; $F_{(2,22)} = 1.60$; $p > 0.23$).

Although facial expression did influence gender judgment accuracy and latency, and may have contributed to the magnitude of blood—oxygen level-dependent (BOLD) response when faces were attended, critically, performance on place judgments (when subjects were instructed to ignore faces) did not differ between face types. This suggests that attention was equally divided for unattended neutral, disgust, and fear face trials, so that performance differences did not account for differences in BOLD responses on unattended trials.

Effect of Attention on Extrastriate Responses

Confirming previous results, decreased attention resulted in a substantial reduction in cortical activations to both faces and places. A region functionally defined as more responsive to faces than places in the right middle fusiform gyrus, consistent with the FFA, demonstrated a greater response (average, 4–7 sec from stimulus onset) when subjects were attending to faces and not places ($F_{(1,154)} = 386.69$; $p < 0.0001$) (Figure 14.1b). Conversely, a bilateral region functionally defined as more responsive to places than faces along the collateral sulcus, consistent with the PPA, demonstrated a greater response when subjects were attending to places and not to faces ($F_{(1,154)} = 74.76$; $p < 0.0001$) (Figure 14.1b).

Effect of Attention on Amygdala Response

When subjects were attending to faces, a comparison of fear relative to neutral faces resulted in a discrete activation in the right amygdala (43 voxels, at a peak height x, 22; y, 1; z, -28; in Talairach coordinates, $F_{(1,11)} = 20.52$; $p < 0.0001$) (Figure 14.2a). During attended conditions, the peak response in this functionally defined amygdala ROI was greater for fearful expressions than either disgusted (fear vs disgust, $F_{(1,154)} = 27.93$; $p < 0.0001$) or neutral expressions (fear vs neutral, $F_{(1,154)} = 40.22$; $p < 0.0001$); disgusted and neutral expressions did not differ ($F_{(1,154)} = 1.12$; $p > 0.28$) (Figure 14.2b). Thus, the amygdala response was specific to fear and did not generalize to disgust. The magnitude of the amygdala response to fearful faces was not significantly modulated by attention ($F_{(1,154)} = 0.24$; $p > 0.62$), remaining greater than neutral expressions (fear vs neutral, $F_{(1,154)} = 25.58$; $p < 0.0001$) during inattention.

However, the amygdala demonstrated a surprising increase in response to expressions of disgust during unattended relative to attended conditions ($F_{(1,154)} = 48.67$; $p < 0.0001$) (Figure 14.3). Because of this increased response to disgust, when faces

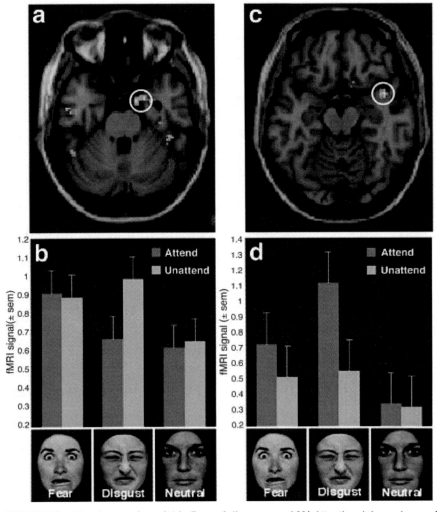

FIGURE 14.2 ■ (*A color version of this figure follows page 146.*) Attentional dependence of amygdala and anterior insular responses to facial expressions. *a*, The amygdala was functionally defined by the group level contrast of fear relative to neutral trials when faces were attended. This resulted in a prominent activation in the right amygdala (at a peak height *x*, 22; *y*,1; *z*,−28; $F_{(1,11)}$ = 20.52; *p* < 0.0001). *b*, Effect of stimulus and attention on amygdala response. Peak amygdala response is displayed for each facial stimulus type during attended (red) and unattended (green) conditions. Attention did not significantly reduce the magnitude of amygdala response to fear, but the enhanced response to disgust during reduced attention suggests attention influenced the specificity of amygdala response. *c*, The insula was functionally defined by contrasting activation on disgust trials compared with neutral trials when faces were attended. This resulted in a prominent activation in the right anterior insula (at a peak height *x*,44; *y*,5; *z*, −14; $F_{(1,11)}$ = 32.72, *p* < 0.0001). *d*, Effect of stimulus and attention on anterior insular response. Peak anterior insular response is displayed for each facial stimulus type during attended (red) and unattended (green) conditions. Reduced attention significantly reduced the magnitude of anterior insular response to disgust.

were unattended, the amygdala response magnitude to fear was no longer significantly greater than that to disgust, with a tendency for a greater response to disgust ($F_{(1,154)}$ = 4.75; p > 0.031). Both fear ($F_{(1,154)}$ = 31.89; p < 0.0001) and disgust ($F_{(1,154)}$ = 54.99; p < 0.0001) resulted in greater responses relative to neutral expressions (Figure 14.2b). Thus, inattention did not significantly reduce the amygdala response to fear faces, but did significantly enhance the amygdala response to disgust faces.

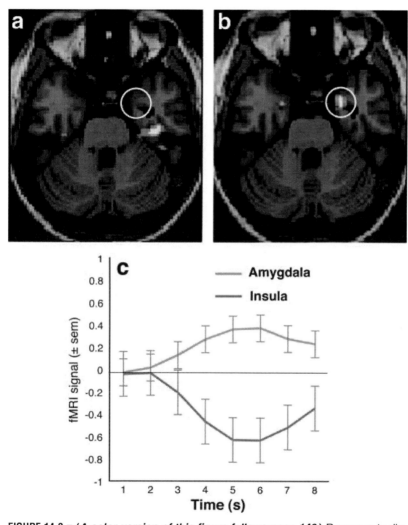

FIGURE 14.3 ■ (*A color version of this figure follows page 146.*) Response to disgust faces when unattended. *a,* Amygdala response to disgust relative to neutral faces when observers were attending to faces. No significant activation was found when faces were attended. *b,* Amygdala response to disgust relative to neutral faces when observers were attending to places. Activation was present when disgust faces were unattended. *c,* Time course of the disgust response difference score (unattended minus attended). A negative deflection of time course represents a decreased response when faces were attended. A positive deflection represents an increased response when faces were unattended. An inverse effect of attention on anterior insula and amygdala response to disgust faces peaked ~6 sec after the stimulus onset.

Effect of Attention on Anterior Insular Response

When subjects were attending to faces, a comparison of disgust relative to neutral faces resulted in activation in the right anterior insula (22 voxels, at peak height x, 44; y, 6; z, -16; $F_{(1,11)} = 32.72$; $p < 0.0001$) (Figure 14.2c). During attended conditions, the peak response in this insular ROI was greater for disgusted expressions than for neutral expressions (disgust vs neutral, $F_{(1,154)} = 117.13$; $p < 0.0001$). Fear responses were also greater than neutral in this region (fear vs neutral, $F_{(1,154)} = 29.04$; $p < 0.0001$), but there remained a greater response to disgusted than to fearful faces ($F_{(1,154)} = 29.53$; $p < 0.0001$). The magnitude of insular response to disgust ($F_{(1,154)} = 61.88$; $p < 0.0001$) and fear ($F_{(1,154)} = 8.64$; $p < 0.004$) were both significantly reduced during unattended compared with attended conditions. During inattention, the magnitude of insular response was no longer greater to disgust than to fear ($F_{(1,154)} = 0.26$; $p > 0.6$), but did remain greater to disgust than neutral ($F_{(1,154)} = 10.58$; $p < 0.002$) (Figure 14.2d). These results indicate that both the magnitude and the specificity of the insular response to disgust were significantly reduced with diminished attention.

In addition to the insula, patient and neuroimaging studies suggest a role of the striatum in evaluating disgust expressions (Sprengelmeyer et al., 1996; Phillips et al., 1997, 1998). When we reduced our statistical and extent thresholds ($p < 0.05$ and 5 voxels), activation in a contiguous bilateral ventral striatal region was greater for disgust than for neutral expressions during attended conditions (peak height on the right at x, 16; y, 18; z, -12; $F_{(1,11)} = 25.91$; $p < 0.0001$; peak height on the left at x, -2; y, 10; z, -8; $F_{(1,11)} = 32.15$; $p < 0.0001$). Like the anterior insular response, inattention resulted in a substantially reduced striatal response to disgust ($F_{(1,154)} = 13.41$; $p < 0.0003$).

Effect of Attention on Cortico-Amygdala Interactions

The inverse relationship between cortical response to disgust (diminished with diminished attention) and the amygdala response to disgust (enhanced with diminished attention) is consistent with the notion that cortical processing can influence the breadth/narrowness of the amygdala response tuning. To examine this hypothesis more closely, we assayed the relation between the amygdala response and how attention influences cortical responsiveness to facial signals of threat in three functionally defined face responsive regions: (1) within the FFA, a region specialized for face processing; (2) within the LOCf, an area lateral to the FFA, purportedly within the lateral occipital complex (Grill-Spector et al., 2001), a region specialized for shape processing; and (3) the anterior insula, a region specialized for disgust face processing.

During attended conditions, responses were greater for fearful relative to neutral faces in the FFA ($F_{(1,154)} = 82.94$; $p < 0.0001$) and LOCf ($F_{(1,154)} = 48.37$; $p < 0.0001$). These greater responses to fear were significantly diminished under unattended relative to attended conditions in the FFA ($F_{(1,154)} = 168.17$; $p < 0.0001$) and LOCf ($F_{(1,154)} = 61.47$; $p < 0.0001$), with response magnitudes in the FFA ($F_{(1,154)} = 3.56$; $p > 0.06$) and LOCf ($F_{(1,154)} = 1.67$; $p > 0.19$) no longer greater for fearful versus neutral expressions. During attended conditions, responses were also greater for disgusted relative to neutral faces in the FFA ($F_{(1,154)} = 32.96$; $p < 0.0001$) and LOCf ($F_{(1,154)} = 32.96$; $p < 0.0001$). These greater responses to disgust were also diminished during unattended relative to attended conditions in the FFA ($F_{(1,154)} = 82.94$; $p < 0.0001$) and LOCf ($F_{(1,154)} = 182.00$; $p < 0.0001$), with FFA and LOCf responses to disgust being numerically smaller than that of neutral expressions during unattended conditions. Thus, like the anterior insula, FFA, and LOCf responses to fear and disgust were significantly reduced with diminished attention (Figure 14.4).

This inverse effect of attention on cortical (FFA, LOCf, and anterior insula) and amygdala responses to disgust suggests that the loss of fear specificity in the amygdala is related to diminished cortical processing of disgust during inattention. To examine such putative cortico-amygdala interactions, we assessed individual differences in the magnitude of attentional modulation (attended vs

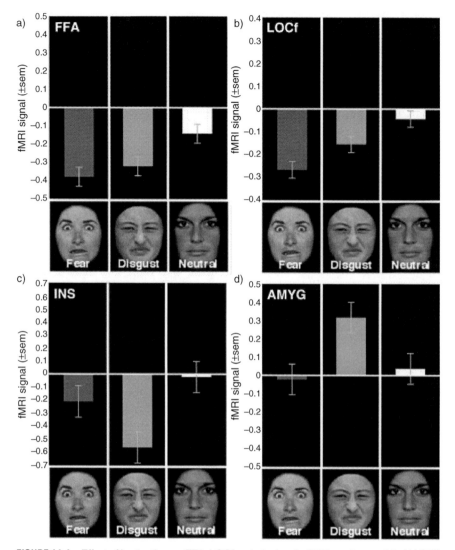

FIGURE 14.4 ■ Effect of inattention on FFA, LOCf, anterior insula (INS), and amygdala (AMYG) ROI responses to facial expressions. Bars represent the difference score between attended and unattended conditions (unattend minus attend) for each fear, disgust, and neutral face. The predominant effect of inattention was to reduce cortical responsiveness in the FFA, LOCf, and insula. In contrast, the amygdala demonstrated a marked increased response to disgust.

unattended) of the amygdala response to disgust and its correlation with magnitude of attentional modulation of FFA, LOCf, and the anterior insular responses to disgust. Although all three cortical regions demonstrated substantial attentional modulation of disgust responses, multiple regression analysis revealed that only the anterior insula

(standardized β coefficient $= -0.471$; $F_{(1,93)} = 19.58$; $p < 0.0001$), and neither FFA ($\beta = -0.17$; $F_{(1,93)} = 2.22$; $p > 0.13$) nor LOCf ($\beta = 0.08$; $F_{(1,93)} = 0.41$; $p > 0.52$), was significantly negatively associated with enhanced amygdala response to disgust. That is, subjects who demonstrated the largest attention-related decrease in anterior insular response tended to be the same as those who showed the largest increase in the amygdala response to disgust. This association between attentional modulation of amygdala and insular responses was stimulus dependent. Consistent with the attention-independent amygdala response to fear, amygdala responses were not significantly correlated with attention-dependent anterior insular responses to fear ($r = -0.10$; $F_{(1,95)} = 0.95$; $p > 0.33$).

Responses to disgust in the FFA, LOCf, and anterior insula all demonstrated a pronounced reduction in response with reduced attention. In addition, this association suggests that anterior insular responses to disgust may be critically dependent on extrastriate face processing. To examine this possibility further, we assayed the relation between individual differences in the magnitude of attentional modulation of FFA, LOCf, and anterior insular responses to disgust. A multiple regression analysis revealed that the LOCf ($\beta = 0.53$; $F_{(1,93)} = 26.23$; $p < 0.0001$), but not the FFA ($\beta = -0.17$; $F_{(1,93)} = 2.34$; $p > 0.12$), was significantly positively associated with a reduced anterior insular response to disgust.

Discussion

Consistent with the notion that the amygdala processes fear automatically, the magnitude of the amygdala response to facial signals of fear was not significantly reduced with reduced attention, despite reduced responses to fear in multiple cortical regions. However, such automaticity did not extend to all forms of facial threat processing: the magnitude of anterior insular response to facial signals of disgust was substantially reduced with reduced attention. That automatic processing did not extend to both amygdala processing of fear and anterior insula processing of disgust demonstrates that automaticity is not a fundamental principle of neural systems dedicated to the processing of facial expressions more generally, and facial expressions related to threat in particular. Automaticity appears unique to amygdala processing of social signals of fear. However, amygdala attentional independence may not be complete. The present study found that amygdala processing of

fear was not entirely automatic, coming at the expense of specificity of response. During inattention, the amygdala demonstrated a markedly enhanced response to disgust. This finding suggests there are important limitations on what precise affective features the amygdala encodes automatically. Thus, amygdala automatic processing is not specific to fearful faces, but rather, may be confined to more coarse affective properties of faces, such as their valence or arousal/intensity.

In contrast to the present and previous studies, Pessoa et al. (2002a) have shown abolished cortical and amygdala responses to fear faces under conditions of extreme attentional load. Such contradictory results can be reconciled if we consider that different levels of attentional load will result in the modulation of activity at different levels of the nervous system. Indeed, given similar attentional load, there are more pronounced modulations in later visual cortical processing stages [e.g., middle temporal (MT)] relative to earlier stages (e.g., VI) (Kastner et al., 1998, 2001). Severe attentional depletion may then result in modulations very early in processing, before cortical processing (O'Connor et al., 2002) such as in the thalamic relays to the amygdala, functionally cutting off the sensory inputs of the amygdala. This would be consistent with demonstrations of preserved amygdala fear responses in patients with striate cortex lesions (Morris et al., 2001). In the context of the present results, the automaticity of amygdala processing of fear is not all-or-none, but a matter of degree. Relative to PPA processing of places, FFA processing of faces, and anterior insula processing of disgust, the magnitude of the amygdala response to fear demonstrates substantial attentional independence.

The pronounced reduction in extrastriate response during inattention contrasted with the amygdala maintenance of response to fear. This is consistent with fear processing in the amygdala occurring independently of extrastriate face processing (Morris et al., 2001; Vuilleumier et al., 2001). Although the magnitude of the amygdala response to fear takes place independently of extra-striate face processing, the specificity of the amygdala response to fear may remain critically dependent on cortical processing. The enhanced amygdala response to expressions of disgust during decreased attention is exceptional with respect to an extensive body of evidence showing reductions of brain response with reduced attention (Corbetta et al., 1990; Haxby et al., 1994; Wojciulik et al., 1998; O'Craven et al., 1999). This enhanced response to disgust may be a reflection of diminished cortical influences on the amygdala. Although previous studies have suggested that there are significant amygdala modulatory influences on cortical perceptual processing (Anderson and Phelps, 2001; Morris et al., 1998a, 1998b), the present findings suggest that cortical processing can significantly modulate the amygdala response (Phelps et al., 2001; Ochsner et al., 2002).

To our knowledge, this interaction between the automaticity and the specificity of the amygdala response provides the first human evidence supporting an important proposed functional consequence of having two parallel pathways to the amygdala: one subcortically mediated and one cortically mediated (LeDoux, 1996). As proposed by LeDoux (1996), by circumventing the cortex, a shorter thalamo-amygdala pathway processes information in a more rapid and automatic manner. By engaging the cortex, a longer thalamo-cortico-amygdala pathway allows for more detailed processing of the stimulus, but in a less rapid and, as we propose here, an attention-limited manner. An important consequence of bypassing cortical processing is that the automaticity of the subcortical pathway should hypothetically come with a cost, at the expense of more fine-grained cortical analysis (Thompson, 1962). Indeed, studies in monkeys have shown altered amygdala discrimination of visual stimuli after reversible cooling of the inferotemporal cortex (Fukuda et al., 1987). Rabbits with lesions of the auditory cortex have demonstrated impaired stimulus discrimination during auditory fear conditioning (Jarrell et al., 1987). In addition to reduced cortical processing, decreased attention is associated with decreased stimulus discriminability (Yeshurun and Carrasco, 1998). Accordingly, reduced cortical responses during inattention can be interpreted as reflecting diminished cortical stimulus analysis that may ultimately

limit the ability for the amygdala to resolve stimuli of specific types.

Individual differences in the degree of attentional degradation of processing in the anterior insular cortex were particularly tied to the amygdala loss of fear specificity, being directly related to the magnitude of the enhanced amygdala response to disgust. With its substantial projections to the amygdala (Mesulam and Mufson, 1982), the anterior insula has been thought to convey cortical processing of affective stimulus content to the amygdala (Shi and Davis, 1999; Phelps et al., 2001). The anterior insular cortex may provide the amygdala with more detailed information regarding stimulus affective properties when attention is focused on the stimulus source. The result of diminished affective cortical processing is that the amygdala may respond more liberally to potentially significant stimulus events. In signal detection terminology, with diminished cortical inputs the amygdala may weigh more heavily "hits" and "misses" than "correct rejections" and "false alarms." That is, recognizing (hits) or failing to recognize (misses) an environmental threat (e.g., responding, or not, to a dangerous snake) should be more critical for amygdala processing than recognizing (correct rejection) or failing to recognize (false alarms) an event as not threatening (e.g., responding, or not, to snake-like objects, such as a curvy stick). This bias toward potentially important events is not a reflection of a loss of sensitivity to discriminate between potentially significant and neutral events. During inattention, amygdala activation discriminated both fear and disgust from neutral expressions. Thus, in healthy individuals the amygdala does not "cry wolf" to all stimuli, losing its predictive usefulness. Rather, under conditions of reduced stimulus analysis, the amygdala appears to extend its response to a broader range of potential threats, ensuring that potentially significant events will not be overlooked.

However, this adaptive form of automaticity may not hold in clinical populations in which there is substantial behavioral evidence of overgeneralization of automatic processing to normatively more neutral events (Williams et al., 1996). This overgeneralization in clinical populations has been shown with respect to amygdala processing as well. For instance, relative to nonsocial phobic individuals, patients with social phobia demonstrate more pronounced amygdala response to neutral faces (Birbaumer et al., 1998). Broadening of the amygdala response to other facial expressions beyond fear has also been shown in patients with major depression, with this overgeneralization found to be reversible with treatment (Sheline et al., 2001). In the context of the present results, the broadening of amygdala responsiveness in clinical populations, and its reversibility, may reflect altered cortical modulatory influences on the amygdala response. Evidence of gender differences in the amygdala response also underscores the variable nature of amygdala processing (Cahill et al., 2001; Canli et al., 2002). The subjects in the present study were mostly women, so future studies with larger and gender-balanced samples will be needed to examine whether the present findings apply equally to men and women.

Why is automaticity unique to the amygdala processing of social signals of fear and does it not extend to other brain regions specialized for social signals of threat? Facial signals of fear, as well as disgust, may serve as important cues for searching one's environment for the source of a potential threat (Whalen, 1998). Fear expressions signal impending attack (e.g., response to a dangerous animal) (Gray, 1987). Disgust expressions signal potential contamination or poisoning (e.g., rejection of harmful food) (Rozin and Fallon, 1987). The character of the stimulus and response for attack-related threat (stimulus: moving target; response: immediate freezing or flight) versus contamination-related threat (stimulus: stationary target; response: further inspection and passive avoidance) differ significantly (Sawchuk et al., 2002). Consistent with this division, predatory animals tend to evoke fear, whereas disgust is associated with animals that do not present significant harm (e.g., spiders, slugs) (Ware et al., 1994). Similarly, fear and disgust demonstrate distinct physiological signatures and action tendencies (Ekman, 1992; Levenson, 1992), with fear associated with increased sympathetic activity (Ekman et al., 1983) and disgust more with parasympathetic activity (Rozin and Fallon, 1987; Levenson, 1992). Commensurate with the prerequisite rapidity of attack-related threat evaluations, the analysis of fear content from faces may occur early on, with relative independence from higher-order attention-limited processes. In contrast, disgust content from faces may have the luxury of occurring later, being dependent on more elaborative and attention-demanding processes. Thus, although selective pressures have promoted the development of specialized neural systems for the processing of social signals of both fear and disgust, selection for automaticity may extend only to fear.

Acknowledgments

This work was supported by National Institute of Mental Health Grant MH12829–01 and by McDonnell-Pew Program in Cognitive Neuroscience Grant 20002024.

REFERENCES

Adolphs R, Tranel D, Damasio H, Damasio A (1994) Impaired recognition of emotion in facial expressions following bilateral damage to the human amygdala. Nature 372:669–672.

Anderson AK, Phelps EA (2001) Lesions of the human amygdala impair enhanced perception of emotionally salient events. Nature 411:305–309.

Birbaumer N, Grodd W, Diedrich O, Klose U, Erb M, Lotze M, Schneider F, Weiss U, Flor H (1998) fMRI reveals amygdala activation to human faces in social phobics. NeuroReport 9:1223–1226.

Breiter HC, Etcoff NL, Whalen PJ, Kennedy WA, Rauch SL, Buckner RL, Strauss MM, Hyman SE, Rosen BR (1996) Response and habituation of the human amygdala during visual processing of facial expression. Neuron 17: 875–887.

Cahill L, Haier RJ, White NS, Fallon J, Kilpatrick L, Lawrence C, Potkin SG, Alkire MT (2001) Sex-related difference in amygdala activity during emotionally influenced memory storage. Neurobiol Learn Mem 75:1–9.

Calder AJ, Keane J, Manes F, Antoun N, Young AW (2000) Impaired recognition and experience of disgust following brain injury. Nat Neurosci 3:1077–1078.

Canli T, Desmond JE, Zhao Z, Gabrieli JD (2002) Sex differences in the neural basis of emotional memories. Proc Natl Acad Sci USA 99:10789–10794.

Corbetta M, Miezin FM, Dobmeyer S, Shulman GL, Petersen SE (1990) Attentional modulation of neural processing of shape, color, and velocity in humans. Science 248:1556–1559.

Ekman P (1992) An argument for basic emotions. Cognition Emotion 6:169–200.

Ekman P, Levenson RW, Friesen WV (1983) Autonomic nervous system activity distinguishes among emotions. Science 221:1208–1210.

Esteves F, Dimberg U, Ohman A (1994) Automatically elicited fear: conditioned skin conductance responses to masked facial expressions. Cognition Emotion 8:393–413.

Fukuda M, Ono T, Nakamura K (1987) Functional relations among inferotemporal cortex, amygdala, and lateral hypothalamus in monkey operant feeding behavior. J Neurophysiol 57:1060–1077.

Gray JA (1987) The psychology of fear and stress, Ed 2. New York: Cambridge UP.

Grill-Spector K, Kourtzi Z, Kanwisher N (2001) The lateral occipital complex and its role in object recognition. Vision Res 41:1409–1422.

Haxby JV, Horwitz B, Ungerleider LG, Maisog JM, Pietrini P, Grady CL (1994) The functional organization of human extrastriate cortex: a PET-rCBF study of selective attention to faces and locations. J Neurosci 14:6336–6353.

Jarrell TW, Gentile CG, Romanski LM, McCabe PM, Schneiderman N (1987) Involvement of cortical and thalamic auditory regions in retention of differential bradycardiac conditioning to acoustic conditioned stimuli in rabbits. Brain Res 412:285–294.

Kastner S, De Weerd P, Desimone R, Ungerleider LG (1998) Mechanisms of directed attention in the human extrastriate cortex as revealed by functional MRI. Science 282:108–111.

Kastner S, De Weerd P, Pinsk MA, Elizondo MI, Desimone R, Ungerleider LG (2001) Modulation of sensory suppression: implications for receptive field sizes in the human visual cortex. J Neurophysiol 86:1398–1411.

LeDoux JE (1995) Emotion: clues from the brain. Annu Rev Psychol 46:209–235.

LeDoux JE (1996) The emotional brain: the mysterious underpinnings of emotional life. New York: Simon & Schuster.

Levenson RW (1992) Autonomic nervous system differences among emotions. Psychol Sci 3:23–27.

Mesulam MM, Mufson EJ (1982) Insula of the old world monkey. III. Efferent cortical output and comments on function. J Comp Neurol 212:38–52.

Morris JS, Frith CD, Perrett DI, Rowland D, Young AW, Calder AJ, Dolan RJ (1996) A differential neural response in the human amygdala to fearful and happy facial expressions. Nature 383:812–815.

Morris JS, Friston KJ, Buchel C, Frith CD, Young AW, Calder AJ, Dolan RJ (1998a) A neuromodulatory role for the human amygdala in processing emotional facial expressions. Brain 121:47–57.

Morris JS, Friston KJ, Dolan RJ (1998b) Experience-dependent modulation of tonotopic neural responses in human auditory cortex. Proc R Soc Lond B Biol Sci 265:649–657.

Morris JS, Ohman A, Dolan RJ (1999) A subcortical pathway to the right amygdala mediating "unseen" fear. Proc Natl Acad Sci USA 96:1680–1685.

Morris JS, DeGelder B, Weiskrantz L, Dolan RJ (2001) Differential extra-geniculostriate and amygdala responses to presentation of emotional faces in a cortically blind field. Brain 124:1241–1252.

O'Connor DH, Fukui MM, Pinsk MA, Kastner S (2002) Attention modulates responses in the human lateral geniculate nucleus. Nat Neurosci 5:1203–1209.

O'Craven KM, Downing PE, Kanwisher N (1999) fMRI evidence for objects as the units of attentional selection. Nature 401:584–587.

Ochsner KN, Bunge SA, Gross JJ, Gabrieli JD (2002) Rethinking feelings: an fMRI study of the cognitive regulation of emotion. J Cogn Neurosci 14:1215–1219.

Ohman A, Lundqvist D, Esteves F (2001) The face in the crowd revisited: a threat advantage with schematic stimuli. J Pers Soc Psychol 80:381–396.

Pessoa L, Kastner S, Ungerleider LG (2002a) Attentional control of the processing of neutral and emotional stimuli. Brain Res Cognit Brain Res 15:31–45.

Pessoa L, McKenna M, Gutierrez E, Ungerleider LG (2002b) Neural processing of emotional faces requires attention. Proc Natl Acad Sci USA 99:11458–11463.

Phelps EA, O'Connor KJ, Gatenby JC, Gore JC, Grillon C, Davis M (2001) Activation of the left amygdala to a cognitive representation of fear. Nat Neurosci 4:437–441.

Phillips ML, Young AW, Senior C, Brammer M, Andrew C, Calder AJ, Bullmore ET, Perrett DI, Rowland D, Williams SC, Gray JA, David AS (1997) A specific neural substrate for perceiving facial expressions of disgust. Nature 389:495–498.

Phillips ML, Young AW, Scott SK, Calder AJ, Andrew C, Giampietro V, Williams SC, Bullmore ET, Brammer M, Gray JA (1998) Neural responses to facial and vocal expressions of fear and disgust. Proc R Soc Lond B Biol Sci 265:1809–1817.

Rozin P, Fallon AE (1987) A perspective on disgust. Psychol Rev 94:23–41.

Sawchuk CN, Meunier SA, Lohr JM, Westendorf DH (2002) Fear, disgust, and information processing in specific phobia: the application of signal detection theory. J Anxiety Disord 16:495–510.

Sheline YI, Barch DM, Donnelly JM, Ollinger JM, Snyder AZ, Mintun MA (2001) Increased amygdala response to masked emotional faces in depressed subjects resolves with antidepressant treatment: an fMRI study. Biol Psychiatry 50:651–658.

Shi C, Davis M (1999) Pain pathways involved in fear conditioning measured with fear-potentiated startle: lesion studies. J Neurosci 19:420–430.

Sprengelmeyer R, Young AW, Calder AJ, Karnat A, Lange H, Homberg V, Perrett DI, Rowland D (1996) Loss of disgust: perception of faces and emotions in Huntington's disease. Brain 119:1647–1665.

Thompson RF (1962) The role of the cerebral cortex in stimulus generalization. J Comp Physiol Psychol 55:279–287.

Vuilleumier P, Armony JL, Driver J, Dolan RJ (2001) Effects of attention and emotion on face processing in the human brain: an event-related fMRI study. Neuron 30:829–841.

Vuilleumier P, Armony J, Clarke K, Husain M, Driver J, Dolan R (2002) Neural response to emotional faces with and without awareness: event-related fMRI in a parietal patient with visual extinction and spatial neglect. Neuropsychologia 40:2156.

Ware J, Jain K, Burgess I, Davey GC (1994) Disease-avoidance model: factor analysis of common animal fears. Behav Res Ther 32:57–63.

Whalen PJ (1998) Fear, vigilance, and ambiguity: initial neuroimaging studies of the human amygdala. Curr Direct Psychol Sci 7:177–188.

Whalen PJ, Rauch SL, Etcoff NL, McInerney SC, Lee MB, Jenike MA (1998) Masked presentations of emotional facial expressions modulate amygdala activity without explicit knowledge. J Neurosci 18:411–418.

Williams JMG, Mathews A, MacLeod C (1996) The emotional Stroop task and psychopathology. Psychol Bull 120:3–24.

Wojciulik E, Kanwisher N, Driver J (1998) Covert visual attention modulates face-specific activity in the human fusiform gyrus: fMRI study. J Neurophysiol 79: 1574–1578.

Yeshurun Y, Carrasco M (1998) Attention improves or impairs visual performance by enhancing spatial resolution. Nature 396:72–75.

Automatic and Intentional Brain Responses during Evaluation of Trustworthiness of Faces

J.S. Winston[1], B.A. Strange[2], J. O'Doherty[1] and R.J. Dolan[1,3]

Successful social interaction partly depends on appraisal of others from their facial appearance. A critical aspect of this appraisal relates to whether we consider others to be trustworthy. We determined the neural basis for such trustworthiness judgments using event-related functional magnetic resonance imaging. Subjects viewed faces and assessed either trustworthiness or age. In a parametric factorial design, trustworthiness ratings were correlated with BOLD signal change to reveal task-independent increased activity in bilateral amygdala and right insula in response to faces judged untrustworthy. Right superior temporal sulcus (STS) showed enhanced signal change during explicit trustworthiness judgments alone. The findings extend a proposed model of social cognition by highlighting a functional dissociation between automatic engagement of amygdala versus intentional engagement of STS in social judgment.

It is conjectured that human survival has depended to a large extent on accurate social judgments and that, as an evolutionary consequence, modular cognitive processes are devoted to such functions[1]. Neuropsychological studies and human functional imaging provide partial support for this idea of a dedicated 'social intelligence', particularly studies that address perception of facial expression[2-7].

However, facial emotional expression is only one aspect of social judgment made about others. In many situations, individuals must also decide whether another person is someone to approach or avoid, trust or distrust. Preliminary evidence regarding the neural underpinnings of this sort of evaluative judgment comes from studies in which patients with bilateral amygdala lesions make

[1]Wellcome Department of Imaging Neuroscience, 12 Queen Square, London WC1N 3BG, UK.
[2]Institute of Cognitive Neuroscience, 17 Queen Square, London WC1N 3AR, UK.
[3]Royal Free and University College Medical School, Roland Hill Street, London NW3 2PF, UK.

abnormal social judgments about others based on facial appearance[8]. These abnormalities are most pronounced in relation to faces that received the most negative ratings by control subjects. Notably, such deficits are not apparent in subjects with unilateral amygdala lesions[8]. Patients with damage to ventromedial prefrontal cortex also have difficulties with trustworthiness decisions[9,10].

The most influential neurobiological model of social cognition[11], based on inferences largely from neurophysiological recordings in non-human primates, postulates that the superior temporal sulcus acts as association cortex for processing conspecifics' behavior and that socially relevant information is subsequently labeled by the emotional systems, such as amygdala and orbitofrontal cortex. More recent models of human social cognition also include sensory regions such as the face-processing area in fusiform gyrus and somatosensory cortex (including insula, SI and SII)[12-14].

Here we used event-related functional magnetic resonance imaging (fMRI) to ascertain the neural substrates mediating evaluative social judgment. Processing of facial emotion can be implicit, occurring when subjects make judgments about facial attributes unrelated to emotion (for example, refs. 5–7, 15, 16). To establish whether trustworthiness judgments might be similarly processed, we used a task in which subjects viewed faces while making either explicit judgments whether an individual was trustworthy or an unrelated age assessment. To account for individual differences in trustworthiness judgment, we acquired ratings of trustworthiness for each stimulus from each subject after scanning and used these ratings as parametric covariates in our subsequent analysis. Based on the models of social cognition outlined above[11-14], along with the neuropsychological findings[8], we predicted that discrete brain regions, the amygdala, orbitofrontal cortex, fusiform gyrus and superior temporal sulcus, would be implicated in trustworthiness assessments. Consequently, these areas formed regions of interest in our statistical analysis. Our data indicate that social judgments about

faces involve such a network and that this network is differentially modulated by implicit and explicit evaluations.

Results

Behavioral

After scanning, on average subjects labeled more than half of the 120 faces as having 'neutral' emotional expressions (mean, 65). Labeled emotional expression interacted significantly with trustworthiness score across the group of subjects (Kruskal-Wallis test, $p < 0.001$). Mann–Whitney U tests showed that the trustworthiness scores (from 1, least trustworthy, to 7) did not differ significantly between 'disgusted,' 'fearful' and 'surprised' faces and 'neutral' faces ($p > 0.05$ in all cases). 'Happy' faces (mean trustworthiness rating, 4.0) were rated as significantly more trustworthy than 'neutral' faces (mean rating, 3.9), and 'angry' (mean rating, 2.7) and 'sad' (mean rating, 3.6) faces as significantly less trustworthy ($p < 0.01$ in all cases). Mean trustworthiness scores (Figure 15.1a) were significantly correlated with mean scores for anger, happiness and sadness from the second group of subjects (see Methods) ($p < 0.01$ for each, two-tailed; Figure 15.1b–e).

Neuroimaging

Linear contrasts were performed to produce statistical parametric maps (SPMs) of the main effect of task (explicit or implicit processing of trustworthiness), the main effect of trustworthiness and the interaction between these two factors. An additional model in which the effects of facial emotion of the stimuli were included as covariates of no interest was used to generate an SPM related to the main effect of trustworthiness independent of effects of facial emotional expression.

A significant activation in the explicit compared to implicit task, independent of trustworthiness, was found in the right posterior superior temporal sulcus (x, y, z coordinates, 56, −44, 4; $Z = 4.27$; $p < 0.05$, corrected for multiple

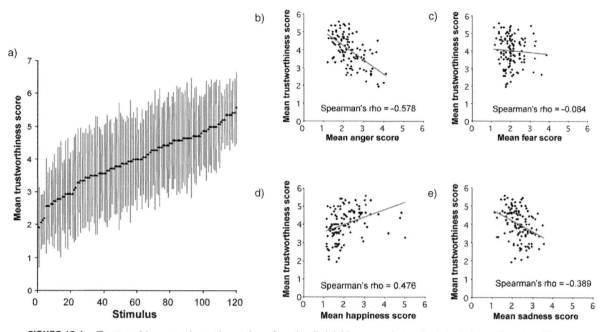

FIGURE 15.1 ■ Trustworthiness and emotion ratings for stimuli. (a) Means and standard deviations of trustworthiness scores of stimuli, rank-ordered by trustworthiness score. (b–e) Mean emotion scores (from second cohort of sixteen subjects) and mean trustworthiness scores (from cohort of subjects scanned with fMRI) for anger (b), fear (c), happiness (d) or sadness (e). Lines of best fit are derived by linear regression. Both rating scales ranged from 1 (low degree of emotion or highly untrustworthy) to 7 (highly emotional or highly trustworthy).

comparisons across a small volume of interest; Figure 15.2; Table 15.1). Additionally, primary visual cortex was significantly activated in this contrast. Attentional and emotional manipulations are known to alter neural responses in early visual cortex[17], and we propose that similar processes engendered by the explicit task account for this latter activation.

As predicted, significant bilateral amygdala activation was evident in the contrast of untrustworthy to trustworthy faces (right, −18, 0, −24; $Z = 4.29$; left, −16, −4, −20; $Z = 3.92$; both $p < 0.05$, corrected for multiple comparisons across a small volume of interest; Figure 15.3a). This examination of parametric data based on each subject's ratings of faces indicates that more untrustworthy faces evoke greater BOLD responses in the amygdala (Figure 15.3c and d).

Further areas showing increased response to untrustworthy faces included left superior temporal sulcus (−50, −58, 10; $Z = 4.15$) and a region of the right superior middle insula (42, −4, 12; $Z = 3.48$; Figure 15.3a and b). Additionally, bilateral activation in the fusiform gyrus was evident in this contrast (right, 44, −46, −24, $Z = 3.58$; left, −48, −48, −24; $Z = 3.60$; both $p < 0.05$, corrected for multiple comparisons across a small volume of interest; Figure 15.4). Table 15.2 presents regions highlighted by this contrast as well as regions highlighted as more responsive to faces rated as trustworthy.

To ensure that the main effect of untrustworthiness was not driven by a highly significant activation in just one of the tasks alone, a masked conjunction of simple effects of trustworthiness under implicit and explicit task conditions was carried out (Methods). This analysis confirmed

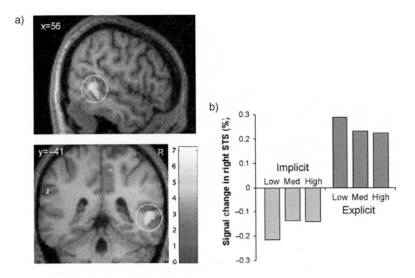

FIGURE 15.2 ■ *(A color version of part a of this figure follows page 146.)* Main effect of explicit social judgments. (a) Random-effects SPM overlaid on a normalized structural scan from a single subject showing activation in right superior temporal sulcus region (x, y, z = 56, −44, 4; Z = 4.27; $p < 0.05$ small volume corrected) when making judgments about trustworthiness compared to age. For illustration, using threshold $p < 0.001$ uncorrected, extent threshold of 5 voxels. (b) BOLD signal measure categorized by task and trustworthiness of faces. 'Low', 'med' and 'high' refer to the least trustworthy third, median third and most trustworthy third of faces calculated in the second model described in Methods. The y-axis represents mean (across subjects) percentage signal change relative to whole brain mean over scanning session for each event type. There is no clear pattern of response to the faces according to trustworthiness. Note that statistical inference is drawn only from the parametric model described in Methods, and not from the illustrative model in (b).

TABLE 15.1. Cerebral Foci of Activation in Main Effect of Task

Brain region	Coordinates of peak activation (mm)			Z score
	x	y	z	
Explicit versus implicit				
Primary visual cortex	2	−98	8	4.49
Right posterior STS*	56	−44	4	4.27
Right superior frontal gyrus	10	14	70	3.99
Left premotor cortex	−48	−2	26	3.84
Left extrastriate cortex	−24	−76	32	3.75
Right cuneus	12	−40	56	3.62
Left primary sensory cortex	−30	−28	72	3.62
Supramarginal gyrus	−62	−40	34	3.50
Right anterior insula	48	34	−6	3.37
Left superior frontal sulcus	−42	12	40	3.34
Left pre-SMA	−6	10	54	3.34
Implicit versus explicit				
Left fusiform gyrus	−36	−36	−18	3.59
Right cuneus	4	−64	12	3.49

All values, $p < 0.001$ uncorrected. *$p < 0.05$ corrected for multiple comparisons across a small volume of interest.

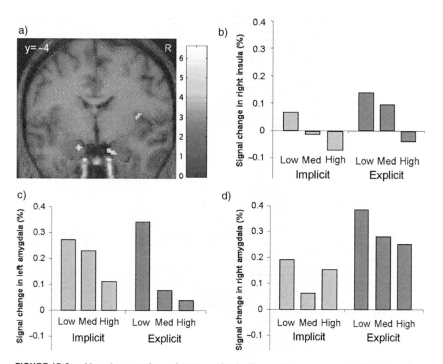

FIGURE 15.3 ■ *(A color version of part a of this figure follows page 146.)* Main effect of trustworthiness in amygdala and insula. (a) Significant increases in BOLD signal to untrustworthy faces in the right and left amygdalae and right insula (right amygdala, −18, 0, −24; $Z = 4.29$; $p < 0.01$ corrected; left amygdala, −16, −4, −20; $Z = 3.92$; $p < 0.025$ corrected; right insula, 42, −4, 12; $Z = 3.48$; $p < 0.001$ uncorrected). (b–d) Responses to faces as a function of degree of individually rated trustworthiness for right insula (b), left amygdala (c) and right amygdala (d). Note greater responses to less trustworthy faces across all these regions. The y-axis is as in Figure 15.2.

that bilateral amygdala, fusiform gyrus and right insula showed significant responses to untrustworthy faces independent of task. Notably, left STS activation was not observed in this contrast, and a *post-hoc* test revealed that the effects in this region were driven principally by trustworthiness judgments under the explicit task.

The contrast pertaining to the interaction of task and trustworthiness demonstrated an area in the lateral orbitofrontal cortex (−28, 42, 10; $Z = 3.73$, $p < 0.0001$, uncorrected) responsive to untrustworthy faces in the implicit task and to trustworthy faces in the explicit task. However, this activation failed to survive correction for multiple comparisons across the entire volume of orbitofrontal cortex. No other areas about which we had a prior

hypothesis were revealed in this contrast or in the reverse interaction term.

Using an additional model that partialed out effects from facial expression of basic emotions in the stimulus set, we performed a random effects analysis across the 14 subjects. Even under these stringent criteria, right amygdala activation was still evident in this model at both uncorrected ($p < 0.001$) and small-volume corrected ($p < 0.05$ corrected for multiple comparisons across bilateral amygdala volume) thresholds (Figure 15.5). This activation (peak at 22, 2, −18; $Z = 4.06$) overlapped with that reported in our primary model. At lower thresholds ($p < 0.005$, uncorrected), there was additional activation in left amygdala.

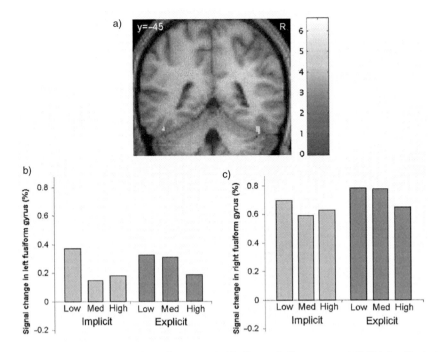

FIGURE 15.4 ■ *(A color version of part a of this figure follows page 146.)* Main effect of trustworthiness in fusiform gyrus. (a) Significant increases in BOLD signal to untrustworthy faces in the fusiform gyrus bilaterally (right, 44, −46, −22; Z = 3.58; p < 0.05, small volume corrected; left, −48, −48, −24; Z = 3.60; p < 0.05, small volume corrected). This activation is independent of task in both the left (b) and right (c) fusiform gyrus. The y-axis is as in Figure 15.2.

TABLE 15.2. Cerebral Foci of Activation in Differential Effects of Trustworthiness of Faces

Brain region	Coordinates of peak activation (mm)			Z score
	x	y	z	
Untrustworthy versus trustworthy				
Right amygdala*	18	0	−24	4.29
Left superior temporal sulcus	−50	−58	10	4.15
Right intraparietal sulcus	22	−54	48	4.00
Left extrastriate cortex	−34	−90	24	3.94
Left amygdala*	−16	−4	−20	3.92
Right pre-SMA	8	8	62	3.83
Left parahippocampal gyrus	−18	−30	−18	3.81
Right auditory cortex	66	−18	4	3.75
Left inferior temporal gyrus	−60	−14	−30	3.64
Left fusiform gyrus*	−48	−48	−24	3.60
Right fusiform gyrus*	44	−46	−22	3.58
Thalamus	4	−12	14	3.52
Right insula	42	−4	12	3.48
Left superior temporal gyrus	−58	−32	14	3.42
Trustworthy versus untrustworthy				
Left insula	−36	4	−4	3.65
Right dorsolateral prefrontal/frontopolar cortex	34	52	6	3.23

All values, p < 0.001 uncorrected. *p < 0.05 corrected for multiple comparisons across a small volume of interest.

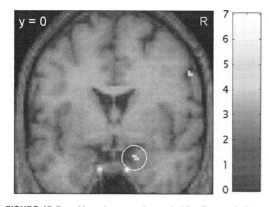

FIGURE 15.5 ■ *(A color version of this figure follows page 146.)* Main effect of trustworthiness in amygdala independent of facial emotion. Significant increases in BOLD signal in response to untrustworthy faces in right amygdala even when scores for four basic facial emotions are additionally used as parametric covariates in the analysis. This activation is significant at $p < 0.05$, corrected for multiple comparisons across the volume of bilateral amygdala. Activation peak at 18, 2, −22 ($Z =$ 4.06), but overlaps with right amygdala activation focus shown in Figure 15.2. At lower threshold of $p < 0.005$ uncorrected, activation is evident in left amygdala.

Discussion

The question addressed in this study was whether the dimension of trustworthiness in faces and the process of making social judgments are associated with distinct patterns of brain activation. By implication, the study is an explicit test of a proposed neurobiological model[11]. The principal findings of activation in amygdala, orbitofrontal cortex and STS are highly consistent with this model. We also extend previous lesion data[8] by showing amygdala activity in response to untrustworthy faces regardless of whether subjects were explicitly making trustworthiness judgments. This finding echoes earlier studies of obligatory threat-related processing in the amygdala[18–21]. In contrast to many imaging studies of facial emotion (for example, ref. 5), the amygdala response to untrustworthy faces was bilateral, supporting neuropsychological evidence that patients with unilateral amygdala lesions can successfully make trustworthiness judgments[8]. To our knowledge, no previous study has demonstrated an automaticity

of amygdala response during complex social judgments.

In addition to the amygdala, the right insula was also activated by faces that subjects considered untrustworthy regardless of task. The insula is activated in a wide variety of functional imaging studies of emotion (for example, refs. 22–25). One suggested role for the insula is the mapping of autonomic changes as they affect the body where such mappings form the basis of 'gut feelings' about emotive stimuli[26,27]. Thus, a possible explanation for the insula activation that we observed is that a consequence of amygdala activation is the generation of autonomically mediated changes in bodily states, which are then re-mapped to the insula.

Differential activation in face-responsive regions of the fusiform gyrus was observed in relation to trustworthiness in face stimuli. Increased activity is found in modality-specific cortical areas in response to stimuli with emotional content relative to non-emotional stimuli (for example, refs. 20, 21, 28–31). Enhanced extrastriate activation in response to emotional stimuli has been attributed to modulatory influences from the amygdala[32], possibly mediated by anatomical back-projections[33]. Indeed, a human lesion study highlights a possible role for the amygdala in enhancing perceptual processing of threat stimuli[34]. We suggest that such processes extend to faces representing potential threat at the social level and that a neural consequence is enhanced fusiform activation.

The right STS showed task-related activation in the explicit judgment condition but no differential activity according to trustworthiness. In other words, the right STS was activated when subjects made explicit judgments about trustworthiness. In this regard, the STS showed activity when subjects were required to make inferences concerning the likely intentionality of others. This region has been implicated in functional imaging studies on biological motion[35] and biological-like motion[36]. More critically, activity in posterior STS and adjacent regions at the temporo-parietal junction is observed when subjects make theory of mind inferences[37–39]. This region is suggested to be involved in intention detection[40,41], rather than biological motion processing *per se*. Intention detection is a critical component in determining whether or not to trust an individual, which may explain the activity in this region in our study.

Evidence from human patients with discrete lesions of orbitofrontal cortex indicate that this region is critical for complex social judgment[9,10]. Unlike the amygdala, this region showed task-dependent activation. When subjects made explicit judgments of trustworthiness, this region responded more strongly to faces deemed trustworthy. By contrast, when judging age, this region showed greater responses to untrustworthy individuals. Other studies have reported similar task-dependent responses in lateral orbitofrontal cortex. For example, responses in a region of lateral orbitofrontal cortex vary between preference and recognition judgment tasks on the same stimuli[42]. A dissociation between implicit/automatic social judgment and explicit (laboratory-tested) social judgment has also been reported in a patient with orbitofrontal cortex damage[9]. This patient remained able to evaluate social situations under explicit task instructions but was impaired in day-to-day ("automatic"[9]) social judgments. Note that activation in this region did not survive correction for multiple comparisons in our study, and we emphasize effects in this region based on its known involvement in social judgments[9,10].

Several regions of interest in this study (amygdala, orbitofrontal cortex and insula) are activated in processing specific facial expressions. Facial expressions of fear consistently activate the amygdala[5,6,43], whereas facial expressions of disgust activate the anterior insula[6,7]. Additionally, we demonstrate correlations between the trustworthiness scores and scores for facial emotions attributed to our stimulus set (Figure 15.1b-e). Consequently, one possibility is that differential patterns of activation seen in this study reflect influences from one or more emotional expressions alone. We assessed this possibility by analyzing the fMRI data with additional nuisance covariates pertaining to the degree of emotional expression of each of four basic emotions (anger, fear, happiness, sadness). A significant right amygdala response to untrustworthy faces persisted, even after this secondary analysis accounted for the variance attributed to facial emotion. These results suggest that facial expressions of emotion provide a constituent element in making trustworthiness judgments but that amygdala responses also were independent of these effects. Notably, patients with bilateral amygdala lesions show deficits in making social judgments in the context of maintained ability to use information about emotional expression of face stimuli[8].

It is interesting to speculate how the results of this study might generalize to social judgments about stimuli in other modalities. Patients with bilateral amygdala lesions are able to make accurate trustworthiness judgments based on verbal reports[8]. It is plausible therefore that amygdala involvement in trustworthiness decisions may be modality-specific. This hypothesis could be tested in follow-up experiments involving trustworthiness judgments about vocal stimuli, or scenarios about individuals based on written descriptions. Our prediction would be that superior temporal sulcus activation would remain in these other contexts and that fusiform modulation would be substituted by modality-specific cortical responses, for example, auditory cortex in the case of vocal stimuli.

In conclusion, we present functional brain imaging evidence for a neural substrate of social cognition that conforms to a previously proposed neurobiological model[11]. Our data extends this model by highlighting a dissociation between automatic and intentional engagement within this proposed circuitry. Thus, social judgments about faces reflect a combination of brain responses that are stimulus driven, in the case of the amygdala, and driven by processes relating to inferences concerning the intentionality of others, in the case of STS.

Methods

Subjects

Informed consent to partake in a study approved by the Joint National Hospital for Neurology and Neurosurgery/Institute of Neurology Ethics

Committee was obtained from 16 right-handed Caucasian volunteers (8 male, 8 female; age range 18–30 years; mean age 23.3 years). Two subjects (both females) were excluded from the analysis; one revealed psychiatric history after scanning and another provided extreme trustworthiness ratings. (Spearman's rho of correlation of ratings with mean of all other subjects, −0.445; for all remaining subjects, Spearman's rho values were over 0.3.) All remaining subjects were free from psychiatric or neurological history. All subjects except one had completed more than two years of post-16 education, and mean length of post-16 formal education was 4.8 years.

Stimuli

Grayscale frontal images of 120 Caucasian male faces were selected from a larger selection of images following a pilot study outside the scanner. The images were selected to cover a range of trustworthiness scores rated by the subjects in the pilot study ($n = 30$; 13 females, 17 males, ages 17–32, mean age 23.5), but to score as low as possible on ratings of 'happiness' and 'anger'. Gaze direction of all stimuli was directly forward. Stimuli were adjusted to be of approximately equal size and luminance and manipulated such that each face was centered on a gray background in a 400×400 pixel image. Of the 120 stimuli used in the imaging study, 60 were high school student photographs and 60 photographs of university students. There was no significant difference in average trustworthiness score between the two groups (Mann–Whitney U test, $p > 0.90$).

Psychological Task

The scanning session for each participant was divided into two parts. In one half of the session, 60 faces were presented sequentially, and participants made a judgment, indicating with a push-button response, whether the face was a high school or university student. In the other half of the session, they judged whether the face was trustworthy or untrustworthy. The order of tasks was counterbalanced between participants. At the start of each task, a word appeared on screen informing the subject of the task requirement ("School/Uni" or "Trustworthiness").

Stimuli were presented on a gray background once each in random order, randomly interspersed with 60 null events. Each stimulus was presented for 1 s with an inter-trial interval of 2 s. Between faces, a fixation cross was presented. Null events were of 3 s duration, during which time a fixation cross remained on screen. Stimuli subtended visual angles of approximately 10° vertically and 5° horizontally.

Image Acquisition

Subjects were scanned during task performance using a Siemens VISION system (Erlangen, Germany) at 2 Tesla to acquire gradient-echo, echoplanar T2*-weighted images with BOLD (blood oxygenation level dependent) contrast. Each volume comprised 33×2.2 mm axial scans with 3-mm in-plane resolution, and volumes were continuously acquired every 2.5 s. Subjects were placed in light head restraint within the scanner to limit head movement during acquisition. Each run began with 5 'dummy' volumes (subsequently discarded) to allow for T1 equilibration effects. Additionally, a T1-weighted structural image was acquired in each subject.

All functional volumes were realigned[44] and slice timing corrected (R. Henson *et al.*, *Neuroimage* 9, 125, 1999), normalized into a standard space[45] to allow group analysis, and smoothed with an 8-mm FWHM Gaussian kernel to account for residual intersubject differences.

Debriefing

After scanning, participants undertook a self-paced task in which they rated all the faces on a scale of trustworthiness from 1 (highly untrustworthy) to 7 (highly trustworthy). When all 120 faces had been rated, a second task was performed, in which participants named emotions that they perceived in the faces by means of a seven-way forced choice procedure (neutral, happy, sad, angry, disgust, fear, surprise). To assist subjects with this task, we gave them a printed sheet with photographs of one face from the Ekman and Friesen series[46] expressing each of these seven emotions.

Emotion Ratings for Stimuli

An additional set of 16 subjects (10 males, 6 females; age range 19–34 years; mean age 23.7 years) undertook a task in which they rated the degree of emotional expression within each face on each of four basic emotions (anger, fear, happiness, sadness) in turn. Ratings were from 1 (neutral for this particular emotion) to 7 (highest degree of this particular emotion).

Data Analysis

Imaging data were analysed with SPM99 using an event-related model[47]. The experimental design allowed a parametric factorial analysis whereby trustworthiness was a parametric regressor and the task (age or trustworthiness judgment) the second factor.

The presentation of each face was modeled by convolving a delta function at each event onset with a canonical hemodynamic response function (HRF) and its temporal derivative to create regressors of interest. These regressors were then parametrically modulated to model subject-specific trustworthiness judgments: that is, the height of the HRF for stimuli was modulated as a function of the trustworthiness score assigned to that stimulus by the subject. Subject-specific parameter estimates pertaining to each regressor were calculated for each voxel[48]. Contrast images were calculated by applying appropriate linear contrasts to the parameter estimates for the parametric regressor of each event. These contrast images were then entered into a one-sample t-test across the 14 subjects (that is, a random effects analysis). In regions about which we had a prior hypothesis, we applied a correction for multiple comparisons across a small volume of interest to the p-values in this region[49]. We report predicted regions surviving this correction at $p < 0.05$. Volumes of interest for amygdala, orbitofrontal cortex and STS were defined by drawing a mask around the regions bilaterally on a normalized T1 structural image with reference to an atlas of human neuroanatomy[50] using the software package MRIcro (http://www.psychology.nottingham.ac.uk/staff/cr1/mricro.html). Total volume of the amygdala

mask was approximately 10 cm^3, volume of the orbitofrontal mask approximately 50 cm^3, and volume of the STS mask approximately 20 cm^3. In the case of the fusiform gyri, small-volume correction was based upon a sphere of 10 mm radius centered on coordinates derived from a previous study[21]. We report descriptively activations outside regions of interest surviving a threshold of $p < 0.001$ uncorrected with an extent threshold of 5 contiguous voxels.

To ensure that the main effect of trustworthiness did not arise from a highly significant activation in just one of the simple effects (i.e., that activation was task independent), we created a mask from random-effects SPMs for the simple effect of untrustworthiness under both tasks (each thresholded at $p < 0.05$, uncorrected). This was used to mask the main effect of trustworthiness. Activations surviving this masking procedure reflect responses during both implicit and explicit judgments.

For the purposes of illustration, a second model was constructed by dividing the events for each subject into three groups by rank score for individual stimuli (that is, the least trustworthy third of faces as one event type, the median third as a second, and the most trustworthy third as a third). This model is used in Figures 15.1–15.3 to demonstrate the direction of BOLD signal change with respect to trustworthiness score. Note that statistical inferences are drawn solely from the parametric model described above.

The mean ratings of facial emotion derived from a second set of 16 age-matched subjects (see above) were used to construct another model for the data. In this model, subject-specific ratings for trustworthiness were entered as parametric covariates, as before. Additionally, mean ratings for each of the four emotions (anger, fear, happiness, sadness) were entered as nuisance parametric covariates. The parameter estimates for trustworthiness are therefore rendered independent of the effects of the four facial expressions, and variance better explained by the effects of a given facial expression will be attributed to the regressor modeling that facial expression. Contrast images for trustworthiness derived from this model were then entered into a random-effects analysis.

Acknowledgments

This work was supported by a programme grant to R.J.D. from the Wellcome Trust.

REFERENCES

1. Humphrey, N. *Consciousness Regained: Chapters in the Development of Mind* (Oxford Univ. Press, New York, 1983).
2. Adolphs, R., Tranel, D., Damasio, H. & Damasio, A. Impaired recognition of emotion in facial expressions following bilateral damage to the human amygdala. *Nature* 372, 669–672 (1994).
3. Hornak, J., Rolls, E. T. & Wade, D. Face and voice expression identification in patients with emotional and behavioural changes following ventral frontal lobe damage. *Neuropsychologia* 34, 247–261 (1996).
4. Adolphs, R., Damasio, H., Tranel, D., Cooper, G. & Damasio, A. R. A role for somatosensory cortices in the visual recognition of emotion as revealed by three-dimensional lesion mapping. *J. Neurosci.* 20, 2683–2690 (2000).
5. Morris, J. S. *et al.* A differential neural response in the human amygdala to fearful and happy facial expressions. *Nature* 383, 812–815 (1996).
6. Phillips. M. L. *et al.* A specific neural substrate for perceiving facial expressions of disgust. *Nature* 389, 495–498 (1997).
7. Sprengelmeyer, R., Rausch, M., Eysel, U. T. & Przuntek, H. Neural structures associated with recognition of facial expressions of basic emotions. *Proc. R. Soc. Lond. B Biol. Sci.* 265, 1927–1931 (1998).
8. Adolphs, R., Tranel, D. & Damasio, A. R. The human amygdala in social judgment. *Nature* 393, 470–474 (1998).
9. Eslinger, P. J. & Damasio, A. R. Severe disturbance of higher cognition after bilateral frontal lobe ablation: patient EVR. *Neurology* 35, 1731–1741 (1985).
10. Damasio, A. R. *Descartes' Error: Emotion, Reason and the Human Brain* (Putnam, New York, 1994).
11. Brothers, L. The social brain: a project for integrating primate behavior and neurophysiology in a new domain. *Concepts Neurosci.* 1, 27–51 (1990).
12. Adolphs, R. Social cognition and the human brain. *Trends. Cogn. Sci.* 3, 469–479 (1999).
13. Adolphs, R. The neurobiology of social cognition. *Curr. Opin. Neurobiol.* 11, 231–239 (2001).
14. Allison, T., Puce, A. & McCarthy, G. Social perception from visual cues: role of the STS region. *Trends Cogn. Sci.* 4, 267–278 (2000).
15. Dolan, R. J. *et al.* Neural activation during covert processing of positive emotional facial expressions. *Neuroimage* 4, 194–200 (1996).
16. Blair, R. J., Morris, J. S., Frith, C. D., Perrett, D. I. & Dolan, R. J. Dissociable neural responses to facial expressions of sadness and anger. *Brain* 122, 883–893 (1999).
17. Lane, R. D., Chau, P. M. & Dolan, R. J. Common effects of emotional valence, arousal and attention on neural activation during visual processing of pictures. *Neuropsychologia* 37, 989–997 (1999).
18. Morris, J. S., Ohman, A. & Dolan, R. J. Conscious and unconscious emotional learning in the human amygdala. *Nature* 393, 467–470 (1998).
19. Whalen, P. J. *et al.* Masked presentations of emotional facial expressions modulate amygdala activity without explicit knowledge. *J. Neurosci.* 18, 411–418 (1998).
20. Strange, B. A., Henson, R. N., Friston, K. J. & Dolan, R. J. Brain mechanisms for detecting perceptual, semantic, and emotional deviance. *Neuroimage* 12, 425–433 (2000).
21. Vuilleumier, P., Armony, J. L., Driver, J. & Dolan, R. J. Effects of attention and emotion on face processing in the human brain. An event-related fMRI study. *Neuron* 30, 829–841 (2001).
22. Buechel, C., Morris, J., Dolan, R. J. & Friston, K. J. Brain systems mediating aversive conditioning: an event-related fMRI study. *Neuron* 20, 947–957 (1998).
23. Buechel, C., Dolan, R. J., Armony, J. L. & Friston, K. J. Amygdala-hippocampal involvement in human aversive trace conditioning revealed through event-related functional magnetic resonance imaging. *J. Neurosci.* 19, 10869–10876 (1999).
24. Casey, K. L. Forebrain mechanisms of nociception and pain: analysis through imaging. *Proc. Natl. Acad. Sci. USA* 96, 7668–7674 (1999).
25. Critchley, H. D., Mathias, C. J. & Dolan, R. J. Neural activity in the human brain relating to uncertainty and arousal during anticipation. *Neuron* 29, 537–545 (2001).
26. Damasio, A. *The Feeling of What Happens: Body and Emotion in the Making of Consciousness* (Harcourt Brace, New York, 1999).
27. Critchley, H. D., Mathias, C. J. & Dolan, R. J. Neuroanatomical basis for first- and second-order representations of bodily states. *Nat. Neurosci.* 4, 207–212 (2001).
28. Breiter, H. C. *et al.* Response and habituation of the human amygdala during visual processing of facial expression. *Neuron* 17, 875–887 (1996).
29. Isenberg, N. *et al.* Linguistic threat activates the human amygdala. *Proc. Natl. Acad. Sci. USA* 96, 10456–10459 (1999).
30. Morris, J. S., Buchel, C. & Dolan, R. J. Parallel neural responses in amygdala subregions and sensory cortex during implicit fear conditioning. *Neuroimage* 13, 1044–1052 (2001).
31. Dolan, R. J., Morris, J. S. & de Gelder, B. Crossmodal binding of fear in voice and face. *Proc. Natl. Acad. Sci. USA* 98, 10006–10010 (2001).
32. Morris, J. S. *et al.* A neuromodulatory role for the human amygdala in processing emotional facial expressions. *Brain* 121, 47–57 (1998).
33. Amaral, D. G. & Price, J. L. Amygdalo-cortical projections in the monkey *(Macaca fascicularis). J. Comp. Neurol.* 230, 465–496 (1984).

34. Anderson, A. K. & Phelps, E. A. Lesions of the human amygdala impair enhanced perception of emotionally salient events. *Nature* 411, 305–309 (2001).

35. Bonda, E., Petrides, M., Ostry, D. & Evans, A. Specific involvement of human parietal systems and the amygdala in the perception of biological motion. *J. Neurosci.* 16, 3737–3744 (1996).

36. Castelli, F., Happe, F., Frith, U. & Frith, C. Movement and mind: a functional imaging study of perception and interpretation of complex intentional movement patterns. *Neuroimage* 12, 314–325 (2000).

37. Fletcher, P. C. *et al.* Other minds in the brain: a functional imaging study of 'theory of mind' in story comprehension. *Cognition* 57, 109–128 (1995).

38. Gallagher, H. L. *et al.* Reading the mind in cartoons and stories: an fMRI study of 'theory of mind' in verbal and nonverbal tasks. *Neuropsychologia* 38, 11–21 (2000).

39. Brunet, E., Sarfati, Y., Hardy-Bayle, M. C. & Decety, J. A PET investigation of the attribution of intentions with a nonverbal task. *Neuroimage* 11, 157–166 (2000).

40. Frith, C. D. & Frith, U. Interacting minds—a biological basis. *Science* 286, 1692–1695 (1999).

41. Frith, C. & Frith, U. in *Understanding Other Minds: Perspectives From Developmental Cognitive Neuroscience* (eds. Baron-Cohen, S., Tager-Flusberg, H. & Cohen, D. J.) 334–356 (Oxford Univ. Press, New York, 2000).

42. Elliott, R. & Dolan, R. J. Neural response during preference and memory judgments for subliminally presented stimuli: a functional neuroimaging study. *J. Neurosci.* 18, 4697–4704 (1998).

43. Phillips, M. L. *et al.* Neural responses to facial and vocal expressions of fear and disgust. *Proc. R. Soc. Land. B Biol. Sci.* 265, 1809–1817 (1998).

44. Friston, K. *et al.* Spatial registration and normalization of images. *Hum. Brain Mapp.* 2, 165–189 (1995).

45. Talairach, J. & Tournoux, P. *Co-planar Stereotaxic Atlas of the Human Brain* (Theime, Stuttgart, Germany, 1988).

46. Ekman, P. & Friesen, W. V. *Pictures of Facial Affect* (Consulting Psychologists Press, Palo Alto, California, 1975).

47. Josephs, O., Turner, R. & Friston, K. Event-related fMRI. *Hum. Brain Mapp.* 5, 243–248 (1997).

48. Friston, K. *et al.* Statistical parametric maps in functional imaging: a general linear approach. *Hum. Brain Mapp.* 2, 189–210 (1995).

49. Worsley, K. *et al.* A unified statistical approach for determining significant signals in images of cerebral activation. *Hum. Brain Mapp.* 4, 58–73 (1996).

50. Duvernoy, H. M. *The Human Brain* (Springer, Vienna, 1999).

PART 9

Decision Making

The processes underlying choice were once thought to be straightforward: individuals were conceptualized as rational decision makers who intuitively calculated the expected value of alternatives and selected the option with the highest expected value. To accomplish this feat, individuals were assumed to know the utility of one good relative to an alternative, follow the laws of probability, exhibit planning and forethought, avoid temptation, and guess fairly accurately what others might do. As seen through the lens of psychology and the neurosciences, this characterization of choice processes is overly simplistic and misleading. Human decisions are subject to a variety of internal biases and context effects from the availability heuristic and confirmatory bias to groupthink. Psychological research has demonstrated how alternative choices, previous experiences, associations, culture, and ways of thinking about a situation all affect decisions in ways that are not predicted by simple Bayesian models and Rational choices. For instance, mental simulation of alternative outcomes through counterfactual reasoning can dramatically influence our evaluations and decisions—so much so that silver medalists in the Olympic Games are generally less happy with their achievements than are bronze medalists.

A study of decision making we conducted with chimpanzees is illustrative of the operation of both cognitive and emotional influences. The chimpanzees in the study had been trained extensively in simple arithmetic operations (counting, addition, subtraction) using Arabic numerals. During testing, the chimps could see two reinforcement pans, each of which was baited with different quantities of candies on each trial. A reverse reinforcement contingency was implemented such that the chimps received the candies from the pan to which it did not point. Thus, it was in the chimps best interest to select the smaller of the two candy arrays in order to obtain the remaining, larger quantity. Even after hundreds of training trials across dozens of sessions, the chimpanzees' performances were significantly below chance. Moreover, their performance worsened at higher reward ratios—where they stood to benefit the most. This was true for all chimps in the study. In another condition, the chimps performed the same task but, rather than using candy arrays as stimuli, placards with corresponding Arabic numerals were substituted, and the chimps received the number of candies that corresponded to the nonselected numeral. This change led to an immediate above-chance performance. When the candies were again used as experimental stimuli, performance fell immediately to below-chance levels, and when the Arabic numerals were used performance rose immediately to above chance. These results suggested that the chimps had acquired the rules of the task but this knowledge, or at least its effect on behavior, was obscured by a potent competing emotional disposition arising from the intrinsic incentive properties of the candy arrays.

The examination of the neural circuitry that is activated during decision making by Sanfey et al. (2003) suggests that emotion and cognition are potent influences in human primates, as well. In their study, a player could propose a division of $10 to another player, who could either accept or reject the offer. Offers around $5 were equitable, whereas offers less than $5 were inequitable splits. If the second player rejected an offer, both players were left with nothing. The goal of the game was to make as much money as possible. Such a task contingency meant it was rational to accept inequitable as well as equitable offers (because a small amount of money is better than no money), and a rational player who anticipated this would offer inequitable divisions to the other player. Neither of these rational choice predictions were found, however, as most of the offers were around $5 and around half of the inequitable offers were rejected. Sanfey and colleagues also used functional brain imaging (fMRI) to explore the regions of brain activation during the task. They found inequitable relative to equitable offers were associated with increased activity in the dorsolateral prefrontal cortex, bilateral anterior insula, and anterior cingulate—a pattern of activation suggesting that inequitable offers evoked more thought, conflict, and negative affect. Furthermore, the greater the activation of the anterior insula—an area involved in negative emotions—the more likely the individual was to reject an inequitable offer. Sanfrey et al.'s study, therefore, suggests that the choice processes are influenced not only by the goals and opportunities that exist in the game or task, but also the attributions made to and emotions aroused by others.

Bar-On et al. (2003) build on this theme in their study of the details of decision making and social reasoning in two groups of individuals—those with lesions in the ventromedial prefrontal cortex and either the amygdala or insula cortices, and those with lesions in other regions of the brain. Several interesting results were obtained. First, the group with lesions within the circuit comprised of the ventromedial prefrontal cortex, amygdala, and insula performed more poorly on measures of social intelligence and decision making than the control group. The competencies most affected by lesions in this circuit were accurate self-awareness, self-expression, and self-regulation (e.g., changing behavior when contingencies change), which Bar-On suggests may mean that the deficits in decision making may be caused in large part by the deficits in social intelligence. Furthermore, the two groups of participants performed comparably on measures of cognitive intelligence and psychopathology, evidence that cognitive and social intelligence are separable constructs, with the latter critical for adaptive decision making in a changing environment. Together, these studies contribute to the accumulating evidence that the brain is not simply an analytic machine but a social information processing mechanism.

The Neural Basis of Economic Decision-Making in the Ultimatum Game

Alan G. Sanfey,[1,3] James K. Rilling,[1]* Jessica A. Aronson,[2] Leigh E. Nystrom,[1,2] Jonathan D. Cohen[1,2,4]

The nascent field of neuroeconomics seeks to ground economic decision-making in the biological substrate of the brain. We used functional magnetic resonance imaging of Ultimatum Game players to investigate neural substrates of cognitive and emotional processes involved in economic decision-making. In this game, two players split a sum of money; one player proposes a division and the other can accept or reject this. We scanned players as they responded to fair and unfair proposals. Unfair offers elicited activity in brain areas related to both emotion (anterior insula) and cognition (dorsolateral prefrontal cortex). Further, significantly heightened activity in anterior insula for rejected unfair offers suggests an important role for emotions in decision-making.

Standard economic models of human decision-making (such as utility theory) have typically minimized or ignored the influence of emotions on people's decision-making behavior, idealizing the decision-maker as a perfectly rational cognitive machine. However, in recent years this assumption has been challenged by behavioral economists, who have identified additional psychological and emotional factors that influence decision-making (1, 2), and recently researchers have begun using neuroimaging to examine behavior in economic games (3). This study applies functional neuroimaging techniques to investigate the relative contributions of cognitive and emotional processes to human social decision-making.

The limitations of the standard economic model are effectively illustrated by empirical findings from a simple game known as the Ultimatum Game. In the Ultimatum Game, two players are given the opportunity to split a sum of money.

[1]Center for the Study of Brain, Mind and Behavior, [2]Department of Psychology, [3]Center for Health and Well-Being, Princeton University, Princeton, NJ 08544, USA. [4]Department of Psychiatry, University of Pittsburgh, Pittsburgh, PA 15260, USA.

One player is deemed the proposer and the other, the responder. The proposer makes an offer as to how this money should be split between the two. The second player (the responder) can either accept or reject this offer. If it is accepted, the money is split as proposed, but if the responder rejects the offer, then neither player receives anything. In either event, the game is over.

The standard economic solution to the Ultimatum Game is for the proposer to offer the smallest sum of money possible to the responder and for the responder to accept this offer, on the reasonable grounds that any monetary amount is preferable to none. However, considerable behavioral research in industrialized cultures indicates that, irrespective of the monetary sum, modal offers are typically around 50% of the total amount. Low offers (around 20% of the total) have about a 50% chance of being rejected (4–8). This latter, quite robust, experimental finding is particularly intriguing, demonstrating that circumstances exist in which people are motivated to actively turn down monetary reward.

Why do people do this? The game is so simple that it is improbable that these rejections are due to a failure to understand the rules of the game, or an inability to conceptualize a single-shot interaction with a partner (9). On the basis of participant reports, it appears that low offers are often rejected after an angry reaction to an offer perceived as unfair (10). Objecting to unfairness has been proposed as a fundamental adaptive mechanism by which we assert and maintain a social reputation (11), and the negative emotions provoked by unfair treatment in the Ultimatum Game can lead people to sacrifice sometimes considerable financial gain in order to punish their partner for the slight. Unfair offers in the Ultimatum Game induce conflict in the responder between cognitive ("accept") and emotional ("reject") motives, motives that we might expect to see represented in brain areas implicated in cognitive and emotional modes of thought, with additional regions possibly mediating these competing goals (12).

To shed light on the neural and psychological processes mediating such behaviors, we scanned 19 participants using functional magnetic resonance imaging (fMRI), each in the role of the responder

in the Ultimatum Game. We were interested in neural and behavioral reactions to offers which were fair (the money is split 50:50) or unfair (the proposer offered an unequal split to his or her advantage). In particular, we hypothesized that unfair offers would engage neural structures involved in both emotional and cognitive processing, and that the magnitude of activation in these structures might explain variance in the subsequent decision to accept or reject these offers.

Before scanning, each participant was introduced to 10 people they were told would partner with them in the games to follow. They were told that they would play a single iteration of the game with each partner and that their decisions with each partner would not be revealed to the other partners and, therefore, could not affect subsequent offers. The participants were then placed inside the MRI scanner and began playing the Ultimatum Game with their partners via a computer interface (Figure 16.1A) (13). They completed 30 rounds in all, 10 playing the game with a human partner (once with each of the 10 partners), 10 with a computer partner, and a further 10 control rounds in which they simply received money for a button press. The rounds were presented randomly, and all involved splitting $10. Offers made by human partners in fact adhered to a predetermined algorithm, which ensured that all participants saw the same set (and a full range) of offers (14, 15). Half of these offers were fair, that is, a proposal to split the $10 evenly ($5:$5), with the remaining half proposing unequal splits (two offers of $9:$1, two offers of $8:$2, and one offer of $7:$3). The 10 offers from the computer partner were identical to those from the human partners (half fair, half unfair). The 10 control trials were designed to control for the response to monetary reinforcement, independent of the social interaction. The distribution of offers generally mimics the range of offers typically made in uncontrolled versions of the game (i.e., involving freely acting human partners).

Behavioral results were very similar to those typically found in Ultimatum Game experiments (Figure 16.1B) (16). Participants accepted all fair offers, with decreasing acceptance rates as the

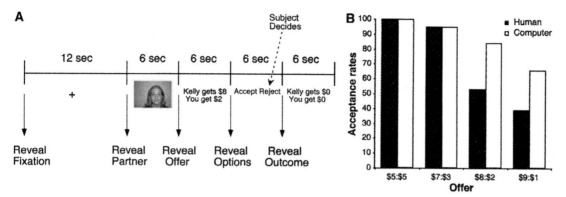

FIGURE 16.1 ■ (A) Time line for a single round of the Ultimatum Game. Each round lasted 36 s. Each round began with a 12-s preparation interval. The participant then saw the photograph and name of their partner in that trial for 6 seconds. A picture of a computer was shown if it was a computer trial, or a roulette wheel if it was a control trial. Next, participants saw the offer proposed by the partner for a further 6 s, after which they indicated whether they accepted or rejected the offer by pressing one of two buttons on a button box. (B) Behavioral results from the Ultimatum Game. These are the offer acceptance rates averaged over all trials. Each of 19 participants saw five $5:$5 offers, one $7:$3 offer, two $8:$2 offers, and two $9:$1 offers from both human and computer partners (20 offers in total).

offers became less fair. Unfair offers of $2 and $1 made by human partners were rejected at a significantly higher rate than those offers made by a computer ($9:$1 offer: $\chi^2 = 5.28$, 1 df, $P = 0.02$; $8:$2 offer: $\chi^2 = 8.77$, 1 df, $P = 0.003$), suggesting that participants had a stronger emotional reaction to unfair offers from humans than to the same offers from a computer (*17*).

Among the areas showing greater activation for unfair compared with fair offers from human partners (Figure 16.2a and b; Table S1) were bilateral anterior insula, dorsolateral prefrontal cortex (DLPFC), and anterior cingulate cortex (ACC). The magnitude of activation was also significantly greater for unfair offers from human partners as compared to both unfair offers from computer partners (left insula: $t = 2.52$, $P < 0.02$; right insula: $t = 2.2$, $P < 0.03$) and low control offers (left insula: $t = 3.46$, $P < 0.001$; right insula: $t = 2.83$, $P < 0.05$). This suggests that these activations were not solely a function of the amount of money offered to the participant but rather were also uniquely sensitive to the context, namely perceived unfair treatment from another human (Figure 16.2c and d). Further, regions of bilateral anterior insula demonstrated sensitivity to the degree of unfairness of an offer, exhibiting

significantly greater activation for a $9:$1 offer than an $8:$2 offer from a human partner (Figure 16.2e) (left insula, $P < 0.001$; right insula, $P < 0.01$), in addition to the aforementioned greater activation for unfair offers than fair ($5:$5) offers.

Activation of bilateral anterior insula to unfair offers from human partners is particularly interesting in light of this region's oft-noted association with negative emotional states. Anterior insula activation is consistently seen in neuroimaging studies of pain and distress (*18–20*), hunger and thirst (*21, 22*), and autonomic arousal (*23*). This region has also been implicated in studies of emotion, in particular involvement in the evaluation and representation of specific negative emotional states (*24*). Chief amongst these are anger and disgust, both of which have been found to engage a distinct region of the anterior insula activated by an unfair offer in the present study (*25, 26*). Though studies of disgust have largely focused on physical sensations of taste and odor (*27*), it has been suggested that emotion-based disgust (as perhaps induced by an insultingly unfair offer) may be conceptually similar. The recruitment of similar neural structures, namely the anterior insula, in both physical and moral disgust gives some credence to this notion.

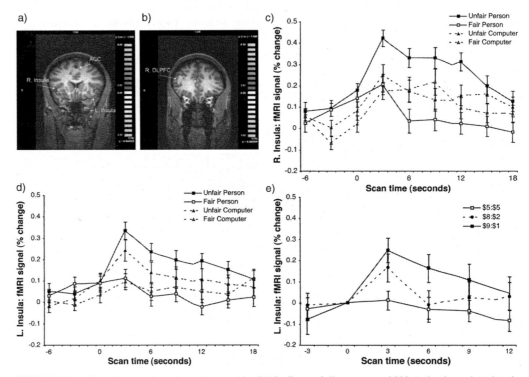

FIGURE 16.2 ■ (*A color version of parts a and b of this figure follows page 146.*) Activation related to the presentation of an unfair offer. (a) Map of the *t* statistic for the contrast [unfair human offer – fair human offer] showing activation of bilateral anterior insula and anterior cingulate cortex. Areas in orange showed greater activation following unfair as compared with fair offers ($P < 0.001$). (b) Map of the *t* statistic for the contrast [unfair human offer – fair human offer] showing activation of right dorsolateral prefrontal cortex. (c) Event-related plot for unfair and fair offers in right anterior insula. The offer was revealed at $t = 0$ on the *x* axis. (d) Event-related plot for unfair and fair offers in left anterior insula. (e) Event-related plot for different human unfair and fair offers in subset of left anterior insula.

If the activation in the anterior insula is a reflection of the responders' negative emotional response to an unfair offer, we might expect activity in this region to correlate with the subsequent decision to accept or reject the offer. Because all fair offers and the vast majority of $7:$3 offers were accepted, we focused on the $8:$2 and $9:$1 offers from a human partner for the analysis of whether neural activity was related to the decision made in the game. Indeed, looking at the participant level, those participants with stronger anterior insula activation to unfair offers rejected a higher proportion of these offers (right insula: correlation coefficient $r = -0.45$, $P = 0.025$, one-tailed; left insula:

$r = -0.39$, $P = 0.05$, one-tailed) (Figure 16.3a). Of particular interest is whether these differences in anterior insular activation extend to the trial level. Looking across participants, an examination of individual trials also revealed a relation between right anterior insular activity and the decision to accept or reject (Figure 16.3b). Activation in this area was significantly greater in response to unfair offers that were later rejected ($P = 0.028$, one-tailed). These results provide additional support for the hypothesis that neural representations of emotional states guide human decision-making.

In contrast to the insula, DLPFC usually has been linked to cognitive processes such as goal

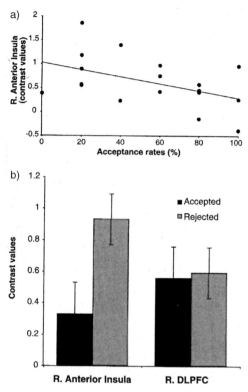

FIGURE 16.3 ■ (a) Acceptance rates of unfair offers plotted against right anterior insula activation for each participant. (b) Right anterior insula and right DLPFC activation for all unfair offer trials, categorized by subsequent acceptance or rejection.

maintenance and executive control (*28, 29*). Thus, the DLPFC activation we observed in response to unfair offers may relate to the representation and active maintenance of the cognitive demands of the task, namely the goal of accumulating as much money as possible. An unfair offer is more difficult to accept, as indicated by the higher rejection rates of these offers, and hence higher cognitive demands may be placed on the participant in order to overcome the strong emotional tendency to reject the offer. Although DLPFC activated to unfair offers, this activation did not correlate with acceptance rates ($r = 0.04$, $P > 0.05$), suggesting that activation of this region alone is not sufficient to predict behavior. However, motivated by the hypothesis that this region may be competing with emotional areas in influencing

the decision, we examined the balance between activation in anterior insula and DLPFC for unfair offers. Unfair offers that are subsequently rejected have greater anterior insula than DLPFC activation, whereas accepted offers exhibit greater DLPFC than anterior insula (Figure 16.3b). The contrast in activation between these two areas is significantly different for accepted and rejected offers ($P = 0.033$, one-tailed), consistent with the hypothesis that competition between these two regions influences behavior. DLPFC activity remains relatively constant across unfair offers, perhaps reflecting the steady task representation of money maximization, with anterior insula scaling monotonically to the degree of unfairness, reflecting the emotional response to the offer. Caution is needed when comparing the magnitude of the fMRI signal across brain regions. However, it is interesting to note that the outcome of the decision may reflect the relative engagement of these regions, with greater anterior insula activation biasing toward rejection and greater DLPFC biasing toward acceptance. Finally, unfair offers were also associated with increased activity in ACC. ACC has been implicated in detection of cognitive conflict (*30, 31*) and activation here may reflect the conflict between cognitive and emotional motivations in the Ultimatum Game.

This study sought to identify the neural correlates of fairness and unfairness, and in particular the relative contributions of cognitive and emotional processes to human decision-making. A basic sense of fairness and unfairness is essential to many aspects of societal and personal decision-making and underlies notions as diverse as ethics, social policy, legal practice, and personal morality. Our results are consistent with the idea that the areas of anterior insula and DLPFC represent the twin demands of the Ultimatum Game task, the emotional goal of resisting unfairness and the cognitive goal of accumulating money, respectively. Further, our finding that activity in a region well known for its involvement in negative emotion is predictive of subsequent behavior supports the importance of emotional influences in human decision-making. We believe that these findings, and work that proceeds from them, will provide a more detailed characterization of specific emotional responses, their neural substrates, and the social circumstances under which they are elicited. Therefore, not only do our results provide direct empirical support for economic models that acknowledge the influence of emotional factors on decision-making behavior, but they also provide the first step toward the development of quantitative measures that may be useful in constraining the social utility function in economic models (*32, 33*). Models of decision-making cannot afford to ignore emotion as a vital and dynamic component of our decisions and choices in the real world.

Supporting Online Material

www.sciencemag.org/cgi/content/full/300/5626/1755/DC1

Materials and Methods
Table S1

REFERENCES AND NOTES

1. C. Camerer, G. Loewenstein, in *Advances in Behavioral Economics*, C. Camerer, G. Loewenstein, M. Rabin, Eds. (Princeton Univ. Press, Princeton, NJ), in press.
2. G. Loewenstein, J. Lerner, in *The Handbook of Affective Science*, R. J. Davidson, H. H. Goldsmith, K. R. Scherer, Eds. (Oxford Univ. Press, Oxford, 2003).
3. K. McCabe, D. Houser, L. Ryan, V. Smith, T. Trouard, *Proc. Natl. Acad. Sci. U.S.A.* 98, 11832 (2001).
4. W. Guth, R. Schmittberger, B. Schwarze, *J. Econ. Behav. Organ.* 3, 376 (1982).
5. R. H. Thaler, *J. Econ. Perspect*, 2, 195 (1988).
6. G. E. Bolton, R. Zwick, *Game Econ. Behav.* 10, 95 (1995).
7. A. E. Roth, in *Handbook of Experimental Economics*, J. H. Kagel, A. E. Roth, Eds. (Princeton Univ. Press, Princeton, NJ, 1995).
8. See J. Henrich *et al.* [*Am. Econ. Rev.* 91, 73 (2001)] for Ultimatum Game research in simple societies.
9. C. Camerer, R. H. Thaler, *J. Econ. Perspect.* 9, 209 (1995).
10. M. M. Pillutla, J. K. Murnighan, *Organ. Behav. Hum. Dec. Proc.* 68, 208 (1996).
11. M. A. Nowak, K. M. Page, K. Sigmund, *Science* 289, 1773 (2000).
12. We use the term "cognitive" here, in place of the term "rational" (as commonly used in the traditional economic literature), in recognition of the fact that emotional responses may also have a rational basis (e.g., to punish

unfair offers). The term "cognitive" is perhaps also problematic, for similar reasons. Terms such as "proximal" and "distal" may be more accurate, respectively indicating the immediate and longer-term sources of gain associated with the behavior. However, until the field converges on a new set of accepted terms for designating these classes of motivation, we use the terms cognitive and emotional as intuitively accessible, if not technically accurate.

13. Materials and methods are available as supporting material on *Science* Online.
14. This methodology deviates somewhat from the standards of experimental economics, a field that generally proscribes the use of deception [see (*34*) for a summary of the issues, though there are some exceptions (*35*)]. We chose to use a limited amount of deception in the current study primarily because of the heavy logistic demands of an fMRI study, requiring a full distribution of offers in a constrained number of participants. Practical issues notwithstanding, we believe the use of deception had little if any impact on our results, and any effect was not likely to confound their interpretation. During the post-experiment debriefing, no subject gave any suggestion that they had been suspicious of the offers they received. Further, the behavioral results in the human partner condition replicate those found in versions of the game using no deception, with approximately half of offers of 20% or less of the total being rejected (*9*). Perhaps most importantly, if subjects suspected deception, this should have diminished emotional responses (i.e., if subjects suspected the offers to be fictitious, their emotional reactions to these offers, particularly unfair offers, should have been muted). The fact that we observed significant effects consistent with emotional responses suggests, once again, that the effects of deception were minimal and, if they were present, have simply caused an underestimate of the observed effects. Although we are sensitive to the issue of deception, we believe that the methodological constraints of fMRI justified our practice and that the findings do not appear to be tainted by subjects' possible perceptions of the deception used.
15. A common concern regarding the use of deception involves possible contamination of the participant pool. As mentioned previously, rejection rates in the current study replicate those typically reported from uncontrolled Ultimatum Game studies; therefore, we do not believe we suffered unduly from this. Furthermore, a comparison of rejection rates over the course of the experiment (i.e., longitudinally over participants) indicates no systematic trends in these rates (mean rejection rate of offers for first six participants was 32%; mean rate for last six participants was 35%).
16. After the conclusion of the Ultimatum Game with all partners, subjects then played a single round of the Prisoner's Dilemma (PD) game with each of the partners. This raises the possibility that subjects did not treat the Ultimatum Game as a true single-shot game. We do not believe playing the PD game affected their play in the Ultimatum

Game in this study for several reasons. First, our behavioral results support the notion that the Ultimatum Game was played as a single-shot game. As noted above, the proportion of rejected offers in our study matches proportions reported in the experimental economic literature when the game is strictly controlled as single-shot. We would have expected much higher rejection rates in an iterated Ultimatum Game. Second, unpublished data of ours using a single-shot Ultimatum Game (with no subsequent task) produced rejection rates of unfair offers that are virtually identical to those reported here ($8:$2 split, 47% versus 49%; $9:$1 split, 61% versus 60%). We believe this evidence strongly suggests that subjects treated the Ultimatum Game as a single-shot game, as instructed.

17. We asked our participants as part of the debriefing process what they considered a "fair" offer to be irrespective of their decision to accept or reject, thus providing an indication of their standards of fairness. Of our participants, 58% considered any offer less than $5:$5 as unfair, with the remaining 42% deeming anything less than $7:$3 to be an unfair division.

18. S. W. Derbyshire *et al. Pain* 73, 431 (1997).

19. M. J. Iadarola *et al. Brain* 121, 931 (1998).

20. K. C. Evans *et al. J. Neurophysiol* 88, 1500 (2002).

21. D. Denton *et al. Proc. Natl. Acad. Sci. U.S.A.* 96, 5304 (1999).

22. P. A. Tataranni *et al. Proc. Natl. Acad. Sci. U.S.A.* 96, 4569 (1999).

23. H. D. Critchley, R. Elliott, C. J. Mathias, R. J. Dolan, *J. Neurosci,* 20, 3033 (2000).

24. A. J. Calder, A. D. Lawrence, A. W. Young, *Nature Rev. Neurosci,* 2, 352 (2001).

25. A. R. Damasio *et al. Nature Neurosci.* 3, 1049 (2000).

26. M. L. Phillips *et al. Nature* 389, 495 (1997).

27. P. Rozin, A. E. Fallon, *Psychol. Rev.* 94, 23 (1987).

28. E. K. Miller, J. D. Cohen, *Annu. Rev. Neurosci* 24, 167 (2001).

29. A. D. Wagner, A. Maril, R. A. Bjork, D. L. Schacter, *NeuroImage* 14, 1337 (2001).

30. A. W. MacDonald III, J. D. Cohen, V. A. Stenger, C. S. Carter, *Science* 288, 1835 (2000).

31. M. Botvinick, L. E. Nystrom, K. Fissell, C. S. Carter, J. D. Cohen, *Nature* 402, 179 (1999).

32. E. Fehr, K. M. Schmidt, *Q. J. Econ.* 114, 817 (1999).

33. G. E. Bolton, A. Ockenfels, *Am Econ. Rev.* 90, 166 (2000).

34. R. Hertwig, A. Ortmann, *Behav. Brain Sci.* 24, 383 (2001).

35. S. Bonetti, *J. Econ. Psychol.* 19, 377 (1998).

36. We would like to thank D. Kahneman, A. Scheres, and three anonymous reviewers for their helpful comments. This work was supported in part by grants from the Seaver Institute and the Mind, Brain, Body, and Health Initiative.

Exploring the Neurological Substrate of Emotional and Social Intelligence

Reuven Bar-On,[1] Daniel Tranel,[2] Natalie L. Denburg[2] and Antoine Bechara[2]

The somatic marker hypothesis posits that deficits in emotional signalling (somatic states) lead to poor judgment in decision-making, especially in the personal and social realms. Similar to this hypothesis is the concept of emotional intelligence, which has been defined as an array of emotional and social abilities, competencies and skills that enable individuals to cope with daily demands and be more effective in their personal and social life. Patients with lesions to the ventromedial (VM) prefrontal cortex have defective somatic markers and tend to exercise poor judgment in decision-making, which is especially manifested in the disadvantageous choices they typically make in their personal lives and in the ways in which they relate with others. Furthermore, lesions to the amygdala or insular cortices, especially on the right side, also compromise somatic state activation and decision-making. This suggests that the VM, amygdala and insular regions are part of a neural system involved in somatic state activation and decision-making. We hypothesized that the severe impairment of these patients in real-life decision-making and an inability to cope effectively with environmental and social demands would be reflected in an abnormal level of emotional and social intelligence. Twelve patients with focal, stable bilateral lesions of the VM cortex or with right unilateral lesions of the amygdala or the right insular cortices, were tested on the Emotional Quotient Inventory (EQ-i), a standardized psychometric measure of various aspects of emotional and social intelligence. We also examined these patients with various other procedures designed to measure decision-making (the Gambling Task), social functioning, as well

[1]Emotional Intelligence Research Laboratory, Trent University, Peterborough, Canada, and [2]Division of Behavioral Neurology and Cognitive Neuroscience, University of Iowa College of Medicine, Iowa City, IA, USA.

as personality changes and psychopathology; standardized neuropsychological tests were applied to assess their cognitive intelligence, executive functioning, perception and memory as well. Their results were compared with those of 11 patients with focal, stable lesions in structures outside the neural circuitry thought to mediate somatic state activation and decision-making. Only patients with lesions in the somatic marker circuitry revealed significantly low emotional intelligence and poor judgment in decision-making as well as disturbances in social functioning, in spite of normal levels of cognitive intelligence (IQ) and the absence of psychopathology based on DSM-IV criteria. The findings provide preliminary evidence suggesting that emotional and social intelligence is different from cognitive intelligence. We suggest, moreover, that the neural systems supporting somatic state activation and personal judgment in decision-making may overlap with critical components of a neural circuitry subserving emotional and social intelligence, independent of the neural system supporting cognitive intelligence.

Keywords: social cognition; decision-making; emotion; somatic markers; emotional intelligence.

Introduction

Patients with lesions to the ventromedial (VM) cortex are subject to impaired personal judgment in decision-making, which is frequently manifested in the manner in which they relate with others. This specific type of impairment is observed even in cases in which cognitive capacity (IQ) falls within the normal or even above-normal range. In spite of normal intellectual capacity, moreover, these patients also reveal a compromised ability to experience, understand, express and effectively use emotions (Damasio, 1994). In essence, they are cognitively intelligent but typically behave in an unintelligent manner with respect to exercising judgment in making decisions of a personal and interpersonal nature. Based on these clinical observations, the somatic marker hypothesis has been proposed to explain this specific type of impairment (Damasio, 1994). The somatic marker hypothesis outlines a neurological explanation for decision-making impairment. This hypothesis suggests that decision-making is a process that depends on emotional signals, which are defined as bio-regulatory responses aimed at maintaining homeostasis and ensuring survival. The roots of this concept, as well as those of emotional intelligence, can be traced back to Charles Darwin's early research that culminated in the publication of the first scientific work on the topic titled *The Expression of the Emotions in Man and Animals* (Darwin, 1872).

The somatic marker hypothesis specifies a number of structures and operations required for the normal function of decision-making. In brief, the hypothesis posits that the amygdala is a critical substrate in the system that triggers somatic states activated by primary inducers (Bechara *et al.,* 1999). Primary inducers are unconditioned stimuli that are innately set as pleasurable or aversive, or conditioned stimuli, which when they are present in the immediate environment, automatically and obligatorily elicit a somatic response. Secondary inducers are entities generated by recall or by thought, and they elicit a somatic response when brought to memory (Damasio, 1995). Once somatic states from primary inducers are induced, signals from them are relayed to the brain. Representations of these signals can remain covert at the level of the brainstem, or can reach the parietal cortices (insular/SI, SII) and posterior cingulate cortices and be perceived as a feeling (Maddock, 1999; Damasio *et al.,* 2000). When we process a secondary inducer, i.e., recall an event associated with a feeling, we may re-enact the somatic state characteristic of the feeling. The VM cortex is a trigger structure for somatic states from secondary inducers (Bechara *et al.,* 1999). Decision-making is a complex process that sometimes involves a conflict between a primary inducer (which may be positive) and a secondary inducer (which may be negative). Sometimes, the conflict could be between only secondary inducers (e.g., a positive thought versus a negative thought). Regardless of how they are triggered, once somatic states induced by primary and/or secondary inducers are enacted in the body, all these somatic states, which can be either positive or negative, are summed into one overall somatic state (figuratively and literally speaking). This overall somatic state then provides signals to the brain that participate in at least two functions. (i) In one function, it provides a substrate for feeling the overall emotional state, possibly via the insular/somatosensory cortices (SI, SII). (ii) In the other function, it provides a substrate for biasing the decision to select a response (Damasio, 1999). This biasing effect may occur covertly at the level of the striatum, in which case the person acts without a conscious decision to do so. The biasing effect may also occur overtly at the level of the lateral orbitofrontal cortex when the person favours a plan of action, and at the anterior cingulate when the person executes a plan of action that is under volitional control.

The concept of the somatic marker hypothesis is thought to overlap with the concept of emotional intelligence regarding the use of emotions to guide human behaviour (Bechara *et al.*, 2000*a*). The conceptual nexus between the somatic marker hypothesis and emotional intelligence can be seen in the way the latter has been defined by some researchers (Bar-On, 2000, 2001): A multifactorial array of interrelated emotional, personal and social competencies that influence our ability to actively and effectively cope with daily demands. Most conceptualizations of this construct address one or more of the following basic components: (i) the ability to be aware of and express emotions; (ii) the ability to be aware of others' feelings and to establish interpersonal relationships; (iii) the ability to manage and regulate emotions; (iv) the ability to realistically and flexibly cope with the immediate situation and solve problems of a personal and interpersonal nature as they arise; and (v) the ability to generate positive affect in order to be sufficiently self-motivated to achieve personal goals. The concept of emotional intelligence is closely related to the concept of social intelligence. This conceptual proximity is evident in the way in which social intelligence was first defined by Thorndike in 1920 (Thorndike, 1920)—the ability to perceive one's own and others' internal states, motives and behaviours, and to act toward them optimally on the basis of that information. Because of the similarity between both concepts, some psychologists have suggested that they may relate to different aspects of the same construct and could actually be referred to as 'emotional and social intelligence' (Bar-On, 2000, 2001). With respect to the present study, moreover, it is important to note that both concepts and closely related constructs are thought by some to be based on a cognitive schemata (Mayer and Salovey, 1997; Taylor *et al.*, 1997; Lane, 2000; Zirkel, 2000). This means that what is perceptually scanned in one's immediate environment, together with one's emotional reaction to that which is perceived, may then be processed, evaluated and understood in order to effectively guide interpersonal behaviour. In the somatic marker hypothesis, it is important to note that there is also a covert route that mediates behaviour, which does not require information to be processed, evaluated and understood. However, it is not yet certain if such a covert route applies to the emotional and social intelligence construct as well.

Together with cognitive intelligence, emotional and social intelligence form important components of general intelligence. One of the major differences between the two is that the former is thought to relate primarily to higher order mental processes like reasoning, while the latter focuses more on perceiving, immediate processing and applying emotional and social content, information and knowledge. It has also been suggested that another fundamental difference between the two may be that cognitive intelligence is more cortically strategic in nature, while emotional and social intelligence is more limbically tactical for immediate behaviour suited more for survival and adaptation (Goleman, 1995; Bar-On, 1997*a*; Stein and Book, 2000). However, thus far these theories are supported more by supposition than by empirical findings.

One of the primary purposes of this study was to provide empirical evidence in support of the hypothesis that emotional and social intelligence is different from cognitive intelligence, in that these two major components of general intelligence are supported by separate neural substrates. Furthermore, we hypothesized that the neural systems that support emotional and social intelligence overlap with neural systems subserving somatic state activation and personal judgment in decision-making, which are separate from the neural systems supporting cognitive intelligence. We predicted that patients with lesions in critical components of the somatic marker circuitry (i.e. amygdala, VM prefrontal and insular/somatosensory cortices), who demonstrate severe impairments in real-life decision-making and an inability to cope effectively with environmental and social demands, would also demonstrate an abnormally low level of emotional and social intelligence. Specifically, we predicted that these patients would present significantly lower scores and ratings than the control group (patients with lesions outside the neural circuitry involved with the somatic state activation) on measures of emotional intelligence, decision-making as well as overall social functioning, despite maintaining normal levels of cognitive intelligence.

Methods

Twenty-three neurological patients were selected and divided into an experimental group and a control group based on the presence or absence of brain injury along the circuitry thought to mediate somatic state activation and decision-making.

Because of the relatively small sample sizes involved in the present study, non-parametric statistics were applied; the Mann–Whitney U test was employed to examine the groups being compared for significant differences (Siegal, 1956). In tandem with this conservative approach, a two-tailed evaluation was applied in interpreting the probability levels of the results. It was decided, moreover, to discuss significant differences on Emotional Quotient Inventory (EQ-i) subscale scores (e.g. emotional self-awareness) only if the parent composite scale score (i.e. intrapersonal EQ) proved to be significantly different when comparing the independent groups being examined.

Subjects

The experimental and control groups were matched with respect to gender, age, level of education and handedness. As can be seen in Table 17.1 the subjects were predominantly right-handed, in their mid-forties and had 14 to 15 years of education with no significant difference between the groups regarding age or education. The experimental group included seven males and five females, and the control group comprised four males and seven females.

Subjects with brain lesions were selected from the Patient Registry of the University of Iowa's Division of Cognitive Neuroscience. All brain-damaged subjects had undergone basic neuropsychological and neuroanatomical characterization according to the standard protocols of the Benton Neuropsychology Laboratory (Tranel, 1996) and

TABLE 17.1. Demographic Data of Participating Subjects

Demographic data	Control group	Experimental group	Z	P-level (2-tailed)
Total number of participants	11	12	–	–
Gender (male/female)	4/7	7/5	–/–	–/–
Age (years)	47.1	43.5	0.46	0.644
Age range (years)	24–74	21–63	–	–
Education (years)	14.6	13.7	0.85	0.398
Handedness (right/left)	10/1	12/0	–/–	–/–

The Mann–Whitney U test was applied to compare the average age and years of education between the control group and the experimental group for significant differences.

the Laboratory of Neuroimaging and Human Neuroanatomy (Damasio and Damasio, 1989; Damasio and Frank, 1992; Damasio, 1995). All subjects provided informed consent, which was approved by the appropriate human subject committees at the University of Iowa. Based on clinical interviews, none of the subjects in this study had a history of mental retardation, psychiatric disorder, substance abuse, learning disability or systemic disease that might affect the CNS.

The selection of subjects with brain lesions conformed to the following criteria: (i) a stable and chronic lesion at least 3 months post onset; and (ii) involvement of a brain region that either included (the experimental group) or excluded (the control group) structures of the somatic marker circuitry as shown below. The experimental, neuropsychological and neuroanatomical studies were all conducted when the subjects were in the chronic phase of recovery (i.e. > 3 months post lesion onset). Data collection for the various studies was contemporaneous for each subject (i.e. experimental, neuropsychological and neuroanatomical data for a given subject were collected at the same time or at a very close point in time).

The experimental group

This group included patients with lesions in either the VM prefrontal cortex, the right insular/somatosensory cortex or the right amygdala.

VM lesions. Six subjects had lesions involving the VM cortex bilaterally. In four subjects, the damage was caused by a stroke. In the other two subjects, the damage was caused by a frontal lobe meningioma that was surgically resected and removed. In all six subjects, the damage was bilateral and involved the anterior and posterior sectors of the VM cortex. In two of the subjects, the damage extended far posteriorly and most likely included the basal forebrain. In one subject, the lesion extended superiorly above the genu of the corpus callosum in both hemispheres. In three of the subjects, the lesions extended anteriorly and involved the frontopolar region. In two of the subjects, the lesions were asymmetrical in that the damage was more extensive on the right

relative to the left. In all subjects, the dorsolateral sectors of the prefrontal cortex were intact.

Amygdala lesions. Three subjects had lesions involving the amygdala. Patients with bilateral amygdala damage are extremely rare. Therefore, we decided to select patients with unilateral amygdala damage. Because the somatic marker hypothesis emphasizes the role of the right hemisphere as opposed to the left in somatic state activation and in light of recent support of this view in relation to patients with prefrontal cortex damage (Tranel *et al.*, 2000; Manes *et al.*, 2002), we selected patients with unilateral damage to the right amygdala.

In all three subjects, the aetiology was a right temporal lobectomy in order to treat an intractable seizure disorder. In all three subjects, the amygdala was completely removed. The entorhinal cortex overlaying the amygdaloid nucleus was damaged. However, there was minimal damage to the surrounding anterior sector of the hippocampal formation.

Insular/somatosensory (SI, SII) lesions. Three subjects had unilateral lesions involving the right insular/somatosensory (SI, SII) cortices. In all subjects, the aetiology was a right middle cerebral artery stroke. And in all three subjects, the insular cortex was damaged. There was also extensive damage to the superior and inferior parietal lobules, which include the somatosensory (SI, SII) cortices.

In two of the subjects, the damage extended to the right dorsolateral prefrontal cortex and included the right pre-central gyrus, but the cortex anterior to it was spared. There was also damage to the superior temporal gyrus. In one subject, the lesion included the right insular cortex and inferior parietal lobule, but did not extend into the prefrontal cortex or the temporal lobe.

The control group

This group included patients with lesions outside the neural circuitry thought to mediate somatic state activation and decision-making. In all 11 subjects, the aetiology of the lesion was a stroke. In four subjects, the damage included any of the following regions: the superior and/or middle frontal gyri in the right prefrontal cortex, the right precentral gyrus, the right paracentral lobule without damage below the body of the corpus callosum or extension to the frontal pole. In two subjects, the lesion involved similar territories in the left hemisphere. In three subjects, the lesions involved the posterior sector of the superior and/or middle temporal gyrus on the right. In one subject, the lesion involved the posterior sector of the middle temporal gyrus on the left. In one subject, the damage involved the right occipital cortex but spared the somatosensory and insular cortices.

Measures

The vagary of subject availability, being neurologically ill, not easily accessible, etc. produced some limitations on data collection but without interfering systemically with the outcome. Every subject completed the EQ-i and the Gambling Task (see below) in the present study. Almost all the subjects in the experimental group completed the social functioning, cognitive intelligence and executive functioning tests. However, a small number of subjects in the control group did not complete all these tests. Quite often, this was because the clinician could not justify administering these specific tests for these particular subjects. This was due to the nature of each subject's lesion, in which there was no suspicion that the subject would have problems in the domains measured by the clinical tests involved. Although not everyone was available to be tested with all of the measures described below, data collection for the critical group, the experimental group, was nearly complete. The missing data from some subjects, who were mostly those in the control group, do not systematically affect the outcome of the results because nonparametric statistics were applied which are designed specifically for examining small samples (Siegal, 1956).

Emotional intelligence

The Bar-On EQ-i was used to assess emotional intelligence (Bar-On, 1997*a*). The EQ-i is a self-report measure of emotionally and socially intelligent behaviour, which provides an estimate of one's underlying emotional and social intelligence. A more detailed discussion of the psychometric properties of this instrument and how it was developed is found in the EQ-i technical manual (Bar-On, 1997*b*) and elsewhere (Plake and Impara, 1999). In brief, the EQ-i comprises 133 items and employs a five-point Likert scale with a textual response format ranging from 'very seldom or not true of me' to 'very often true of me or true of me'. A list of the inventory's items is included in the EQ-i technical manual (Bar-On, 1997*b*). The subject's responses render a total emotional quotient (EQ) score and the following five composite scale scores give 15 subscale scores in all:

(i) Intrapersonal EQ (comprising self-regard, emotional self-awareness, assertiveness, independence and self-actualization);
(ii) Interpersonal EQ (comprising empathy, social responsibility and interpersonal relationship);
(iii) Stress management EQ (comprising stress tolerance and impulse control);
(iv) Adaptability EQ (comprising reality-testing, flexibility and problem-solving); and
(v) General mood EQ (comprising optimism and happiness).

A brief description of the emotional and social intelligence competencies measured by the 15 subscales is given in the Appendix. The EQ-i has a built-in correction factor which automatically adjusts the scale scores based on scores obtained from its two validity indices (the positive impression and negative impression scales); this is an important psychometric factor for self-report measures in that it reduces the distorting effects of response bias, thereby, increasing the accuracy of the results obtained. Also, this correction factor is of particular importance in the current application of the EQ-i because some of the brain-damaged subjects' self-awareness of their acquired deficits is limited (i.e. anosognosia). Raw scores are computer-tabulated and automatically converted into standard scores based on a mean of 100 and standard deviations of 15. It is important to stress that the EQ-i is acknowledged as a valid measure of emotional intelligence based on independent review (Plake and

Impara, 1999). Moreover, the EQ-i is significantly correlated with other measures that tap various aspects of this construct, for example with the Mayer– Salovey–Caruso Emotional Intelligence Test (MSCEIT) (0.46), Trait Meta-Mood Scale (TMMS) (0.58), Emotional Intelligence Questionnaire (EIQ) (0.63) and the 20-item Toronto Alexithymia Scale (TAS-20) (-0.72) (Bar-On, 2000). This means that the EQ-i is tapping—relatively well—what these other measures are tapping (i.e. various aspects of emotional intelligence).

All participants completed the EQ-i ($n = 23$).

Personal judgment in decision-making

The ability to exercise personal judgment in decision-making was assessed by the Gambling Task. A detailed account of this measure is given elsewhere (Bechara *et al.*, 1994, 2000*b*). In brief, subjects are required to select a total of 100 cards from four packs labelled A, B, C and D. The subject's decision to select from one pack versus another is largely influenced by various schedules of immediate reward and future punishment. These schedules are pre-programmed and known only to the examiner and entail a number of basic game rules that must be adhered to by the subject. First, every time the subject selects a card from pack A or B, the subject receives $100; and every time the subject selects a card from pack C or D, the subject receives $50. However, in each of the four packs, subjects encounter unpredictable punishments (money loss). The punishment is more severe in the high-paying packs A and B, and less severe in the low-paying packs C and D. Overall, selections from packs A and B are disadvantageous because they cost more in punishments in the long run, i.e. one loses $250 every 10 cards. Packs C and D are advantageous because they result in an overall gain in the long run, i.e. one wins $250 every 10 cards.

All participants completed the Gambling Task ($n = 23$).

Social functioning

Post-morbid employment status, social functioning, interpersonal relationships and social standing were evaluated with a series of semi-structured interviews and rating scales described in detail by Tranel and colleagues (Tranel *et al.*, 2002). Briefly, these entailed a comprehensive assessment by a clinical neuropsychologist (who was unaware of the objectives and design of the current study) of each patient's post-morbid employment status, social functioning, interpersonal relationships and social standing. For each of these domains, the extent of social change or impairment for each patient was rated on a three-point scale on which one corresponded to 'no change or impairment'; two corresponded to 'moderate change or impairment'; and three corresponded to 'severe change or impairment.' For each patient, a Total Social Change score was then calculated by summing the four scores from each of the domains. Higher overall scores are indicative of greater levels of change (impairment). Sixteen participants (10 experimental and six control subjects) were assessed for post-morbid social functioning.

Cognitive intelligence, perception, memory and executive functioning

Subjects were assessed according to standard protocols of the Benton Neuropsychology Laboratory (Tranel, 1996). This included standardized measurement of cognitive intelligence, perception, memory and executive functioning.

Cognitive intelligence. This was measured with the Wechsler Adult Intelligence Scale (WAIS-III); 21 subjects (12 experimental and nine control) were administered the WAIS.

Perception. This was measured with the Benton Facial Discrimination Test and the Benton Judgment of Line Orientation Test; 18 subjects (10 experimental and eight control) completed these tests.

Memory. This was measured with the Rey Auditory Verbal Learning Test (RAVLT), the Benton Visual Retention Test-Revised (BVRT), and the Complex Figure Test; 20 subjects (10 experimental and 10 control) were assessed with these instruments.

Executive functioning. This was measured with the Wisconsin Card Sorting Test (WCST), the

Trail-making Test (TMT) and the Controlled Oral Word Association Test (COWA); 16 subjects (10 experimental and six control) completed the WCST and the TMT, and 20 (10 experimental and 10 control) were tested with the COWA.

Personality and psychopathology

Personality and psychopathology was assessed with the Minnesota Multiphasic Personality Inventory (MMPI) (Butcher et al., 1989). Ten subjects (seven experimental and three control) completed the MMPI.

Results

Differences in Cognitive Intelligence Between the Control and Experimental Groups

There are no significant differences between the control and experimental groups with respect to cognitive intelligence, executive functioning, perception, memory or signs of psychopathology (see Table 17.2). In addition to a lack of significant difference between the control group and the experimental group regarding the level of their cognitive intelligence as can be seen in Table 17.2 ($Z = 1.17, P = 0.241$), it is also important to point out that no significant correlation was found between cognitive intelligence and emotional intelligence ($r = 0.08, P = 0.740$) for the clinical sample examined in the present study.

Differences in Decision-Making, Social Functioning and Emotional Intelligence Between the Control and Experimental Groups

A comparison of advantageous ($+$) to disadvantageous ($-$) choices made in the Gambling Task for the first 40 cards selected did not reveal significant differences between the experimental and control groups (-10.67 versus -04.73, respectively; $Z = 1.52, P = 0.128$). During the next and final 60 selections, however, significant differences began to appear between the two groups with the experimental group making more disadvantageous than advantageous choices; this ratio

was reversed for the control group who began to make more advantageous than disadvantageous choices (-18.83 versus $+08.36$, respectively; $Z = 3.67, P < 0.000$). This increase in exercising better judgment in decision-making among subjects in the control group appears to follow a typical learning curve that would be expected; however, it is important to note that this normal learning process did not occur among the subjects in the experimental group whose personal judgment tends to get worse as can be seen in Figure 17.1. In addition to indicating the existence of a neurological substrate mediating the somatic marker hypothesis, this suggests that it takes ~40 attempts of trial and error before people, who are not damaged along the targeted somatic marker circuitry, to catch on to the rules of the game and to do what is more advantageous for them. Based on these findings and in an attempt to obtain the most accurate evaluation of differences between the groups that were examined, it was decided to focus only on the last 60 attempts in the Gambling Task when comparing personal judgment in decision-making with emotional intelligence and overall social functioning in the present study.

Post-morbid social functioning was also found to be significantly worse for the experimental group compared with the control group (see Table 17.3).

Table 17.4 reveals that subjects in the experimental group have significantly lower emotional intelligence than those in the control group (82.3 versus 101.1, respectively; $Z = -3.33, P = 0.001$). A review of these results suggest that the key emotional intelligence competencies involved appear to be the ability to be aware of oneself (self-regard), to express oneself (assertiveness), to manage and control emotions (stress tolerance and impulse control), to adapt flexibly to change (flexibility) and to solve problems of a personal nature as they arise (problem-solving), as well as the ability to motivate oneself and mobilize positive affect (self-actualization, optimism and happiness).

A precursory examination of the differences between the control group and all of the three subgroups forming the experimental group reveals

TABLE 17.2. Neuropsychological Test Scores for the Control and Experimental Groups

Neuropsychological tests	Control group ($n = 11$)	Experimental group ($n = 12$)	Z	P-level (2-tailed)
Cognitive intelligence				
WAIS-III:				
Full IQ	97.7	105.3	1.17	0.241
Verbal IQ	99.2	107.9	1.32	0.186
Performance IQ	95.7	102.8	1.42	0.155
Perception				
Benton faces	44.4	43.9	0.50	0.620
Benton lines	25.4	24.6	0.81	0.420
Memory				
WAIS:				
Digit span	11.0	10.8	0.16	0.869
BVRT:				
Correct	7.4	7.4	0.12	0.908
Errors	3.8	4.0	0.58	0.565
RAVLT:				
Trial 1 to 5	10.1	12.0	1.53	0.127
30 minute recall	8.1	9.3	0.46	0.648
Recognition	28.9	28.8	0.91	0.361
Complex figure (Rey-O):				
Copy	32.2	30.9	0.55	0.585
Delay	20.7	19.5	0.22	0.827
Executive functioning				
Trails-making test A	34.8	39.6	0.06	0.957
Trails-making test B	86.8	79.9	0.33	0.745
WCST:				
Perseverative errors	10.2	17.7	0.44	0.662
Categories	5.8	5.1	0.71	0.476
COWA	37.0	40.4	0.53	0.596
Personality/psychopathology				
MMPI:				
Scale 1 (Hs)	57.3	57.6	0.34	0.732
Scale 2 (D)	53.0	63.0	1.26	0.209
Scale 3 (Hy)	64.3	57.6	0.69	0.493
Scale 4 (Pd)	58.7	61.9	1.03	0.304
Scale 5 (Mf)	52.7	55.0	0.57	0.568
Scale 6 (Pa)	50.3	57.1	0.92	0.359
Scale 7 (Pt)	49.3	61.3	1.38	0.168
Scale 8 (Sc)	52.0	63.3	1.48	0.139
Scale 9 (Ma)	54.3	53.9	0.23	0.818
Scale 0 (Si)	49.7	52.9	0.34	0.731

The Mann–Whitney U test was applied to compare the scores for significant differences between the groups.

significant differences with respect to emotional and social intelligence (those with damage to the VM prefrontal lobe (101 versus 92; $Z = 2.22$, $P = 0.026$), the right amygdala (101 versus 80; $Z = 2.43$, $P = 0.015$) and, especially, to the right insular/somatosensory cortices (101 versus 65; $Z = 2.58$, $P = 0.010$)). However, a closer examination of the specific differences between these subgroups is not justified because of the very small sample sizes involved.

Discussion

Only those subjects with injury to the somatic marker circuitry (the experimental group) revealed significantly low emotional intelligence

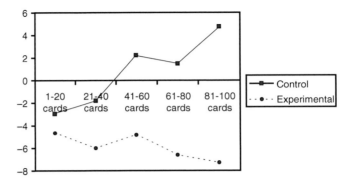

FIGURE 17.1 ■ The ratio of advantageous (+) to disadvantageous (−) decisions made in the Gambling Task by the control group (*n* = 11) and the experimental group (*n* = 12) progressing from the first 20 to the last 20 cards selected.

and poor judgment in decision-making as well as disturbances in social functioning, in spite of normal levels of cognitive intelligence (IQ) and in the absence of psychopathology. Specifically, the experimental group made significantly more disadvantageous decisions (on the Gambling Task) than the control group and their personal judgment got worse rather than better as time went on, i.e. they failed to make advantageous choices and to learn from experience. In addition to obtaining significantly lower scores on the Gambling Task, the experimental group demonstrated many disturbances in social functioning, and they received significantly lower scores on the EQ-i indicating impaired emotional and social intelligence. Yet, there were no differences between the experimental and control groups with respect to cognitive capacity (IQ), executive functioning, perception, memory or signs of psychopathology. Similarly, there were no differences between the two groups with respect to demographic factors.

Thus, the differences between the experimental and control groups with respect to emotional and social intelligence (EQ) exist in spite of the fact that the two groups were well matched on demographic and cognitive grounds. It was also demonstrated that there was no significant correlation between IQ and EQ in the clinical sample studied in the present study. In addition to reconfirming the neurological substrate that mediates somatic state activation and decision-making, these findings support our hypothesis that emotional and social intelligence is fundamentally different from cognitive intelligence. Moreover, the neural systems that support emotional and social intelligence appear to overlap with the neural systems subserving somatic state activation and personal judgment in decision-making, which are apparently separate from the neural systems supporting cognitive intelligence.

The key emotional intelligence competencies affected by damage to the neural circuitry of

TABLE 17.3. Differences in Post-Morbid Social Functioning Between the Control and Experimental Groups

Post-morbid changes in:	Control group (*n* = 6)	Experimental group (*n* = 10)	*Z*	*P*-level (2-tailed)
Employment	1.17	2.70	−3.11	0.002
Social functioning	1.00	2.30	−2.84	0.005
Interpersonal relationships	1.00	2.40	−2.87	0.004
Social status	1.00	1.90	−3.40	0.001
Total social change	4.17	9.30	−3.00	0.003

The Mann–Whitney *U* test was applied to compare scores for significant differences.

TABLE 17.4. Differences in Emotional Intelligence Between the Control and Experimental Groups

EQ-i scales (emotional intelligence)	Control group ($n = 11$)	Experimental group ($n = 12$)	Z	P-level (2-tailed)
Total EQ	101.1	82.3	3.33	0.001
Intrapersonal EQ	100.0	81.8	3.23	0.001
Self-regard	99.1	83.8	2.40	0.016
Emotional self-awareness	100.9	90.1	1.48	0.139
Assertiveness	103.6	82.6	3.21	0.001
Independence	97.7	87.3	1.58	0.115
Self-actualization	99.4	86.8	2.25	0.024
Interpersonal EQ	99.6	91.6	1.36	0.175
Empathy	98.6	89.8	1.24	0.216
Social responsibility	101.5	95.3	1.14	0.254
Interpersonal relationship	98.8	92.8	0.83	0.406
Stress management EQ	104.8	89.1	2.62	0.009
Stress tolerance	100.1	83.2	2.56	0.011
Impulse control	108.3	96.9	2.13	0.033
Adaptability EQ	100.0	86.3	2.28	0.023
Reality testing	99.8	91.0	1.08	0.280
Flexibility	100.3	86.8	2.38	0.017
Problem-solving	100.6	88.3	2.16	0.031
General mood EQ	99.9	83.3	3.27	0.001
Optimism	99.0	83.5	3.02	0.003
Happiness	100.9	85.8	2.71	0.007

Emotional intelligence was assessed by EQ-i and the Mann–Whitney U test was applied to compare scores for significant differences.

somatic markers appear to be the ability to be aware of oneself and one's emotions, to express oneself and one's feelings, to manage and control emotions, to adapt flexibly to change and solve problems of a personal nature, as well as the ability to motivate oneself and mobilize positive affect. Indeed, self-regard (accurate self-awareness) and, especially assertiveness (self-expression), stand out as those competencies that are affected most by brain injury to the neural circuitry being examined in the present study. This is understandable in that these are two of the most important emotional intelligence competencies.

It is important to note that the specific type of brain injury sustained by subjects belonging to the experimental group usually produces a certain degree of anosognosia (i.e. lack of self-awareness of acquired impairments). Given the reliance of the EQ-i on self-report, the question arises as to whether this instrument can provide a valid measure of emotional and social intelligence when used with this particular group of clinical subjects. The issue of self-awareness of acquired impairments is critical in situations where self-report

measures fail to detect acquired impairments in tested individuals. This situation often occurs in the case of VM patients as was previously noted, in which case collateral information is usually needed in order to document changes in the personality and social behaviour of impaired patients (Barrash et al., 2000). However, in the case of the EQ-i, the instrument proved to be successful in detecting abnormal levels of emotional and social intelligence in the target subjects. This suggests that the instrument has adequate construct validity when used with individuals whom otherwise may be unaware of the limitations of their own emotional and social abilities. Indeed, low scores—particularly on the two scales of self-regard (accurate self-awareness) and assertiveness (self-expression)—most likely mean that these subjects possess low self-awareness consistent with their symptomatology; their scores on these two scales would have been even lower without the EQ-i's correction factor that automatically adjusts scale scores to compensate for various types of inaccuracies in responding that occur for one reason or another.

The findings of the present study indicate that poor personal judgment in decision-making is related to deficiencies in emotional intelligence, in spite of average or above average levels of cognitive intelligence. Relative to patients with brain damage in areas outside of the neural circuitry studied in the present study (the control group), those who exercise poor judgment in decision-making linked to impaired somatic state activation (the experimental group) are less emotionally intelligent based on lower EQ-i scores. Furthermore, poor decision-making appears to be related to an inadequate knowledge of who one is (accurate self-awareness), what one wants and how to convey this effectively and constructively (self-expression). Equally important is that subjects who often fail to make the right decision are also less effective in controlling their emotions, in maintaining a positive and optimistic attitude, and in generating and selecting potentially effective solutions.

Emotional and social intelligence provides a valuable approach to understanding why some people behave more intelligently than others, which is often revealed in making the right versus wrong decisions in one's personal life and interactions with others. There are a number of other closely related concepts that are based on the way emotions are perceived, understood and used to guide effective human behaviour like 'emotional awareness' (Lane and Schwartz, 1987), 'empathy' (Brothers, 1990; Preston and de Waal, 2002), 'psychological mindedness' (McCallum, 1989), 'theory of mind' (Gopnik, 1993; Gallup, 1998; Blair, 1999; Frith and Frith, 1999), 'practical intelligence' (Sternberg, 1985), 'successful intelligence' (Sternberg, 1997), etc. Most of these concepts can be considered different components of emotional and social intelligence rather than separate constructs. For example, psychological mindedness is the salutogenic (i.e. non-pathological) end of alexithymia and emotional awareness is a major component of this continuum. While this continuum represents the essence of the intrapersonal aspect of emotional intelligence, empathy and theory of mind represent the essence of social intelligence; both types of intelligence have

been combined into one meta construct by some theorists (Gardner, 1983; Goleman, 1995; Bar-On, 2001).

One of the implications of the significant statistical and neurological connections between the somatic marker hypothesis and the concept of emotional intelligence, based on the present findings, is that emotional and social intelligence is a valid construct which is neurally distinct from cognitive intelligence. The major differences between these two important components of intelligence may be that cognitive intelligence is more dependent on cortical structures that support logical reasoning, whereas emotional and social intelligence is more dependent on limbic and related neural systems that support the processing of emotions and feelings. In this study, we have examined clinical subjects who possess average or above average cognitive intelligence and significantly below average emotional intelligence. However, we do not know the impact of below average cognitive intelligence (IQ) on emotional and social intelligence. The neural systems supporting emotional and cognitive intelligence may be completely independent, i.e. impaired cognitive intelligence does not compromise emotional intelligence. Alternatively, the dissociation may only be partial (i.e. impaired emotional intelligence does not compromise cognitive intelligence) as we have shown in this study. However, impaired cognitive intelligence may compromise emotional intelligence. Such asymmetrical relationship between neural systems has been demonstrated before in relation to two functions of the prefrontal cortex: decision-making and working memory. Bachara and colleagues found that VM lesions that impaired decision-making did not compromise working memory, but dorsolateral lesions that impaired working memory did compromise decision-making (Bechara et al., 1998). Thus, it would be intriguing to study patients with Down's syndrome or William's syndrome, for example, who have significantly limited cognitive intelligence but are known to be relatively effective in social interactions. Another approach is to examine the level of emotional and social intelligence in neurological patients with impaired cognitive intelligence. In this study, we used the WAIS-III to measure cognitive intelligence, whereas Duncan (2001), for instance, has used more sensitive tasks to measure various aspects of cognitive intelligence, attributing them to the lateral orbitofrontal/dorsolateral prefrontal cortices. Therefore, using these more sensitive measures of cognitive intelligence in future studies will yield additional important information about the relationships between the neural systems that support cognitive versus emotional intelligence.

One of the most important implications of the current findings is that the complex cognitive processes that subserve social competence, which appears to constitute a distinct form of intelligence dedicated to behaviour suited more for survival and adaptation (Goleman, 1995; Bar-On, 1997b; Stein and Book, 2000), does not draw upon neural processes specialized for social information. Rather, these processes depend on known brain mechanisms related to emotion and decision-making. Indeed, we have argued that the process of judgment and decision-making depends on systems for: (i) memory, which is supported by high-order association cortices as well as the dorsolateral sector of the prefrontal cortex; (ii) emotion, which is mediated by subcortical limbic structures that trigger the emotional response; and (iii) feelings which are supported by limbic as well as closely associated regions such as the insula, surrounding parietal cortices and the cingulate cortex (Damasio, 1994, 1995, 1999; Bechara et al., 2000a). Therefore, damage to the systems that impact emotion, feeling and/or memory usually compromise the ability to make advantageous decisions (Bechara et al., 2000a). The VM prefrontal cortex links these systems together; when damaged, there are a number of manifestations that occur including alterations of emotional experience and social functioning (Bechara et al., 2000a). The findings of the present study suggest that emotional and social intelligence has neural roots, which may be associated with these known basic mechanisms of the brain. Impairment of these mechanisms may manifest itself in low levels of emotional intelligence, which comprises a wide array of emotional and social competencies, which can have an ill effect on one's ability to effectively cope with daily demands. Such impairment may include a decrease in one's ability to: (i) be aware of and express oneself; (ii) function interpersonally; (iii) manage and control emotions; (iv) generate positive affect required in achieving personal goals; and (v) cope flexibly with the immediate situation, make decisions and solve problems of a personal and interpersonal nature.

Finally, the findings that emotional intelligence is significantly related to the ability to exercise personal judgment in decision-making help explain why this concept is highly connected with human performance (Bar-On et al., 2003). To perform well and be successful in one's professional and personal life apparently requires the ability to make emotionally and socially intelligent decisions more than just having a high IQ.

Acknowledgment

This study was supported by NIH Program Project Grant PO1 NS19632.

Abbreviations

BVRT = Benton Visual Retention Test-Revised; COWA = Controlled Oral Word Association Test; EQ = emotional quotient; EQ-i = Emotional Quotient Inventory; MMPI = Minnesota Multiphasic Personality Inventory; RAVLT = Rey Auditory Verbal Learning Test; TMT = Trailmaking Test; VM = ventromedial; WAIS = Wechsler Adult Intelligence Scale; WCST = Wisconsin Card Sorting Test.

REFERENCES

Bar-On R. *The Bar-On Emotional Quotient Inventory (EQ-i): a test of emotional intelligence*. Toronto (Canada): Multi-Health Systems; 1997a.

Bar-On R. *The Bar-On Emotional Quotient Inventory (EQ-i): technical manual*. Toronto (Canada): Multi-Health Systems; 1997b.

Bar-On R. Emotional and social intelligence: insights from the Emotional Quotient Inventory. In: Bar-On R, Parker JDA, editors. *The handbook of emotional intelligence.* San Francisco: Jossey-Bass; 2000. p. 363–88.

Bar-On R. Emotional intelligence and self-actualization. In: Ciarrochi J, Forgas JP, Mayer JD, editors. *Emotional intelligence in everyday life: A scientific inquiry.* Philadelphia: Psychology Press; 2001. p. 82–97.

Bar-On R, Fund S, Handley R. The impact of emotional intelligence on performance. In: Druskat V, Sala F, Mount G, editors. *Emotional intelligence and performance at work.* San Francisco: Jossey-Bass. In press 2003.

Barrash J, Tranel D, Anderson SW. Acquired personality disturbances associated with bilateral damage to the ventromedial prefrontal region. *Dev Neuropsychol* 2000; 18: 355–81.

Bechara A, Damasio AR, Damasio H, Anderson SW. Insensitivity to future consequences following damage to human prefrontal cortex. *Cognition* 1994; 50: 7–15.

Bechara A, Damasio H, Tranel D, Anderson SW. Dissociation of working memory from decision making within the human prefrontal cortex. *J Neurosci* 1998; 18: 428–37.

Bechara A, Damasio H, Damasio AR, Lee GP. Different contributions of the human amygdala and ventromedial prefrontal cortex to decision-making. *J Neurosci* 1999; 19: 5473–81.

Bechara A, Tranel D, Damasio AR. Poor judgment in spite of high intellect: neurological evidence for emotional intelligence. In: Bar-On R, Parker JDA, editors. *The handbook of emotional intelligence.* San Francisco: Jossey-Bass; 2000a. p. 192–214.

Bechara A, Tranel D, Damasio H. Characterization of the decision-making deficit of patients with ventromedial prefrontal cortex lesions. *Brain* 2000b; 123: 2189–202.

Blair RJR. Psychophysiological responsiveness to the distress of others in children with autism. *Personality Individ Diff* 1999; 26: 477–85.

Brothers L. The neural basis of primate social communication. *Motivation Emotion* 1990; 14: 81–91.

Butcher JN, Dahlstrom WG, Graham JR, Tellegen A, Kaemmer B. *Minnesota Multiphasic Personality Inventory-2 (MMPI-2) manual for administration and scoring.* Minneapolis (MN): University of Minnesota Press; 1989.

Damasio AR. *Descartes' error: emotion, reason, and the human brain.* New York: G. P. Putnam; 1994.

Damasio AR. Toward a neurobiology of emotion and feeling: operational concepts and hypotheses. *Neuroscientist* 1995; 1: 19–25.

Damasio AR. *The feeling of what happens: body and emotion in the making of consciousness.* New York: Harcourt Brace; 1999.

Damasio AR. Grabowski TG, Bechara A, Damasio H, Ponto LLB, Parvizi J, et al. Subcortical and cortical brain activity during the feeling of self-generated emotions. *Nat Neurosci* 2000; 3: 1049–56.

Damasio H, Damasio AR. *Lesion analysis in neuropsychology.* New York: Oxford University Press; 1989.

Damasio H, Frank R. Three-dimensional *in vivo* mapping of brain lesions in humans. *Arch Neurol* 1992; 49: 137–43.

Darwin C. *The expression of the emotions in man and animals.* London: Murray; 1872.

Duncan J. An adaptive coding model of neural function in prefrontal cortex. *Nat Rev Neurosci* 2001; 2: 820–9.

Frith CD, Frith U. Interacting minds: a biological basis. *Science* 1999; 286: 1692–5.

Gallup GGJ. Self-awareness and the evolution of social intelligence. *Behav Process* 1998; 42: 239–47.

Gardner H. *Frames of mind.* New York: Basic Books; 1983.

Goleman D. *Emotional intelligence.* New York: Bantam Books; 1995.

Gopnik A. How we know our minds: the illusion of first-person knowledge of intentionality. *Behav Brain Sci* 1993; 16: 1–14, 29–113.

Lane RD. Levels of emotional awareness: Neurological, psychological, and social perspectives. In: Bar-On R, Parker JDA, editors. *The handbook of emotional intelligence.* San Francisco: Jossey-Bass; 2000; p. 171–91.

Lane RD, Schwartz GE. Levels of emotional awareness: a cognitive developmental theory and its application to psychopathology. *Am J Psychiatry* 1987; 144: 133–43.

Maddock RJ. The retrosplenial cortex and emotion: new insights from functional neuroimaging of the human brain. *Trends Neurosci* 1999; 22: 310–6.

Manes F, Sahakian B, Clark L, Rogers R, Antoun N, Aitken M, et al. Decision-making processes following damage to the prefrontal cortex. *Brain* 2002; 125: 624–39.

Mayer JD, Salovey P. What is emotional intelligence: In: Salovey P, Sluyter DJ, editors. *Emotional development and emotional intelligence: educational implications.* New York: Basic Books; 1997. p. 3–34.

McCallum M. *A controlled study of effectiveness and patient suitability for short-term group psychotherapy* (doctoral dissertation). Montreal (Canada): McGill University; 1989.

Plake BS, Impara JC, editors. The BarOn Emotional Quotient Inventory (EQ-i). Supplement to the 13th mental measurement yearbook. Lincoln (NE): Buros Institute for Mental Measurement; 1999.

Preston S, de Waal F. Empathy: Its ultimate and proximate bases. *Behav Brain Sci* 2002; 25: 1–71.

Siegal S. *Nonparametric statistics for the behavioral sciences.* New York: McGraw-Hill; 1956.

Stein SJ, Book HE. *The EQ edge: emotional intelligence and your success.* Toronto (Canada): Stoddart Publishing; 2000.

Sternberg RJ. *Beyond IQ: a triarchic theory of human intelligence.* New York: Cambridge University Press; 1985.

Sternberg RJ. *Successful intelligence.* New York: Plume; 1997.

Taylor GJ, Bagby RM, Parker JDA. *Disorders of affect regulation: alexithymia in medical and psychiatric illness.* Cambridge: Cambridge University Press; 1997.

Thorndike EL. Intelligence and its uses. *Harper's Magazine* 1920; 140: 227–35.

Tranel D. The Iowa-Benton school of neuropsychological assessment. In: Grant I, Adams KM, editors. *Neuropsychological assessment of neuropsychiatric disorders,* Vol. 1. 2nd ed. New York: Oxford University Press; 1996. p. 81–101.

Tranel D, Bechara A, Damasio H, Damasio AR. Decision-making in patients with unilateral ventromedial prefrontal cortex lesions (abstract). *Soc Neurosci Abstr* 2000; 26: 549.

Tranel D, Bechara A, Denburg N L. Asymmetric functional roles of right and left ventromedial prefrontal cortices in social conduct, decision-making, and emotional processing. *Cortex* 2002; 38: 589–612.

Zirkel S. Social intelligence: the development and maintenance of purposive behavior. In: Bar-On R, Parker JDA, editors. *The handbook of emotional intelligence.* San Francisco: Jossey-Bass; 2000. p. 3–27.

Appendix I *The EQ-i Scales and What They Assess*

EQ-i scales	The EI competency assessed by each scale
Intrapersonal	
Self-regard	To accurately perceive, understand and accept oneself.
Emotional self-awareness	To be aware of and understand one's emotions.
Assertiveness	To effectively and constructively express one's emotions and oneself.
Independence	To be self-reliant and free of emotional dependency on others.
Self-actualization	To strive to achieve personal goals and actualize one's potential.
Interpersonal	
Empathy	To be aware of and understand how others feel.
Social responsibility	To identify with one's social group and cooperate with others.
Interpersonal relationship	To establish mutually satisfying relationships and relate well with others.
Stress management	
Stress tolerance	To effectively and constructively manage emotions.
Impulse control	To effectively and constructively control emotions.
Adaptability	
Reality-testing	To objectively validate one's feelings and thinking with external reality.
Flexibility	To adapt and adjust one's feelings and thinking to new situations.
Problem-solving	To effectively solve problems of a personal and interpersonal nature.
General mood	
Optimism	To be positive and look at the brighter side of life.
Happiness	To feel content with oneself, others and life in general.

PART 10

Biological Does Not Mean Predetermined: Reciprocal Influences of Social and Biological Processes

The readings in this book have illustrated that social and biological approaches are complementary rather than antagonistic. Together, these perspectives are helping to illuminate questions ranging from the social sciences to the neurosciences by examining how organismic processes are shaped, modulated, and modified by social factors and vice versa. Rather than viewing social psychology and biological psychology as generating inevitably oppositional forces, the readings in this book illustrate some of the synergisms that result from a social neuroscientific approach.

The readings in the final section demonstrate that biological does not mean fixed or predetermined regardless of environmental influences, and indeed that sociocultural and biological processes even have reciprocal influences. In some ways this is so patently obvious as to be trivial. The culture in which we live influences what we deem to be valuable and beautiful, and these learned evaluations in turn modulate activity, for instance, in the reward circuitry in the brain. Genetic factors (genotype) may place broad constraints on an individual's development or functioning, but genetic expression (phenotype) typically can be powerfully modulated by environmental influences. For instance numerous genes, each with small effects, contribute to the expression and outcome of many of the most costly human diseases we endure (e.g., cardiovascular disease, hypertension, inflammatory arthritis). Genetic influences are documented but they do not tell the whole story. Environmental factors also determine much if not most of the expression and outcome of these diseases.

The first reading in this section by Morgan and colleagues (2002) illustrates how environmental factors can modulate genetic expression in the brain. Dopamine is a powerful neurotransmitter, which acts on dopamine *receptors* in the brain. Morgan and colleagues studied the dopamine D_2 family of dopamine binding sites, which is related to cocaine's reinforcing and addictive effects. Morgan et al. (2002) examined the D_2 receptors in dominant and subordinate male cynomolgus monkeys when they were individually housed and, later, when they were socially housed. No differences were found in D_2 family receptor binding potential in the monkeys when they were individually housed. After only 3 months of being socially housed, however, a dominance hierarchy emerged, and those at the top of the dominance hierarchy showed a significant increase in D_2 family receptor binding potential, whereas the submissive animals showed no change in dopaminergic characteristics. More interestingly, behavioral testing further showed that dominant animals self-administered cocaine at levels comparable to saline—that is, the dominant animals acted as if cocaine had minimal reinforcing value. Subordinate monkeys, in contrast, reliably self-administered cocaine at higher doses than saline. These results suggest that the vulnerability to the abuse-related effects of cocaine are not predictable from dopaminergic characteristics of individual

animals nor from dominance hierarchies alone but, rather, they are apparent only after a dominance hierarchy emerged in socially housed groups. A strictly physiological (or social) analysis, regardless of the sophistication of the measurement technology, may not have revealed the orderly relationship that exists because the receptors expressed by the brain were modulated by the social context of the animal.

There is a large body of evidence showing that negative affect is associated with activation in a neural circuit that includes the amygdala. Inhibitory connections between the prefrontal cortex and the amygdala have also been identified and are thought to be involved in self-regulation and self-control. Evidence for the involvement of this circuit during the exercise of voluntary control over responses to aversive events is provided in the final reading by Ochsner et al. (2002). Individuals were exposed to neutral and aversive photographs under two instructional sets. In one task, participants were shown neutral or negative pictures and were instructed to attend to the picture and to be aware of the feelings it aroused but to not attempt to alter these feelings. In another task, participants were shown negative photographs and were instructed to reinterpret the pictures so that they no longer elicited a negative response. Participants performed both tasks while functional magnetic resonance images (fMRI) were constructed. Behavioral responses to the pictures confirmed that participants were able to voluntarily reduce the emotional impact of the aversive pictures when instructed to do so. Moreover, the fMRI data further revealed increased activity in the lateral and medial prefrontal regions of the brain and decreased activity in the amygdala and medial orbitofrontal cortex when the participants deliberately thought about the aversive pictures in a way that reduced their aversion to the pictures rather than simply viewing these pictures. Together these readings indicate that just because palpable biological processes underlie social behavior, it does not mean that social behavior is determined entirely by one's biological inheritance. An implication of this line of reasoning is that a personally or socially damaging behavior may have biological roots, but it does not necessarily follow that the person has no personal responsibility for having enacted this behavior.

In sum, all human behavior, at some level, is biological, but this is not to say that biological representation yields a simple, singular, or satisfactory explanation for complex behaviors, or that molecular forms of representation provide the only or best level of analysis for understanding human behavior. Molar constructs such as those developed by social psychologists provide a means of understanding highly complex activity without needing to specify each individual action of the simplest components, thereby providing an efficient means of describing the behavior of a complex system. Social and biological approaches to human behavior have traditionally been contrasted, as if the two were antagonistic or mutually exclusive. The readings in this book demonstrate the fallacy of this reasoning and suggest that the mechanisms underlying mind and behavior may not be fully explicable by a biological or a social approach alone but, rather, that a multilevel integrative analysis may be required.

READING 18

Social Dominance in Monkeys: Dopamine D₂ Receptors and Cocaine Self-Administration

Social Dominance in Monkeys: Dopamine D_2 Receptors and Cocaine Self-Administration

Drake Morgan[1], Kathleen A. Grant[1], H. Donald Gage[2],
Robert H. Mach[1,2], Jay R. Kaplan[3], Osric Prioleau[1], Susan H. Nader[1],
Nancy Buchheimer[2], Richard L. Ehrenkaufer[2] and Michael A. Nader[1,2]

Disruption of the dopaminergic system has been implicated in the etiology of many pathological conditions, including drug addiction. Here we used positron emission tomography (PET) imaging to study brain dopaminergic function in individually housed and in socially housed cynomolgus macaques ($n = 20$). Whereas the monkeys did not differ during individual housing, social housing increased the amount or availability of dopamine D_2 receptors in dominant monkeys and produced no change in subordinate monkeys. These neurobiological changes had an important behavioral influence as demonstrated by the finding that cocaine functioned as a reinforcer in subordinate but not dominant monkeys. These data demonstrate that alterations in an organism's environment can produce profound biological changes that have important behavioral associations, including vulnerability to cocaine addiction.

Drug abuse is a significant public health problem. With regard to cocaine use in the United States, the annual number of new users rose between 1994 and 1998 from 500,000 to over 900,000 ("1999 National Household Survey on Drug Abuse," Substance Abuse and Mental Health Services Administration, 2000). Although some of these new cocaine users will eventually become addicted, not all will. Unfortunately, little is known about the biological substrates and environmental influences underlying this differential vulnerability[1], and ethical considerations make it impossible to

[1]Department of Physiology and Pharmacology, [2]Department of Radiology, [3]Departments of Pathology (Comparative Medicine) and Anthropology, Wake Forest University School of Medicine, Medical Center Boulevard, Winston-Salem, North Carolina 27157, USA.

study in humans. One purpose of the present study was to develop an animal model of vulnerability to drug abuse that incorporates the assessment of social behavior, the noninvasive brain imaging technique PET, and cocaine self-administration in socially housed monkeys. Such a model could identify variables that would aid in the characterization and treatment of individuals vulnerable to drug abuse.

Certain environmental conditions, such as availability of alternative reinforcers[2] or living in an 'enriched' environment[3], alter the reinforcing effects of drugs, particularly cocaine[4]. Many of these stimuli also produce changes in dopaminergic function[5,6], a neurotransmitter system whose dysregulation is linked to cocaine's abuse potential[7]. In particular, the dopamine D_2 family of receptors is related to cocaine's effects[8]. Thus, there is a clear potential for interaction between particular environmental events, the actions of dopamine, and the reinforcing effects of cocaine.

A profound environmental influence on dopaminergic function is the particular housing conditions of animals and the dominance rank among socially housed animals[6,9–12]. It is unclear whether these observed differences reflect a neurobiological predisposition that determines dominance rank (a trait marker), or a neurobiological alteration induced by the attainment of dominance rank (a state marker). Our hypothesis that D_2 receptor binding potential is related to environmental influences and associated with vulnerability to the abuse-related effects of cocaine[13] was confirmed by the findings that there were differential changes in binding potential across social ranks, and that the dominant monkeys were less vulnerable to the reinforcing effects of cocaine compared to subordinate animals.

Results

Behavioral Profiles of Socially Housed Monkeys

For the first 1.5 years of the study, the monkeys were individually housed and various hormonal measures (such as cortisol, testosterone) and behavioral measures (such as locomotor activity) were obtained[14], as well as initial PET scans. Monkeys were subsequently assigned to social groups of four. Consistent with previous research, the dominant monkeys engaged in significantly more aggressive behaviors (1.9 versus 0 episodes/h) and were submitted to more often than were the subordinate monkeys (3.0 compared to 0.1 episodes/h). Conversely, subordinate monkeys received aggression and submitted more often (3.6 and 3.5 episodes/h) than did dominant monkeys (0.1 and 0 episodes/h). Percentage of time engaged in various affiliative behaviors also depended on social rank. For example, dominant monkeys were groomed more often (12.1% versus 4.9% of the time), whereas the subordinate monkeys spent more time alone (27.8% versus 14.8% of the time; for details, see ref. 14).

Social Rank and Dopaminergic Functioning

Monkeys were first scanned using PET imaging while individually housed and again after they were placed in social groups and a stable social hierarchy was established. During all PET scans, there was a high level of uptake of [18F]fluoroclebopride (FCP) and a linear rate of washout from the region of interest (ROI), the basal ganglia (Figure 18.1). In the reference region, the cerebellum, there was a low level of [18F]FCP uptake and high rate of washout. After three months of social housing, dominant monkeys (rank 1) had significantly higher D_2 receptor distribution volume ratios (DVRs) compared to subordinate (rank 4) monkeys (Table 18.1). These data replicate previous findings[12] showing a greater than 20% higher DVR in dominant monkeys compared to subordinate monkeys. Importantly, these findings extended the previous data from female to male monkeys, and demonstrate that this difference is apparent after only three months of social housing compared to three years in the previous study. In addition, the longitudinal design of the present experiment allowed the comparison of the same ROIs obtained while

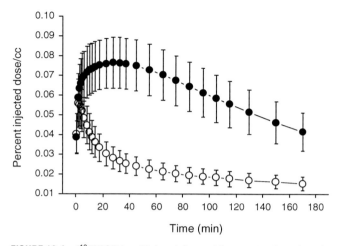

FIGURE 18.1 ■ [^{18}F]FCP has high uptake and linear rate of washout in the basal ganglia (BG; black symbols) relative to the cerebellum (Cb; white symbols). Each point is the mean (± 1 s.d.) value determined from 20 individually housed monkeys.

individually and socially housed, and revealed a significant change in [^{18}F]FCP binding only in the eventual dominant monkeys (Table 18.1). That is, the significant interaction between housing condition and social rank ($F_{2,39} = 8.88, p = 0.002$) demonstrates that the DVR of dominant monkeys increased from a mean of 2.49 to a mean of 3.04, an increase of approximately 22%, whereas the mean DVR of subordinate monkeys was not altered (means of 2.40 and 2.49) as a function of housing condition (Figure 18.2). The latter findings are similar to previous results showing low between-study variability with this PET ligand[15].

This measure of dopaminergic function suggests that, rather than a predisposing trait, the changes were a consequence of becoming the dominant monkey in a social group (Figure 18.3). Previously examined neuroendocrine markers, such as cortisol and testosterone levels, were similarly not predictive of eventual social rank[14]. In contrast, high levels of locomotor activity in individually housed monkeys were associated with eventual social subordination[14]. Age or weight of the monkeys did not correlate with D_2 binding (all p values > 0.05) during either housing condition, indicating no relationship between these characteristics and dopaminergic function.

TABLE 18.1. Dopaminergic Characteristics of Monkeys

Social rank[a]	[^{18}F]FCP distribution volume ratios		
	Individually housed	Socially housed	Percent change
1	2.49 ± 0.08	3.04 ± 0.23[b,c]	+22.0 ± 8.8
2	2.58 ± 0.13	2.99 ± 0.13	+16.7 ± 6.0
3	2.58 ± 0.13	2.88 ± 0.30	+13.4 ± 15.3
4	2.40 ± 0.06	2.49 ± 0.10	+3.9 ± 5.3

Mean ± s.e.m. [^{18}F]FCP DVR as determined with PET imaging in male cynomolgus monkeys as a function of social rank while individually and socially housed. [a]For individually housed scans, these numbers represent eventual social rank. [b]Significantly higher than individually housed 'dominants.' [c]Significantly higher than socially housed subordinates.

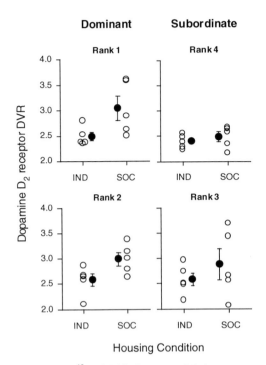

Dominant   **Subordinate**

FIGURE 18.2 ■ [¹⁸F]FCP binding potential changes as a function of social rank. Panels show the mean and individual [¹⁸F]FCP DVR values for monkeys with different social ranks, while they were individually (IND) and socially (SOC) housed.

Social Rank and Cocaine Self-Administration

Subordinate monkeys reliably self-administered cocaine across several doses, with the entire dose–effect curve characterized as an inverted U-shaped function (Figure 18.4 left, black symbols). There was a significant interaction between dose and social rank ($F_{4,134} = 3.54, p < 0.01$), and further analyses showed that subordinate monkeys self-administered more 0.01 and 0.03 mg/kg cocaine injections than saline. In contrast, in the dominant monkeys, cocaine failed to maintain responding higher than saline, and therefore did not function as a reinforcer (Figure 18.4 left, white symbols). During these sessions, subordinate monkeys had significantly higher intakes compared to dominant monkeys (Figure 18.4 right; significant interaction between dose and social rank, $F_{3,107} = 10.59, p < 0.0001$). A dose-dependent increase in cocaine intake occurred for the dominant monkeys, suggesting that these animals were not avoiding cocaine altogether, but their total intakes were significantly below those of subordinate monkeys. Correlation analyses indicated that social rank was inversely related to the number of reinforcers obtained per session ($r^2 = 0.62$,

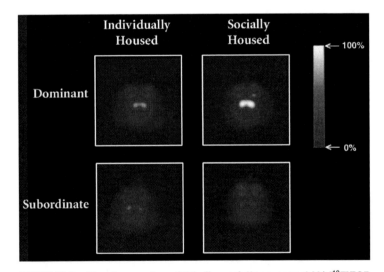

FIGURE 18.3 ■ (*A color version of this figure follows page 146.*) [¹⁸F]FCP binding potential increases in dominant monkeys. Normalized, co-registered PET images (percent injected dose per ml) of [¹⁸F]FCP binding in the basal ganglia of a dominant and a subordinate monkey, while individually housed and socially housed.

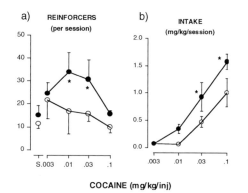

FIGURE 18.4 ■ Reinforcing effects of cocaine are greater in subordinate monkeys compared to dominant animals. Left, mean number of intravenous injections (either saline or various doses of cocaine) per session for 5 dominant (rank 1 and 2, white symbols) and 4 subordinate (rank 3 and 4, black symbols) monkeys. Right, mean intake per session for dominant (white symbols) and subordinate (black symbols) monkeys. Each dose was available for at least 7 sessions and until responding was stable. Data represent the mean of the last 3 days of availability for each animal. Asterisk indicates a statistically significant difference ($p < 0.05$) from dominant monkeys at that particular dose, and from the appropriate saline point.

$p = 0.01$) and to cocaine intake ($r^2 = 0.55$, $p = 0.02$). These data demonstrate a resistance to the reinforcing effects of cocaine in the dominant monkeys, and, conversely, show an increased vulnerability in the subordinate monkeys.

Discussion

The major findings from these studies were that environmental conditions produced a relatively quick alteration in the dopaminergic system of socially housed dominant but not subordinate monkeys and that this difference was associated with a differential vulnerability to the reinforcing effects of cocaine. These findings emerged from a design using a combination of several experimental methods including repeated PET imaging in individually and socially housed monkeys to study changes in brain DA function, the evaluation of social interactions in monkeys, and the study of intravenous cocaine self-administration in socially housed animals.

Whereas the present study represents the first examination of intravenous drug self-administration in socially housed monkeys, there have been several studies examining other behavioral effects of psychomotor stimulants in similarly housed monkeys[16–19]. These experiments have demonstrated differential effects of cocaine and d-amphetamine as a function of social rank[19]. Several rodent studies have examined the influence of housing conditions (individual versus social) on cocaine and amphetamine self-administration, although the results have been contradictory[3,4,20–22]. Differences in intravenous self-administration of cocaine across social ranks of rats or monkeys had not been previously explored. The present study provides experimental evidence in monkeys that individual differences in susceptibility to cocaine abuse within a population may be mediated by social dominance rank.

In the present study, the higher levels of [^{18}F]FCP binding in dominant monkeys could have resulted from increased levels of D_2 receptors and/or decreases in the basal levels of synaptic dopamine. Previous rodent studies have examined the neurochemical changes within the dopamine system as a consequence of housing conditions[6,9–11]. For example, rats reared in isolation or in 'environmentally impoverished' conditions have increased synaptic levels of dopamine and/or increased efflux of dopamine in response to particular environmental events (for example, after exposure to stressful stimuli) when compared to socially housed rodents or those living in 'enriched' environments. Concurrent decreases in D_2 responsivity and D_2 receptor levels have been observed in individually housed rats. Taken together with the present findings, these results suggest that individually housed monkeys and socially subordinate animals have relatively high levels of synaptic dopamine (that is, dopaminergic hyperactivity). We would suggest that after social housing, the dominant animals return to a 'normal' state of dopamine function, presumably as the result of being in control of environmental events such as social contact, mobility through the environment, and food and sexual resources. The ability to control resources may induce neurochemical changes that are reflected in the over 20% increase in D_2 receptor

DVR and a decrease in vulnerability to the reinforcing effects of cocaine in the dominant animals. This latter finding is even more striking when one considers that in non-human primate models, cocaine functions as a reinforcer in nearly all individually housed subjects.

The dopaminergic system is centrally involved in the neurochemical pathology of various psychiatric and neurodegenerative diseases involving the basal ganglia[13,23–25]. The link between dopaminergic functioning and behavioral processes has been extensively studied in the field of drug abuse[26–28]. Importantly, individual differences in dopaminergic function can result in varying degrees of susceptibility to drug abuse[29,30]. The most well studied animals in this respect are the high- and low-responders (HR and LR, respectively) to novelty as measured by locomotion in an open field. LR rats are less likely to acquire amphetamine self-administration compared to HR rats[31], similar to our findings that low locomotor levels in monkeys predicted 'resistance' to the reinforcing effects of cocaine (also see ref. 14). Neurobiologically, HR rats have higher basal, cocaine-stimulated and stress-induced dopamine levels, and have lower D_2 receptor levels in the nucleus accumbens[32]. Using extracellular single-neuron recordings, HR rats have higher basal firing rates of dopamine neurons in the ventral tegmental area and decreased sensitivity to D_2 receptor stimulation compared to LR rats; these differences in firing rates are associated with differences in sensitivity to cocaine's reinforcing effects[33]. These data suggest that a hyperactive dopamine system is characteristic of a drug-prone phenotype.

There is an extensive literature describing the involvement of D_2-like receptors in modulating cocaine's reinforcing effects using direct-acting agonists and antagonists in several animal models of cocaine abuse[34–36]. Consistent with these animal studies, PET data obtained in non-drug abusing humans suggest that levels of D_2 receptors predict the subjective effects of stimulants[37]. In particular, individuals with low D_2 receptor DVRs reported that methylphenidate was more pleasurable and less aversive than did individuals with high D_2 DVRs.

This behavioral and biological phenotype is similar to the one defined in the present study, and suggests that environmental events (such as becoming a particular social rank) may be as important as biological predispositions in determining vulnerability to drug abuse. It is not clear, however, whether changes or differences in extracellular dopamine or the D_2 receptors themselves are contributing to the differences in cocaine reinforcement.

The present study demonstrates that social context can have profound effects on brain dopaminergic function in adult, non-human primates. Furthermore, these neurobiological alterations in D_2 receptor levels or availability produced by an environmental change can lead to qualitatively different behavioral phenotypes. In the present study, this difference manifested as dominant monkeys being resistant to cocaine's effects, while subordinate monkeys were shown to be susceptible to the reinforcing effects of cocaine. The promise of this model, specifically for vulnerability to drug abuse but more generally to any behavioral phenotype, lies in the ability to use brain-imaging techniques to identify individual neurobiological characteristics associated with a particular social or environmental state, so that the course of related diseases and treatment can be followed and ultimately altered.

Methods

Subjects

Twenty experimentally naive adult male cynomolgus monkeys (*Macaca fascicularis*) were purchased from a commercial vendor (Primate Products, Miami, Florida, or Biomedical Resources Foundation, Houston, Texas). The monkeys were bred in captivity and, after weaning, were primarily individually housed. At the start of the study, monkeys lived in cages (Allentown Caging, Allentown, New Jersey) equipped with removable metal partitions, providing four compartments each containing 11.5 cubic feet of space and a water spigot. Throughout the experiment, monkeys were weighed weekly and maintained at approximately 95% of their free-feeding body weight by limited access to Purina Monkey Chow (100–120 g/day). In addition, monkeys received a multiple vitamin tablet and fresh fruit approximately 2–3 times per week. At the time of the first PET scans, monkeys weighed an average of 5.0 kg (range, 3.8–7.6 kg) and were approximately 4.8 years old (range, 3.4–6.4 years old). Approximately 8 months (range, 5–12 months) after the first PET scan and after at least 3 months of social housing, the second PET scan was conducted, at which point the monkeys weighed ~5.2 kg (range, 4.4–7.8 kg). The experimental manipulations described in this manuscript were conducted in accordance with the Guide for the Care and Use of Laboratory Animals as adopted and promulgated by the NIH, and with the approval of the Institutional Animal Care and Use Committee.

Behavioral Profiles of Socially Housed Monkeys

Monkeys were individually housed for approximately 10 months before the initial PET scans. The monkeys were placed into social groups of four after initial PET scans were completed. Approximately 20 behavioral observation sessions, to measure various aggressive, submissive and affiliative behaviors, were conducted per pen at regular intervals over the next 3 months[14]. Dominance rank was determined by the outcomes of dyadic agonistic encounters. That is, the monkey that aggressed toward and typically elicited submission from all others was designated as the first-ranking monkey. The monkey that aggressed toward all except the first-ranking monkey was designated the second-ranking monkey, and so on. In each pen, a linear hierarchy formed where the relationships between monkeys were transitive.

Social Rank and Dopaminergic Function

Monkeys were first scanned with the D_2 radioligand [^{18}F]FCP while individually housed and again after they were placed in social groups and a stable social hierarchy was established. The average time between scans was 8 months (range, 4.5–12.1 months). All animals in a particular pen were scanned before beginning the next pen and the

order of scanning as a function of social rank was randomly determined. Details regarding the PET data acquisition protocol, blood sampling procedure, and metabolite analysis have been fully described[15,38–39]. Briefly, monkeys were initially anesthetized with 8 mg/kg ketamine, maintained on isoflurane anesthesia (1.5%), administered a paralytic (0.07 mg/kg vecuronium bromide), and prepared with percutaneous arterial and venous catheters. Although it is possible that ketamine-induced changes in dopamine levels can alter tracer kinetics when injected during a PET study[40], we previously demonstrated that under the present conditions, this dose of ketamine does not alter the DVR values obtained with [^{18}F]FCP[15].

PET scans were obtained with a Siemens/CTI ECAT 951/31 PET scanner, which has been described elsewhere[15,38,39]. The effective resolution (full width at half maximum) of the PET scanner was 9 mm in all axes for the reconstructed image after filtering (Hanning filter with a 0.4-cycle/pixel cutoff; resolution determined experimentally using a line source).

ROI determinations were made from frame 13 (25–30 minutes post-injection acquisition frame) of the 26 dynamically acquired emission frames, as this frame occurs at the time that the basal ganglia uptake reaches a plateau, providing good whole brain anatomic definition and sufficient contrast of the basal ganglia versus the rest of the brain. ROIs for both basal ganglia and cerebellar regions were determined using the isocontour mode. For the basal ganglia, an isocontour threshold of 95% was set. For the cerebellum, a reference region with low D_2 receptor density, an isodensity contour of 65–85% was routinely used. The use of set isocontour levels for ROI determination insures that the ROIs are easily and reproducibly defined. The narrow range of 95% was used for the basal ganglia, as it selects the highest 5% of the pixel activities in the slice, thus minimizing the errors due to partial volume effect. In contrast, using an isocontour level of 65–85% in the cerebellum generates a fairly large region of nearly uniform tracer concentration. For all studies, the first 4 frames (0–4 min) were used for registration. The individual housing scan from each monkey was registered to the social housing scan and the ROI from the social housing scan placed onto the individual housing scan, ensuring that identical ROIs were used[41]. This method of defining ROIs resulted in the same overall effects as using other methods (e.g. separate ROIs for each scan or ROIs from the summed scans). Time–activity curves were generated by the ECAT software by placing the isocontour regions determined from frame 13 over the same region in each of the 26 frames. The ROI value is the average of all pixels contained within the ROI, for each time frame. In the basal ganglia, right and left sides were determined separately, then averaged. The distribution volumes (DV) for these regions were determined using the linear portion of the Logan plot[42], which in all cases included the last 80 min of the PET scan. DVR was used as a metric of specific binding.

At the start of the scan, approximately 4 mCi of [^{18}F]FCP was injected, followed by 3 ml of heparinized saline. Tracer doses of FCP were injected (2.39 ± 0.35 µg), and the mass of FCP was not different across groups. There was no relationship between injected mass and binding potential.

Surgery

After the second PET scan, each monkey was surgically prepared under sterile conditions with a vascular access port (Model GPV, Access Technologies, Skokie, Illinois), implanted under ketamine (15 mg/kg) and butorphanol (0.025 mg/kg) anesthesia. An incision was made near the femoral or jugular vein, and the catheter was inserted into the vein for a distance calculated to terminate in the vena cava. The distal end of the catheter was threaded subcutaneously to an incision made slightly off the midline of the back. The vascular access port was placed within a pocket formed by blunt dissection near the incision. The port and catheter were then flushed with a 50% dextrose/saline solution containing heparin (500 Units/ml). Antibiotic (25 mg/kg kefzol, BID; Cefazolin sodium, Marsam Pharmaceuticals, Cherry Hill, New Jersey) was administered prophylactically for 7–10 days beginning on the day of the surgery.

Cocaine Self-Administration

Monkeys were first trained to respond with food as the reinforcer, and subsequently, saline and increasing doses of cocaine were made available for self-administration. Each morning (5–7 days/week), monkeys from each pen were individually housed by partitioning the cage into four quadrants. Next, each monkey was seated in a primate chair (Primate Products) and the chair was wheeled to the operant chamber (Med Associates, East Fairfield, Vermont). The back of the animal was cleaned with 95% ethyl alcohol and betadine, and a 20 gauge Huber Point Needle (Access Technologies) was inserted into the port, connecting the infusion pump to the catheter. The pump was operated for approximately 3 s, filling the port and catheter with the dose of cocaine available during the experimental session. During the session, a fixed number of responses on the response lever (for example, a fixed ratio of 30) resulted in presentation of a banana pellet or activation of the infusion pump for 10 seconds. Each condition (saline or each dose of cocaine availability) was available for at least 7 consecutive sessions and until responding was stable (±15% of the mean for the last 3 sessions). There was a return to food-reinforced responding after evaluating a cocaine dose. In some social groups, the hierarchy changed while the cocaine dose-response curves were being determined. Because the effects of changes in rank, as well as cocaine exposure, on D_2 binding potential were not assessed, only self-administration data obtained during the time in which we were confident that the monkey's rank was not different from when the PET scans were conducted was included in the analysis. Thus, data from 9 monkeys that were evaluated with 4 doses of cocaine and saline, whose rank did not change across the period of the study, were evaluated.

Statistical Analysis

For purposes of PET image analysis, animals with a rank of 1 or 4 were considered dominant or subordinate, respectively, whereas those ranking 2 or 3 were considered intermediate, and their data were combined ($n = 5$ for each rank). Data were analyzed with a 3 (rank: dominant, intermediate and subordinate) by 2 (housing: individual and social) repeated measures ANOVA using commercially available software. Because of the smaller number of animals tested for acquisition of cocaine self-administration ($n = 9$), animals were considered either dominant (rank of 1 or 2, $n = 5$) or subordinate (rank of 3 or 4, $n = 4$). A repeated-measures ANOVA with dose (5 levels including saline) as the within-subject variable and social rank (that is, dominant and subordinate) as the between-subject variable was conducted. Pairwise comparisons for all analyses were made using the student Neuman-Keuls test. Correlation coefficients were computed using the same software package. Differences were considered statistically significant when $p < 0.05$.

Acknowledgments

We would like to thank C.S. Carter for comments on the manuscript; C. Hubbard, T. Moore and J. Lile for assistance with handling the monkeys; R. Kuhner for conducting the PET scans; and E. Nicks and P. Warren for assistance analyzing the social behavior data. This research was supported by the National Institute on Drug Abuse Grant DA-10584.

REFERENCES

1. Leshner, A. I. Vulnerability to addiction: new research opportunities. *Am. J. Med. Genet.* 96, 590–591 (2000).
2. Nader, M. A. & Woolverton, W. L. Effects of increasing the magnitude of an alternative reinforcer on drug choice in a discrete-trials choice procedure. *Psychopharmacology* 105, 169–174 (1991).
3. Schenk, S., Lacelle, G., Gorman, K. & Amit, Z. Cocaine self-administration in rats influenced by environmental conditions: implications for the etiology of drug abuse. *Neurosci. Lett.* 81, 227–231 (1987).
4. LeSage, M. G., Stafford, D. & Glowa, J. R. Preclinical research on cocaine self-administration: environmental determinants and their interaction with pharmacological treatment. *Neurosci. Biobehav. Rev.* 23, 717–741 (1999).
5. Schultz, W., Tremblay, L. & Hollerman, J. R. Reward processing in primate orbitofrontal cortex and basal ganglia. *Cereb. Cortex* 10, 272–284 (2000).
6. Bowling, S. L., Rowlett, J. K. & Bardo, M. T. The effect of environmental enrichment on amphetamine-stimulated locomotor activity, dopamine synthesis and dopamine release. *Neuropharmacology* 32, 885–893 (1993).
7. Hurd, Y. L., Svensson, P. & Ponten, M. The role of dopamine, dynorphin, and CART systems in the ventral striatum and amygdala in cocaine abuse. *Ann. NY Acad. Sci.* 877, 499–506 (1999).
8. Volkow, N. D., Fowler, J. S. & Wang, G. J. Imaging studies on the role of dopamine in cocaine reinforcement and addiction in humans. *J. Psychopharmacol.* 13, 337–345 (1999).
9. Blanc, G. *et al.* Response to stress of mesocortico-frontal dopaminergic neurones in rats after long-term isolation. *Nature* 284, 265–267 (1980).
10. Rilke, O., May, T., Oehler, J. & Wolffgramm, J. Influences of housing conditions and ethanol intake on binding characteristics of D_2, 5-HT1A, and benzodiazepine receptors of rats. *Pharmacol. Biochem. Behav.* 52, 23–28 (1995).
11. Hall, F. S. *et al.* Isolation rearing in rats: pre- and postsynaptic changes in striatal dopaminergic systems. *Pharmacol. Biochem. Behav.* 59, 859–872 (1998).
12. Grant, K. A. *et al.* Effect of social status on striatal dopamine D2 receptor binding characteristics in cynomolgus monkeys assessed with positron emission tomography. *Synapse* 29, 80–83 (1998).
13. Blum, K., Cull, J. G., Braverman, E. R. & Comings, D. E. Reward deficiency syndrome. *Am. Scientist* 84, 132–145 (1996).
14. Morgan, D. *et al.* Predictors of social status in cynomolgus monkeys (*Macaca fascicularis*) after group formation. *Am. J. Primatol.* 52, 115–131 (2000).
15. Nader, M. A. *et al.* PET imaging of dopamine D_2 receptors with [^{18}F] fluoroclebopride in monkeys: effects of isoflurane- and ketamine-induced anesthesia. *Neuropsychopharmacology* 21, 589–596 (1999).
16. Crowley, T. J., Stynes, A. J., Hydinger, M. & Kaufman, I. C. Ethanol, methamphetamine, pentobarbital, morphine, and monkey social behavior. *Arch. Gen. Psychiatry* 31, 829–838 (1974).
17. Crowley, T. J. *et al.* Cocaine, social behavior, and alcohol-solution drinking in monkeys. *Drug Alcohol Depend.* 29, 205–223 (1992).
18. Martin, S. P., Smith, E. O. & Byrd, L. D. Effects of dominance rank on damphetamine-induced increases in aggression. *Pharmacol. Biochem. Behav.* 37, 493–496 (1990).
19. Miczek, K. A. & Gold, L. H. d-Amphetamine in squirrel monkeys of different social status: effects on social and agonistic behavior, locomotion, and stereotypes. *Psychopharmacology* 81, 183–190 (1983).
20. Bozarth, M. A., Murray, A. & Wise, R. A. Influence of housing conditions on the acquisition of intravenous heroin and cocaine self-administration in rats. *Pharmacol. Biochem. Behav.* 33, 903–907 (1989).
21. Phillips, G. D. *et al.* Isolation rearing enhances the locomotor response to cocaine and a novel environment, but impairs the intravenous self-administration of cocaine. *Psychopharmacology* 115, 407–418 (1994).

22. Boyle, A. E., Gill, K. J., Smith, B. R. & Amit, Z. Differential effects of an early housing manipulation on cocaine-induced activity and self-administration in laboratory rats. *Pharmacol. Biochem. Behav.* 39, 269–274 (1991).

23. Verhoeff, N. P. Radiotracer imaging of dopaminergic transmission in neuropsychiatric disorders. *Psychopharmacology* 147, 217–249 (1999).

24. Calabresi, P., De Murtas, M. & Bernardi, G. The neostriatum beyond the motor function: experimental and clinical evidence. *Neuroscience* 78, 39–60 (1997).

25. Wang, G. J. *et al.* Brain dopamine and obesity. *Lancet* 357, 354–357 (2001).

26. Piazza, P. V. & Le Moal, M. The role of stress in drug self-administration. *Trends Pharmacol. Sci.* 19, 67–74 (1998).

27. Volkow, N. D. *et al.* Effects of chronic cocaine abuse on postsynaptic dopamine receptors. *Am. J. Psychiatry* 147, 719–724 (1990).

28. Volkow, N. D. *et al.* Decreased dopamine D_2 receptor availability is associated with reduced frontal metabolism in cocaine abusers. *Synapse* 14, 169–177 (1993).

29. Piazza, P. V. & LeMoal, M. Pathophysiological basis of vulnerability to drug abuse: role of an interaction between stress, glucocorticoids, and dopaminergic neurons. *Annu. Rev. Pharmacol. Toxicol.* 36, 359–378 (1996).

30. Lucas, L. R. *et al.* Neurochemical characterization of individual vulnerability to addictive drugs in rats. *Eur. J. Neurosci.* 10, 3153–3163 (1998).

31. Piazza, P. V., Deminiere, J.-M., Le Moal, M. & Simon, H. Factors that predict individual vulnerability to amphetamine self-administration. *Science* 245, 1511–1513 (1989).

32. Piazza, P. V., Deroche-Gamonent, V., Rouge-Pont, F. & Le Moal, M. Vertical shifts in self-administration dose-response functions predict a drug-vulnerable phenotype predisposed to addiction. *J. Neurosci.* 20, 4226–4232 (2000).

33. Marinelli, M. & White, F. J. Enhanced vulnerability to cocaine self-administration is associated with elevated impulse activity of midbrain dopamine neurons. *J. Neurosci.* 20, 8876–8885 (2000).

34. Nader, M. A., Green, K. L., Luedtke, R. R. & Mach, R. H. The effects of benzamide analogues on cocaine self-administration in rhesus monkeys. *Psychopharmacology* 147, 143–152 (1999).

35. Caine, S. B., Negus, S. S. & Mello, N. K. Effects of dopamine $D_{(1}$-like) and $D_{(2}$-like) agonists on cocaine self-administration in rhesus monkeys: rapid assessment of cocaine dose-effect functions. *Psychopharmacology* 148, 41–51 (2000).

36. Khroyan, T. V., Barrett-Larimore, R. L., Rowlett, J. K. & Spealman, R.D. Dopamine D_1- and D_2-like receptor mechanisms in relapse to cocaine-seeking behavior: effects of selective antagonists and agonists. *J. Pharmacol. Exp. Ther.* 294, 680–687 (2000).

37. Volkow, N. D. *et al.* Prediction of reinforcing responses to psychostimulants in humans by brain dopamine D_2 receptor levels. *Am. J. Psychiatry* 156, 1440–1443 (1999).

38. Mach, R. H. *et al.* Comparison of two fluorine-18 labeled benzamide derivatives that bind reversibly to dopamine D_2 receptor: *in vitro* binding studies and positron emission tomography. *Synapse* 24, 322–333 (1996).

39. Mach, R. H. *et al.* Use of positron emission tomography to study the dynamics of psychostimulant-induced dopamine release. *Pharmacol. Biochem. Behav.* 57, 477–486 (1997).

40. Laruelle, M. Imaging synaptic neurotransmission with *in vivo* binding competition techniques: a critical review. *J. Cereb. Blood Flow Metab.* 20, 423–451 (2000).

41. Woods, R. P. *et al.* Automated image registration: I. General methods and intrasubject, intramodality validation. *J. Comput. Assist. Tomogr.* 22, 141–152 (1998).

42. Logan, J. *et al.* Graphical analysis of reversible radioligand binding from time-activity measurements applied to [N-11C-methyl]-cocaine PET studies in human subjects. *J. Cereb. Blood Flow Metab.* 10, 740–747 (1990).

READING 19

Rethinking Feelings: An fMRI Study of the Cognitive Regulation of Emotion

Kevin N. Ochsner[1], Silvia A. Bunge[2], James J. Gross[1], and John D. E. Gabrieli[1]

The ability to cognitively regulate emotional responses to aversive events is important for mental and physical health. Little is known, however, about neural bases of the cognitive control of emotion. The present study employed functional magnetic resonance imaging to examine the neural systems used to reappraise highly negative scenes in unemotional terms. Reappraisal of highly negative scenes reduced subjective experience of negative affect. Neural correlates of reappraisal were increased activation of the lateral and medial prefrontal regions and decreased activation of the amygdala and medial orbito-frontal cortex. These findings support the hypothesis that prefrontal cortex is involved in constructing reappraisal strategies that can modulate activity in multiple emotion-processing systems.

Introduction

We humans are extraordinarily adaptable creatures. Drawing upon a vast array of coping skills, we can successfully manage adversity in even the most trying of circumstances. One of the most remarkable of these skills was described by Shakespeare's (1998/1623, p. 216) Hamlet, who observed, "there is nothing either good or bad, but thinking makes it so." Although Hamlet himself failed to capitalize on this insight, his message is clear: We can change the way we feel by changing the way we think, thereby lessening the emotional consequences of an otherwise distressing experience.

The cognitive transformation of emotional experience has been termed "reappraisal." In both experimental and individual-difference studies, reappraising an aversive event in unemotional terms reduces negative affect with few of the physiological, cognitive, or social costs associated with other emotion-regulatory strategies, such as the suppression of emotion-expressive behavior (Jackson, Malmstadt, Larson, & Davidson, 2000; Richards & Gross, 2000; Gross, 1998, 2002; Gross

[1]Stanford University, [2]Massachusetts Institute of Technology.

& John, in press). The mechanisms that mediate such reappraisals, however, are not yet understood. The goal of the present study was to use functional magnetic resonance imaging (fMRI) to elucidate the neural bases of reappraisal.

Although little prior work has directly examined the neural systems involved in the cognitive control of emotion, we expected that it would involve processing dynamics similar to those implicated in other well-studied forms of cognitive control. In general, cognitive control is thought to involve interactions between regions of lateral (LPFC) and medial prefrontal cortex (MPFC) that implement control processes and subcortical and posterior cortical regions that encode and represent specific kinds of information (Miller & Cohen, 2001; Knight, Staines, Swick, & Chao, 1999; Smith & Jonides, 1999). By increasing or decreasing activation of particular representations, prefrontal regions enable one to selectively attend to and maintain goal-relevant information in mind and resist interference (Miller & Cohen, 2001; Knight et al., 1999; Smith & Jonides, 1999). Based on these cognitive neuroscience models, as well as process models of emotion and emotion regulation (Gross, 2002; Ochsner & Feldman Barrett, 2001), we hypothesized that comparable interactions between cognitive control and emotion-processing systems would underlie reappraisal.

With respect to cognitive-processing systems, we hypothesized that reappraisal would involve three processes implemented by lateral and medial frontal cortices. The first is the active generation of a strategy for cognitively reframing an emotional event in unemotional terms, and keeping that strategy in mind as long as the eliciting conditions endure. In neuropsychological (Barcelo & Knight, 2002; Stuss, Eskes, & Foster, 1994), functional imaging (Cabeza & Nyberg, 2000; Smith & Jonides, 1999; Barch et al., 1997), and electrophysiological (Barcelo, Suwazono, & Knight, 2000; Nielsen-Bohlman & Knight, 1999) studies, these functions have been associated with working memory processes localized in the LPFC. The second process may monitor interference between top-down reappraisals that neutralize affect and bottom–up evaluations that continue to generate an affective response, signaling the need for reappraisal to continue. In a variety of tasks involving response conflict (Barch et al., 2001; van Veen, Cohen, Botvinick, Stenger, & Carter, 2001; Phelps, Hyder, Blamire, & Shulman, 1997) or overriding prepotent response tendencies (Carter et al., 2000; Peterson et al., 1999), these functions have been associated with the dorsal anterior cingulate cortex (for reviews, see Botvinick, Braver, Barch, Carter, & Cohen, 2001; Bush, Luu, & Posner, 2000). The third process involves reevaluating the relationship between internal (experiential or physiological) states and external stimuli, which may be used to monitor changes in one's emotional state during reappraisal. The dorsal regions of the MPFC are activated when making attributions about one's own (Paradiso et al., 1999; Lane, Fink, Chau, & Dolan 1997) or another person's (Gallagher et al., 2000; Happe et al., 1996) emotional state as well as during viewing of emotional films (Beauregard et al., 1998; Lane, Reiman, Ahern, Schwartz, & Davidson, 1997; Reiman et al., 1997) or photos (Lane, Reiman, Bradley, et al., 1997). Importantly, activation of the medial frontal cortex when anticipating painful shock (Chua, Krams, Toni, Passingham, & Dolan, 1999; Hsieh, Stone-Elander, & Ingvar, 1999; Ploghaus et al., 1999) may be inversely correlated with the experience of anxiety (Simpson et al., 2000), suggesting its importance for regulatory control (cf. Morgan & LeDoux, 1995).

With respect to emotion-processing systems, we hypothesized that reappraisal would modulate the processes involved in evaluating a stimulus as affectively significant. Many theories of emotion posit that at least two types of evaluative processing are involved in emotion generation (Lazarus, 1991; for a review, see Scherer, Schorr, & Johnstone, 2001). One type is important for determining whether a stimulus is affectively relevant and may be relatively automatic, whereas a second type is important for evaluating contextual meaning and the appropriateness of possible responses (Scherer et al., 2001; Lazarus, 1991). Evidence suggests that two highly interconnected brain structures (Cavada, Company, Tejedor, Cruz-Rizzolo, & Reinoso-Suarez, 2000), the amygdala and medial orbital frontal cortex (MOFC), are associated with these two types of emotion processing (Ochsner & Feldman Barrett, 2001; LeDoux, 2000; Bechara, Damasio, Damasio, & Lee, 1999). On one hand, the amygdala is important for the preattentive detection and recognition of affectively salient stimuli (Anderson & Phelps, 2001; Morris, Ohman, & Dolan, 1999; Whalen et al., 1998), learning and generating physiological and behavioral responses to them (LeDoux, 2000; Bechara et al., 1999), and modulating their consolidation into declarative memory (Hamann, Ely, Grafton, & Kilts, 1999; Cahill, Babinsky, Markowitsch, & McGaugh, 1995). On the other hand, the MOFC is important for representing the pleasant or unpleasant affective value of a stimulus (Kawasaki et al., 2001; O'Doherty, Kringelbach, Rolls, Hornak, & Andrews, 2001; Davidson & Irwin, 1999; Rolls, 1999; Elliott, Frith, & Dolan, 1997) in a flexible format that is sensitive to momentary changes in social and motivational context (Ochsner & Feldman Barrett, 2001; Bechara, Damasio, & Damasio, 2000; Rolls, 1999). Together, the amygdala and the MOFC differentially encode and represent the affective properties of stimuli (Bechara et al., 1999; Rolls, 1999), and we sought to determine whether reappraisal modulates activity in the MOFC, amygdala, or both.

To test these hypotheses, we adapted an experimental procedure used to study regulation of the fear-potentiated startle eyeblink response (Jackson et al., 2000). In that study, participants viewed aversive photos and were instructed either to increase, maintain, or decrease (postexperimental debriefing suggested that participants reappraised) their emotional reactions. Startle eyeblink magnitude (which was used as an indicator of the relative strength of an emotional reaction across trial types) increased, remained constant, or decreased according to the regulatory strategy being employed. This result suggests that participants can successfully regulate their emotional responses on a trial-by-trial basis. To isolate the processes related to the cognitive control of emotion, we needed to compare reappraisal to another condition that draws on processes invoked by reappraisal, but are not related to the regulation of affect per se. Because we hypothesized that reappraisal involves both attention to and awareness of one's emotional state, as well as regulatory processes directed towards altering it (Gross, 1998), we employed two conditions: On "Attend trials," participants were asked to let themselves respond emotionally to each photo by being aware of their feelings without trying to alter them. On "Reappraise trials," participants were asked to interpret photos so that they no longer felt negative in response to them. Because both Attend and Reappraise trials involve attention to emotion, regions more active when reappraising than attending were thought to reflect processes used to exert cognitive control. In contrast, regions more active for Attend than Reappraise trials were thought to be important for emotion processing that would be deactivated by reappraisal.

Each trial began with a 4-sec presentation of a negative or neutral photo, during which participants were instructed simply to view the stimulus on the screen. This interval was intended to provide time for participants to apprehend complex scenes and to allow an emotional response to be generated that participants then would be asked to regulate. The word Attend (for negative or neutral photos) or Reappraise (negative photos only) then appeared beneath the photo and participants followed this instruction for 4 sec, at which time the photo disappeared from the screen. Because we were interested in the processes used to actively reappraise an affective event as it unfolds, we focused our analyses on this portion of each trial. During this portion of the trial, we predicted that (a) Reappraise trials would result in greater lateral prefrontal activation than Attend trials and (b) that Attend trials would show greater activation of the MOFC and the amygdala than would Reappraise trials. For approximately three more seconds, participants could continue attending to or reappraising any feelings that lingered after presentation of the photo. A rating scale then appeared, which participants used to rate the strength of their current negative affect and which we used to verify that that reappraisal had successfully reduced negative feelings as compared to Attend trials. Finally, participants were instructed to relax for 4 sec before the next trial began.

Results

The experimental procedure included a measure that allowed us to segregate and analyze separately the trials on which participants experienced their strongest emotional responses without biasing the initial perception of photos during scanning. In a post-scanning session, participants viewed each negative photo a second time and rated the strength of their initial affective response (i.e., when they first viewed it, before they had attended or reappraised). These ratings were used to identify the third of the negative photos of each trial type that were rated most negative by each participant. As has been found in prior studies (Canli, Zhao, Brewer, Gabrieli, & Cahill, 2000), preliminary analyses indicated that reliable activation of emotion-processing systems was observed only for these most negative images. Given that the goal of this study was to examine the modulation of these systems by reappraisal, the analyses reported here focused only on these trial types.

Subjective Reports of Negative Affect

Segregating Most Negative Photos. Post-scan ratings of affective response indicated that the third of photos rated most negative ($M = 3.77$) elicited significantly greater negative affect than the moderately negative ($M = 2.99$) or least negative ($M = 1.93$) third of photos (all differ $p < .01$). Affect ratings for negative photos selected from Attend as compared to Reappraise trials did not differ significantly at any level of affect (all $p > .16$). The fact that retrospective ratings of negative affect were equivalent on Attend and Reappraise trials suggests that in-scan reappraisals did not bias post-scan emotional responses to photos. However, because these ratings were provided retrospectively, it is important to provide independent evidence that post-test ratings can be correlated with a participant's initial affective response to a stimulus (Ochsner & Schacter, in press). A separate pilot behavioral study was conducted to provide such evidence. Eight female participants rated their affective response to photos an average of 3 days before completing a test session that procedurally was equivalent to the scanning session used in the present study. They then completed post-test retrospective ratings of

the affective response they had to each photo when it was viewed during the test session. Results indicated that pre- and post-test ratings of negative affect were highly correlated for all trial types and all levels of negative photos (i.e, most, moderately, or least negative, all $p < .01$), which suggests that post-test ratings can provide a reliable index of one's initial affective response to a photo.

Success of Reappraisal. Ratings made during scanning showed that overall, moderate, and least negative photos elicited less negative affect than the most negative photos (both $p < .01$), which is consistent with post-test reports of initial affective response. Significantly, reappraisal was successful for the most negative photos: The average ratings of the strength of negative affect were high on Attend trials ($M = 3.48$) and were significantly lower on Reappraise trials[1] [$M = 1.90, t(14) = 17.41, p < .01$] (Figure 19.1). Reappraisal was potent enough that affect was diminished to that experienced when attending to the least negative photos ($p > .5$). Although negative affect was not as great as that reported for most negative photos, ratings for both the moderately negative and least negative photos showed a similar

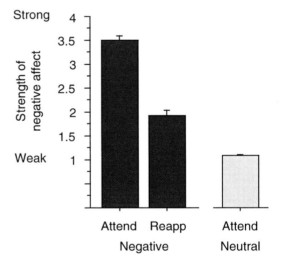

FIGURE 19.1 ■ Average negative ratings made during scanning for the most negative photos (the third of photos that elicited the most negative affect for a given participant). Negative affect was strong on Attend trials and decreased significantly on Reappraise (Reapp) trials ($p < .01$). When participants attended to their feelings towards neutral photos, the negative affect elicited was significantly weaker than for all other trial types (both $p <$ at least.01).

pattern of successful reappraisal [moderate: Attend $M = 2.75$, Reappraise $M = 1.52$, $t(14) = 7.66$, $p < .01$; least: Attend $M = 2.05$, Reappraise $M = 1.43$, $t(14) = 4.27$, $p < .01$]. However, comparisons with affect reported on Attend-neutral trials ($M = 1.08$) showed that in no case did reappraisal entirely eliminate negative affect ($p < .01$ for all comparisons).

Manipulation Check. In a pre-scan training session, participants were instructed to reappraise photos during scanning by generating an interpretation of, or story about, each photo that would explain apparently negative events in a less negative way. To verify that participants had, in fact, reappraised in this manner, during the post-scan rating session participants also were asked to indicate for each photo whether they had reinterpreted the photo (as instructed) or had used some other type of reappraisal strategy. Compliance with instructions was very high: On less than 4% of trials with highly negative photos did participants report using another type of strategy.

Brain Imaging Results

Activation by Reappraisal. Reappraisal-sensitive regions were identified by greater activation in response to the most negative photos on Reappraise than on Attend trials. Consistent with predictions, significantly activated regions included the dorsal and ventral regions of the left LPFC, as well as the dorsal MPFC (Figure 19.2, Table 19.1). Additional

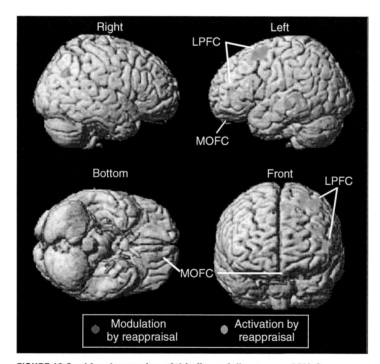

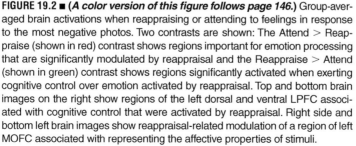

FIGURE 19.2 ■ (*A color version of this figure follows page 146.*) Group-averaged brain activations when reappraising or attending to feelings in response to the most negative photos. Two contrasts are shown: The Attend > Reappraise (shown in red) contrast shows regions important for emotion processing that are significantly modulated by reappraisal and the Reappraise > Attend (shown in green) contrast shows regions significantly activated when exerting cognitive control over emotion activated by reappraisal. Top and bottom brain images on the right show regions of the left dorsal and ventral LPFC associated with cognitive control that were activated by reappraisal. Right side and bottom left brain images show reappraisal-related modulation of a region of left MOFC associated with representing the affective properties of stimuli.

TABLE 19.1. Group Activations for Reappraise > Attend Contrast

| Region of Activation | Brodmann's Area | Coordinates | | | Z Score | Volume (mm³) |
		x	y	z		
Group Contrast						
Superior frontal gyrus	L6	−36	14	58	3.90	2736
Superior frontal gyrus	L6/8	−24	6	64	3.71	(L)
Middle frontal gyrus	L6/8	−24	10	56	3.68	(L)
Middle frontal gyrus	L6/8	−40	2	60	3.60	416
Inferior frontal gyrus	L46	−54	42	12	3.79	736
	L44/10	−48	46	4	3.31	(L)
Dorsomedial prefrontal cortex	8	−12	18	54	3.47	1040
	8	−4	20	54	3.39	
Dorsomedial prefrontal cortex	8/32	8	28	40	3.88	224
Temporal pole	28	−22	4	−26	4.21	128
Lateral occipital cortex	19	−38	−74	40	4.23	240
Supramarginal gyrus	R39/40	54	−70	30	4.23	688
Positive Correlation between Activation and Drop in Negative Affect then Reappraising						
Anterior cingulate	R24	6	14	32	4.67	88
Supramarginal gyrus	R40	54	−48	34	4.05	40

Clusters of 5 or more contiguous voxels whose global maxima meet a *t* threshold of 3.09, $p < .001$ uncorrected, are reported. Local maxima for these clusters are denoted with (L). Coordinates are in MNI space.

reappraisal-related activations were observed in left temporal pole, right supramarginal gyrus, and left lateral occipital cortex (Figure 19.2, Table 19.1). Contrary to expectations, activation of the cingulate cortex was not observed.

Cingulate involvement in reappraisal was revealed, however, in an SPM99 regression analysis used to identify regions for which level of brain activation across participants correlated significantly with reappraisal success. An index of reappraisal success was computed for each participant by subtracting the mean level of negative affect reported on Reappraise trials from that reported on Attend trials when highly negative images were shown. Larger difference scores thus corresponded to a greater decrease in negative affect, which is indicative of a more effective reappraisal. At a threshold of $p < .001$ (uncorrected), activity in no brain regions was negatively correlated, and in only two regions was positively correlated, with reappraisal success such that greater activation predicted greater decreases in negative affect. These two regions were located in the right anterior cingulate and right supramarginal gyrus (Figure 19.3, Table 19.1). To more precisely characterize these correlations, mean parameter estimates of the

response increase when reappraising as compared to attending were correlated with reappraisal success. These correlations were highly significant both for the foci in the anterior cingulate ($R^2 = .649$, $r = .805$, $p = .0001$) and the supramarginal gyrus ($R^2 = .570$, $r = .755$, $p < .0006$).

Modulation by Reappraisal. Emotion-sensitive regions modulated by reappraisal were identified by greater activation in response to the most negative photos on Attend than on Reappraise trials. Activation was observed in a region of left MOFC (Figure 19.2, Table 19.2). Additional regions of activation were found in the left posterior insula, right medial occipital cortex, and right inferior parietal cortex (Figure 19.2, Table 19.2). The amygdala, an a priori region-of-interest (ROI), was not significantly activated at a map-wise statistical threshold of $p < .001$. However, significant activation was observed in the right amygdala at a more liberal threshold ($p < .005$) (Figure 19.4). This finding was confirmed by the results of a planned ROI analysis in which parameter estimates that model the amplitude of the fMRI response were extracted from structurally defined ROIs (see, e.g., Figure 19.4). For the right amygdala, this analysis revealed a significantly greater amplitude of

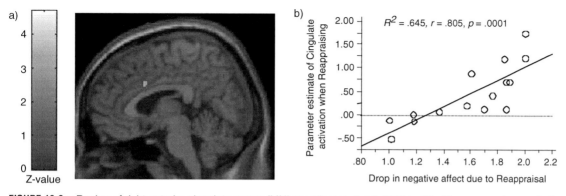

FIGURE 19.3 ■ Region of right anterior cingulate cortex (MNI coordinates: 6, 14, 32) identified in a regression analysis as showing a significant correlation between increasing activation and decreasing negative affect on Reappraise as compared to Attend trials with negative photos. Activation is shown on SPM99 canonical T1 image.

response on Attend than Reappraise trials ($p < .025$, one-tailed for planned comparison). The response to most negative photos on Reappraise trials was not significantly different from the response to neutral photos on Attend trials [$t(14) < 1$, $p > .5$] (Figure 19.5). No significant differences in response were shown across trial types for the left amygdala ROI [all $t(14) < 1$, $p > .5$].

To further characterize the relationships between reappraisal-related increases and decreases in brain activation, mean parameter estimates across trial types were contrasted for a set of functionally defined ROIs: The first was the region of MOFC identified by the Attend > Reappraise contrast, and the others were regions of the LPFC activated by the Reappraise > Attend contrast (Table 19.1). These analyses indicated that MOFC exhibited greater activation to most nega-

tive photos on Attend than on Reappraise trials, whereas activated regions of the LPFC exhibited precisely the opposite pattern ($p < .025$, one-tailed for planned comparisons). For one of the activated prefrontal regions—the ventral LPFC—the reappraisal-related increase in brain activation was correlated across participants with the reappraisal-related decrease in amygdala activation ($r = -.677$, $p < .004$; for all other regions, $p > .19$). Ventral LPFC activation also was negatively correlated with MOFC activation, albeit to a lesser extent ($r = -.494$, $p < .06$) (Figure 19.6). Activation on Attend-neutral trials was not significantly different from either activation on Attend–most negative trials in this ventral prefrontal region [$t(14) < 1.2$, $p > .24$] or from activity on Reappraise–most negative trials in MOFC and amygdala [both $t(14) < 1$, $p > .5$] (Figure 19.5).

TABLE 19.2. Group Activations for Attend > Reappraise Contrast

| Region of Activation | Brodmann's Area | Coordinates | | | Z Score | Volume (mm³) |
		x	y	z		
Medial orbito-frontal cortex	L11	−6	44	−22	4.17	112
Posterior insula	L13	−44	−16	2	3.84	240
Inferior parietal cortex	R39/19	38	−64	34	3.86	640
Medial occipital cortex	R19	22	−76	40	3.46	240
Amygdala	R	16	−12	−20	2.88*	112

Clusters of 5 or more contiguous voxels whose global maxima meet a t threshold of 3.09, $p < .001$ uncorrected, are reported. Local maxima for these clusters are denoted with (L). Coordinates are in MNI space.
*$T = 2.98$, $p < .005$.

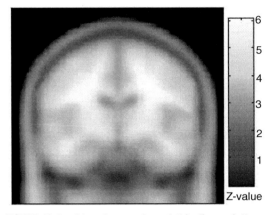

FIGURE 19.4 ■ (*A color version of this figure follows page 146.*) Coronal image showing the group-averaged cluster of activation in right amygdala for the Attend > Reappraise contrast for trials with the most negative photos ($p < .005$). The focus is centered on MNI coordinates (16, −12, −20). Activation is shown on group-averaged anatomy.

Discussion

This study is one of the first to use functional imaging to draw inferences about the neural bases of the cognitive control of emotion. Behaviorally, reappraisal of negative photos successfully diminished negative affect. Neural correlates of effective reappraisal were (1) activation in the regions of the LPFC and MPFC essential for working memory, cognitive control (Miller & Cohen, 2001; Knight et al., 1999; Smith & Jonides, 1999), and self-monitoring (Gusnard, Akbudak, Shulman, & Raichle, 2001) and (2) decreased activation in two regions involved in emotion processing, the MOFC and the amygdala (Adolphs, 2001; Ochsner & Feldman Barrett, 2001; Bechara et al., 1999; Davidson & Irwin, 1999; Rolls, 1999). In addition, the magnitude of ventral LPFC activation during reappraisal was inversely correlated with activation in both emotion-processing regions. Taken together, these findings provide the first evidence that reappraisal may modulate emotion processes implemented in the amygdala and MOFC that are involved in evaluating the affective salience and contextual relevance of a stimulus (Ochsner & Feldman Barrett, 2001; Phelps et al., 2001; Bechara et al.,

2000; LeDoux, 2000; Bechara et al., 1999; Rolls, 1999).

Cognitive Processes Supporting Reappraisal

The particular regions of the LPFC and MPFC activated by reappraisal are similar to the regions commonly activated across working memory and response-selection tasks that involve maintaining information in awareness and resisting interference from competing inputs (Cabeza & Nyberg, 2000; Smith & Jonides, 1999; Courtney, Petit, Maisog, Ungerleider, & Haxby, 1998; Petit, Courtney, Ungerleider, & Haxby, 1998; Alexander, Delong, & Strick, 1996). These similarities suggest that an overlapping set of prefrontal regions support the cognitive regulation of feelings and thoughts (Miller & Cohen, 2001; Ochsner & Feldman Barrett, 2001; Davidson & Irwin, 1999; Knight et al., 1999; Smith & Jonides, 1999).

The finding that activation of the ventral LPFC was inversely correlated with the activation of the amygdala and the MOFC suggests that this region may play a direct part in modulating emotion processing, perhaps related to the role of ventral frontal regions in interference control and behavioral inhibition more generally (Miller & Cohen, 2001; Smith & Jonides, 1999). It is notable, however, that other prefrontal regions were even more strongly activated by reappraisal, although these activations did not correlate significantly with activity in emotion-processing regions. Although this initial study was not designed to determine the precise contributions to the reappraisal process made by each region, they may mediate processes necessary for, but not directly related to, successful reappraisal. For example, dorsomedial prefrontal cortex was the region most strongly activated by reappraisal. This region has been associated with emotional awareness (Lane, 2000; Lane et al., 1997), drawing inferences about one's own (Paradiso et al., 1999) or others' (Gallagher et al., 2000; Happe et al., 1996) emotional states, and self-related processing (Gusnard et al., 2001) more generally. The need to monitor and evaluate the self-relevance of emotional stimuli could be important whenever one reappraises

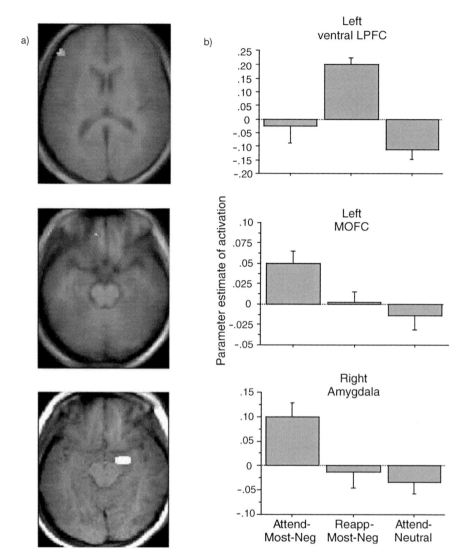

FIGURE 19.5 ■ ROI analyses. (a) Functionally or structurally defined ROIs and (b) group mean parameter estimates ($M \pm SEM$) for each ROI on Attend and Reappraise (Reapp) trials using negative photos, and Attend trials using neutral photos. Note that the negative images contributing to this analysis were identified as the third of negative images that were given the most negative rating by each participant (see Methods and Results). Top row: A functionally defined ROI within the left ventral LPFC (BA 46/10) activated by Reappraise > Attend contrast, centered on MNI coordinates ($-54, 42, 12$) and shown on group-averaged anatomy. This is the only prefrontal region whose activation during reappraisal was inversely correlated with activation in emotion-processing regions (shown in Figure 19.6). Middle row: A functionally defined ROI within left MOFC (BA 11) identified by the Attend > Reappraise contrast, centered on MNI coordinates ($-6, 46, -20$) and shown on group-averaged anatomy. Bottom row: Sample structurally defined ROI for the right amygdala from a single subject centered on MNI coordinates ($24, -7, -15$). Ventral LPFC activation on Reappraise–most negative trials was significantly greater than on Attend–most negative trials ($p < .025$, one-tailed), whereas the MOFC and amygdala showed the opposite pattern (both $p < .025$, one-tailed).

a)

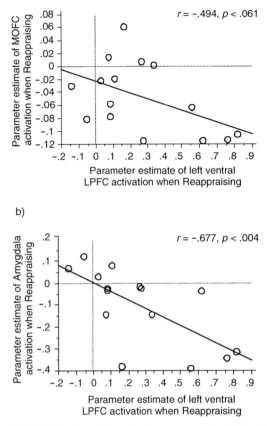

$r = -.494, p < .061$

Parameter estimate of MOFC activation when Reappraising

Parameter estimate of left ventral LPFC activation when Reappraising

b)

$r = -.677, p < .004$

Parameter estimate of Amygdala activation when Reappraising

Parameter estimate of left ventral LPFC activation when Reappraising

FIGURE 19.6 ■ Correlations between reappraisal-induced changes in parameter estimates of activation for the functional and structural ROIs shown in Figure 19.5. During reappraisal, increases in response in the ventral LPFC (a) correlated with decreases in response in the amygdala and (b) to a lesser degree correlated with decreases in response in the MOFC.

(Scherer et al., 2001; Lazarus, 1991) and may be used to regulate anxiety in anticipation of aversive events (Simpson et al., 2000). Similarly, the superior prefrontal regions have been associated with spatial working memory and control of eye movements (Smith & Jonides, 1999; Courtney et al., 1998), both of which could be needed for analyzing and reinterpreting perceptual inputs during reappraisal.

We also hypothesized that the anterior cingulate cortex would be involved in reappraisal.

Although cingulate activation was not observed in the group contrast of Reappraise and Attend trials, there was, across participants, a positive correlation between cingulate activation and effective reappraisal. The anterior cingulate cortex is thought to be important for monitoring ongoing processing and evaluating the need for cognitive control (e.g., Botvinick et al., 2001), and it might be expected that successful reappraisal would depend upon the use of this process to monitor for conflicts between initial emotional appraisals and cognitively restructured reappraisals. In the present study, cingulate activation may therefore reflect active monitoring that enhanced the cognitive transformation of an aversive experience.

Emotion Processes Modulated by Reappraisal

The observation that reappraisal can influence brain systems implicated in emotion processing may have significance for contemporary appraisal theories of emotion (for a review, see Scherer et al., 2001). It has been clear that reappraisal diminishes negative emotion experience and negative emotion-expressive behavior (Gross, 1998), but theorists have not specified the types of emotion processing that might be influenced by reappraisal. Although the present study was not designed to determine which specific emotion-processing functions attributable to the amygdala and MOFC are modulated by reappraisal, modulation of these two brain structures is consistent with the idea that reappraisal can influence processes involved in evaluating the affective salience of a stimulus (Anderson & Phelps, 2001; Morris et al., 1999; Whalen et al., 1998), as well as those important for evaluating the salience of that stimulus in the context of current situational or personal goals (Kawasaki et al., 2001; Ochsner & Feldman Barrett, 2001; O'Doherty et al., 2001; Bechara et al., 2000; Davidson & Irwin, 1999; Rolls, 1999; Elliott et al., 1997).

Further work will be needed to determine which specific aspects of amygdala and OFC functioning can be modulated by reappraisal. On one hand, the appraisal function of the amygdala often is characterized as automatic (e.g., LeDoux,

2000; Morris et al., 1999). In the present study, it is likely that reappraisal did not modulate this early amygdala response, which is thought to depend upon subcortical inputs from the senses. Instead, reappraisal may have influenced a more sustained response that may depend (as discussed below) on cortical inputs and is more amenable to control by cognitive processes. It will be important to determine whether and how reappraisal could influence the early automatic response as well. On the other hand, the MOFC often is characterized as serving a regulatory function,[2] as evidenced, for example, by its roles in decision-making involving risky choices (e.g., Bechara et al., 2000) and extinction of conditioned fear responses (e.g., Morgan et al., 1995; see, however, footnote 2). On our view, the cognitive processes supporting reappraisal, as well as the emotional processes supporting context-sensitive evaluation, may both exert regulatory effects, albeit in different ways. Whereas the evaluation processes supported by OFC may support the selection of appropriate, and the transient suppression of inappropriate, affective responses, the reappraisal processes supported by lateral and medial prefrontal regions may be important for modulating these evaluation processes themselves. By down-regulating multiple types of evaluation processes, reappraisal may shift from an emotional to an unemotional mode of stimulus analysis.

Further work will also be needed to determine exactly how prefrontal regions modulate the amygdala and MOFC during reappraisal. In the present study, we observed an inverse correlation between lateral prefrontal and amygdala activation during reappraisal, although these two structures share few direct connections. One route by which the LPFC could influence the amygdala is via the MOFC, which has reciprocal connections with both regions (Cavada et al., 2000). By directly modulating representations of the affective significance of a stimulus in the MOFC, activation in the LPFC could blunt processing in the amygdala indirectly. This seems somewhat unlikely, however, because the correlation between the LPFC and the MOFC activity was not as strong as the correlation between LPFC and

amygdala activity (which could be due, in part, to signal loss in MOFC). A second possible route involves prefrontal modulation of posterior perceptual and semantic inputs to the amygdala from the occipital and parietal regions (de Fockert, Rees, Frith, & Lavine, 2001; Miller & Cohen, 2001; Knight et al., 1999; Smith & Jonides, 1999). Reappraising the affective significance of images in working memory may reorganize these inputs so that the amygdala and the MOFC no longer register the presence of an aversive stimulus. This view is supported by the fact that reappraisal modulated activation in the lateral occipital cortex, a region associated with visual object processing, and the supramarginal gyrus, an inferior parietal region associated with attentional selection and storage of information held in working memory (Cabeza & Nyberg, 2000; Culham & Kanwisher, 2001; Smith & Jonides, 1999). Future research may help determine which account is correct.

The Nature of Emotion Regulation

The present study provides insight into the processes supporting reappraisal. However, a number of additional steps will be necessary to develop a more complete framework for understanding the cognitive and affective mechanisms of emotion and emotion regulation more generally (Ochsner & Feldman Barrett, 2001). In particular, the present research raises at least two important questions about the nature of emotion regulation.

The first question concerns the way in which emotion processing might be modulated differently by cognitive reappraisal as compared to other forms of emotion regulation. A pair of studies have examined attentional influences on emotion processing and found that enhanced amygdala responses to fearful faces did not change as attention to a fear stimulus decreased (Anderson et al., 2001; Vuilleumier, Armony, Driver, & Dolen, 2001). These results contrast with the present finding that attempts to cognitively transform feelings can modulate amygdala activity. A handful of other studies have examined the influence on amygdala processing of cognitive judgments that involve explicit evaluation of the emotional properties of faces as compared to evaluation of stimulus dimensions unrelated to emotion, such as gender or age. Results have been mixed, with some studies finding that evaluative judgments diminish amygdala activation (Hariri, Bookheimer, & Mazziotta, 2000; Liberzon et al., 2000) and others finding the opposite (Winston, Strange, O'Doherty, & Dolan, 2002; Critchley et al., 2000). Although the precise relevance of these judgments to emotion regulation is not clear, some of the discrepant findings could be attributable to a differential dependence of some evaluative judgments on processes involved in reappraisal. More generally, the present results may be difficult to directly relate to these studies because of the differences in the stimuli employed and the responses they evoke. Whereas the present study used stimuli that elicit relatively strong responses that induce changes in emotional experience, the words and faces employed in other studies elicit weaker responses overall and only rarely alter experience (Ochsner & Feldman Barrett, 2001; Davidson & Irwin, 1999). Future work may serve to clarify the precise ways in which different types of regulation modulate different aspects of emotion (Ochsner & Feldman Barrett, 2001; cf. Gray, in press).

A second question concerns the lateralization of activations and deactivations related to reappraisal and emotion processing, respectively. One possibility is that these findings are related to properties of the particular regulatory processes involved in the present study. Left lateralization of reappraisal-related prefrontal activations may, for example, reflect a common verbal component of reappraisal strategies employed by participants, who typically reported mentally talking themselves through their reappraisals.[3] Left prefrontal regions have been implicated in interference tasks involving verbal stimuli (e.g., Bunge, Ochsner, Desmond, Glover, & Gabrieli, 2001; Macdonald, Cohen, Stenger, & Carter, 2000; D'Esposito, Postle, Jonides, & Smith, 1999; Jonides, Smith, Marshuetz, Koeppe, & Reuter-Lorenz, 1998), which suggests that this region may represent verbal reappraisal strategies and help resolve interference with competing negative evaluations generated by the perception of aversive stimuli. Were one to examine other types of reappraisal or other emotion-regulation strategies that do not share this interpretive verbal component (e.g., those involving attentional deployment, as discussed above, or the suppression of expressive emotional behavior; Gross, 1998), it is possible that activation of the right prefrontal systems would be observed. This hypothesis is supported by a study showing that regulating responses to a sexually arousing film clip by viewing them from a detached third-person perspective activated right PFC and deactivated structures related to sexual arousal, including the hypothalamus and the amygdala (Beauregard, Levesque, & Bourgouin, 2001). In this context, the deactivation of the right amygdala and the left MOFC may reflect stimulus- (as compared to verbally) driven processing of affective information by the amygdala (Phelps et al., 2001; Morris et al., 1999), and the observation that the right amygdala and the left orbitofrontal cortex activity may be coupled during sensory processing of aversive stimuli (Zald & Pardo, 1997).

A second possible explanation for lateralized activations relates to findings associating negative affect with the right hemisphere and positive affect with the left hemisphere (e.g., Canli, Desmond, Zhao, Glover, & Gabrieli, 1998; see Davidson & Irwin, 1999, for a review). Thus, right amygdala deactivation could reflect down-regulation of systems that generate negative appraisals whereas left PFC activation could reflect engagement of systems supporting positivizing reappraisals. This interpretation is consistent with the finding that relatively greater resting activation of the left than the right PFC is correlated with resistance to depression, which may in turn reflect baseline differences in the ability to represent cognitive control strategies used to down-regulate emotion processing (Davidson, Putnam, & Larson, 2000). Consistent with this view, studies of resting brain metabolism in individuals with depression or obsessive–compulsive disorder—who may be unable to effectively represent these strategies—have shown hypoactivation of the prefrontal regions coupled with hyperactivation of the amygdala and/or the orbito-frontal cortex that normalizes with effective treatment (Davidson et al., 2000; Brody et al., 1999; Saxena et al., 1999).

Conclusions

The aim of the present study was to use information about brain function to draw inferences about the mechanisms supporting one type of cognitive control of emotion. As such, it represents one example of a growing trend towards using neuroscience methods to address questions that traditionally have been of interest to social and personality psychologists (Ochsner & Lieberman, 2001). Although findings suggest that cognitive reappraisal can modulate multiple types of emotion processing, questions remain about the functional significance of observed frontal and amygdala activations, their relation to other forms of regulation, and their relevance to clinical populations. As future work addresses these questions, we may be able to better connect Hamlet's timeless observation that thinking can make things good or bad with an increased understanding of how the brain makes this possible.

Methods

Participants

Fifteen healthy right-handed female volunteers[4] recruited from Stanford University and the surrounding community (ages 18–30, $M = 21.9$) gave informed consent and were paid $50 for their participation.

Task

On the basis of normative ratings, two sets of 38 negative color photos and one set of 38 neutral color photos were selected from the International Affective Picture System (Lang, Greenwald, Bradley, & Hamm, 1993). The task design was adapted from Jackson et al., (2000). At the beginning of each trial, a photo (subtending approximately $20 \times 20°$ of visual angle) appeared in the center of a black screen for 4 sec with the instruction VIEW printed in white underneath. Many photos depicted complex scenes, and during this viewing period participants were instructed to view the photo, understand its content, and allow themselves to experience/feel any emotional response it might elicit. The photo remained on the screen for an additional 4 sec with an instruction either to ATTEND or REAPPRAISE replacing the instruction to VIEW. On Attend trials, either a negative or a neutral photo was shown and participants were instructed to attend to and be aware of, but not to try to alter, any feelings elicited by it. On Reappraise trials, a negative photo was shown and participants were instructed to reinterpret the photo so that it no longer elicited a negative response. The 4-sec epoch during which participants were attending or reappraising negative photos is the subject of the functional imaging analyses reported in the present study. The photo then disappeared and, for 3.1 sec, participants could continue attending to, or reappraising, any feelings that lingered after its presentation. A four-point scale (1 = "weak" to 4 = "strong") for rating the strength of current negative affect then was presented for 3 sec, and participants indicated how they felt currently. Finally, an instruction to RELAX appeared in the center of the screen for 5 sec. A 900-msec interval separated each trial.

Testing Procedure

One to three days before scanning, participants received extensive instruction in reappraisal. Pilot testing suggested reappraisal was commonly accomplished by generating an interpretation of, or a story about, each photo that would explain apparently negative events in a less negative way (e.g., women depicted crying outside of a church could be described as attending a wedding instead of a funeral). No single type of reinterpretation was universally applicable to all photos, which was expected given that individuals must generate context-appropriate reappraisals in everyday life. To strike a balance between generalizability and experimental control, we instructed participants to select the reinterpretation that was most effective for each photo. Training began by asking participants to spontaneously generate reappraisals of sample photos. After appropriate coaching and shaping by the researcher to ensure that participants could reinterpret photos quickly and effectively, the training ended with the completion of 18 practice trials. It was stressed that when asked to reappraise, participants should neither look away (unless necessary; no subjects reported that it was) nor distract themselves with irrelevant and/or positive thoughts.

During scanning, participants completed one hundred and fourteen 20-sec trials over six separate scans. Each scan included approximately equal numbers of each trial type, and trial order was counterbalanced across scans so that every trial type followed every other with equal probability. Assignment of photos to trial types and scans was counterbalanced across participants. Psyscope was used to control stimulus presentation and response collection. Upon completion of scanning, participants viewed all the negative photos they had seen in the scanner and indicated the strength of their initial negative reaction to each one (i.e., during the viewing period, before attending, or reappraising). These ratings were used to identify the trials that involved the photos rated most negatively by each participant. To verify that participants had, in fact, reappraised, for each photo they were asked to indicate whether they had generated an alternative interpretation or whether they had used some other types of reappraisal strategy.

Data Acquisition

Whole-brain imaging data were acquired on a 3-T MRI Signa LX Horizon Echospeed scanner (GE Medical Systems, 8.3_m4 systems revision). T2-weighted flow-compensated spin-echo anatomical images (TR, 2000 msec; TE, 85 msec) were acquired in 16 contiguous 7-mm axial slices. Functional images were acquired with the same slice prescription using a T2*-sensitive gradient-echo spiral pulse sequence (Glover & Lai, 1998) (TE, 30 msec; TR, 1000 msec; two interleaves; flip angle 60°, field of view, 24 cm; 64×64 data acquisition matrix).

Data Analysis

Functional images were motion-corrected and normalized to a standard template brain using SPM99 (Wellcome Department of Cognitive Neurology). Normalized images were interpolated to $2 \times 2 \times 4$-mm voxels and spatially smoothed with a Gaussian filter (6 mm full width

half maximum). Low-frequency noise and differences in global signal between participants were removed. Single participants' data were analyzed with a fixed-effects model (Friston, Jezzard, & Turner, 1994) and group data were analyzed using a random-effects model (Holmes & Friston, 1998). Effects were modeled using a box-car convolved with a canonical hemodynamic response function for the 4-sec trial epoch during which participants reappraised or attended while a photo was on the screen. An anatomically defined gray matter mask was created and explicitly specified during analysis. This ensured that statistical analysis was performed in all brain regions, including those where signal may be low due to susceptibility artifacts. For the group analysis, functional images were averaged to create a single image of mean activation per trial type and participant. To identify regions recruited across participants that wee activated or relatively deactivated by reappraisal, one-sample t tests were performed on these average images to create a series of SPM{Z} maps depicting differences in brain activation between trial types. To identify regions for which the level of reappraisal-related activation across participants was correlated with the reappraisal-related decreases in negative affect, a simple regression analysis was performed on the average images for the Reappraise > Attend contrast. Except as noted below, for group contrasts and regression analysis, a voxel-level threshold of $p < .001$ uncorrected for multiple comparisons ($t = 3.09$) was used. An extent threshold of five contiguous voxels was applied to activated clusters meeting the voxel-level threshold. Maxima are reported in MNI305 coordinates, as in SPM99.

To determine whether reappraisal modulated the amygdala's response to negative photos, structurally defined ROIs were drawn around each participant's amygdalae on their in-plane anatomical images (Desmond & Lim, 1997). Parameter estimates (that model the amplitude of the fMRI response) averaged across all voxels for each ROI were then extracted for Reappraise and Attend trials on which the most negative photos had been presented. For comparison, parameter estimates on Attend neutral trials also were extracted.

Planned *t* tests ($\alpha = .05$, one-tailed) were used to compare amygdala activation across these three trial types. This analysis also was performed for functionally defined ROIs in regions of a priori interest in the LPFC and MOFC.

Acknowledgments

This research was supported by NSF grant BCD-0084496, McDonnel-Pew grant 98–23, and grant 5 F32 MH11990–03 from the National Institute of Health. The authors thank Adam Anderson and Kalina Christoff for discussion of relevant issues and comments on earlier drafts of this reading.

The data reported in this experiment have been deposited in The fMRI Data Center (http://www.fmridc.org). The accession number is 2–2002–1137G.

NOTES

1. To provide an independent check for bias in participants' subjective reports, and the affect ratings in particular, in a pre-scan session participants were asked to complete the Marlowe–Crowne social desirability scale, which is commonly used as a measure of the tendency to provide responses that would be demanded in an experiment. Overall, scores on this scale were low ($M = 13.125$) and were uncorrelated ($r = -.099$, $p > .80$) with reappraisal success (as indexed by the drop in negative affect on reappraise as compared to attend trials). Furthermore, if affect ratings reflected compliance with experimental demand, then ratings might have been expected to drop on reappraise trials to the level of affect reported on aware trials with neutral photos. This did not occur. In fact, ratings on reappraise trials remained sensitive to differences in intensity across photos: ratings on reappraise trials with most negative photos were greater than on reappraise trials for least negative images, which in turn, were still greater than rating on aware neutral trials.

2. Two points concerning the MOFC's role in regulation are relevant here. First, recent studies suggest that the relation of MOFC to extinction is not yet clear. Some animal lesion studies indicate that medial lesions impair extinction (Morgan et al., 1995), others suggest that they do not (Gewirtz, Falls, & Davis, 1997), whereas others suggest that the impairments may be observed only during some phases of extinction (Quirk, Russo, Barron, & Lebron, 2000). Although the reasons for these discrepancies await clarification, one possible contributing factor may be that subtle differences in learning contexts lead to differential dependence on context-sensitive appraisal processes associated with

MOFC. In some circumstances, when a UCS no longer follows a CS, these appraisal processes might be used to try and figure out what action to take next. This decision process might transiently suppress a CR, which research has shown can spontaneously reemerge at a later point. Second, prior work has shown that OFC is involved in modifying associations established in the amygdala (e.g., Rolls, 1999). This modification does not always involve down-regulation of amygdala activity, however, and in many cases may involve coactivation of the two structures during emotional learning and evaluation (e.g., Schoenbaum, Chiba, & Gallagher, 1998). In the case of extinction, OFC activity could also reflect the use of appraisal processes to encode new properties of the stimulus–context relationship. We would suggest, therefore, that these data, along with the results of the present study, are consistent with the conclusion that reappraisal may down-regulate two processing components of a system important for analyzing different kinds of emotion features. Under certain circumstances, these two emotion-related processors may themselves configure to regulate responses. In the present circumstances, regulatory effects are achieved by shutting them both down. Ultimately, brain systems might best be thought of as performing task non-specific computations that may play a part in different types of behavior, whether or not that behavior is best described as regulatory.

3. In this regard, it is worth noting that variability introduced by the fact that we did not constrain participants to reappraise photos in exactly the same way (they were free to implement a common cognitive reframing strategy in a whatever manner was appropriate for each photo) could provide a conservative estimate of reappraisal-related prefrontal activations.

4. Only women were studied because women often exhibit stronger emotional responses than men (Kring & Gordon, 1998), and prior research from our laboratory and others suggested that women respond more strongly and more reliably to the emotional stimuli used in this study (Ito, Cacioppo, & Lang, 1998).

REFERENCES

Adolphs, R. (2001). The neurobiology of social cognition. *Current Opinion in Neurobiology, 11*, 231–239.

Alexander, G. E., Delong, M., & Strick, P. L. (1996). Parallel organization of functionally segregated circuits linking basal ganglia and cortex. *Annual Review of Neuroscience, 9*, 357–381.

Anderson, A. K., Panitz, D. A., Ochsner, K. N., Bunge, S. A., Christoff, K., & Gabrieli, J. D. E. (2001). Examination of attentional modulation of neural responses in affective and neural object processing domains. *Society for Neuroscience Abstracts*, 120.2.

Anderson, A. K., & Phelps, E. A. (2001). Lesions of the human amygdala impair enhanced perception of emotionally salient events. *Nature, 411*, 305–309.

Barcelo, F., & Knight, R. T. (2002). Both random and perseverative errors underlie WCST deficits in prefrontal patients. *Neuropsychologia, 40,* 349–356.

Barcelo, F., Suwazono, S., & Knight, R. T. (2000). Prefrontal modulation of visual processing in humans. *Nature Neuroscience, 3,* 399–403.

Barch, D. M., Braver, T. S., Akbudak, E., Conturo, T., Ollinger, J., & Snyder, A. (2001). Anterior cingulate cortex and response conflict: Effects of response modality and processing domain. *Cerebral Cortex, 11,* 837–848.

Barch, D. M., Braver, T. S., Nystrom, L. E., Forman, S. D., Noll, D. C., & Cohen, J. D. (1997). Dissociating working memory from task difficulty in human prefrontal cortex. *Neuropsychologia, 35,* 1373–1380.

Beauregard, M., Leroux, J. M., Bergman, S., Arzoumanian, Y., Beaudoin, G., Bourgouin, P., & Stip, E. (1998). The functional neuroanatomy of major depression: An fMRI study using an emotional activation paradigm. *NeuroReport, 9,* 3253–3258.

Beauregard, M., Levesque, J., & Bourgouin, P. (2001). Neural correlates of conscious self-regulation of emotion. *Journal of Neuroscience, 21,* RC165.

Bechara, A., Damasio, H., & Damasio, A. R. (2000). Emotion, decision making and the orbitofrontal cortex. *Cerebral Cortex, 10,* 295–307.

Bechara, A., Damasio, H., Damasio, A. R., & Lee, G. P. (1999). Different contributions of the human amygdala and ventromedial prefrontal cortex to decision-making. *Journal of Neuroscience, 19,* 5473–5481.

Botvinick, M. M., Braver, T. S., Barch, D. M., Carter, C. S., & Cohen, J. D. (2001). Conflict monitoring and cognitive control. *Psychology Review, 108,* 624–652.

Brody, A. L., Saxena, S., Silverman, D. H., Alborzian, S., Fairbanks, L. A., Phelps, M. E., Huang, S. C., Wu, H. M., Maidment, K., & Baxter, L. R., Jr. (1999). Brain metabolic changes in major depressive disorder from pre- to posttreatment with paroxetine. *Psychiatry Research, 91,* 127–139.

Bunge, S. A., Ochsner, K. N., Desmond, J. E., Glover, G. H., & Gabrieli, J. D. E. (2001). Prefrontal regions involved in keeping information in and out of mind. *Brain, 124,* 2074–2086.

Bush, G., Luu, P., & Posner, M. I. (2000). Cognitive and emotional influences in anterior cingulate cortex. *Trends in Cognitive Sciences, 4,* 215–222.

Cabeza, R., & Nyberg, L. (2000). Imaging cognition: II. An empirical review of 275 PET and fMRI studies. *Journal of Cognitive Neuroscience, 12,* 1–47.

Cahill, L., Babinsky, R., Markowitsch, H. J., & McGaugh, J. L. (1995). The amygdala and emotional memory. *Nature, 377,* 295–296.

Canli, T., Desmond, J. E., Zhao, Z., Glover, G., & Gabrieli, J. D. (1998). Hemispheric asymmetry for emotional stimuli detected with fMRI. *NeuroReport, 9,* 3233–3239.

Canli, T., Zhao, Z., Brewer, J., Gabrieli, J. D. E., & Cahill, L. (2000). Event-related activation in the human amygdala associates with later memory for individual emotional experience. *Journal of Neuroscience, 20,* RC99.

Carter, C. S., Macdonald, A. M., Botvinick, M., Ross, L. L., Stenger, V. A., Noll, D., & Cohen, J. D. (2000). Parsing executive processes: Strategic vs. evaluative functions of the anterior cingulate cortex. *Proceedings of the National Academy of Sciences, U.S.A., 97,* 1944–1948.

Cavada, C., Company, T., Tejedor, J., Cruz-Rizzolo, R. J., & Reinoso-Suarez, F. (2000). The anatomical connections of the macaque monkey orbitofrontal cortex. A review. *Cerebral Cortex, 10,* 220–242.

Chua, P., Krams, M., Toni, I., Passingham, R., & Dolan, R. (1999). A functional anatomy of anticipatory anxiety. *Neuroimage, 9,* 563–571.

Courtney, S. M., Petit, L., Maisog, J. M., Ungerleider, L. G., & Haxby, J. V. (1998). An area specialized for spatial working memory in human frontal cortex. *Science, 279,* 1347–1351.

Critchley, H., Daly, E., Phillips, M., Brammer, M., Bullmore, E., Williams, S., Van Amelsvoort, T., Robertson, D., David, A., & Murphy, D. (2000). Explicit and implicit neural mechanisms for processing of social information from facial expressions: A functional magnetic resonance imaging study. *Human Brain Mapping, 9,* 93–105.

Culham, J. C., & Kanwisher, N. G. (2001). Neuroimaging of cognitive functions in human parietal cortex. *Current Opinion in Neurobiology, 11,* 157–163.

Davidson, R. J., & Irwin, W. (1999). The functional neuroanatomy of emotion and affective style. *Trends in Cognitive Sciences, 3,* 11–21.

Davidson, R. J., Putnam, K. M., & Larson, C. L. (2000). Dysfunction in the neural circuitry of emotion regulation—a possible prelude to violence. *Science, 289,* 591–594.

de Fockert, J. W., Rees, G., Frith, C. D., & Lavie, N. (2001). The role of working memory in visual selective attention. *Science, 291,* 1803–1806.

Desmond, J. E., & Lim, K. O. (1997). On- and offline Talairach registration for structural and functional MRI studies. *Human Brain Mapping, 5,* 58–73.

D'Esposito, M., Postle, B. R., Jonides, J., & Smith, E. E. (1999). The neural substrate and temporal dynamics of interference effects in working memory as revealed by event-related functional MRI. *Proceedings of the National Academy of Sciences, U.S.A., 96,* 7514–7519.

Elliott, R., Frith, C. D., & Dolan, R. J. (1997). Differential neural response to positive and negative feedback in planning and guessing tasks. *Neuropsychologia, 35.*

Friston, K. J., Jezzard, P., & Turner, R. (1994). Analysis of functional MRI time-series. *Human Brain Mapping, 1,* 153–171.

Gallagher, H. L., Happe, F., Brunswick, N., Fletcher, P. C., Frith, U., & Frith, C. D. (2000). Reading the mind in cartoons and stories: An fMRI study of 'theory of mind' in verbal and nonverbal tasks. *Neuropsychologia, 38,* 11–21.

Gewirtz, J. C., Falls, W. A., & Davis, M. (1997). Normal conditioned inhibition and extinction of freezing and fear-potentiated startle following electrolytic lesions of medial prefrontal cortex in rats. *Behavioral Neuroscience, 111,* 712–726.

Glover, G. H., & Lai, S. (1998). Self-navigated spiral fMRI: Interleaved versus single-shot. *Magnetic Resonance Imaging, 39,* 361–368.

Gross, J. J. (1998). Antecedent- and response-focused emotion regulation: Divergent consequences for experience, expression, and physiology. *Journal of Personality and Social Psychology, 74,* 224–237.

Gross, J. J. (2002). Emotion regulation: Affective, cognitive, and social consequences. *Psychophysiology, 9,* 281–291.

Gross, J. J., & John, O. P. (in press). Wise emotion regulation. In L. Feldman Barrett & P. Salovey (Eds.), *The wisdom of feelings: Psychological processes in emotional intelligence.* New York: Guilford.

Gusnard, D. A., Akbudak, E., Shulman, G. L., & Raichle, M. E. (2001). Medial prefrontal cortex and self-referential mental activity: Relation to a default mode of brain function. *Proceedings of the National Academy of Sciences, U.S.A., 98,* 4259–4264.

Hamann, S. B., Ely, T. D., Grafton, S. T., & Kilts, C. D. (1999). Amygdala activity related to enhanced memory for pleasant and aversive stimuli. *Nature Neuroscience, 2,* 289–293.

Happe, F., Ehlers, S., Fletcher, P., Frith, U., Johansson, M., Gillberg, C., Dolan, R., Frackowiak, R., & Frith, C. (1996). 'Theory of mind' in the brain. Evidence from a PET scan study of Asperger syndrome. *NeuroReport, 8,* 197–201.

Hariri, A. R., Bookheimer, S. Y., & Mazziotta, J. C. (2000). Modulating emotional responses: Effects of a neocortical network on the limbic system. *NeuroReport, 11,* 43–48.

Holmes, A. P., & Friston, K. J. (1998). Generalisability, random effects and population inference. *Neuroimage: Abstracts of the Fourth International Conference on Functional Mapping of the Human Brain, 7,* S754.

Hsieh, J. C., Stone-Elander, S., & Ingvar, M. (1999). Anticipatory coping of pain expressed in the human anterior cingulate cortex: A positron emission tomography study. *Neuroscience Letters, 262,* 61–64.

Ito, T. A., Cacioppo, J. T., & Lang, P. J. (1998). Eliciting affect using the International Affective Picture System: Trajectories through evaluative space. *Personality and Social Psychology Bulletin, 24,* 855–879.

Jackson, D. C., Malmstadt, J. R., Larson, C. L., & Davidson, R. J. (2000). Suppression and enhancement of emotional responses to unpleasant pictures. *Psychophysiology, 37,* 515–522.

Jonides, J., Smith, E. E., Marshuetz, C., Koeppe, R. A., & Reuter-Lorenz, P. A. (1998). Inhibition in verbal working memory revealed by brain activation. *Proceedings of the National Academy of Sciences, U.S.A., 95,* 8410–8413.

Kawasaki, H., Kaufman, O., Damasio, H., Damasio, A. R., Granner, M., Bakken, H., Hori, T., Howard, M. A., III, & Adolphs, R. (2001). Single-neuron responses to emotional visual stimuli recorded in human ventral prefrontal cortex. *Nature Neuroscience, 4,* 15–16.

Knight, R. T., Staines, W. R., Swick, D., & Chao, L. L. (1999). Prefrontal cortex regulates inhibition and excitation in distributed neural networks. *Acta Psychologica, 101,* 159–178.

Kring, A. M., & Gordon, A. H. (1998). Sex differences in emotion: Expression, experience, and physiology. *Journal of Personality and Social Psychology, 74,* 686–703.

Lane, R. (2000). Neural correlates of emotional experience. In R. D. Lane & L. Nadel (Eds.), *Cognitive Neuroscience of Emotion.* New York: Oxford University Press.

Lane, R. D., Fink, G. R., Chau, P. M., & Dolan, R. J. (1997). Neural activation during selective attention to subjective emotional responses. *NeuroReport, 8,* 3969–3972.

Lane, R. D., Reiman, E. M., Ahern, G. L., Schwartz, G. E., & Davidson, R. J. (1997). Neuroanatomical correlates of happiness, sadness, and disgust. *American Journal of Psychiatry, 154,* 926–933.

Lane, R. D., Reiman, E. M., Bradley, M. M., Lang, P. J., Ahern, G. L., Davidson, R. J., & Schwartz, G. E. (1997). Neuroanatomical correlates of pleasant and unpleasant emotion. *Neuropsychologia, 35,* 1437–1444.

Lang, P. J., Greenwald, M. K., Bradley, M. M., & Hamm, A. O. (1993). Looking at pictures: Affective, visceral, and behavioral reactions. *Psychophysiology, 30,* 261–273.

Lazarus, R. S. (1991). *Emotion and adaptation.* New York: Oxford University Press.

LeDoux, J. E. (2000). Emotion circuits in the brain. *Annual Review of Neuroscience, 23,* 155–184.

Liberzon I., Taylor, S. F., Fig, L. M., Decker, L. R., Koeppe, R. A., & Minoshima, S. (2000). Limbic activation and psychophysiologic responses to aversive visual stimuli. Interaction with cognitive task. *Neuropsychopharmacology, 23,* 508–516.

MacDonald, A. W., Cohen, J. D., Stenger, V. A., & Carter, C. S. (2000). Dissociating the role of the dorsolateral prefrontal and anterior cingulate cortex in cognitive control. *Science, 288,* 1835–1838.

Miller, E. K., & Cohen, J. D. (2001). An integrative theory of prefrontal cortex function. *Annual Review of Neuroscience, 24,* 67–202.

Morgan, M. A., & LeDoux, J. E. (1995). Differential contribution of dorsal and ventral medial prefrontal cortex to the acquisition and extinction of conditioned fear in rats. *Behavioral Neuroscience, 109,* 681–688.

Morris, J. S., Ohman, A., & Dolan, R. J. (1999). A subcortical pathway to the right amygdala mediating "unseen" fear. *Proceedings of the National Academy of Sciences, U.S.A., 96,* 1680–1685.

Nielsen-Bohlman, L., & Knight, R. T. (1999). Prefrontal cortical involvement in visual working memory. *Brain Research. Cognitive Brain Research, 8,* 299–310.

Ochsner, K. N., & Feldman Barrett, L. (2001). A multi-process perspective on the neuroscience of emotion. In G. Bonnano & T. J. Mayne (Eds.), *Emotion: Current issues and future directions* (pp. 38–81). New York: Guilford.

Ochsner, K. N., & Lieberman, M. D. (2001). The emergence of social cognitive neuroscience. *American Psychologist, 56,* 717–734.

Ochsner, K. N., & Schacter, D. L. (in press). Remembering emotional events: A social cognitive neuroscience approach. In R. J. Davidson, H. Goldsmith, & K. R. Scherer (Eds.), *Handbook of the affective sciences*. Oxford University Press: New York.

O'Doherty, J. O., Kringelbach, M. L., Rolls, E. T., Hornak, J., & Andrews, C. (2001). Abstract reward and punishment representations in the human orbitofrontal cortex. *Nature Neuroscience, 4*, 95–102.

Paradiso, S., Jhonson, D. L., Andreasen, N. C., O'Leary, D. S., Watkins, G. L., Ponto, L. L., & Hichwa, R. D. (1999). Cerebral blood flow changes associated with attribution of emotional valence to pleasant, unpleasant, and neutral visual stimuli in a PET study of normal subjects. *American Journal of Psychiatry, 156*, 1618–1629.

Peterson, B. S., Skudlarski, P., Gatenby, J. C., Zhang, H., Anderson, A. W., & Gore, J. C. (1999). An fMRI study of Stroop word–color interference: Evidence for cingulate subregions subserving multiple distributed attentional systems. *Biological Psychiatry, 45*, 1237–1258.

Petit, L., Courtney, S. M., Ungerleider, L. G., & Haxby, J. V. (1998). Sustained activity in the medial wall during working memory delays. *Journal of Neuroscience, 18*, 9429–9437.

Phelps, E. A., Hyder, F., Blamire, A. M., & Shulman, R. G. (1997). FMRI of the prefrontal cortex during overt verbal fluency. *NeuroReport, 8*, 561–565.

Phelps, E. A., O'Connor, K. J., Gatenby, J. C., Gore, J. C., Grillon, C., & Davis, M. (2001). Activation of the left amygdala to a cognitive representation of fear. *Nature Neuroscience, 4*, 437–441.

Ploghaus, A., Tracey, I., Gati, J. S., Clare, S., Menon, R. S., Matthews, P. M., & Rawlins, J. N. (1999). Dissociating pain from its anticipation in the human brain. *Science, 284*, 1979–1981.

Quirk, G. J., Russo, G. K., Barron, J. L., & Lebron, K. (2000). The role of ventromedial prefrontal cortex in the recovery of extinguished fear. *Journal of Neuroscience, 20*, 6225–6231.

Reiman, E. M., Lane, R. D., Ahern, G. L., Schwartz, G. E., Davidson, R. J., Friston, K. J., Yun, L. S., & Chen, K. (1997). Neuroanatomical correlates of externally and internally generated human emotion. *American Journal of Psychiatry, 154*, 918–925.

Richards, J. M., & Gross, J. J. (2000). Emotion regulation and memory: The cognitive costs of keeping one's cool. *Journal of Personality and Social Psychology, 79*, 410–424.

Rolls, E. T. (1999). *The brain and emotion*. New York: Oxford University Press.

Saxena, S., Brody, A. L., Maidment, K. M., Dunkin, J. J., Colgan, M., Alborzian, S., Phelps, M. E., & Baxter, L. R., Jr. (1999). Localized orbitofrontal and subcortical metabolic changes and predictors of response to paroxetine treatment in obsessive–compulsive disorder. *Neuropsycho-pharmacology, 21*, 683–693.

Scherer, K. R., Schorr, A., & Johnstone, T. (2001). *Appraisal processes in emotion*. New York: Oxford University Press.

Schoenbaum, G., Chiba, A. A., & Gallagher, M. (1998). Orbitofrontal cortex and basolateral amygdala encode expected outcomes during learning. *Nature Neuroscience, 1*, 155–159.

Shakespeare, W. (1998/1623). *The Oxford Shakespeare: Hamlet*. New York: Oxford University Press.

Simpson, J. R., Ongur, D., Akbudak, E., Conturo, T. E., Ollinger, J. M., Snyder, A. Z., Gusnard, D. A., & Raichle, M. E. (2000). The emotional modulation of cognitive processing: An fMRI study. *Journal of Cognitive Neuroscience, 12*, 157–170.

Smith, E., & Jonides, J. (1999). Storage and executive processes in the frontal lobes. *Science, 283*, 657–660.

Stuss, D. T., Eskes, G. A., & Foster, J. K. (1994). Experimental neuropsychological studies of frontal lobe functions. In F. Boller & J. Grafman (Eds.), *Handbook of neuropsychology*. Amsterdam: Elsevier.

van Veen, V., Cohen, J. D., Botvinick, M. M., Stenger, V. A., & Carter, C. S. (2001). Anterior cingulate cortex, conflict monitoring, and levels of processing. *Neuroimage, 14*, 1302–1308.

Vuilleumier, P., Armony, J. L., Driver, J., & Dolan, R. J. (2001). Effects of attention and emotion on face processing in the human brain: An event-related fMRI study. *Neuron, 30*, 829–841.

Whalen, P. J., Rauch, S. L., Etcoff, N. L., McInerney, S. C., Lee, M. B., & Jenike, M. A. (1998). Masked presentations of emotional facial expressions modulate amygdala activity without explicit knowledge. *Journal of Neuroscience, 181*, 411–418.

Winston, J. S., Strange, B. A., O'Doherty, J., & Dolan, R. J. (2002). Automatic and intentional brain responses during evaluation of trustworthiness of faces. *Nature Neuroscience, 5*, 277–283.

Zald, D. H., & Pardo, J. V. (1997). Emotion, olfaction, and the human amygdala: Amygdala activation during aversive olfactory stimulation. *Proceedings of the National Academy of Sciences, U.S.A., 94*, 4119–4124.

How to Read a Journal Article in Social Psychology

Christian H. Jordan and Mark P. Zanna • University of Waterloo

When approaching a journal article for the first time, and often on subsequent occasions, most people try to digest it as they would any piece of prose. They start at the beginning and read word for word, until eventually they arrive at the end, perhaps a little bewildered, but with a vague sense of relief. This is not an altogether terrible strategy; journal articles do have a logical structure that lends itself to this sort of reading. There are, however, more efficient approaches—approaches that enable you, a student of social psychology, to cut through peripheral details, avoid sophisticated statistics with which you may not be familiar, and focus on the central ideas in an article. Arming yourself with a little foreknowledge of what is contained in journal articles, as well as some practical advice on how to read them, should help you read journal articles more effectively. If this sounds tempting, read on.

Journal articles offer a window into the inner workings of social psychology. They document how social psychologists formulate hypotheses, design empirical studies, analyze the observations they collect, and interpret their results. Journal articles also serve an invaluable archival function: they contain the full store of common and cumulative knowledge of social psychology. The documentation of past research allows researchers to build on past findings and advance our understanding of social behavior, without pursuing avenues of investigation that have already been explored. Perhaps most important, a research study is never complete until its results have been shared with others, colleagues and students alike. Journal articles are a primary means of communicating research findings. As such, they can be genuinely exciting and interesting to read.

That last claim may have caught you off guard. For beginning readers, journal articles may seem anything but interesting and exciting. They may, on the contrary, appear daunting and esoteric, laden with jargon and obscured by menacing statistics. Recognizing this fact, we hope to arm you, through this essay, with the basic information you will need to read journal articles with a greater sense of comfort and perspective.

Social psychologists study many fascinating topics, ranging from prejudice and discrimination, to culture, persuasion, liking and love, conformity and obedience, aggression, and the self. In our daily lives, these are issues we often struggle to understand. Social psychologists present systematic observations of, as well as a wealth of ideas about, such issues in journal articles. It would be a shame if the fascination and intrigue these topics have were lost in their translation into journal publications. We don't think they are, and by the end of this essay we hope you won't either.

Journal articles come in a variety of forms, including research reports, review articles, and theoretical articles. Put briefly, a *research report* is a formal presentation of an original research study, or series of studies. A *review article* is an evaluative survey of previously published work, usually organized by a guiding theory or point of view. The author of a review article summarizes previous investigations of a circumscribed problem, comments on what progress has been made toward its resolution, and suggests areas of the problem that require further study. A *theoretical article* also evaluates past research but focuses on the development of theories used to explain empirical findings. Here, the author may present a new theory to explain a set of findings, or may compare and contrast a set of competing theories, suggesting why one theory might be the superior one.

This essay focuses primarily on how to read research reports, for several reasons. First, the bulk of published literature in social psychology consists of research reports. Second, the summaries presented in review articles, and the ideas set forth in theoretical articles, are built on findings presented in research reports. To get a deep understanding of how research is done in social psychology, fluency in reading original research reports is essential. Moreover, theoretical articles frequently report new studies that pit one theory against another, or test a novel prediction derived from a new theory. In order to appraise the validity of such theoretical contentions, a grounded understanding of basic findings is invaluable. Finally, most research reports are written in a standard format that is likely unfamiliar to new readers. The format of review and theoretical articles is less standardized, and more like that of textbooks and other scholarly writings, with which most readers are familiar. This is not to suggest that such articles are easier to read and comprehend than research reports; they can be quite challenging indeed. It is simply the case that, because more rules apply to the writing of research reports, more guidelines can be offered on how to read them.

The Anatomy of Research Reports

Most research reports in social psychology, and in psychology in general, are written in a standard format prescribed by the American Psychological Association (1994). This is a great boon to both readers and writers. It allows writers to present their ideas and findings in a clear, systematic manner. Consequently, as a reader, once you understand this format, you will not be on completely foreign ground when you approach a new research report—regardless of its specific content. You will know where in the paper particular information is found, making it easier to locate. No matter what your reasons for reading a research report, a firm understanding of the format in which it is written will ease your task. We discuss the format of research reports next, with some practical suggestions on how to read them. Later, we discuss how this format reflects the process of scientific investigation, illustrating how research reports have a coherent narrative structure.

Title and Abstract

Although you can't judge a book by its cover, you can learn a lot about a research report simply by reading its title. The title presents a concise statement of the theoretical issues investigated, and/or the variables that were studied. For example, the following title was taken almost at random from a prestigious journal in social psychology: "Sad and guilty? Affective influences on the explanation of conflict in close relationships" (Forgas, 1994, p. 56). Just by reading the title, it can be inferred that the study investigated how emotional states change the way people explain conflict in close relationships. It also suggests that when feeling sad, people accept more personal blame for such conflicts (i.e., feel more guilty).

The abstract is also an invaluable source of information. It is a brief synopsis of the study, and packs a lot of information into 150 words or less. The abstract contains information about the problem that was investigated, how it was investigated, the major findings of the study, and hints at the theoretical and practical implications of the findings. Thus, the abstract is a useful summary of the research that provides the gist of the investigation. Reading this outline first can be very helpful, because it tells you where the report is going, and gives you a useful framework for organizing information contained in the article.

The title and abstract of a research report are like a movie preview. A movie preview highlights the important aspects of a movie's plot, and provides just enough information for one to decide whether to watch the whole movie. Just so with titles and abstracts; they highlight the key features of a research report to allow you to decide if you want to read the whole paper. And just as with movie previews, they do not give the whole story. Reading just the title and abstract is never enough to fully understand a research report.

Introduction

A research report has four main sections: introduction, method, results, and discussion. Although it is not explicitly labeled, the introduction begins the main body of a research report. Here, the researchers set the stage for the study. They present the problem under investigation, and state why it was important to study. By providing a brief review of past research and theory relevant to the central issue of investigation, the researchers place the study in an historical context and suggest how the study advances knowledge of the problem. Beginning with broad theoretical and practical considerations, the researchers delineate the rationale that led them to the specific set of hypotheses tested in the study. They also describe how they decided on their research strategy

(e.g., why they chose an experiment or a correlational study).

The introduction generally begins with a broad consideration of the problem investigated. Here, the researchers want to illustrate that the problem they studied is a real problem about which people should care. If the researchers are studying prejudice, they may cite statistics that suggest discrimination is prevalent, or describe specific cases of discrimination. Such information helps illustrate why the research is both practically and theoretically meaningful, and why you should bother reading about it. Such discussions are often quite interesting and useful. They can help you decide for yourself if the research has merit. But they may not be essential for understanding the study at hand. Read the introduction carefully, but choose judiciously what to focus on and remember. To understand a study, what you really need to understand is what the researchers' hypotheses were, and how they were derived from theory, informal observation, or intuition. Other background information may be intriguing, but may not be critical to understand what the researchers did and why they did it.

When reading the introduction, try answering these questions: what problem was studied, and why? How does this study relate to, and go beyond, past investigations of the problem? How did the researchers derive their hypotheses? What questions do the researchers hope to answer with this study?

Method

In the method section, the researchers translate their hypotheses into a set of specific, testable questions. Here, the researchers introduce the main characters of the study—the subjects or participants—describing their characteristics (gender, age, etc.) and how many of them were involved. Then, they describe the materials (or apparatus), such as any questionnaires or special equipment, used in the study. Finally, they describe chronologically the procedures of the study; that is, how the study was conducted. Often, an overview of the research design will begin the method section. This overview provides a broad outline of the design, alerting you to what you should attend.

The method is presented in great detail so that other researchers can recreate the study to confirm (or question) its results. This degree of detail is normally not necessary to understand a study, so don't get bogged down trying to memorize the particulars of the procedures. Focus on how the independent variables were manipulated (or measured) and how the dependent variables were measured.

Measuring variables adequately is not always an easy matter. Many of the variables psychologists are interested in cannot be directly observed, so they must be inferred from participants' behavior. Happiness, for example, cannot be directly observed. Thus, researchers interested in how being happy influences people's judgments must infer happiness (or its absence) from their behavior—perhaps by asking people how happy they are, and judging their degree of happiness from their responses; perhaps by studying people's facial expressions for signs of happiness, such as smiling. Think about the measures researchers use while reading the method section. Do they adequately reflect or capture the concepts they are meant to measure? If a measure seems odd, consider carefully how the researchers justify its use.

Oftentimes in social psychology, getting there is half the fun. In other words, how a result is obtained can be just as interesting as the result itself. Social psychologists often strive to have participants behave in a natural, spontaneous manner, while controlling enough of their environment to pinpoint the causes of their behavior. Sometimes, the major contribution of a research report is its presentation of a novel method of investigation. When this is the case, the method will be discussed in some detail in the introduction.

Participants in social psychology studies are intelligent and inquisitive people who are responsive to what happens around them. Because of this, they are not always initially told the true purpose of a study. If they were told, they might not act naturally. Thus, researchers frequently need to be creative, presenting a credible rationale for complying with procedures, without revealing the study's purpose. This rationale is known as a *cover story,* and is often an elaborate scenario. When reading the method section, try putting yourself in the shoes of a participant in the study, and ask yourself if the instructions given to participants seem sensible, realistic, and engaging. Imagining what it was like to be in the study will also help you remember the study's procedure, and aid you in interpreting the study's results.

When reading the method section, try answering these questions: How were the hypotheses translated into testable questions? How were the variables of interest manipulated and/or measured? Did the measures used adequately reflect the variables of interest? For example, is self-reported income an adequate measure of social class? Why or why not?

Results

The results section describes how the observations collected were analyzed to determine whether the original hypotheses were supported. Here, the data (observations of behavior) are described, and statistical tests are presented. Because of this, the results section is often intimidating to readers who have little or no training in statistics. Wading through complex and unfamiliar statistical analyses is understandably confusing and frustrating. As a result, many students are tempted to skip over reading this section. We advise you not to do so. Empirical findings are the foundation of any science, and results sections are where such findings are presented.

Take heart. Even the most prestigious researchers were once in your shoes and sympathize with you. Though space in psychology journals is limited, researchers try to strike a balance between the need to be clear and the need to be brief in describing their results. In an influential paper on how to write good research reports, Bem (1987) offered this advice to researchers:

> No matter how technical or abstruse your article is in its particulars, intelligent nonpsychologists with no expertise in statistics or experimental design should be able to comprehend the broad outlines of what you did and why. They should understand in general terms what was learned. (p. 74)

Generally speaking, social psychologists try to practice this advice.

Most statistical analyses presented in research reports test specific hypotheses. Often, each analysis presented is preceded by a reminder of the hypothesis it is meant to test. After an analysis is presented, researchers usually provide a narrative description of the result in plain English. When the hypothesis tested by a statistical analysis is not explicitly stated, you can usually determine the hypothesis that was tested by reading this narrative description of the result, and referring back to the introduction to locate an hypothesis that corresponds to that result. After even the most complex statistical analysis, there will be a written description of what the result means conceptually. Turn your attention to these descriptions. Focus on the conceptual meaning of research findings, not on the mechanics of how they were obtained (unless you're comfortable with statistics).

Aside from statistical tests and narrative descriptions of results, results sections also frequently contain tables and graphs. These are efficient summaries of data. Even if you are not familiar with statistics, look closely at tables and graphs, and pay attention to the means or correlations presented in them. Researchers always include written descriptions of the pertinent aspects of tables and graphs. When reading these descriptions, check the tables and graphs to make sure what the researchers say accurately reflects their data. If they say there was a difference between two groups on a particular dependent measure, look at the means in the table that correspond to those two groups, and see if the means do differ as described. Occasionally, results seem to become stronger in their narrative description than an examination of the data would warrant.

Statistics *can* be misused. When they are, results are difficult to interpret. Having said this, a lack of statistical knowledge should not make you overly cautious while reading results sections. Although not a perfect antidote, journal articles undergo extensive review by professional researchers before publication. Thus, most misapplications of statistics are caught and corrected before an article is published. So, if you are unfamiliar with statistics, you can be reasonably confident that findings are accurately reported.

When reading the results section, try answering these questions: did the researchers provide evidence that any independent variable manipulations were effective? For example, if testing for behavioral differences between happy and sad participants, did the researchers demonstrate that one group was in fact happier than the other? What were the major findings of the study? Were the researchers' original hypotheses supported by their observations? If not, look in the discussion section for how the researchers explain the findings that were obtained.

Discussion

The discussion section frequently opens with a summary of what the study found, and an evaluation of whether the findings supported the original hypotheses. Here, the researchers evaluate the theoretical and practical implications of their results. This can be particularly interesting when the results did not work out exactly as the researchers anticipated. When such is the case, consider the researchers' explanations carefully, and see if they seem plausible to you. Often, researchers will also report any aspects of their study that limit their interpretation of its results, and suggest further research that could overcome these limitations to provide a better understanding of the problem under investigation.

Some readers find it useful to read the first few paragraphs of the discussion section before reading any other part of a research report. Like the abstract, these few paragraphs usually contain all of the main ideas of a research report: what the hypotheses were, the major findings and whether they supported the original hypotheses, and how the findings relate to past research and theory. Having this information before reading a research report can guide your reading, allowing you to focus on the specific details you need to complete your understanding of a study. The description of the results, for example, will alert you to the major variables that were studied. If they are unfamiliar to you, you can pay special attention to how they are defined in the introduction, and how they are operationalized in the method section.

After you have finished reading an article, it also can be helpful to reread the first few paragraphs of the discussion and the abstract. As noted, these two passages present highly distilled summaries of the major ideas in a research report. Just as they can help guide your reading of a report, they can also help you consolidate your understanding of a report once you have finished reading it. They provide a check on whether you have understood the main points of a report, and offer a succinct digest of the research in the authors' own words.

When reading the discussion section, try answering these questions: What conclusions can be drawn from the study? What new information does the study provide about the problem under investigation? Does the study help resolve the problem? What are the practical and theoretical implications of the study's findings? Did the results contradict past research findings? If so, how do the researchers explain this discrepancy?

Some Notes on Reports of Multiple Studies

Up to this point, we have implicitly assumed that a research report describes just one study. It is also quite common, however, for a research report to describe a series of studies of the same problem in a single article. When such is the case, each study reported will have the same basic structure (introduction, method, results, and discussion sections) that we have outlined, with the notable exception that sometimes the results and discussion section for each study are combined. Combined "results and discussion" sections contain the same information that separate results and discussion sections normally contain. Sometimes, the authors present all their results first, and only then discuss the implications of these results, just as they would in separate results and discussion sections. Other times, however, the authors alternate between describing results and discussing their implications, as each result is presented. In either case, you should be on the lookout for the same information, as outlined earlier in our consideration of separate results and discussion sections.

Reports including multiple studies also differ from single study reports in that they include more general introduction and discussion sections. The general introduction, which begins the main body of

a research report, is similar in essence to the introduction of a single study report. In both cases, the researchers describe the problem investigated and its practical and theoretical significance. They also demonstrate how they derived their hypotheses, and explain how their research relates to past investigations of the problem. In contrast, the separate introductions to each individual study in reports of multiple studies are usually quite brief, and focus more specifically on the logic and rationale of each particular study presented. Such introductions generally describe the methods used in the particular study, outlining how they answer questions that have not been adequately addressed by past research, including studies reported earlier in the same article.

General discussion sections parallel discussions of single studies, except on a somewhat grander scale. They present all of the information contained in discussions of single studies, but consider the implications of all the studies presented together. A general discussion section brings the main ideas of a research program into bold relief. It typically begins with a concise summary of a research program's main findings, their relation to the original hypotheses, and their practical and theoretical implications. Thus, the summaries that begin general discussion sections are counterparts of the summaries that begin discussion sections of single study reports. Each presents a digest of the research presented in an article that can serve as both an organizing framework (when read first), and as a check on how well you have understood the main points of an article (when read last).

Research Reporting as Story Telling

A research report tells the story of how a researcher or group of researchers investigated a specific problem. Thus, a research report has a linear, narrative structure with a beginning, middle, and end. In his paper on writing research reports, Bem noted that a research report:

> . . . is shaped like an hourglass. It begins with broad general statements, progressively narrows down to the specifics of [the] study, and then broadens out again to more general considerations. (1987, p. 175)

This format roughly mirrors the process of scientific investigation, wherein researchers do the following: (1) start with a broad idea from which they formulate a narrower set of hypotheses, informed by past empirical findings (introduction); (2) design a specific set of concrete operations to test these hypotheses (method); (3) analyze the observations collected in this way, and decide if they support the original hypotheses (results); and (4) explore the broader theoretical and practical implications of the findings, and consider how they contribute to an understanding of the problem under investigation (discussion). Though these stages are somewhat arbitrary distinctions—research actually proceeds in a number of different ways—they help elucidate the inner logic of research reports.

When reading a research report, keep this linear structure in mind. Although it is difficult to remember a series of seemingly disjointed facts, when these facts are joined together in a logical, narrative structure, they become easier to comprehend and recall. Thus, always remember that a research report tells a story. It will help you to organize the information you read, and remember it later.

Describing research reports as stories is not just a convenient metaphor. Research reports *are* stories. Stories can be said to consist of two components: a telling of what happened, and an explanation of why it happened. It is tempting to view science as an endeavor that simply catalogues facts, but nothing is further from the truth. The goal of science, social psychology included, is to *explain* facts, to explain *why* what happened happened. Social psychology is built on the dynamic interplay of discovery and justification, the dialogue between systematic observation of relations and their theoretical explanation. Although research reports do present novel facts based on systematic observation, these facts are presented in the service of ideas. Facts in isolation are trivia. Facts tied together by an explanatory theory are science. Therein lies the story. To really understand what researchers have to say, you need to consider how their explanations relate to their findings.

The Rest of the Story

> There is really no such thing as research. There is only search, more search, keep on searching. (Bowering, 1988, p. 95)

Once you have read through a research report, and understand the researchers' findings and their explanations of them, the story does not end there. There is more than one interpretation for any set of findings. Different researchers often explain the same set of facts in different ways.

Let's take a moment to dispel a nasty rumor. The rumor is this: researchers present their studies in a dispassionate manner, intending only to inform readers of their findings and their interpretation of those findings. In truth, researchers aim not only to inform readers but also to *persuade* them (Sternberg, 1995). Researchers want to convince you their ideas are right. There is never only one explanation for a set of findings. Certainly, some explanations are better than others; some fit the available data better, are more parsimonious, or require fewer questionable assumptions. The point here is that researchers are very passionate about their ideas, and want you to believe them. It's up to you to decide if you want to buy their ideas or not.

Let's compare social psychologists to salesclerks. Both social psychologists and salesclerks want to sell you something: either their ideas, or their wares. You need to decide if you want to buy what they're selling or not—and there are potentially negative consequences for either decision. If you let a salesclerk dazzle you with a sales pitch, without thinking about it carefully, you might end up buying a substandard product that you don't really need. After having done this a few times, people tend to become cynical, steeling themselves against any and all sales pitches. This, too, is dangerous. If you are overly critical of sales pitches, you could end up foregoing genuinely useful products. Thus, by analogy, when you are too critical in your reading of research reports, you might dismiss, out of hand, some genuinely useful ideas—ideas that can help shed light on why people behave the way they do.

This discussion raises the important question of how critical one should be while reading a research report. In part, this will depend on why one is reading the report. If you are reading it simply to learn what the researchers have to say about a particular issue, for example, then there is usually no need to be overly critical. If you want to use the research as a basis for planning a new study, then you should be more critical. As you develop an understanding of psychological theory and research methods, you will also develop an ability to criticize research on many different levels. And *any* piece of research can be criticized at some level. As Jacob Cohen put it, "A successful piece of research doesn't conclusively settle an issue, it just makes some theoretical proposition to some degree more likely" (1990, p. 1311). Thus, as a consumer of research reports, you have to strike a delicate balance between being overly critical and overly accepting.

When reading a research report, at least initially, try to suspend your disbelief. Try to understand the researchers' story; that is, try to understand the facts—the findings and how they were obtained—and the suggested explanation of those facts—the researchers' interpretation of the findings and what they mean. Take the research to task only after you feel you understand what the authors are trying to say.

Research reports serve not only an important archival function, documenting research and its findings, but also an invaluable stimulus function. They can excite other researchers to join the investigation of a particular issue, or to apply new methods or theory to a different, perhaps novel, issue. It is this stimulus function that Elliot Aronson, an eminent social psychologist, referred to when he admitted that, in publishing a study, he hopes his colleagues will "look at it, be stimulated by it, be provoked by it, annoyed by it, and then go ahead and do it better. . . . That's the exciting thing about science; it progresses by people taking off on one another's work" (1995, p. 5). Science is indeed a cumulative enterprise, and each new study builds on what has (or, sometimes, has not) gone before it. In this way, research articles keep social psychology vibrant.

A study can inspire new research in a number of different ways, such as: (1) it can lead one to conduct a better test of the hypotheses, trying to rule out alternative explanations of the findings; (2) it can lead one to explore the limits of the findings, to see how widely applicable they are, perhaps exploring situations to which they do not apply; (3) it can lead one to test the implications of the findings, furthering scientific investigation of the phenomenon; (4) it can inspire one to apply the findings, or a novel methodology, to a different area of investigation; and (5) it can provoke one to test the findings in the context of a specific real world problem, to see if they can shed light on it. All of these are excellent extensions of the original research, and there are, undoubtedly, other ways that research findings can spur new investigations.

The problem with being too critical, too soon, when reading research reports is that the only further research one may be willing to attempt is research of the first type: redoing a study better. Sometimes this is desirable, particularly in the early stages of investigating a particular issue, when the findings are novel and perhaps unexpected. But redoing a reasonably compelling study, without extending it in any way, does little to advance our understanding of human behavior. Although the new study might be "better," it will not be "perfect," so it would have to be run again, and again, likely never reaching a stage where it is beyond criticism. At some point, researchers have to decide that the evidence is compelling enough to warrant investigation of the last four types. It is these types of studies that most advance our knowledge of social behavior. As you read more research reports, you will become more comfortable deciding when a study is "good enough" to move beyond it. This is a somewhat subjective judgment, and should be made carefully.

When social psychologists write up a research report for publication, it is because they believe they have something new and exciting to communicate about social behavior. Most research reports that are submitted for publication are rejected. Thus, the reports that are eventually published are deemed pertinent not only by the researchers who wrote them, but also by the reviewers and editors of the journals in which they are published. These people, at least, believe the research reports they write and publish have something important and interesting to say. Sometimes, you'll disagree; not all journal articles are created equal, after all. But we recommend that you, at least initially, give these well-meaning social psychologists the benefit of the doubt. Look for what they're excited about. Try to understand the authors' story, and see where it leads you.

NOTE

Preparation of this essay was facilitated by a Natural Sciences and Engineering Research Council of Canada doctoral fellowship to Christian H. Jordan. Thanks to Roy Baumeister, Arie Kruglanski, Ziva Kunda, John Levine, Geoff MacDonald, Richard Moreland, Ian Newby-Clark, Steve Spencer, and Adam Zanna for their insightful comments on, and appraisals of, various drafts of this paper. Thanks also to Arie Kruglanski and four anonymous editors of volumes in the series, *Key Readings in Social Psychology*, for their helpful critiques of an initial outline of this paper.

REFERENCES

American Psychological Association. (1994). *Publication manual* (4th ed.). Washington, DC.

Aronson, E. (1995). Research in social psychology as a leap of faith. In E. Aronson (Ed.), *Readings about the social animal* (7th ed., pp. 3–9). New York: W. H. Freeman and Company.

Bem, D. J. (1987). Writing the empirical journal article. In M. P. Zanna & J. M. Darley (Eds.), *The compleat academic: A practical guide for the beginning social scientist* (pp. 171-201). New York: Random House.

Bowering, G. (1988). *Errata*. Red Deer, Alberta.: Red Deer College Press.

Cohen, J. (1990). Things I have learned (so far). *American Psychologist, 45,* 1304-1312.

Forgas, J. P. (1994). Sad and guilty? Affective influences on the explanation of conflict in close relationships. *Journal of Personality and Social Psychology, 66,* 56-68.

Sternberg, R. J. (1995). *The psychologist's companion: A guide to scientific writing for students and researchers* (3rd ed.). Cambridge: Cambridge University Press.

Author Index[*]

---

[*]Numbers in parentheses indicate reference number.

Subject Index